Serial Offenders

Theory and Practice

Editors

Kevin Borgeson
Department of Criminal Justice
Salem State College
Salem, MA

Kristen Kuehnle
Department of Criminal Justice
Salem State College
Salem, MA

JONES & BARTLETT
LEARNING

World Headquarters

Jones & Bartlett Learning
40 Tall Pine Drive
Sudbury, MA 01776
978-443-5000
info@jblearning.com
www.jblearning.com

Jones & Bartlett Learning
Canada
6339 Ormindale Way
Mississauga, Ontario L5V 1J2
Canada

Jones & Bartlett Learning
International
Barb House, Barb Mews
London W6 7PA
United Kingdom

Jones & Bartlett Learning books and products are available through most bookstores and online booksellers. To contact Jones & Bartlett Learning directly, call 800-832-0034, fax 978-443-8000, or visit our website, www.jblearning.com.

Substantial discounts on bulk quantities of Jones & Bartlett Learning publications are available to corporations, professional associations, and other qualified organizations. For details and specific discount information, contact the special sales department at Jones & Bartlett Learning via the above contact information or send an email to specialsales@jblearning.com.

Production Credits
Publisher, Higher Education: Cathleen Sether
Acquisitions Editor: Sean Connelly
Senior Associate Editor: Megan R. Turner
Associate Production Editor: Jessica deMartin
Associate Marketing Manager: Lindsay White
Manufacturing and Inventory Control: Amy Bacus
Photo and Permissions Associate: Emily Howard
Composition: Nicolazzo Productions
Cover Design: Kristin E. Parker
Cover Image: © danilo ducak/ShutterStock, Inc.
Printing and Binding: Malloy, Inc.
Cover Printing: Malloy, Inc.

Library of Congress Cataloging-in-Publication Data
Borgeson, Kevin.
Serial offenders : theory and practice / Kevin Borgeson, Kristen Kuehnle.—1st ed.
    p. cm.
Includes bibliographical references and index.
ISBN-13: 978-0-7637-7730-2
ISBN-10: 0-7637-7730-7
1. Recidivists. 2. Recidivism. 3. Murder in mass media. I. Kuehnle, Kristen. II. Title.
HV6049.B67 2012
364.3—dc22
                                2010041566
6048

Printed in the United States of America
14 13 12 11 10   10 9 8 7 6 5 4 3 2 1

Contents

Preface ——————————————————————

OVER THE YEARS THE EDITORS have taught classes on violent offenders and used several texts. Teaching a class on serial offenders involved the process of gathering information from various sources and then integrating the materials into a comprehensive manner. Most of the research, though, has focused on serial murder. By omitting other types of serial offenders, students were limited in their understanding of the array of serial offenders. This means that the importance of other types of violent serial offenders has been overlooked.

The book provides an understanding of the different types of offenders while bringing up investigative issues surrounding these elusive offenders. The book specifically looks at murder, rape, cyber pedophiles, arson, muti-murder, and sex offenders. While other types of offenders could have been used, the editors felt that these offenders are the most complex to understand and investigate. The book explores several investigative issues: profiling, case linkage analysis, task force, and (the most overlooked) the victims.

We set out to produce a volume that is academically rigorous, grounded in research and theory, as well as accessible to the general public. It is our hope that this book will raise the public's awareness and concern about serial offenders, fostering a growing body of research about these offenders and stimulate efforts in understanding and investigating their actions.

Acknowledgments

WE EXPRESS OUR DEEPEST THANKS to the contributing authors for their hard work, attention, and adherence to strict deadlines.

We extend our gratitude to our editor, Sean Connelly, for his patience, support, and encouragement throughout this process. We also extend our gratitude and respect to the staff at Jones & Bartlett Learning who helped bring this volume to completion.

Contributors ————————————

KEVIN BORGESON is assistant professor in the Criminal Justice Department at Salem State University, Salem, Massachusetts, where he teaches courses in crime scene investigation, profiling, and bias crimes. Borgeson's work has appeared in *Journal of Applied Sociology, Michigan Sociological Review*, and *American Behavioral Science*.

KRISTEN KUEHNLE is a professor in the Criminal Justice Department at Salem State University. She was a clinical psychologist for nearly twenty years at Massachusetts General Hospital, specializing in child sexual abuse cases, working with both victims and offenders. She has lectured extensively in the area of child sexual abuse. Other research interests and publications have been on same sex battering and bias crimes, as well as rehabilitation of the offender.

LORNA ALVAREZ-RIVERA is a visiting assistant professor at Ohio University and a PhD candidate at the University of Florida, Department of Sociology and Criminology and Law. Her research interests expand over a number of criminological, psychological, and criminal justice–related areas, but her primary focus is the cross-cultural study of criminological theories. Some of her recent publications have appeared in the *Journal of Criminal Justice, Journal of Drug Issues*, and the *Journal of Criminal Justice Education*.

DETECTIVE KRISTYN BERNIER is an 18-year veteran of the Portsmouth, New Hampshire Police Department, specializing in undercover internet crime investigation, child exploitation, sexually based crimes, domestic violence, sex offender management, and undercover narcotics work. She is currently a member of the New Hampshire Internet Crimes Against Children Task Force, actively investigating offenders who possess, manufacture, and distribute child sexual assault images. Det. Bernier is the co-author of *Cyber Crime Fighters: Tales from the Trenches*, and gives Internet safety presentations throughout New Hampshire.

LEILA B. DUTTON, PhD, earned her PhD (2004) in Experimental Psychology from the University of Rhode Island. She was a post-doctoral research fellow at the Family Research Laboratory at the University of New Hampshire from 2004 to 2006 working on the International Dating Violence Study, particularly investigating factors associated with perpetration of sexual coercion and dating violence. Dr. Dutton is an assistant professor of criminal Justice at the University of New Haven. Her research focuses on testing theoretical explanations for why individuals engage in unwanted pursuit and stalking after the termination of a romantic relationship and on effective victim responses to unwanted pursuit and stalking.

JAMES ALAN FOX is the Lipman Family Professor of Criminology, Law, and Public Policy at Northeastern University. Among his many book publications are several on serial and mass murder co-authored with Jack Levin, as well as his newest, *Violence and Security on Campus: From Preschool through College*. He has published dozens of journal and magazine articles and hundreds of newspaper opinion columns, primarily in the areas of multiple murder, youth crime, school and campus violence, workplace violence, and capital punishment.

AMANDA HOWERTON is currently an assistant professor at Salem State University. After receiving her PhD at the University of New Hampshire in 2005, she was awarded a post-doctoral fellowship at the University of Exeterin, England, where she designed and implemented a qualitative study in an English correctional facility. Her primary areas of expertise and research are prisoner rehabilitation and reentry and prisoner mental health.

JOHN C. KILBURN, JR., PhD, is professor of sociology and criminal justice at Texas A&M International University in Laredo, Texas. He previously served on the faculty at Eastern Connecticut State University. He earned his PhD degree in sociology from Louisiana State University and has continued to study issues related to violence and community security. He is currently working on a manuscript that explores halfway houses as both public goods and neighborhood nuisances. His previous research has appeared in *Criminal Justice Review*, *The Journal of Pediatrics*, *Social Forces*, and *Urban Affairs Review*.

CHARLES WESLEY KIM, JR. received his J.D. (1982) from Columbia and is counsel at Yelman & Associates in San Diego. He was adjunct professor at California Western, Thomas Jefferson, and University of Diego Schools of Law; past member of the California Commission on Impartial Courts, past-president of the Asian Pacific Bar of California, and former board member of the State Bar Conference of Delegates and

San Diego County Bar. His law enforcement experience includes service with the San Diego Citizens Review Board on Police Practices, Citizens Advisory Board on Police Community Relations, San Diego Stalking Strike Force/Stalking Case Assessment Team, Association of Threat Assessment Professionals, and as an NYPD Auxiliary Police Officer.

Senior Superintendent GÉRARD LABUSCHAGNE, PhD, is the commander of the South African Police Service's Investigative Psychology Unit, which is responsible for assisting with all serial murder investigations throughout South Africa. He is a licensed clinical psychologist and a criminologist and testifies regularly in the High Court and magistrates courts of South Africa, often about case linkage issues. He is on the editorial board for the *Journal of Investigative Psychology and Offender Profiling*, a consultant to the National Institute of Justice of the Department of Justice in the USA, a research fellow at the University of the Free State's (SA) Centre for Psychology and the Law, and a fellow of the International Association of Investigative Psychology. He is a member of the British Psychological Society and the International Homicide Investigators Association. He is an adjunct faculty member of the California School of Forensic Studies at Alliant International University in the USA, and a Professor Extraordinarius at the Dept Criminology at UNISA (University of South Africa).

KENNETH V. LANNING is a consultant in the area of crimes against children. Before he retired in 2000, Kenneth Lanning was a special agent with the FBI for over 30 years. He was assigned to the FBI Behavioral Science Unit and the National Center for Analysis of Violent Crime at the FBI Academy in Quantico. He has trained police officers and criminal justice professional in his areas of specialty.

JACK LEVIN is the Irving and Betty Brudnick Professor of Sociology and Criminology and director of the Brudnick Center on Violence and Conflict at Northeastern University in Boston. He has published 30 books and numerous journal articles and newspaper columns, primarily in the areas of serial and mass murder, hate crimes, school violence, juvenile murder, and workplace violence. Levin was recently the recipient of the American Sociological Association's Public Understanding of Sociology Award.

RICHARD PARENTEAU graduated Magna Cum Laude fom the Master's Program at Salem State College in 2009. Currently, he works for the West Newbury Police Department in West Newbury, Massachusetts and is enrolled in the Northeast Regional Police Institute for law enforcement training. In addition, he has been conducting research on both juvenile and serial arson offenses.

AMY L. POLAND, PhD, is an assistant professor of Criminal Justice at Texas A&M International University in Laredo, Texas. She previously served on the faculty at Buena Vista University in Storm Lake, Iowa. She earned her PhD in criminal justice from the University of Nebraska at Omaha and has continued to study issues related to juvenile justice and delinquency. She is currently working on a study of the mental health needs of juvenile offenders in an Hispanic community and the effect of perceptions of racial discrimination on delinquency. She previously co-authored *Assessing the Need for and Availability of Mental Health Services for Juvenile Offenders*, a report for the State of Nebraska.

KENNA QUINET is an associate professor of criminal justice, law, and public safety in the School of Public and Environmental Affairs at Indiana University Purdue University Indianapolis (IUPUI) and a faculty scholar at the Center for Urban Policy and the Environment in Indianapolis. Her research focuses on various aspects of homicide, including serial homicides and medical murder. She is also currently studying the demographics of external causes of death—accidents, suicides, and homicides. Most recently, she is a coauthor with Jamie Fox and Jack Levin of the third edition of *The Will to Kill: Making Sense of Senseless Murder.*

MARK W. SCHMINK is a sergeant in charge of operations for the Rockport Police Department in Massachusetts. He has 26 years of law enforcement experience including 4 years in the United States Marine Corps (Military Police K-9 division), 6 years with the Essex County Sheriff's Department (Training Lieutenant), and 16 years in his current position. Sgt. Schmink holds a Master of Science Degree from Salem State University. He is a member of the Massachusetts Law Enforcement and Armorer's Association, the International Association for Law Enforcement Firearms Instructors and Armorer's Association, and Massachusetts Coalition of Police Sergeant at Arms, and is a commander for the Cape Ann Regional Response and Tactical Team.

BRIAN H. SPITZBERG received his PhD from the University of Southern California. He is currently Senate Distinguished Professor in the School of Communication at San Diego State University. His is widely published, with books and articles in interpersonal communication skills, communication assessment, conflict management, jealousy, infidelity, intimate violence, sexual coercion, and stalking. He has authored four books on "the dark side" of communication and relationships. *The Dark Side of Relationship Pursuit: From Attraction to Obsession and Stalking* won the International Association for Relationship Research book award in 2006. He serves as a member of the San Diego District Attorney's Stalking Case Assessment Team and is an active member of the Association of Threat Assessment Professionals.

CHAPTER 1

Introduction: Why Study Serial Crime?

Kevin Borgeson and Kristen Kuehnle

Understanding motivation and behaviors of offenders, particularly serial offenders, is critical to apprehending and convicting an offender. Practitioners in law enforcement continually seek patterns in their investigation and often look to researchers who present typologies from their studies of convicted offenders. These typologies appear to simplify the process, which is reinforced when the media portray these techniques in solving a crime within 45 minutes. Presently, we have consumers who feel competent to be experts on a jury, whether in the United States or elsewhere (as in Italy with the Amanda Knox case), based on their avid following of television shows such as *CSI* and *Law and Order*, or films such as *Dead Man Walking*, to name a few. How did we arrive at this perceived level of expertise? What drove the development of these typologies? Do other aspects need to be considered in the typology? And how have others developed typologies? These are questions that this book considers. A starting point is to answer the question, "Why study serial crime?"

WHY STUDY SERIAL CRIME?

Over the past 2 decades, Western society has become fascinated with serial murder. Although the media have presented this as a new phenomenon, in reality, it is not. According to one media source:

> The phenomenon of serial murder can be found throughout history and around the world, the most famous case being Jack the Ripper in England of the 1800s. But the 1800s brought a new and intensified spotlight on serial murder, inspired by the media, popular culture, and the political agenda of law enforcement agencies and certain advocate groups. (USA Today Magazine cited in Jenkins, 1994, p. 7)

Although interest in serial homicide has existed for over 150 years, interest has increased since the early 1980s, exploding in the 1990s. Part of this explosion was a direct result of the overestimation in the late 1980s by professionals that there were over 5000 serial killers at large in the United States (Hickey, 2002, p. 2). Erick Hickey, who has compiled the largest data set on serial killers from 1800 to 1995, points out that from 1920 through 1989 there were a total of 67 films dealing with the theme of serial killers. In the 10-year period from 1990 to 1999, the film industry produced a total of 117 serial killer films (2002, p. 3).[1]

Networks, including CBS, NBC, ABC, and Fox, as well as the movie industry, have cashed in on the serial killer phenomenon. Serial murder became a staple on such shows as *The X-Files, CSI, Millennium,* and *Profiler,* and in Hollywood films such as *The Glimmer Man, The Silence of the Lambs, Manhunter,* and *The Bone Collector.* Although these programs are made for entertainment, they play a significant role in distorting the normalcy of serial offenders to the consuming public. Those who are saturated with media exposure of murder have problems differentiating fact from fiction, overestimating the number of killers in society, the number of such homicides, and the number of victims they are responsible for. As stated by one authority:

> People's enthrallment with serial killers represents a way of dealing with crime. Crime is boiled down to a single human face, representing the most frightening evil. Actually, it's easier to deal with emotionally than the faceless random crime of muggings and shootings. (USA Today Magazine cited in Jenkins, 1994, p. 7)

While it may or may not be true that this "enthrallment" has desirable social effects, some effects are clearly undesirable. The overdramatization of murders, murderers,

---

[1] Collective behavior literature refers to such overemphasis on a subject, and the general population's need for information on the subject, as a moral panic.

and their apprehension clearly distort the facts. People are led to believe that serial killers are different from the rest of us, that they possess identifiable characteristics that can be readily identified—e.g., they look different, they act different, and they are different. Such a construct has negative effects during investigations of serial killers. For instance, during the Maryland Sniper crimes of October 2002, the general public believed the police would eventually capture the sniper; however, a palpable sense of anxiousness developed around the perceived slowness in identifying and apprehending the perpetrators. Part of the anxiousness stemmed from the familiar media portrayal of a "typical" investigation process and viewers' acceptance that media depictions are accurate. In movies or on television, law enforcement officials readily identify culprits and bring them to justice. Anxiety around such things as catching serial killers, in movies, is supposed to only last an hour or two. As a result, the public is conditioned to expect such a time frame for catching a real-world serial killer, not the 21 days that it took to apprehend the Maryland Snipers.

The media construct of a serial killer as a monster of heroic proportion is designed to sell a product—a movie or television show. Today's serial offender has replaced the werewolf and Frankenstein as the modern boogeyman (Fox & Levin, 2001). This is part of the reason why the audiences for these depictions are growing; drama is enhanced by suspense and fear. Additionally, the simplistic view of the world as a division between good and evil is gaining in legitimacy. Showing the existing faces of evil to all who are willing to watch reinforces the perception that there is clearly and easily identified evil in the world.

Public fascination does not end with serial murder. Over the last decade, it has been extended to mass killings, such as school shootings (which will be discussed later). One possible explanation for the public's fascination with serial murder and mass killings could be 20th century geopolitics, which have made death an increasingly public and, therefore, publicized feature of life itself. The images necessary for producing a sense of drama and moral significance are increasingly becoming images of death and the battle of the righteous against those who stand against humanity. This trend may help us to understand why, over the years, slasher films have become so popular. Films such as *Friday the 13th* and *Halloween* are box office smashes because they fulfill society's fascination with death and evil. While some may believe that such films are merely entertainment, others disagree. For example, Grossman's work argues that there is more harm than good done by these films. He believes that the techniques used to create such scenarios resemble techniques used by government to desensitize assassins during war. Grossman speculates that desensitization begins subtly:

> *It begins innocently with cartoons and then goes on to the countless thousands of acts of violence depicted on TV as the child grows up and the scramble of ratings steadily*

raises the threshold of violence on TV. As children reach a certain age, they then begin to watch movies with a degree of violence sufficient to receive a PG-13 rating due to the brief glimpses of spurting blood, a hacked-off limb, or bullet wounds. The parents, through neglect or conscious decision, begin to permit the child to watch movies rated R due to vivid depictions of knives penetrating and protruding from bodies, long shots of blood spurting from severed limbs, and bullets ripping into bodies and exploding out the back in showers of blood and brains.

Finally our society says that young adolescents, at the age of 17, can legally watch these R-rated movies (although most are well experienced with them by then), and at 18 they can watch movies rated even higher than R. These are films in which eye gouging is often the least of the offenses that are vividly depicted. And thus, at that malleable age of 17 and 18, the age at which armies have traditionally begun to indoctrinate the soldier into the business of killing, American youth, systematically desensitized from childhood, takes another step in the indoctrination into the cult of violence. (1996, pp. 308–309).

Grossman concludes:

[With this] classical conditioning process, adolescents in movie theaters across the nation, and watching television at home, are seeing the detailed, horrible suffering and killing of human beings, and they are learning to associate killing and suffering with entertainment, pleasure, their favorite soft drink, their favorite candy bar, and the close intimate contact of their date. (1996, p. 302)

While Grossman's speculations may be extreme, he is not alone in his opinion. Fox and Levin (2001) point out that this "selling of evil" is damaging to youth, saying, "The lesson for youngsters may be: Behave yourself and adults won't notice; go on a rampage at school, and you become a big-shot superstar." Whatever research ultimately proves, it is widely believed that the celebration of serial killers and pervasive representations of violence are problematic. It is interesting to note that "serial killer web sites" rank order offenders by the number of people they have killed. In this way, murderers who have the highest body count are afforded the highest status, while those having lower body counts are afforded lesser status. Fitting murders into the more general template of status associated with celebrity and heroism may well account for desensitization toward the effects that go beyond the moral pale. Any study of serial crime needs, first of all, to sift out what is factual from what is false. Researchers also need to explore the possibility that the same conditions that produce the public's enthusiasm for viewing violence also produce a serial criminal's motivation for violence. Research may help reduce the public's fear and allow people to be more rational about their vulnerability to atrocious violence.

FEAR OF CRIME

Apart from enthusiasm, media coverage contributes to the fear of crime, even something as improbable as serial murder. Gerbner and Gross (1976) examined the impact of violent television programs on children and adults. Their results revealed that children and adults exposed to heavy doses of violent television saw the world as more dangerous. In later studies (cf., Gerbner & Morgan, 2002; Gerbner & Signorielli, 1988), Gerbner discovered that individuals who watched 5 or more hours of television daily overestimated their chances of victimization from crimes, rated their communities as more unsafe, and overestimated crime rates—prompting these researchers to title their theory "mean world syndrome." In short, this theory supports that those who are exposed to media saturation of murder have problems differentiating fact from fiction.

Lee and Dehart (2007, p. 1) conducted a study on serial killers and fear, finding that:

> *The temporal trend in fear of crime is punctuated by a moderate increase during the serial killing spree, and a sharp decline after the apprehension of the serial killer. Moreover, post apprehension data reveal that nearly 56% of respondents report experiencing an increase in their fear of crime specifically in response to the serial killer.*

The study also found that the fear was:

> *Evenly distributed across races and marital statuses, but, as expected, females and younger people were more likely to report increases in fear. Additionally, 46% of the respondents took the extra step of implementing some sort of protective measure, with the most frequent being carrying mace or pepper spray or adding a security device to their home.*

The irony of the situation is that this rise in fear of crime (of both serial killers and crime in general) comes during a time when violent crime has actually decreased. The Federal Bureau of Investigation (FBI) classifies violent crime as composed of four offenses: murder and nonnegligent manslaughter, forcible rape, robbery, and aggravated assault. According to the FBI, from 2000 to 2004, the rate of violent crimes decreased 4.1%. During the same period, aggravated assault was the largest category of crimes, with an estimated 291.1 offenses per 100,000 people. Murder, on the other hand, only constituted 5.5 murders per 100,000 people.

In *The Culture of Fear*, Glassner (2000) reports that while the nation's murder rate went down, "the number of murder stories on network news increased 600% (not counting stories about O. J. Simpson)" (p. xxi). Most of this can be explained by what

Lavrakas (1982) calls "vicarious victimization." Fear of crime can be vicariously experienced by those who have not been victims as a result of media contact alone, regardless of the crime rate. This may be part of why people believe that serial killing is at a crisis level. Although the individual has not been victimized, each instance of media coverage heightens the individual's degree of fear, which manifests itself as both curiosity and a desire for increased protection.

Contrary to popular belief that serial killings have increased dramatically, Figure 1.1 shows that homicides involving multiple victims "increased gradually during the last 2 decades from just under 3% of all homicides in 1976" to just under 5% in 2005 (Bureau of Justice Statistics, 2010). As Figure 1.2 demonstrates, homicides involving two victims have increased slightly over the years, while the percentage of those involving more than two victims has remained relatively steady. Moreover, serial homicides are extremely rare among crimes. The fear associated with so rare an event draws on the belief, fostered by the media, that it is not rare. Similarly, because of the media's coverage of school shootings, high school students now fear becoming a victim. According to an April 30, 1999, CNN/*Time* magazine poll, students are fearful that a shooting could take place at their school.

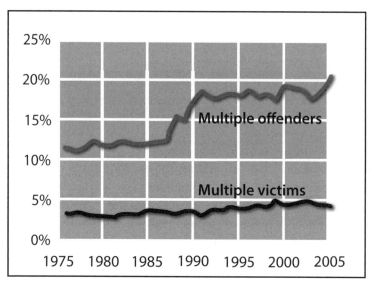

FIGURE 1.1 Percentage of homicides involving multiple offenders or multiple victims, 1976–2005.
Source: Bureau of Justice Statistics, n.d.

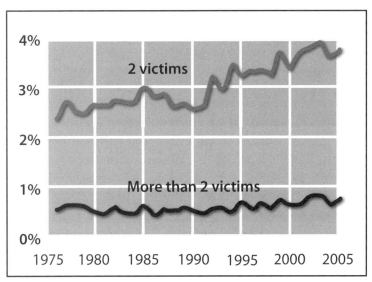

FIGURE 1.2   Homicides involving multiple victims by number of victims.
Source: Bureau of Justice Statistics, n.d.

Still, there are instances of multiple homicide that are so dramatic and frightening that even recognizing their rarity does not reduce their impact on individuals, communities, and the legislation passed in response to the offender's actions. One example is the Port Arthur murders in Tasmania. As reported by Bellamy (2004):

On April 28, 1996, Martin Bryant entered a café in the tourist town of Port Arthur, Tasmania, to get a bite to eat. The town is known for having been one of the first Penal settlements in Australia[n] history, where thousands of tourists flock annually to see a piece of Australian history.

After several minutes of solitude, Bryant stated, "There's a lot of wasps about today." After a few more minutes he made another remark about the lack of "Japanese tourists." Without notice, Bryant picked up his belongings, moved to the rear of the building, opened up his bag, pulled out an automatic rifle and opened fire upon those in the building. In a brief span of seconds, Bryant killed twelve tourists, along with injuring several others.

Bryant moved outside where he continued his rampage, execution style, randomly choosing victims hiding under vehicles and behind trees. He eventually made his way to a cottage on the periphery of the property where there was a standoff with authorities. In a period of just over 19 hours, Martin Bryant, a man described by locals as being "a quiet lad and a bit of a loner," had killed 35 men, women, and children and wounded another 18 making him the most notorious spree killer of all time.

As a result of the Port Arthur murders, the Australian government adopted the National Agreement on Firearms, "which effectively banned self-loading rifles and self-loading and pump action shotguns; and introduced stringent limitations to firearm ownership (namely, minimum age of 18 years and satisfactory reason and fitness for ownership). And [a] 12-month firearms amnesty and compensation scheme (the gun buy back scheme) was also introduced" (Mouzos, 1999, p. 2). These measures responded not just to the probability of such an event recurring but to the effect its magnitude had on citizens and their confidence in the social environment. While this example refers to mass murder, it shows the complex relationship between high-media cases of homicide and the public's fear as well as the public reaction to these events.

Another example is David Berkowitz. Berkowitz became infamous when he began a 13-victim killing spree from July 1976 through August 1977. Berkowitz's trademarks were choosing young women who had long dark hair, using a .44-caliber pistol, and leaving behind taunting notes for the police. Upon his arrest in August 1977, he told law enforcement officials that he went on the killing spree because he was taking orders from his neighbor's dog. Upon hearing this, the media went into a frenzy to get any information on Berkowitz. After a lengthy trial, Berkowitz was offered money to sell the rights to his story for a movie. The public became so enraged by the idea of an infamous brutal killer profiting from his deeds that people began lobbying for laws that would restrict any prisoner from profiting from a crime while in prison, such as by running a business, signing a book deal, or selling rights for a movie. Consequently, "Son of Sam laws" were enacted to prevent prisoners from profiting from their crimes. Instead, money made from the crime would go to the family of the victims.

As a result of increasing fear of crime, coupled with beliefs about incidence and evaluations based on magnitude and drama, more and more Americans are taking reactionary precautions to defend themselves, their property, and their families. For instance, in a national survey on fear of crime, Saad (2001) reports that 32% of respondents had bought a dog for protection, 32% had locks installed, 21% purchased a gun, and 11% kept a gun on their person for defensive purposes. The effects of fear go beyond encouraging people to take such measures. Fear introduces tensions in communities (see Ferraro, 1995; Warr & Ellison, 2000; Wilson & Kelling, 1982). Making celebrities out of serial criminals contributes to anomie. Conklin (2004) concludes that "emphasizing dramatic crimes and persistently high crime rates seem[s] to breed mistrust, insecurity, and weakened attachment to the community" (p. 319). Given these adverse effects, it seems clear that more rigorous studies of serial crime and more accurate information about it can help to mitigate some of the effects of media coverage.

PROBLEMS OF GENERALIZING

Our knowledge of certain offense types is limited. Many studies have relied on the statements of apprehended offenders who are willing to admit they have committed the act and give their consent to talk to authorities or social scientists about their crimes. Even though these offenders talk, it does not mean researchers are getting a complete and accurate snapshot of their motivations, in part because most offenders stick to the "con code" that you only discuss those cases you have been convicted of. Another shortcoming of these studies is that they rely on a small sample of offenders (Balachandra & Swaminath, 2002; Kocsis, 1997; Taylor, Thorne, Robertson, & Avery, 2002), which from a social science model limits their generalizability to a larger population of criminals. Additionally, previous studies do not include perpetrators who have not been caught for their offenses. As a result, these studies may tell us more about those involved in the criminal justice system than about the reality of serial offenses. While these studies are useful in developing hypotheses about those killers willing to talk, there is a lot we do not know about those who have either eluded detection or prefer not to talk to authorities or researchers.

The problem with current typologies used within the criminology community is that typologies such as organized and disorganized offenders are based on data limited in sample size to a population of 36 serial offenders. With such a small sample serving as the basis for theories and predictions, generalizability to larger populations of criminals is limited. Therefore, existing typologies should be seen as a beginning but not the definitive description of offender behavior. In addition, these studies' methodologies are exploratory, not explanatory. Studies of this nature have a tendency to group offenders into broad categories. In the criminal justice field, attempting to use these broad typologies to identify an unknown serial offender can lead to false positives. The characteristics that make up the typology fit too many people and do not accurately identify the concept being investigated.

An additional barrier to solving a case that may result from relying on a typology is that of a mental set. A mental set occurs when individuals persist in using a problem-solving strategy, in this case a typology, they have relied on in the past that does not work in the current situation. As a result, a set of zero-sum thinking emerges in which an individual doing research or investigating serial criminals becomes entrenched in one way of looking at the world.

The FBI typology of serial killers is the best example of these drawbacks. Problems arise when hypotheses are treated as fact. For instance, the FBI's study of serial murderers is broken down into two main types: organized and disorganized. An organized offender is someone who lacks a moral compass and attends to a great deal of detail at the crime scene. Most organized offenders are thought to have some or all of the following qualities:

- Highly intelligent
- Socially adequate
- Skilled worker
- High birth status
- Sexually competent
- Lives with a partner
- Experienced harsh discipline in childhood
- Controlled mood
- Masculine image
- Charming
- Follows crime in the media

The disorganized offender does not pay close attention to detail, and crime scenes are relatively sloppy and show evidence of passion and incompetence. Most disorganized offenders are thought to have some or all of the following qualities:

- Below average intelligence
- Socially inadequate
- Unskilled worker
- Low birth status
- Sexually incompetent
- Lives alone
- Received harsh/inconsistent discipline as a child
- Anxious mood
- Exhibits poor personal hygiene
- Minimal interest in crime in the media

For a study's conclusion to carry weight, the sample must be representative of a greater population. More participants are therefore needed, and they are obtained through a probability sampling technique. Additionally, more caution must be exhibited when choosing and applying the typologies. A useful step in refining the typologies may be to compare and contrast noncriminals who possess the qualities described in the typologies with actual criminals. (See the work of David Canter.) In other words, having a small nonprobability sample creates problems regarding generalizability and hinders identification.

An example can be found in the Maryland sniper case mentioned earlier. From October 2 through October 23, 2002, John Allen Muhammad and Lee Boyd Malvo went on a 23-day killing spree, involving 14 sniper incidents that resulted in 10 deaths. During this time, the media airways were flooded with experts giving profiles of the sniper. On October 3, speculation about the use of a white vehicle in the sniper attacks began to surface. The involvement of a white vehicle, although later shown to be inaccurate, would be the focus of the investigation for several weeks. The lookout for a white van resulted in hundreds of daily calls by people claiming to see suspicious individuals in white vans to the hotlines set up by Chief Moose and his task force. In hindsight, we know that there was neither a white van nor a white man involved. However, these inaccurate leads cost investigators valuable time. What we can learn from this lesson is that overinvesting in one typology, hypothesis, or witness statement can get in the way of serial crime investigation, thus affording offenders more time to carry out such heinous acts. More studies need to be carried out on serial killers, and serial crime in general, in order for law enforcement and academics to understand the complexity of these types of criminals.

A number of social scientists have attempted to overcome the pitfalls of the original FBI study (Hickey, 2002). For example, Hickey constructed a data set of 62 women and 337 men over a period of 195 years (1800–1995), drawing from biographical case study analyses. Although Hickey's study has a larger sample than the original FBI study, it represents an average of only 2.05 cases per year. In addition, it is a post-hoc analysis of existing data without a comparison group. To conduct good social scientific research—as well as scientific crime scene investigations—we need to keep developing, testing, and refining hypotheses to determine if the typologies currently being used are representative of the behaviors demonstrated by current offenders under study. Despite the limitations of his sample population, Hickey has created such a model (Hickey, 2002, p. 33). Hickey utilizes two variables: victims and methods. As Table 1.1 demonstrates, the two variables exhaust combinations of specific victims, a variety of victims, specific methods, or a variety of methods. Hickey believes that this model will help researchers in reevaluating specific typologies as social behavior changes.

As a field, we need to emphasize care in using typologies and also emphasize the value of cases in appreciating the conditions under which certain criminals repeat or serialize their acts. It is important to identify and understand different typologies, their constructs, and their applications.

TABLE 1.1 Factors of Constructing Typologies	
Specific victims	Variety of victims
Specific methods	Specific methods
Specific victims	Variety of victims
Variety of methods	Variety of methods

Source: Hickey, 2002.

INVESTIGATION

A good starting point is to recognize that the investigation of serial offender cases is the most difficult to undertake. Part of the problem is the sheer number of victims involved. According to the FBI (1990), serial murderers average about 9.7 victims. Although the public believes that serial killers have a large number of victims, other serial offenders average more victims. Table 1.2 shows serial killers to have the fewest victims among serial offenders. Several chapters in this book delve into the complexities of serial offenders and consider why they are so elusive to law enforcement.

In Chapter 2, Jack Levin and James Alan Fox discuss the normalcy of serial killers. The serial killer, and all serial offenders for that matter, are not easily identified in the general public. Levin and Fox's chapter discusses the complexity of serial killers and shows that warning signs are not that obvious for these types of offenders. Some offenders do have a history of cruelty to animals or violence against others, but this type of offenders is rare. More often than not, serial killers can go undetected.

TABLE 1.2 Base Rates of Serial Offences	
Offender Type	**Average Number of Victims**
Serial Murderer	9.7
Serial Rapist	20.4
Serial Arsonist	31.5
Pedophile	100–200

Source: FBI, 1990; Sapp, Huff, Gary, Icove, & Horbert, 1994; Hazelwood & Warren, 1995.

In Chapter 8, Labuschagne shows how culture can complicate the distinction between serial murder and muti murder. What law enforcement sees as serial murder, others may see as having religious-cultural importance. Not knowing the motivations for an offender can slow down an investigation. When cultural-religious elements are added to the crime, it makes the investigation of such a crime that much more difficult.

In Chapter 3, Poland, Kilburn, and Alvarez-Rivera discuss the complexities of rapists in our midst. These offenders are so complicated that research on the motivations of serial rapists is continually changing. The chapter details the progression in serial rape and the social-psychological makeup of these offenders. In Chapter 4, Bernier, Kuehnle, and Howerton take a similar approach to the complexities of sex offenders and how the use of technology has assisted in their ability to groom victims. The chapter adds to the field by looking to see if rehabilitation works, and, if so, on which type of offenders.

While serial killers, serial rapists, and sex offenders have had the most attention by researchers, arson has received the least. Research on serial arson has barely scratched the surface of this topic, and a good portion of the research is outdated. In Chapter 8, Parenteau deals with the complexities of this subject, considering the role juvenile offenders play in the makeup of these offenders. Stalking is a relatively new phenomenon, and the vast majority of the research has looked at the unwanted pursuit of one offender and one victim. In Chapter 6, Spitzberg, Dutton, and Kim review the current research on stalking and discuss the omission of serial stalking by other researchers.

While several chapters deal with the social psychology of serial offenders, the remainder of the book looks at issues that may be pertinent to investigation of such cases. Borgeson (2008) points out two distinct problems with serial offender investigation: linkage blindness and department image. Linkage blindness is a term that:

> *refers to the lack of sharing crime scene data with other agencies to help determine whether or not similar cases exist in a surrounding area or state. In order to see if similarities exist agencies need to compare notes on the MO (the way a perpetrator commits the crime) and any type of signature (behaviors unique to that individual person) that the offender uses in committing the crime. (p. 15)*

Another investigative issue centers on public image by police departments:

> *Sometimes agencies are reluctant to reveal that they have a serial killer working in the neighborhood. Having a killer on the loose looks bad for departments and sends the image that the department is ineffective in protecting the public from harm. As a result, the agencies that have suspicions will try to keep this under wraps and work the case slowly in order to find evidence that points to the theory of a multiple killer. (p. 15)*

Schmink's review of task forces in Chapter 12 takes these details into consideration. Because not much information has been made available on this subject, this chapter advances the academic discussion in this area and identifies the complexities of trying to deal with multiple agencies in carrying out the investigation.

To overcome the shortcomings of serial offender investigation, some agencies have turned to the use of profiling and case linkage analysis. Chapter 9 deals with the types of profiling used in serial offender investigation and offers an inside look at how a profiling unit is run. Chapter 10 looks at using case linkage analysis as a tool in helping to link behavioral aspects of offenders over a series of crimes to see whether they may be committed by the same offender. Such a tool is relatively new, and this chapter helps define what case linkage analysis is and how it has been used in criminal investigation. Chapter 11 looks at the least studied part of serial crime, the victim. This chapter is important for researchers because it can help in understanding the victimology of women who are killed by serial murderers.

We believe that a book focusing on behavioral and investigative issues of serial offenders can be useful in policy formation, particularly in regard to comparing different paradigms for developing profiles and in regard to mitigating some of the effects of media coverage by providing facts not only about incidence but about the conditions that influence rates. It can also contribute to a greater clarity in distinguishing between the moral aspect of popular responses to dramatic instances of crime and the types of evidence relevant for reducing harm to society.

CONCLUSION

This book brings together two unique aspects in regard to serial offenders: social-psychological explanations of their behavior and investigative issues. Firstly, when we look at offenders' serial aspect, we may discover that the mere presence of repetition is relevant to our understanding of causation, the role of personality traits and pathology, and other factors connected with such crimes. Secondly, by bringing together the various types of problems with investigation, we may be able to form hypotheses about how to better handle these offenders.

There is another purpose in writing this book, namely to contribute to the ongoing efforts of some scholars and researchers to mitigate the negative social and political consequences of the ways in which crimes such as serial murder are represented in the media to society at large. We assume that increasing the amount of information by applying rigorous methods and presenting it in a more comprehensive format than those available on television and in the press can increase the likelihood of better public understanding and, therefore, better policies.

The difficulties in achieving these goals cannot be overemphasized. To some extent, they are methodological. That is, given that increasing the number of cases is largely out of the hands of researchers, the small number of cases available requires greater attention to each case than is typical. This means increasing the intensiveness with which each case is investigated, which calls for something that anthropologists refer to as the "thick" description. It also means that there needs to be more emphasis on comparative studies, including the employment of control groups. Yet, the sort of access necessary for the advancement of such a program is difficult, often impossible, to obtain, even more so when some of the more prolific serial criminals remain at large. Despite these problems, it is at least possible to avoid the sorts of hasty generalizations that one finds in both the media and, to a certain extent, in the area of policy.

It is understandable that pressures from the public and from law enforcement agencies can lead otherwise responsible researchers to generalize prematurely and to overgeneralize. In this regard, the research community faces the same problems as responsible policy makers who have little choice but to respond to the same pressures. In attempting to bring information together that ordinarily appears apart and out of context, we are also trying to introduce a note of caution in interpreting findings and evaluating both case studies and statistics.

Beyond the study of crimes and criminals, more can be done to clarify the various influences on public perceptions of crime and its dangers and how those perceptions influence the process of policy formation. While this is not represented in the book, it remains a vital topic about which all the authors are aware, and it is one that comes up in one way or another in many studies that have nothing ostensibly to say about it. So it is appropriate in this introduction that several questions be raised in anticipation of future research. The media are often accused of creating misperceptions, increasing fear, decreasing empathy, and perhaps even creating future serial offenders. To what extent are these accusations accurate? For example, to what degree are the media responsible for misperceptions of serial crimes? Is media coverage determined by other more general factors than those directly associated with the television, radio, and print (e.g., social, cultural, political, and economic factors)?

Clearly causation is complex, all the more so when public perception and social policy reflect the total operation of the social system. In any case, it seems clear that policy is more rational and more likely to be focused on the reduction of harm to society when there is an abundance of information and considerate evaluation of it. At the very least, information can increase policy makers' abilities to negotiate the difficult waters of public opinion and to base their ideas and proposals on relevant and accurate evidence.

CHAPTER 2

Normalcy of the Sadistic Serial Killer

Jack Levin and James Alan Fox

In popular culture as in serious writing on the topic, serial killers are frequently characterized as "monsters" who share little, if anything, with "normal" human beings. This image is represented, for example, in the title of Robert Ressler's interesting book *Whoever Fights Monsters*, just as it is in the cinematic depiction of serial killer Aileen Wuornos in the popular film *Monster*. The same image is reinforced by excessive media attention to grisly crimes involving satanic human sacrifice, the sexual torture of children, and acts of cannibalism and necrophilia. While the "normal us" versus "evil them" perspective may be comforting and convenient, it tends to promote several major distortions in our understanding of these hideous crimes.

In this chapter, we focus on certain characteristics that have been widely regarded in the literature as distinctive of sadistic serial killers—in particular, their inability to empathize, concern with impression management, ability to compartmentalize and dehumanize their victims, and need for power and control. We argue that these distinguishing characteristics are hardly distinguishing at all from the vast majority of humanity. In a sense, are the manipulative skills of a serial killer who flatters his victims into modeling for his photo shoots any different from those of the sales clerk who wants to convince a shopper to buy the most expensive dress on the rack? Does the role-playing of the serial killer who kisses his wife goodbye as he goes off to troll the streets for prostitutes to rape and murder really differ from the role-playing of the loving family man who brutally mistreats his employees at work but loves his family? It may be a different playing field but a very similar game.

LACK OF EMPATHY

In the 1930s, social philosopher George Herbert Mead (1934) identified "role taking" as a basic human quality, whereby an individual is able to adopt the viewpoint of another person. Initially, the child takes one role at a time. The child may, for example, "put himself [or herself] in the shoes" of a parent, teacher, sibling, or close friend. Later on, according to Mead, the maturing child develops a consistent self-concept by defining him- or herself from the viewpoint of the entire community or "the generalized other."

Many serial killers apparently share this role-taking ability, even if they use it to enhance the pleasure they derive from inflicting pain and suffering on their victims. Indeed, role-taking ability has been shown to take the form of a continuum rather than a dichotomous variable, along which any given individual's degree of empathy can be located. Thus, there are some individuals whose empathy is so profound and broad that they commiserate with the plight of starving children on the other side of the globe. Many individuals are closer to the middle of the continuum, identifying with the grief of victims in proximity to themselves but emotionally oblivious to the pain and suffering of most strangers. At the other end of the continuum, however, there may also be millions who are completely lacking in empathy. They may not be serial killers, but they are insensitive to human tragedy. They may not kill, but they are more than willing to cheat, swindle, lie, womanize, make unethical business decisions, or sell someone a bad used car.

Mental health specialists seem to agree that the sadistic serial killer tends to be a sociopath, which is a disorder of character rather than of the mind. Such individuals lack a conscience, feel no remorse, care exclusively for their own pleasures in life, and lack the ability to empathize with the suffering of their victims. Other people are seen merely as tools to fulfill their own needs and desires, no matter how perverse or reprehensible (see Hare, 1993; Harrington, 1972; Magid & McKelvey, 1988).

The term sociopath is often employed interchangeably with *psychopath* and *antisocial personality disorder*. Initially, the word psychopath was widely used by psychiatrists and psychologists to identify the syndrome of character traits involving an impulsive, reckless, and selfish disregard of others. In the 1950s, however, the psychiatric profession recommended using the diagnostic term *sociopath*, in part to distinguish the psychopathic personality from the much more serious psychotic disorders. Then in the late 1960s, psychiatrists once again proposed a change in terminology, replacing both the sociopathic and psychopathic diagnoses with the antisocial personality disorder (APD). Some experts in psychopathology maintain fine distinctions among the three diagnostic categories, even offering various subtypes for each (see Samenow, 2004). To understand sadistic serial murder, however, these differences are not particularly important because the fundamental characteristics prevalent among these offenders are, for the most part, common to all three terms.

More disconcerting is Robert Hare's (1993) estimate that at least 1% of the population consists of what he refers to as "subclinical psychopaths." They are not repeat killers but possess the characteristics usually associated with individuals who kill for pleasure. Subclinical psychopaths include charming men who use women for sex and money only to then abandon them, con artists who engage in insider trading and illegal market timing as stockbrokers and money managers, individuals who are HIV-positive and still have unprotected sex, and salespersons who make vastly exaggerated claims about their products. Psychopaths are neighbors, coworkers, bosses, and dates. Some are sadistic serial killers.

We believe that lack of empathy is one characteristic of sadistic killers that has been accepted far too uncritically by psychologists and criminologists alike. Many investigators have indeed argued that sadistic serial killers are incapable of appreciating their victims' pain and suffering. Serial killer Henry Lee Lucas reportedly compared his attitude toward killing humans to our concern for squashing a bug—no big deal. Similarly, Hillside Strangler Kenneth Bianchi boasted that "killing a broad" meant nothing to him. Yet as we will argue, "killing a broad" meant everything to him.

In the case of repeat killers for whom murder is instrumental, the lack of empathy may truly be essential for avoiding apprehension. Profit-motivated serial killers, for example, may not enjoy the suffering of their victims but still take their victims' lives for the sake of expediency. In the 1970s, Gary and Thaddeus Lewingdon committed a series of 10 armed robberies around central Ohio, in which they took their victims' wallets and then cavalierly shot each one in the head. Twenty years later, Sacramento landlady Dorothea Puente, with moral impunity, poisoned to death her nine elderly tenants in order to steal their social security checks. In October 2002, Washington, DC snipers John Allen Muhammad and Lee Boyd Malvo dispassionately shot and killed 10 innocent victims to further their demands for $10 million in ransom—pay up or perish. For them, the physical distance from the victims they gunned down with a long-range rifle inoculated them against any tendency to empathize. The victims were merely and literally targets of opportunity.

For sadistic serial killers, however, murder is an end in itself, making the presence of empathy—even intensely heightened empathy—important in two respects. First, their crimes require highly tuned powers of cognitive empathy in order to capture their victims. Killers who do not understand their victims' feelings would be incapable of conning them effectively. For example, Ted Bundy understood all too well the sensibilities of female college students who were taken in by his feigned helplessness. He trapped attractive young women by appearing to be disabled and asking them for help. Calaveras County killers Leonard Lake and Charles Ng gained entry into the homes of their victims by answering classified ads in the local newspaper, pretending that they wished only to purchase a camcorder or furniture. And Milwaukee's cannibal killer Jeffrey Dahmer met his victims in a bar and lured them to his apartment, where they expected to party, not be murdered.

Second, a well-honed sense of emotional empathy is critical for sadistic killers' enjoyment of their victims' suffering. For sadistic objectives to be realized, killers who torture, sodomize, rape, and humiliate must be able both to understand and to experience their victims' suffering. Otherwise, there would be no enjoyment or sexual arousal. Thus, they feel their victims' pain but interpret it as their own pleasure. Indeed, the more empathic sadistic killers are, the greater their enjoyment of their victims' suffering.

In the literature of psychiatry as well as criminology, lack of empathy—along with a manipulative and calculating style, an absence of remorse, and impulsiveness—is frequently regarded as a defining characteristic of a sociopathic or antisocial personality disorder. Yet a 1982 study by Heilbrun came to quite a different conclusion. In interviews with 168 male prisoners, he found two kinds of sociopaths—those who had poor impulse control, low IQ, and little empathy (the Henry Lee Lucas type) and those who had better impulse control, high IQ, sadistic objectives, and heightened empathy (the Ted Bundy type). In fact, the most empathic group of criminals in Heilbrun's study was comprised of intelligent sociopaths with a history of extreme violence, particularly rape, a crime occasionally involving a sadistic component.

According to Heilbrun, violent acts inflicting pain and suffering are more intentional than impulsive. In addition, empathic skills promote the arousal and satisfaction of sadistic objectives by enhancing the criminal's awareness of the pain being experienced by his or her victim. Because the subjects in Heilbrun's study were surveyed within months of their scheduled parole hearing dates, it is certainly possible that at least some of the observed differences could represent systematic response error. That is, perhaps the more intelligent subjects, anticipating their upcoming parole review, were more apt to feign empathy through their responses. Thus, IQ differences may have produced artificial differences in empathy responses.

Whether or not methodological concerns were partially responsible, Heilbrun's finding of empathic sadistic sociopaths was all but ignored in the literature—that is, until very recently, when psychiatrists began to question the commonly held view that antisocial types necessarily lack the ability to feel their victims' pain. Instead, psychiatrists noted that in many cases these killers possess, as Glen Gabbard (2003) wrote in Psychiatric News, "tremendous powers of empathic discernment—albeit for the purposes of self-aggrandizement."

PRESENTATION OF SELF

Serial killers are often characterized as being extremely skillful at presentation of self. They are seen as unusually capable of looking and acting beyond suspicion, of appearing to be more innocent than a truly innocent person, of being able to lure their victims with charm and cunning.

For example, Derrick Todd Lee, alleged to be the serial killer who raped and murdered a number of women in the Baton Rouge area, eluded capture at least in part because he was able to blend in so well. To many, he came across as "friendly" and "charming." He cooked barbeque and led a Bible study group. Those who got to know him informally regarded him as more a preacher than a killer. Green River Killer Gary Ridgway, who in 2004 was convicted in the deaths of 48 prostitutes in Washington State, brought his young son with him to a crime scene in order to look "fatherly" and give his victim a false sense of security. John Wayne Gacy, who brutally murdered 33 men and boys, was regarded by his suburban Chicago neighbors as a gregarious man who often dressed as a clown at children's birthday parties and organized get-togethers for the people on his block. He often lured victims to his home by offering to interview them for a job with his construction company.

Even if serial killers seem to be skillful at presentation of self, they are certainly not alone in their concern for projecting an image that is acceptable to others. Erving Goffman (1959) long ago suggested that managing the impression that we wish to convey to others is a normal and healthy human characteristic. In fact, successful individuals in many legitimate occupations seem to have a knack for using self-awareness to their personal advantage. This is true, for example, of effective politicians who come across as "one of the boys" or "one of the girls," of skillful actors who base their entire professional lives on their ability to stage a character, and of salespersons who are able to convince their clients that they really do have their best interests at heart.

Even in the most mundane areas of everyday life, normal people stage a character. Goffman distinguished the frontstage, where the performance is given, from the backstage region, where it is rehearsed. In a restaurant, for example, the wait staff stages a scene in the dining area by their cordial and hospitable demeanor with customers. In the kitchen, however, the same waiters complain about their working conditions and swap unflattering stories about experiences with customers.

The difference between serial killers and other people may not lie so much in the greater effectiveness of the killers' presentation of self as a means to an end but in their greater willingness to torture and kill as a result of employing the tactic. When individuals use techniques of self-presentation for benign purposes in everyday life, it escapes our attention. Or, we might characterize our friends and family members in a complimentary way, emphasizing their polite manners, attractive smile, or charming style. When serial killers are polite and charming in order to lure their victims, however, we characterize them as manipulative and crafty.

COMPARTMENTALIZATION AND DEHUMANIZATION

Serial killers typically target absolute strangers. On a practical level, killing in this manner creates a greater challenge for law enforcement by denying them the benefit of knowing the killer's motivation or relationship to the victim. But this may be only half of the story.

Compartmentalization is a psychological facilitator that serial killers use to overcome or neutralize whatever pangs of guilt they might otherwise experience (Fox & Levin, 1998). They are able to compartmentalize their attitudes by conceiving of at least two categories of human beings—those whom they care about and treat with decency and those with whom they have no relationship and therefore can victimize with total disregard for their feelings.

For example, Hillside Strangler Kenneth Bianchi clearly divided the world into two camps. The individuals toward whom he had no feelings including the 12 women he brutally tortured and killed. Bianchi's inner circle consisted of his mother, his common-law wife, and his son, as well as his cousin Angelo Buono, with whom he teamed up for the killings. Bianchi's wife Kelli Boyd once told investigators, "The Ken I knew couldn't ever have hurt anybody or killed anybody. He wasn't the kind of person who could have killed somebody." It could be argued, of course, that Bianchi was simply manipulating his spouse to appear innocent. However, it is also a compelling interpretation that he compartmentalized human beings in a manner that was not very different from the way normal people compartmentalize others in everyday life.

Indeed, the compartmentalization that allows for killing without guilt is really an extension of this universal phenomenon. An executive might be a heartless "son of a bitch" to all his employees at work, but a loving and devoted family man at home. A harsh disciplinarian at home can be highly regarded by friends and acquaintances. Similarly, many serial killers have jobs and families, do volunteer work, and kill part-time with a great deal of selectivity. Thus, a sexual sadist who may be unmercifully cruel in his treatment of a stranger he meets in a bar might not dream of harming his family members, friends, or neighbors.

Despite his conviction on 33 counts of murder, John Wayne Gacy was seen by those in his community as a rather decent and caring man. Lillian Grexa, who had lived next door to Gacy while he was burying victims in the crawl space beneath his house, remained supportive, even writing to him on death row. "I know they say he killed 33 young men," explained Grexa, "but I only knew him as a good neighbor . . . the best I ever had."

Compartmentalization is aided by another universal process: the capacity of human beings to dehumanize "the other" by regarding outsiders as animals or demons who are therefore expendable. Serial killers have taken advantage of this process in the selection of their victims. They often view prostitutes as mere sex machines, gays as AIDS carriers, nursing home patients as vegetables, and homeless alcoholics as nothing more than trash.

On the highways, many drivers become aggressive road warriors, facilitated by the dehumanizing effect of the automobile. Otherwise calm and civil individuals can mistreat other motorists through obscene gestures or worse. They feel anonymous and protected—distanced from the masses by the 3000 pounds of steel that envelops them. In a sense, they are cursing at another vehicle without much consideration for the human being sitting behind the wheel.

In warfare, soldiers similarly learn psychologically to separate the allies from the enemy, treating the latter as less than human. As a result, countless normal and healthy individuals who would never dream of killing for fun have slaughtered the enemy in combat. Not unlike serial killers, they are not, in their minds, killing human beings—only "gooks," "krauts," or "kikes." Amid combat, they continue to hold dehumanized images. After returning home, however, they typically adopt prevailing attitudes toward and live at peace with members of the same groups with whom they previously fought. At the end of the Cold War, for example, we very easily modified our thinking about the "red peril" and "the evil empire," viewing Russians as our allies rather than our mortal enemies. After World War II, the negative image of our Japanese opponents—"the yellow peril"—quickly dissipated.

NEED FOR POWER

Many observers regard the true intention of sexual sadism as the achievement of power, dominance, and control. To the extent that the victim is demeaned and humiliated, the killer is able to feel superior, exalting in the victim's suffering.

Actually, the same motive—to gain a sense of power and control—is widely shared by millions of people around the world, especially men. Some observers have argued, in fact, that power is an integral component of how men express their masculinity. Most of them are, however, able to satisfy their need for power in a socially acceptable way. Business leaders have been known to wheel and deal, hire and fire; some teachers are unnecessarily tough on their students; and parents can be harsh and threatening in their child-rearing practices. For various reasons, serial killers lack whatever it takes to achieve a position of dominance in the legitimate system. Had serial killer Ted Bundy ever completed his law degree, he might have been able to kill them—figuratively, of course—inside the courtroom, rather than on the streets. If Aileen Wuornos had been blessed with a decent childhood, she might have become an aggressive entrepreneur rather than a deadly highway prostitute.

Sadism has even found a prominent position in American popular culture. Many prime-time television series now owe their staying power to the sadistic impulses they exploit on the tube. Audience members have found tremendous enjoyment in viewing horrified contestants devour worms and insects on NBC's *Fear Factor*; Donald Trump exclaim, "You're fired!" on his wildly popular series *The Apprendice*; *American Idol's* Simon Cowell brutally insult contestants; Ann Robinson refer to the losing player as "the weakest link"; contestants backstab one another or eat rodents on *Survivor*; and aspiring singers (lacking any talent) being deceived and humiliated for the sake of a laugh on the WB's contest *Superstar USA*.

CONCLUSION

In their capacity for committing extreme violence against innocent victims, serial killers obviously differ qualitatively from the average person. Very few members of society would be able to torture and kill multiple victims (although the sadistic impulse is probably much more pervasive than we would like to think). In terms of their underlying psychology, however, serial murderers may not differ from normal people as much as we have been led to believe.

An alternative possibility is that the sociopathic designation has been incorrectly applied to sadistic serial killers. If they really do not differ from other people in terms of their ability to project a public image of themselves, their need for power, their ability to compartmentalize, and their empathy for the suffering of victims, then they may not be the extreme sociopaths we have believed them to be. This does not mean that the psyche of the serial murderer is like that of normal people, only that we have been looking in the wrong place for the important differences.

CHAPTER 3

Serial Rape

Amy Poland, John Kilburn, and Lorna Alvarez-Rivera

In 2007, 90,427 rapes were reported to police in the United States, a rate of 30 rapes per 100,000 inhabitants (U.S. Department of Justice, 2008). These numbers represent a decrease of 2.5% from the previous year, the lowest rate since 2000 and lower than rates reported in the late 1980s and early 1990s. This figure, obtained from the FBI Uniform Crime Report, includes only rapes against females reported to law enforcement. There are two significant issues excluded from these numbers: unreported rapes of females and all rapes involving male victims. In terms of rape victimization, the negative stigma substantially inhibits the degree of reporting victimization (Feldman-Summers & Palmer, 1980; Gartner & McMillan, 1995; Jensen & Kapros, 1993); therefore, this concept is often referred to as "the dark figure of crime" (Skogan, 1977). It is necessary, then, to also examine victimization data from the National Crime Victimization Survey (NCVS). According to the NCVS, approximately 248,300 people were sexually assaulted in 2007; this figure includes both males and females over the age of 12 years (Rand, 2008, p. 1). The NCVS shows the same trend in lower rates of rapes in 2007, with a rate of approximately 1 in 1000 people being the victim of a sexual assault, a 33% reduction from 1998.

Part of the confusion in understanding rape is due to the numerous ways of collecting information on rape. There are official statistics from the government, such as the Uniform Crime Reports or National Incident-Based Reporting System, that include crimes that are reported to the police and are recorded in official governmental records. Then, there are victimization surveys that vary from the NCVS, which is sponsored by the Bureau of Justice Statistics, and other victimization surveys that may be done by social agencies or research studies. Each of these studies leads to a different set of statistics defining the severity of the problem.

While there is substantial agreement that rape is a global problem, van Dijk, van Kesteren, and Smit (2008) declare that "measuring sexual incidents [is] difficult in victimization surveys, since perceptions as to what is unacceptable sexual behavior may differ across countries" (p. 77). However, these researchers did attempt to capture general 1-year sexual assault prevalence rates. Their data demonstrate a greater prevalence of sexual assault in the United States, Iceland, Sweden, Northern Ireland, and England and Wales, while showing relatively low rates in Mexico, Hungary, Bulgaria, Spain, and Portugal. According to the authors of the report, one possible explanation is that women in countries with greater equality are more likely to report sexual victimization, especially more minor forms, resulting in higher levels of reported sexual victimization. Another report studying lifetime prevalence of sexual assault listed Mexico relatively high on a list of women whose intimate partners forced sex on them (World Health Organization, 2002).

The typical image of sexual assault may be illustrated by high-profile cases in the media of women being attacked, brutally beaten, and raped in a sadistic manner by one or more strangers. Logically, the thought of being attacked and raped by a stranger would elicit tremendous fear among the general populace. According to researcher Mark Warr:

> *The magnitude and prevalence of such fear are striking, particularly among younger women, who fear rape more than any other crime. The high fear attached to rape stems from the fact that it is perceived to be both extremely serious and relatively likely; and from the fact that it is closely associated with other serious offenses such as homicide and robbery. (1985, p. 238)*

Contrary to the perceptions that there is a high prevalence of rapes committed by a stranger, approximately three out of four rape victims are actually acquainted with their attacker (Greenfield, 1997). Similarly, the NCVS reports that in 63% of cases, the victim knows the attacker; the rapist is a stranger in 32% of cases; and the victim–offender relationship is unknown in 5% of cases (Rand, 2008). Because of this, many protection courses teach that safety should begin with people they know, and less attention and worry should be given to concerns about random attacks.

However, serial rape does not fit this standard profile. Gary Leon Ridgway, the Green River Killer, confessed murderer of 48 women, admitted that strangling, raping, and killing young runaways and prostitutes was his career.

Ridgway is a perfect example of what is considered a sadistic rapist. His modus operandi was luring females into his truck, showing them pictures of his son to put them at ease, and at times even taking them to his home. He typically strangled his victim during sexual intercourse. All but two of his victims were found in or around the Green River near Seattle, nude and in advanced states of decomposition. Ridgway, while reported to have a low IQ, managed to commit most of the killings in a relatively short period of time in the early 1980s by confusing law enforcement agents. Ridgway would lead officers in multiple directions by tampering with the crime sites, leaving behind false evidence to send officers on wild goose chases.

Serial rapists are successful in eluding law enforcement and perpetrating a series of rapes only because they are able to remain anonymous. In addition, much of their anonymity comes from finding victims who do not know them. For example, Gary Ridgway first became a suspect in 1983, but he managed to pass a polygraph test. In 1987, officers obtained hair and saliva samples from Ridgway that were later analyzed and used to acquire a warrant for his arrest in 2001. In his confession, Ridgway told police officers that he chose prostitutes because they would not be reported missing quickly if at all.

By combining the fear of the unknown perpetrator with the knowledge that rapes are occurring in a specific region, serial rapists are more likely to be reported to the police, elicit fear throughout the community, and place a great deal of pressure on law enforcement to find and arrest the offender as quickly as possible (LeBeau, 1985). For example, consider the "Waldo Area Rapist," who terrorized the Kansas City, Missouri, metropolitan area for more than 5 months. A series of five rapes in the Waldo neighborhood caused a great deal of fear among community residents. Law enforcement, with the help of the rapist's victims, created a composite of the rapist that was distributed to area residents. The publicity of the case resulted in feelings of discrimination by black men in the area because the composite showed the rapist as being black. One black man interviewed by the *Kansas City Star* reported, "It's like I have a scarlet letter on me" (Vendel, 2010). In addition, the case has resulted in reports of vigilantism and potential additional violence as neighboring residents have followed people they considered suspicious in the area. After initially calling police, one man followed a potential suspect for several hours into neighboring Kansas City, Kansas, where the potential suspect entered a home, came back out, and fired shots at the person who had followed him. It was later discovered that he was not, in fact, the person responsible for the Waldo-area rapes (KMBC.com, 2010).

This chapter begins by describing the characteristics of serial rape, including the definition of rape and serial rape, as well as the characteristics of serial rapists and their victims. It will also discuss how and where serial rapists approach their victims and the use of force in serial rapes. Finally, this chapter examines typologies of serial rapists, investigative approaches to serial rapes, and criminal profiling of serial rapists.

DEFINING RAPE

Definitions of rape come from official sources, authors of books on the subject, and results from studies of rape victimization. The most commonly cited definition of rape comes from the Uniform Crime Report (UCR). The UCR is an annual compilation of crime statistics from the FBI. The UCR defines rape as "the carnal knowledge of a female forcibly and against her will" and makes no distinction between attempted and completed rape (U.S. Department of Justice, 2008). Another official definition source is the National Incident-Based Reporting System (NIBRS), a more comprehensive crime-reporting system from the FBI. The NIBRS definition of rape includes both male and female victims and differentiates between attempted and completed rapes.

Researchers interested in studying rape have commonly relied on the FBI definition of rape, continuing to exclude males as victims of rape. Kaplan and Sadock (1998), Thornhill and Palmer (2000), and Bartol and Bartol (2005) all refer to rape as sexual intercourse with a woman against her will and without her consent. However, some authors are more inclusive in their definitions of rape. For example, Holmes and Holmes (2002, p. 139) define rape as forcible sexual intercourse with an individual against his or her will. And Groth and Birnbaum (1979, pp. 2–4) define rape to include any forcible sexual assault including sexual intercourse as well as other sexual acts. While the research on male rape is scarce and exploratory at best, there is a growing increase in its study (Graham, 2006). Scarce (1997) suggests that in 5–10% of all rapes reported, the victim is a male.

The National Violence Against Women Survey defines rape as "an event that occurred without the victim's consent that involved the use or threat of force in vaginal, anal, or oral intercourse." This definition includes both attempted and completed rapes. Koss, Gidycz, and Wisniewski (1987) constructed a definition of rape that included unwanted sexual intercourse because they were given alcohol or drugs by a man, unwanted sexual intercourse because they were threatened or physically forced, or unwanted sexual acts (anal or oral intercourse or penetration with objects other than a penis) because they were threatened or physically forced. The National Women's study (Kilpatrick, 2000) also constructed a definition of rape from multiple questions asked of respondents. Women were considered to have been raped if they answered affirmatively to being threatened or forced to have vaginal, oral, or anal sex or if they had someone put fingers or objects in their vagina or anus by using force or threat.

DEFINING SERIAL RAPE

As a unique form of rape involving multiple victims, there is no clear consensus on what makes a rape a "serial rape." It may be as simple as two or more rapes by the same person (LeBeau, 1987; Santtila, Junkkila, & Sandnabba, 2005). However, other sources require that at least 3 rapes be committed by the same person or persons (FBI), or at least 10 offenses by the same offender (Hazelwood & Burgess, 1987a; Hazelwood & Warren, 1989) for a classification of serial rape to be applied. Another significant criterion in classifying rape as serial rape is the existence, or lack thereof, of a cooling-off period between offenses (Douglas, Burgess, Burgess, & Ressler, 1992; Graney & Arrigo, 2002; Kocsis & Irwin, 1998).

The one consistent element between studies is the attempt to identify those who have a propensity to commit repeated rapes. Typically, studies in which the definition of serial rape requires larger numbers of rapes are attempting to examine changes in rapists' behaviors over time and to understand how rapists who have eluded law enforcement have been able to do so. Kocsis (2006) argues that it is possible for a person to have the same propensity to reoffend even with a single victim. It is this propensity to reoffend that separates serial rapists from other rapists. In contrast, Graney and Arrigo (2002) argue that it is the ability to elude apprehension that distinguishes serial rapists from single-victim rapists.

Characteristics of Serial Rapists

Several teams of researchers (Beauregard, Rossmo, & Proulx, 2007; Hazelwood & Warren, 1989; Park, Schlesinger, Pinizzotto, & Davis, 2008; Santtila et al., 2005; Warren et al., 1999) have identified many typical characteristics of serial rapists. Among the most significant findings are that these offenders commit anywhere from 2 to 17 rapes before being apprehended and are males ranging in age from their late 20s to early 30s, many of whom had previously been married or cohabited and had children. In terms of sociodemographic characteristics, there is little racial difference found among most studies of serial rapists, and although nearly one-third were unemployed at the time of the attack, in one study most reported being economically comfortable or advantaged (Hazelwood & Warren, 1989, p. 19). Serial rapists typically live in the area where they commit their rapes and are under the influence of alcohol at the time of the rape. Of the sample population, 78% were exclusively heterosexual, and 92% were sexually interested in people in the same age group (1989, p. 24).

When examining the childhood and family of serial rapists, several patterns emerge. Half of the serial rapists in the Hazelwood and Warren study (1989) were raised in homes where the mother was the dominant parental figure, with the father being dominant in 40% of homes and some other adult figure being dominant in the remaining 10% of homes. Holmes and Holmes (2008) explain that rapists may take out their hostility and anger toward their dominating mother on future rape victims, inflicting the pain they felt at their mother's hands on their victims. Just over one-third of the men reported that their relationship with their mother was close; only 18% said they had a close relationship with their father. It is the relationship with the rapist's mother that seems to have the most impact on the offender's likelihood to be a serial rapist.

While physical abuse was reported by 30% of the men, psychological abuse (73%) and sexual abuse (76%) was much more common among the men. Holmes and Holmes (2002) report that rapists often are seduced by their mothers or other adults at a young age; this may range from covert seductive behaviors to actual sexual victimization. Some rapists also have a history of parental rejection and cruelty in their childhood, leading to increased hostility toward women in general. When the men were asked about past or present sexual behavior, over two-thirds of the serial rapists reported that they began with window peeping while in childhood or adolescence, 41% reported fetishism, and 38% had made obscene phone calls (2002, p. 21). Other common behaviors among the men included collecting pornography and detective magazines, sexual bondage, cross-dressing, and prostitution. According to Holmes and Holmes (2008), early sexual behavior and exposure to violent pornography may cause serial rapists to view their victims as willing participants rather than victims. All of these actions lead to trauma and problems that in turn lead to gradually more violent and antisocial behavior. This progression is referred to as the "graduation hypothesis."

Rapists typically have a criminal history consisting of mostly nonviolent property crimes escalating over time. Many of the rapists in the study were identified at an early age as being either delinquent or emotionally disturbed. Almost three-fourths of serial rapists in the study reported previous stealing and shoplifting offenses, while temper tantrums/hyperactivity and alcohol abuse were reported in approximately two-thirds of the rapists. Other common childhood behaviors among the rapists in the study included isolation/withdrawal, assaultive behavior toward adults, and chronic lying.

Hazelwood and Warren (1989, p. 23) found that the rapists in the study reported adolescent behavior patterns believed to predict violent behavior in adulthood as well, including enuresis (32%), fire setting (24%), and cruelty to animals (19%). Many would likely fit the *Diagnostic and Statistical Manual* (DSM) diagnosis criteria for conduct disorder in adolescence and later for antisocial personality disorder.

Victim Characteristics and Approach

The factors that Beauregard et al. (2007) found most common in serial rapists' victim selection are location and availability, general physical appearance, vulnerability, age, personality, and behavior. Hazelwood and Warren (1989) suggest that the majority of victims were strangers to the offender, a fact that aids offenders in not being apprehended. In only 16 instances (13%) did one of the rapists report raping an acquaintance, neighbor, or friend.

While victims were predominantly adult white women between the ages of 5 and 65 years, 19% of the victims were children and 2% were males (Hazelwood & Warren, 1989). As with most violent crimes, serial rape is largely intraracial, though black offenders reported raping both white and black women. Becker (2007) explains that racial segregation of white and minority populations residentially as well as within occupations and in the educational system offers limited access to victims outside one's own race.

Rossmo (1997) separates a serial rapist's approach or selection of victims into the search for a suitable victim and the method of attack. The selection of victims refers to where serial rapists search for victims, with four search methods identified: hunting, poaching, trolling, and trapping. Hunters (as cited in Rossmo) look for victims within their own city of residence, searching for victims in areas with which they are already familiar. According to Greenfield (1997), more than half of these rapes take place within a mile of the victim's home. Poachers, on the other hand, travel outside their city to find victims. Serial rapists tend to be hunters, trollers, or trappers, preferring victims within their own city rather than travelling to another city as a poacher would.

Trollers are opportunistic and encounter victims in their everyday lives. Almost half of serial rapists spend most of their time searching for potential victims, even as they are going about their daily lives shopping, working, walking, or driving. With regard to where they approach their victims, these serial rapists tend to interact with victims in places they are most likely to be. Rapists initially encounter their victim in a public place they frequent, such as a bar or a movie theater, or on the way home. They approach the victim outside. Most of the rapes take place at night on a weekday with the actual rape occurring in private or semiprivate area such as an apartment or a stairwell or laundry area in an apartment building (Santtila et al., 2005).

Trappers have occupations or positions that bring potential victims to them. For example, Beauregard, Rossmo, and Proulx (2007) found that one-fourth of serial rapists work where they can come into contact with potential victims; they may work with vulnerable populations in hospitals or day-care centers or coach sports or work in bicycle repair. Some hunt for victims through an acquaintance's family; they may befriend a single mom and gain her trust, then offer to help her in an effort to get access to her children.

With regard to the attack used in serial rape, the majority of serial rapes are perpetrated with a single offender attacking a single victim (Santtila et al., 2005). The most common form of attack has been described as a blitz attack (LeBeau, 1987) or surprise attack (Hazelwood & Warren, 1990). These types of attacks target previously unknown victims by breaking into their houses and attacking them in their sleep. They differ mostly in the degree of injury inflicted upon the victim. In a blitz attack, the rapist most often overpowers the victim physically or with chemicals or gases. This approach also prevents the rapist from being aroused by fantasy components of the rape such as having a willing partner. The surprise attack, in contrast, involves the rapist waiting for the victim or approaching the victim when sleeping. In a surprise attack, there is rarely enough force used to cause injury; however, the rapist may threaten the victim and may have a weapon present (Hazelwood & Warren, 1990).

Santtila and colleagues (2005) found that offenders were more likely to use the confidence approach (which Hazelwood and Warren refer to as the con approach). This approach assumes that the rapist has the ability to interact with the victims, as the rapist using this technique "openly approaches the victim and requests or offers some type of assistance or direction" (Hazelwood & Warren, 1990, p. 12). In the study by Santtila and colleagues, it was common for the victim to voluntarily join the offender (for example after leaving a restaurant drunk). While initially the victims will go willingly with rapists using this approach, they forcefully resist the offender about half the time (Santtila et al., 2005). Moreover, the rapist may also become more aggressive once the victim is within his control (Hazelwood & Warren, 1990).

Although most serial rapes are strangers using blitz, surprise, or con tactics on total strangers, rapes may also occur through more conventional dating methods. For example, a recent case, accused rapist Zebulon Whisler alleged that he developed relationships by meeting women through Internet sites and friends. Whisler at the time of the allegations was 24 years old and employed as a cook in a bowling alley diner. One specific case detailed that his behavior was not much different than if he were on a "normal date." He picked his date up and took her to a bar, and they later went stargazing at the top of a mountain. Whisler's size (6 feet 8 inches tall and 240 pounds) created an intimidating presence. This led to individual victims being fearful about reporting their victimization; there was little testimony until the state troopers launched their investigation (White, 2009). Shortly after his arrest, it was discovered that Whisler suffered from a genetic disorder and was convicted 10 years previously of sexual assault on 9- and 10-year-old girls when he was a teenager residing in Oregon (Hollander, 2009).

Serial Rape and Use of Force

The use of force varies among serial rapists. Father John Geoghan was accused of molesting 130 children in his 30-year career, and the resulting legal investigation concluded that at least 780 children were abused by 250 employees of the Boston Archdiocese from 1940 to 2002. While there was definitely an abuse of power in the serial rapes by the priests and other employees of the church, there have been no significant reports of the use of force in these attacks. On the other end of the spectrum, rape and murder are consistently linked in the attacks perpetrated by Andrei Romanovich Chikatilo. In 1978, he attempted to rape a 9-year-old girl; as the girl tried to escape, he stabbed her to death and ejaculated while stabbing her. He was also responsible for a spree of several sexually related murders in 1982 and another series of sexually related murders in the late 1980s.

In the cases studied, most male serial rapists used their physical presence or verbal threats to control their victims. More than three-fourths used little or no force in any of their attacks (Hazelwood & Warren, 1989; Stevens, 1997). When force was used, it was used to shock victims into submission; the goal for these offenders was to achieve sexual contact and/or intimacy with their victims (Stevens, 1997). They showed no change over time in amount of force used, the pleasure they experienced, the number of victim injuries, or the length of the assault (Hazelwood, Reboussin, & Warren, 1989; Santtila et al., 2005; Stevens, 1997). This would seem to indicate that the modus operandi of the serial rapist does not change much from one rape to the next. Hazelwood, Reboussin, and Warren (1989, pp. 71–75) did find that approximately one-fourth of the serial rapists demonstrated a significant escalation of force from the first rape to the last, with four victims receiving fatal injuries. Additionally, 9 of the 10 subjects who increased the force used inflicted "moderate to fatal" injuries during the final assault. When compared with serial rapists who showed no change in force used over time, these offenders (labeled increasers) raped more women (40 vs. 22) in half the time (19 days between rapes vs. 55 days between rapes). Moreover, they exhibited a higher degree of victim injury during the last rape committed and more sadistic acts, such as anal sex, during the final assault. Stevens (1997) labeled these men "ultimate violence" offenders, as their goal in the attack was the destruction of another with sexual acts feeding from that goal. Such offenders use rape to totally dominate their victim and cannot be stopped short of their own destruction.

The rapist's pleasure was related to victim resistance, with the rapist's pleasure being greater when the victim resisted in the first or middle assault but not in the last assault; victim resistance also increased the duration of the rape. The most common reaction to victim resistance was verbal threats. Some rapists attempted to negotiate or compromise with resisting victims while others stopped the attack when the victim resisted. There was no relationship between victim resistance and injury to the victim (Hazelwood & Warren, 1989). Similar to the limited use of force exhibited in most serial rapists, injuries were most often bruises, black eyes, or cuts. Less than one-fourth of the victims had gunshot or knife wounds, and even rarer were internal injuries, head injuries resulting in loss of consciousness, broken bones, or knocked-out teeth (Santtila et al., 2005).

The most common sexual activities victims were forced to engage in were vaginal penetration, oral sex, fondling, removal of the victims' clothing, ejaculation by the offender, and kissing (Hazelwood & Warren, 1990; Santtila et al., 2005). Santtila et al. found that offenders achieved penetration multiple times in about half of the attacks. Hazelwood and Warren observed that forced anal sex and penetration with a foreign object were reported less frequently. Moreover, they found that in examining multiple offenses by the same offender, there was an increased interest in oral sex and decreased interest in vaginal sex over time.

TYPOLOGIES OF SERIAL RAPISTS

The characteristics of rapists when known can be used to develop typologies, or models of personality types, of rapists. While some scholars argue that there are many different kinds of rapists (Rabkin, 1979), others have narrowed down the number to just a few. Groth, Burgess, and Holmstrom (1977) examined more than 100 convicted rapists and their victims and reported three central themes when discussing rape: anger, power, and sexuality. The primary explanation is that the perpetrator is acting out an exercise of power or expressing anger. They subsequently categorized rapes into two typologies: anger and power.[2]

---

[2] In a succeeding collaboration, Groth and Birnbaum added a third typology: sadism rapes, in which the rapist engages in rituals and torture during the crime. In sadism rapes, the rapist might position the victim in a specific way or might introduce a weapon of sorts (1979). However, the authors of this chapter perceive significant overlap between sadism rapes and anger rapes within the original typologies.

Anger Rapes Versus Power Rapes

Groth and colleagues (1977) argue that anger rapes are characterized by loathing and anger toward the victim, not necessarily due to the victim's behavior or wrongdoing but due to past rejection or ridicule the rapist has suffered. One subcategory of anger rape is the anger-retaliation rape that occurs as an expression of hate toward women in general. Anger-retaliation rapists gain a release by expressing their anger through a brief attack with the use of physical force on anonymous victims. Another subcategory of anger rape is the anger-excitation rape in which the victim's prolonged suffering produces pleasure to the rapist. This form of anger rape is characterized by careful planning, as the victim is subject to torture for several hours or days in the commission of the sexual attack.

Power rapes are more likely to be about power and control over the victim than specific sexual role-playing. The expression of power divides into two subcategories: power-assertive and power-reassurance. In power-assertive rapes, rapists forcefully assert their power by establishing dominance over the victim. They claim that the act of rape is an expression of their own virility and strength. While still focused on the power dynamic, *power-reassurance* rapists are more likely to frame their actions as a response to their own sexual inadequacy. The lack of overt force assists in the perpetrators' own faulty rationalization that they did not cause any significant harm but rather were seducing the victim.

Hazelwood and Burgess (1987b) outline the dimensions of four types of rapists: the power-reassurance rapist, the *power-assertive* rapist, the *anger-retaliatory* rapist, and the *anger-excitation* rapist. Power-reassurance rapists follow a ritual because the rape is committed to act out a fantasy. Thus, the intent is not to harm the victim but to make the victim play a specific role. They target individuals who will best fulfill the dream. The power perspective is used as a demonstration of masculinity, where the victim is "overpowered" by the fantasy that the rapist is actually being seductive, rather than violent. Part of the fantasy is the rapist's self-assertion that he is not being selfish or harmful, but is truly full of sensual, masculine, seductive powers. Power-assertive typology may be stated in a simpler manner. These offenders will attack with a sense of entitlement to express that they do have the power to overpower their victims. Anger-retaliatory rapists, while not as common, are feared due to the severity and brutality they show. The act of rape is accompanied by significant physical violence that focuses on harming the victim and getting back at the victim—or, more likely, women in general. These acts can be spontaneous, where the perpetrator is unexpectedly "set off" into a rage. Anger-excitation rapists experience excitement from the victims' suffering, which, in most cases, results in the victims' murder.

Bear in mind, while the majority of rapists can be classified into a category, research suggests that 25% of rapists cannot be classified (Barbaree, Seto, Serin, Amos, & Preston, 1994).

Other Typologies of Serial Rape

Another framework for understanding the actions of a serial rapist was developed by the Massachusetts Treatment Center for Sexually Dangerous Persons (Knight & Prentky, 1987; Prentky, Cohen, & Seghorn, 1985). Using data from offenses dating back to 1958, this study classified sexual offenders into categories in attempting to understand the motives of the offender. These classifications were originally developed as the Massachusetts Treatment Center: Rape 1 (MTC:R1) classification and were later refined to models that offered more detailed classifications, eventually becoming the MTC:R3 system. As shown in Table 3.1 below, this system classifies offenders by the meaning of the aggression during the offense, the meaning of the sexuality in the offense, and the general impulsivity of the perpetrator. The various combinations of offenses identify nine unique types of offenders.

TABLE 3.1 Typologies of Serial Rape Derived from the MTC:R3	
Type	**Characteristics**
Opportunistic	Opportunistic, high or low social competence
Pervasive anger	Pervasive anger
Sexual	Overt or muted sadism Sexualized, high or low social competence
Vindictive	Vindictive, high or low social competence

The nature of the sexual acts may be sadistic, overtly causing harm and damaging the victim, or they may be nonsadistic, possibly in an awkward attempt to provide a sexual release. The degree of social competence becomes an important aspect of understanding the actions. While assisting in our level of understanding the classifications of offenders by investigating the degree of anger, power, social competence, and sexual factors related to the crime, some critiques of this classification system point out that there is a degree of overlap between the categories (McCabe & Wauchope, 2005). For example, this degree of overlap may lead to negating significant behaviors because an individual is classified as motivated by anger, but the motivations for anger and the way an offender deals with anger may vary among individuals.

Santtila and colleagues (2005) found four different types of rapists based on their behaviors during the rape: sexually hostile, physically hostile, involvement-deceptive, and involvement-expressive. Sexually hostile serial rapists approach their victims outdoors, achieve penetration more than once, and achieve or attempt other sexual acts. Physically hostile offenders attack their victims outdoors, manually gag their victims, and cause injuries to their victims as a result of the attack. Involvement-expressive rapists remove victims' clothing to reveal their breasts, verbally threaten their victims to not report the rape, and reveal information about themselves; they are also more likely to reside in the area where the crime occurred. Involvement-deceptive rapists target victims who are under the influence of alcohol and/or drugs, use the confidence approach to get victims to join them voluntarily, and typically attack on weekdays; they are more likely to be unemployed.

Developmental Issues

The development of serial rapists is somewhat complex in that they have significant histories of committing antisocial and criminal acts (Weinrott & Saylor, 1991). From an individual offender perspective, most serial rapists were exposed to traumatic events defined as "forced" or "exploitive" sexual experiences (Hazelwood & Warren, 1989). Serial rapists differ from those who have raped only once in that they are more likely to claim to be acting out sexual fantasies during their attacks (Grubin & Gunn, 1990). Even then, among serial rapists, some become "impulsive" offenders, striking out in a relatively unsophisticated and reactive manner, while others are "ritualistic" offenders, acting out fantasies and carefully designing details in setting the crime scene and the actions that will take place, frequently leading to medically documented injuries on the victim (Hazelwood & Warren, 2000).

Grubin and Gunn's (1990) study of 142 rapists found that more than four out of five had a criminal history, and half had four or more convictions for some type of offense. We should note that many of these acts were not necessarily sexually related offenses; rather, they show an escalation that began with a series of significant family problems and alcohol dependency. Later, other offenses such as animal cruelty, antisocial behavior, property crime, and violence became common (Arluke, Levin, Luke, & Ascione, 1999). Additionally, 30% had been previously convicted of some type of sexually related offense, such as indecent exposure. Wright and Hensley (2003) offer a detailed description of the escalating offenses—called the "graduation hypothesis," as mentioned earlier—with their detailed description of the life of Jeffrey Dahmer. Dahmer's childhood was spent in relative isolation, marked by difficulties in making friends. At 10 years of age, he carried around and dissected the bodies of dead animals then began desecrating the bodies of the animals. He developed alcohol dependency in his teens, then "graduated" to attacking humans and raping them either shortly before or soon after their deaths. Dahmer is believed to be responsible for the murder, rape, and mutilation of 17 men and boys.

INVESTIGATING SERIAL RAPE

The characteristics and typologies of serial rapists previously described can be used to identify, investigate, and apprehend serial rapists. In their *Rape Investigation Handbook*, Savino and Turvey (2005) report that serial rape suspects are brought to the attention of investigators in many different ways. They may confess to the series of rapes, or someone else (e.g., a victim, another criminal, a family member, a friend, a neighbor) may provide investigators with information about them. Serial rapists are sometimes identified through traffic stops or arrests for unrelated offenses. The South Side Rapist, Dennis Rabbitt, was eventually caught after being chased for prowling into a window. Law enforcement officers had been told that Rabbitt was likely attempting far more rapes than he was successful in completing and turned their attention toward reports of burglaries. On the night he was chased, he had false plates on his van and had been stopped earlier in the evening for the plates. Using the information about the van from the police report, one detective spent his off-duty time watching for the van in the area where the South Side Rapist was believed to live. When he saw it at a party, he walked into the party and asked whose van it was. He then took Rabbitt into custody and obtained a DNA sample from him. Rabbitt was released pending the DNA results and fled to Albuquerque, New Mexico, where he was caught several months later. Rabbitt confessed to all but one of the rapes for which he was accused. He pled guilty to about 50 felony counts in Missouri and additional counts in Illinois.

A second issue important in investigations of serial rape is the ability to identify the subset of serial rapists who will also increase the amount of force and injury used during their attacks. Warren et al. (1999) found that rapists who are white and who, during their first rape, rape their victims for longer periods of time and use more profanity are more likely to escalate their level of blunt force in subsequent rapes. They use the term "increaser" for rapists who escalate during the actions. It is thought that these increasers are less likely to have general criminal histories and instead are focused more on sexual violence. Those less likely to escalate and use profanity may be more likely to commit the sexual assault as one of many different crimes. It is helpful when investigating serial rapes to understand that these men shared a number of characteristics that differentiated them from other serial rapists. These characteristics include raping more women over the age of 40 years, raping their victims indoors, conveying more information about themselves to their victims, making excuses for their behavior, expressing more hostility in general and toward women, inflicting more injuries, using more force than necessary, and humiliating their victims. They also were more likely to plan their attacks, were more specific in choosing their victims, and were more likely to penetrate their victims with a foreign object. These characteristics can be useful for law enforcement as they prioritize investigations. They are also useful for identifying serial rapists who will not only rape more victims but also do so in a more violent and life-threatening manner.

DNA Evidence in Rape Cases

DNA evidence is often used to link cases in serial rape investigations. It is used to positively identify suspects as well as to eliminate other potential suspects. It also provides a tangible link between different attacks, allowing law enforcement to know one offender is responsible for the attacks. DNA evidence is collected from the crime scene and compared to known DNA samples of potential suspects. With the exception of identical twins, no one has the same DNA, making it possible to positively identify the person(s) responsible for a crime. Moreover, it is also possible to compare DNA from an unknown suspect to DNA samples collected by law enforcement nationwide through the use of the Combined DNA Index System (CODIS), an FBI-managed database (Buckles, 2007).

While DNA evidence has gained legitimacy in the criminal court system and is useful for investigations, it is not infallible. It is still subject to human error. DNA information has to be entered into a database for a match to be found. In Denver, police submitted evidence from three victims to CODIS, but it was not uploaded, causing a delay in identifying the suspect in a rape case. Brent J. Brents was later apprehended for additional rapes and linked to the earlier rape as well; he pled guilty to 68 charges related to 7 rapes and 1 additional assault. Brents's DNA profile was already in the DNA database due to previous convictions for child molestation (Callebs, 2005; Nguyen, 2005). The DNA from the victims was not matched due to an FBI contractor's transfer of data to a new server, which happened to additional samples around the same time.

Another issue with DNA evidence is the time it takes for evidence to be processed and the backlog of cases being put into the database. If DNA is being collected and analyzed on a suspect, the suspect will likely be released pending results of the DNA examination. According to an article in *St. Louis Magazine*, that is what happened to police detectives in St. Louis who tracked down the South Side Rapist from a lead about stolen license plates (Cooperman, 2005). As mentioned earlier, using the information on the license plate, one detective waited for the van to show up. When Rabbitt identified himself as the owner of the van, he was arrested and gave a DNA sample to police. In 1998, when he was first caught, DNA matching could take as long as 4 weeks, so Rabbitt had to be released. A week later, the DNA results came back identifying Rabbitt as the South Side Rapist. But he was already out of town by then and was not caught until months later in Albuquerque.

In the past, forensic science has produced valuable evidence that has contributed to the successful prosecution and conviction of criminals. In fact, many crimes that were previously unsolved are now being solved because forensic science is helping to identify perpetrators. However, in some cases poor forensic analysis and imprecise or exaggerated testimony on forensic evidence has led to the admission of erroneous or misleading evidence. According to a recent study from the National Academy of Sciences (NAS) (2009), changes and advancements are needed to ensure reliability of work, establish enforceable standards, and promote best practices with consistent application. The NAS argues that the lack of a systematic methodology for collecting evidence, as well as testing for the presence of DNA, may lead to confusion in trials, with various experts claiming validity regarding specific findings. For example, this report notes that blood and saliva tests may yield variable responses to tests. Some use chemical tests while others may use light wavelengths as evidence. Some tests search for specific antigens while others look for proteins. Other concerns are related to the collection and handling of evidence. Systems for collecting forensic evidence must be upgraded, better training must be offered for collecting and analyzing forensic evidence, and uniform and enforceable best practices must be established. Moreover, the NAS argues that mandatory certification and accreditation programs need to be required.

CRIMINAL PROFILING AND LINKAGE BLINDNESS

Similar to the use of DNA evidence, criminal profiling has attained unprecedented recognition in law enforcement. This has happened despite little empirical evidence to support its validity and the absence of any information on the skills involved. The origin of profiling stems from investigation of atypical crimes with a psychologically aberrant offender whose motives appear outside typical criminological patterns and police investigative procedures. Most evidence of the accuracy of profiling is anecdotal and found in true crime books. Criminal profiling has grown due to media attention and glamorization of profiling techniques. Movies and television shows revolving around criminal profiling are abundant. Unlike other law enforcement techniques, criminal profiling is primarily used for investigations and is rarely presented in court; as such, it is rarely scrutinized in the same manner as other law enforcement techniques, allowing it to gain in popularity even without solid evidence of its usefulness. The rationale for the continued use of criminal profiling is circular in that accuracy and validity of profiling is demonstrated through its continued use and demand by police agencies.

In terms of understanding the nature of serial rape, criminal profilers attempt to understand circumstances such as the motive of the offender (the reason the crime was committed), the ways in which the offender chooses the victim, and actions taken by the offender. Profiling should be used as a decision support tool as opposed to a magic bullet for solving cases (Rossmo, 2000). While each offense is unique, in the case of serial offenses, offenders often use the same modus operandi, sometimes referred to as the "MO," and/or leave "signatures." The modus operandi is the way in which the serial rape is committed and everything at the crime scene such as the time of the attack, point of entry, type of weapon(s) used, type of victim involved, the means of the attack, and any other unique elements presented at the crime scene (Buckles, 2007). A signature, on the other hand, is a "calling card" left by the rapist; it is an action or ritual some serial rapists perform at a crime scene. Authorities believe rapists leave a signature either because they are compelled to do so because they are left unsatisfied by the crime itself or as a way to gain publicity and taunt law enforcement officials. In terms of investigating serial rape, we are not interested in the similarities among serial rapists but their unique differences. It is the unique manner in which they choose their victims, perform their criminal actions, and act afterward that we must identify.

In terms of choosing their victim, some profilers have shown that certain serial rapists are likely to continue striking in a small geographic area. The knowledge they have allows them more control over their environment when they strike their victim. There are myriad factors related to the attack that provide a signature to the specific perpetrator. A few examples include:

- The amount of and type of violence used
- The use of bindings for disabling the victim
- The use of transportation in moving the victim
- The tone of voice and language used in addressing the victim
- The duration of rape and the specific actions performed by the perpetrator

Therefore, some may be soft-spoken and awkward in their attack, for example; these traits may be associated with the use of a specific weapon. Serial rapists range in the degree to which they deny causing any significant harm to their victims. Some take advantage of circumstances and repeatedly perform the act because they see an opportunity; others are pervasively angry and wish to release their anger. Still others are more personally vindictive, while some individuals see the action as having sexual relations (Knight &

Prentky, 1990). One individual's seduction can be another's aggressive attack. Because of this, many of them do not wish to participate in any form of treatment.

With regard to the circumstances of the attack, most victims are unsuspecting strangers. However, while the victims may not know the offender, Hazelwood and Warren (1990) claim that only 15–22% of serial rapes are impulsive attacks. Instead, the victims were carefully selected by the offender, who determines specific targets, times, and places to attack. Due to the nature of the surprise attack, frequently offenders only threaten violence to gain control over the victim.

Geographic profiling specifically examines the role of geography within the crime scene. It is a process used to discover the most probable area of residence of a serial offender (LeBeau, 2005). For example, Rossmo, Davies, and Patrick (2004) found that serial rapists traveled farther than nonserial rapists; however, LeBeau (1987) found that serial offenders traveled about half as far as nonserial offenders. The distance offenders travel to find a victim is influenced by their method of transportation, how familiar they are with an area, the number and types of barriers present, and the presence of alternative routes of travel (Holmes & Holmes, 2002). Criminals are more likely to conduct their criminal activities close to their homes, workplaces, or other centers of activity. Moreover, Canter (2000) argues that offenders will act consistently over time and in different situations. The consistency hypothesis asserts that the way the crime is committed will reflect the everyday behavior and traits of the offender. It can be applied both to the interactions between the offender and the victim and to the geographic area where the crimes are committed. Canter and Larkin (1993) put forth the "circle hypothesis," stating that an offender will live within a circle, using the two farthest offenses as its diameter. While this knowledge is helpful in identifying potential suspects, it is not very precise.

The ideal case for geographic profiling would have more incidents rather than fewer, incidents that cluster around a single location or home base, and incidents close together temporally as well as spatially. Ideally, the incidents would also be within one law enforcement jurisdiction and within that jurisdiction there would be an observant and motivated investigator on the case who is trained in extracting meaningful information from geographic information. Regarding information about the offender, geographic profiling is easier with offenders who have a previous record of serial rape and are offending in an otherwise low-crime environment.

It is difficult for investigators to know when several rapes are committed by the same serial rapist. When Dennis Rabbitt, the South Side Rapist, was apprehended, it was for rapes that had occurred between 1992 and 1997. Investigators had not linked him to additional rapes in the previous 20 years because the rapes were committed over several different jurisdictions. When investigators are able to link crimes to a single offender, it reduces the number of suspects and increases the evidence gained on the offender, thus leading to more productive and efficient investigative strategies (Santtila et al., 2005).

Ideally, cases would be linked through hard physical evidence such as DNA or fingerprints, but these findings are often not present or are inconclusive. They are also time consuming and expensive to process. Linking cases using offender crime scene behavior can be helpful when physical evidence is unavailable. There are two main assumptions behind linking crimes based on offender behavior: (1) An offender will behave in a similar manner over repeated crimes (consistency) and (2) no two offenders will exhibit the same behaviors, making it possible to distinguish between them (variability) (Santtila et al., 2005; Woodhams, Hollin, & Bull, 2008).

In linking cases, behavioral similarities between crimes are identified from police records, which may suggest they are committed by the same unknown offender (Woodhams, Grant, & Price, 2007). Incomplete information can cause inaccuracies in the behavioral linking of crimes. For linkage to be successful, one must be able to accurately differentiate linked crime pairs (crimes committed by the same offender) from unlinked crime pairs. Hierarchical measures that take into account both similarities between factors present in cases and factors absent in cases are more accurate. Absence of a behavior is as important as presence of a behavior.

Egger (1984) put forth the idea of linkage blindness or the inability to recognize serial criminality between and/or among different jurisdictions. For example, if an offender committed a series of crimes, each committed in an adjacent jurisdiction, if the agencies do not recognize the similarities in crimes and/or refuse to share information, the investigation will be hampered. They would not be aware that they are looking for the same offender and that the offender had committed multiple offenses. As discussed previously, there are differences between single-victim rapists and serial rapists that also help the investigation if the agencies know about the other crimes in the area. The South Side Rapist case suffered from linkage blindness; the rapes for which Rabbitt was originally apprehended and charged occurred on the south side of St. Louis, but some were in nearby jurisdictions such as Collinsville (Cooperman, 2005). Without sharing information and cooperation among law enforcement agencies, even the most sophisticated technology will not aid in identifying and apprehending serial rapists. The technology and databases are merely tools to aid in the investigation and apprehension of serial rapists. The information put into a database and the crime scene evidence is only as good as the person entering the data or collecting the evidence.

CONCLUSION

Serial rape is difficult to define and measure because many rapes go unreported and the definitions of rape and attempted rape may vary. However, the victims, as well as communities at large, suffer physical, social, and psychological consequences. While relatively rare, if and when public attention is given to a serial rapist on the loose, significant populations of entire cities increase their levels of fear and vigilance. Due to the adverse impact on community psychology as well as the suffering of victims, various researchers have spent significant time attempting to understand perpetrators' motives and actions (Groth et al., 1977; Hazelwood & Burgess, 1987b; Knight & Prentky, 1990). Common themes among groups of offenders have been turned into profiles of serial rapists. The primary goal of this research is to assist in understanding the causation of the act so that effective policing and offender treatment may take place.

Among the most confounding findings in the research is that offenders vary in their motives for acting as serial rapists. Some are playing out a fantasy of being a seductive individual while others fully recognize their goals of seriously harming the victim. In terms of identifying offenders just by their appearance and/or social skills, once again, there is a great deal of variance among offenders. While developmental factors may be related to the creation of serial rapists (as noted by the case of Jeffrey Dahmer), not all offenders had highly dysfunctional childhoods, and not all adults with dysfunctional childhoods become offenders.

However, the research and profiles are very helpful because serial offenders tend to replicate their behaviors. Douglas and Munn (1992) point out three common aspects of sexual offenses: (1) the modus operandi, or process of selecting the victim and process of attacking the victim, (2) the signature, or types of and degree of sexuality in the criminal act, and (3) staging of the crime, or how the crime scene may be altered in order to confuse investigators. All three of these actions lead to significant contributions in policing. More specifically, we have learned through extensive research that the characteristics shared by serial rapists set them apart from other rapists.

Research on serial rapists is important for helping law enforcement identify, investigate, and apprehend the offenders. There is no standardized policing method for investigating these crimes. However, these typologies provide us with approaches to the investigation. Investigations are also moved forward with the use of DNA evidence and collaboration with other law enforcement agencies. While professionals are beginning to address concerns about the use of DNA evidence, progress is currently being made in the standardization of collection and analysis of evidence. Without collaboration of law enforcement agencies, related rapes in a specific geographic area may go unrecognized as the work of a single perpetrator, as was the case with Dennis Rabbitt, the South Side Rapist.

Rape is a rare crime compared to other criminal acts, and serial rape is even rarer. However, serial rape is real in its effects on its victims and communities. As such, it remains an important area of study for law enforcement and other criminal justice professionals.

CHAPTER 4

Adult Sexual Offenders: An Overview

Kristyn Bernier, Kristen Kuehnle, and Amanda Howerton

In 2007, there were approximately 565,000 registered sex offenders in the United States, and by 2010, the estimate was 704,000 (National Center for Missing and Exploited Children, 2010). While this number may seem high, it is a conservative estimate because of the range of offending patterns and corresponding recidivism rates. Thus it is important to understand the different types of sexual offender, their intended victims, and their recidivism rates. In this chapter, we provide an overview profile of the different types of sexual offenders, including a distinction between the preferential versus situational offender of children, the "target victim" of the offender of children, incest offenders, and rehabilitation as measured by recidivism. In addition, we discuss the challenges of convicting sexual offenders and recent issues in childhood sexual offending.

THE "TYPICAL" OFFENDER

When the average person hears the words "child molester" or "sex offender," a stereotypical image often comes to mind. The stereotype is commonly the vision of a very skinny or overweight middle-aged man who wears thick prescription glasses, shuffles around in orthopedic shoes, and lives alone or with his mother. The stereotype for the offender who rapes adult women is often the leather jacket-clad, knife-wielding thug who hides in the shadows and chooses a victim unknown to him. People tend to attribute certain jobs, often menial, to the sex offender. It is uncommon to associate the sex offender with a high-paying profession, a beautiful home and family, or good looks.

In actuality, there is no stereotypical offender. Offenders have a wide range of individual characteristics as well as varied social situations. Offenders may be very organized or very disorganized; they may have complex social skills or lack social skills; they may function in a successful profession or be incapable of holding a job. There are, however, common personality traits and behavioral patterns that many offenders share. First, we will review adult sex offenders who victimize adult. We will then review adult sex offenders who victimize children.

ADULT SEX OFFENDERS WITH ADULT VICTIMS

When examining adult offenders who offend adult victims, it is important to understand that sexual assault is not motivated by sexual desire; rather, it is an attempt to control, manipulate, humiliate, and hurt a victim. After Groth, Burgess, and Holmstrom (1977) interviewed more than 100 convicted rapists as well as their victims, they found three central themes—namely power, anger, and sexuality. The researchers developed two typologies, anger rapes and power rapes. Hazelwood and Burgess (1987) further delineated four types of rapists along these two dimensions: the power-reassurance rapist, the power-assertive rapist, the anger-retaliatory rapist, and the anger-excitation rapists. In these typologies, there are psychological motivators behind the rape, not the desire for an intimate relationship.

In the majority of sexual assault cases, the victim knows the offender, either as an intimate partner, as an acquaintance, as a date, or as a family member. According to the National Crime Victimization Survey in 2005, 73% of sexual assaults were perpetrated by a nonstranger, 38% by a friend or acquaintance, 28% by an intimate, and 7% by a relative (other than a spouse). Based upon the National College Women Sexual Victimization Study, it has been estimated that 20% to 25% of college women experience completed or attempted rape during their college years (feminist.com, 2008).

Using a definition of rape that includes attempted and completed rape achieved through the use or intended use of force, the *National Violence Against Women Survey* found that 17.6% of surveyed women were raped at some point in their lives (Tjaden & Thoennes, 2006). Essentially one out of every six women has been raped in her life. Nearly 22% of the women were younger than 12 years of age when first raped, and 54% were raped before their 18th birthday. At least 20% of American men report having perpetrated sexual assault, with 5% admitting to having committed rape. Female victims are more likely to be raped in a private setting (84.5%) than in a public setting (15.5%). Of the victims in this survey, 62% report being raped by an intimate, 8.5% by a relative other than a spouse, and 21% by an acquaintance. Only 18.5% were raped by a stranger, compared to 28.4% of male victims (Tjaden & Thoennes, 2006).

In more than 80% of sexual assaults, the victim knows the assailant, meaning that most sexual assaults are committed by a nonstranger. In 85% of all sexual assaults and in 92% of nonstranger sexual assaults, weapons were not used. Drugs and alcohol also appear to play a major role. Nearly 67% of women and 59% of men reported that their rapist was using drugs and/or alcohol at the time of the rape (Tjaden & Thoennes, 2006). Injuries are very rarely sustained in sexual assaults, with 83% of assaults and 61% of attempted assaults resulting in no injury. Society and the criminal justice system have mixed perceptions about the credibility of the sexual assault report, especially when a victim may have engaged in high-risk behaviors and "voluntarily" consumed alcohol in a situation that resulted in a sexual assault, as seen later in Case Study 3.

In acquaintance, stranger, and nonfamilial relationships, adult offenders often plan their course of behavior, pick the right victim, and determine the setting and circumstances. These offenders are organized and generally perceived as charming and confident. They are generally high functioning, self-absorbed, narcissistic, single, and college age or older than 30 years of age. These perpetrators typically have good verbal skills, establish trust in the victim (often "wining and dining" the victim), and do not hide their identity. They are not perceived as violent, are not psychiatrically ill, and usually are sober. They are very much in control of the situation. These perpetrators may live out their fantasies in regard to anal sex, ejaculating onto a victim's face or into the victim's mouth, or other fantasy situations. They might take "trophies" of their accomplishments and even video record or photograph the assault. This type of perpetrator often shows little remorse and will deny wrongdoing. Case Study 1 exemplifies this type of offender.

CASE STUDY 1: CHARLIE

At 20 years of age, Charlie gave a 16-year-old girl a motorcycle ride and brought her to a spot in the woods where he raped her a couple of times, beat her, choked her by stuffing underwear in her mouth, kicked her, and hit her in the head with a rock. He left her for dead under leaves. She crawled to the local fire station and lived to see him convicted. The prosecutor referred to the case as one of the most egregious he had ever worked on. The judge also commented on how inhumane the crime was. Charlie then committed more than 28 major infractions in the first several years of his confinement, including assaulting a guard and creating a homemade shank to attack a fellow inmate. He was convicted of attempted escape and ultimately maxed out on a 22-year sentence. He had also been convicted of attempting to run over a bicyclist with his car, a case that had occurred a year prior to the rape. Charlie refused to meaningfully complete sex offender treatment, but having served all of his committed time, he was released.

At 42 years of age, he was released with no family of which to speak, no probation, no job, and no order for treatment. Charlie lied about his offense to some and minimized it to others. In counseling sessions, he told me that he was convicted of statutory rape, claiming that the girl was of age. He never admitted to the heinous crime he had committed. He even told a judge in a subsequent arraignment that the sex had been consensual during the incident that had resulted in his underlying rape conviction.

Charlie told me he was only violent when he was drinking or using drugs. He was tightly wound and angry, and it was very apparent that he had to consciously try to control his anger. He would talk, though he had to force words from his mouth when he answered a question. He spoke deliberately, and one could sense the tension in his face and body language. He began drinking very soon after his release. He was involved in a relationship with a subservient female to whom he was reportedly emotionally and physically abusive. He reportedly lost his temper in front of his friends and would act out by throwing his bike and on one occasion assaulting a former female friend. He was arrested numerous times, for crimes ranging from failure to report as a sex offender, to attempted second-degree assault by trying to strangle a female associate, to felony possession of a dangerous weapon, to sexual assault and possession of marijuana with intent to sell. He would react to an arrest first with anger, then by becoming emotional and crying, claiming to have made a mistake. Charlie is back in prison, serving a combined sentence of suspended time for his original offenses and time for the newer charges.

Date Rape and Drug-Facilitated Sexual Assault

A common adult sex offender is the date rapist, who often uses substances to manipulate, coerce, and overcome an unsuspecting acquaintance. A Maryland training program for law enforcement on sexual assault investigation teaches its students that almost 62% of sexual assaults are found to be drug facilitated, and nearly 5% of the victims are given what we commonly refer to as "date rape drugs." Drug-facilitated sexual assault is not a new phenomenon, although it is a newly recognized crime in law enforcement. Interestingly, the drug of choice is most commonly alcohol. The effect of the substance on the victim prevents resistance and ability to consent; thus, the victim is incapacitated and subjected to nonconsensual sexual acts (Maryland Coalition Against Sexual Assault, 2007).

The perpetrator of the drug-facilitated rape can be a stranger; however, it is most commonly a date or a trusted friend. Often, the victim, with the perpetrator's encouragement, voluntarily consumes alcohol. The alcohol impairs the victim's decision making, which is what the offender wants. This is a planned crime. For the victim who is unwittingly slipped an illicit substance, such as gamma-hydroxybutyric acid (GHB) or ketamine, the ability to identify that the situation is dangerous or to resist the perpetrator is greatly decreased. The perpetrator has put the victim in a situation in which it appears as though the victim is consenting, and the advances of the perpetrator are not resisted.

This type of sexual assault requires planning and often produces repeat offenders. Many offenders who use drugs or alcohol to facilitate the sexual assault are not caught or prosecuted because the victim may not report, or when the victim does report, the crime never reaches prosecution. Case Study 2 presents a typical instance of drug-facilitated rape:

CASE STUDY 2: ANTHONY

Anthony was a successful pharmaceutical representative from a wealthy New England family. He was confident and attractive, and he paraded this confidence and good looks on a popular dating web site. He claimed to be a world traveler who liked the finer things in life. He used his job, his company car, and his company-issued cell phone in luring a woman he met online to his hotel.

The victim in this incident reported that she had been drugged and raped. She remembered some details of the night but drew a blank on others. She told the police that Anthony was confident and egocentric, bragging about his accomplishments and saying how lucky she was to be with him. The victim told Anthony that she would not be having sex with him; however, at some point during the night, she had several drinks and began losing control over her actions. She remembers that Anthony had very little to drink. She remembers dancing, riding in a cab, being in a hot tub and then in his bed; however, she recalled that she could not move or scream. She described being under Anthony but felt as though she was having an out-of-body experience and was unable to stop the rape. She said she was very sick and that he was very callous and unconcerned about her. He became angry when she tried to call someone the following morning.

Upon returning home, she was sick, exhausted, and withdrawn. She put the pieces together and reported the incident to a detective she trusted. While she was perceived by the police as credible, the case did not proceed to indictment.

ADULT SEX OFFENDERS WITH CHILD VICTIMS

Child Molesters and Pedophiles

Lanning (2002) identifies the difficulties in differentiating between child molesters and pedophiles. Pedophilia is frequently misused and misinterpreted by the public, by clinicians, and within the criminal justice system. Diagnostically, pedophiles are those individuals with recurrent, intense sexually arousing fantasies, urges, or behaviors involving prepubescent children (Lanning, 2002). Pedophiles are more likely to be males, though there are cases of female pedophiles. Pedophiles often prefer a very particular age of child. They generally do not view the child as a victim; rather, they perceive themselves to be teaching the child about sex. Emotionally, they are immature and appeal to children because they do not interact on adult levels (Profile of a Pedophile, 2010).

Case Study 3 illustrates how a potential offender may have difficulty relating to other adults and may attempt to "groom" the child.

CASE STUDY 3: BRIAN

Ricky, the victim, was an 11-year-old boy whose single mother believed he should spend more time around male figures, playing sports and going to games. As her therapist, I encouraged her to contact the Big Brothers Association. She applied to the Big Brothers Association and was delighted to find a referral, Brian. Brian was a college graduate, 22-years-old, currently employed and living in an apartment with roommates.

Brian arrived at his first visit laden with gifts for Ricky. He brought a football, and they went outside and played. Brian talked little with Ricky's mother during the visit, though he stayed in clear view. At the second visit, he offered to take Ricky to a Friendly's restaurant and offered to bring ice cream back to Ricky's mother. They were gone a short while, and Ricky was responding very well to Brian. Brian asked for permission to take Ricky to his apartment to watch movies. Ricky begged, and his mother allowed the next visit to take place at Brian's apartment. This visit was short and nothing appeared unusual to Ricky's mother. The request escalated to an overnight stay at Brian's apartment, and each visit involved more presents for Ricky.

To this point, Ricky's mother was extremely happy, describing Brian's involvement with Ricky during her therapy sessions with me. When asked whether she thought it was unusual for Brian to continually bring presents for Ricky and to talk primarily to Ricky, she hesitated and then replied that Ricky was happy. When Ricky's mother returned for further interviews, she was extremely upset that Brian had a confrontation with her when she refused to allow Ricky to go on a camping trip with him. Brian angrily exploded, asking her what more she wanted considering that he was always bringing Ricky presents. He left, after making a comment about whether his involvement with Ricky was worth it. At that point, we contacted the Big Brother Association about Brian, and he was not reassigned to another little brother. While Brian had not committed a crime, he clearly was grooming his victim.

Buckley (2006) has identified other commonalities among sex offenders with child victims. Based on over 8000 interviews with offenders, he found that most offenders of children have poor impulse control, are hypersensitive, emotionally immature, and self-centered, and are unable to control their sexual urges. They are often shy, have poor social skills, have low self-esteem, but are "skilled manipulators." They are narcissistic and egocentric, lack a sense of control over their own lives, have inadequate coping skills, and have a difficult time developing intimate adult relationships; they may have been abused as children and may have poor relationships with their own parents. They may also have minor criminal histories. Many are sexually promiscuous, cannot control their own sexual urges, experience sexual obsessions and compulsions, and experience sexual anxiety and/or sexual frustration. Case Study 4 demonstrates how the typical adult sexual offender of a child victim typically operates.

CASE STUDY 4: JERRY

Jerry is someone we like to refer to as a triple threat. He lived in his parents' trailer and was attending classes to become a massage therapist. He was an Internet chatter looking to have sex with a minor female and was arrested for attempting to meet with a person whom he thought was a child, who was in fact a police detective. Following the arrest, a 7-year-old child disclosed that Jerry had been molesting her for months. He had been babysitting the child, the niece of a girlfriend. Her family situation was unstable, and it was easy for the adults in her life to let Jerry watch her and spend time with her. He took her overnight to hotels and even had her overnight at his own parents' home. He allegedly took pictures of her and video recorded the abuse. He also made her watch pornography and showed her illicit web sites on the computer. He told her he would kill her and her family if she ever told.

During the investigation, a forensic exam of his computer uncovered a large collection of child sexual assault images and videos. Jerry agreed to an interview after his arrest, and he minimized his activity, blaming the 7-year-old for visiting web sites with sexual content. The girl's mother (no longer Jerry's girlfriend) came forth and gave a statement that Jerry never had sexual intercourse with her, never seeming interested. She did not think anything of this or his interest in babysitting her niece until after his arrest. Jerry was convicted of using the Internet to solicit a minor for sexual activity and possessing child sexual assault images. Jerry was also convicted of the course of conduct sexual abuse on the 7-year-old child to include anal and vaginal intrusion. She testified against him at 9 years old and saw him receive a sentence that will ensure he is incarcerated for decades.

Jerry had been well known to the local police department and had earned the nickname "Accidental Jerry." While working as a janitor for a local school, allegations had been made that he had inappropriately touched a child. His defense was that it was "accidental." The jurisdiction was not able to prosecute Jerry. Later, he was convicted of a nonsexual charge after it was alleged that he had been having sex with a minor teenage female whom he had held against will at a hotel in the area. The victim was not able to testify and had been uncooperative with authorities.

As seen in the Case Studies, sexual offenders who abuse children know where to locate them and are adept at choosing a vulnerable victim. These offenders are skilled at convincing a child to trust them and will try to manipulate and control the victim. They exploit a child's trust and sense of safety in order to meet their own needs. They groom the child by buying gifts and giving money, creating more and more trust and taking progressive liberties with the child. These offenders often fantasize about the abuse prior to the event and also may have an incident of high stress in their lives prior to abusing. Although the typology described here is useful in developing a basic profile for adults who victimize children, it is important to distinguish between preferential child molesters and situational child molesters (see also Chapter 5).

The Preferential Sexual Offender of Children

Preferential sexual offenders can be distinguished from situational offenders in several ways. First, preferential molesters generally prefer prepubescent children (aged 13 years or younger) and are therefore considered "classic" pedophiles. While it is true that any adult who engages in sexual activity with a child is considered a child molester, pedophilia is a psychiatric classification with specific criteria necessary for diagnosis. It is characterized by intense urges, fantasies, or behaviors over a period of at least 6 months and oriented toward a prepubescent child (APA, 2000). Preferential molesters also typically have a specific interest in either male or female victims, have a large number of victims, remain uncaught or undiscovered for a long time, and have extensive child pornography collections of which they are very possessive. Without a doubt, preferential sexual offenders comprise most of the offenders who violate children (Lanning, 1992a). Additionally, preferential sexual offenders will often select themselves into situations, as illustrated in Case Study 5.

CASE STUDY 5: RAY

Ray was named "Man of the Year" in his native city, was his city's mayor, and was a very wealthy businessman who was married and had adopted several children. He was lauded for the wonderful work he did, volunteering his time to mentor these young boys and provide them with new opportunities. What he actually did was molest the boys over many years. It is estimated that he and one of his employees victimized more than 100 children at a lake house where he brought underprivileged boys during the summer. He paid the victims, often by personal check, purportedly for yard work; however, he lured them, gained their trust, groomed them, and then sexually assaulted them. He preferred younger blond males around 10 years old. He even paid the victims who outgrew his tastes to find him victims in his age preference. He gave victims he lost interest in to the employee who had helped recruit the children. Ray was convicted as a senior citizen. He got cancer and was arrogant enough to request that his sentence be shortened so he could die at home, arguing that cancer was his sentence. His request was denied.

Ray, from Case Study 5, meets several of the criteria for a preferential molester. He had well over 100 victims. He groomed the children for long periods of time, gaining their trust before he molested them, and he had a specific interest in prepubescent boys.

Preferential offenders will typically threaten the child with bodily harm or with harm toward the child's family. They may also try to make the child feel responsible for them. They prey on the emotions and feelings of the child. The child often cares for the offender but also has conflicting feelings of fear for getting the offender into trouble or for his or her own safety if the sexual activity is disclosed. It is interesting to note that most of the research indicates that preferential molesters seduce children similar to the ways that adults seduce each other (Lanning, 1992b).

The Situational Sexual Offender of Children

Whereas the preferential offender has a genuine preference for the type of victim, the situational offender's main criterion is availability. That is, situational offenders typically have no preference for prepubescent children, nor any real preference for gender. They pick children to be victims because children are vulnerable prey. In a similar vein, situational molesters will also turn to other populations to offend that they perceive as easy targets—e.g., the elderly, sick, or mentally impaired. Furthermore, because they often do not have the social skills necessary to attain a sexual partner of their own age, they commonly view children as substitutes for consensual same-aged sexual partners (Beyer & Beasley, 2003). Lastly, unlike preferential molesters who often view their activities as "natural" rather than deviant, situational molesters often have far fewer victims because they commonly victimize as a result of pent-up sexual impulse and/or anger. Case Studies 7 and 8 present examples of situational offenders.

CASE STUDY 6: LARRY

Larry met his wife, June, working at a grocery chain. He was 30 years old at the time, and June was 18, a recent high school graduate. In the storage room at night, he raped her. Instead of reporting to the police, she confided in an aunt, asking whether she should marry Larry since she had been a virgin. June married Larry shortly after and became pregnant with their daughter.

Larry's job history was sketchy, and he was frequently unemployed. June took a job working third shift in a large chain store because the money was better. Larry would stay home with his daughter who was turning 9 years old. His drinking intensified. He was having physical fights with June, and he would sleep through the day when June was home. June noticed that her daughter was becoming increasingly quiet, her school performance was rapidly declining, and she had stopped talking to her friends. She stayed home and never wanted to have friends over to their house. June started to suspect something was wrong with her daughter. She took her daughter and moved back into her parents' house. Slowly, her daughter revealed that her father was forcing her to have oral and eventually vaginal sex. When arrested, Larry admitted that he had abused his daughter and was sentenced to a lengthy sentence. While in prison, Larry attempted to hire a hit man to kill his father-in-law. The hit man was an undercover officer, and Larry was convicted of attempted murder. He remains incarcerated at a federal facility in Illinois, serving two separate sentences.

CASE STUDY 7: MARK

Mark was a 34-year-old firefighter who was married and had an 11-year-old stepdaughter. One night, he exposed himself and sexually assaulted the child. He was arrested and convicted, served his sentence, and was released on probation. When completing his sex offender registration, he minimized his actions, acting as though he was in the police station for a social call, making reference to being a firefighter and knowing many of the local police officers. He stated that while he understood that he had to register by law, he did not understand why he was seen as a threat, saying, "It's not like I'm a pedophile." When asked how old his victim was, Mark commented that she was 11 years old. When asked why he did not consider his actions egregious, he replied, "It was one of those things . . . You know how it is. Sometimes things get out of hand." Mark essentially perceived this as a minor situation and demonstrated no remorse.

The "Target" Victim

One thing that both preferential and situational molesters have in common is that they both tend to choose their victims very carefully, choosing vulnerable children over children with strong social support systems. They often pick children of single parents, children with low self-esteem, children who are being bullied in school, and/or children who are socially isolated in general. The earlier example involving Ricky (Case Study 3) demonstrated the selection of a vulnerable target. Case Study 8 offers another example of an offender who chose the typical "target child."

CASE STUDY 8: JOSEPH

Joseph was convicted of molesting several young boys over a period of time, grooming them and seducing them with gifts and trips to Burger King. After his release, he continued with sex offender treatment but years later reoffended with a 15-year-old boy.

Joseph gained the trust of a single father with three children. The middle child was a teenage boy with some emotional and educational issues. Joseph spent time with the family, taking part in family dinners and even celebrating holidays with them. He began taking an interest in the then 15-year-old, taking him out to dinner, buying him gifts, cigarettes, and alcohol, letting him drive his vehicle, and allowing him to use a spare computer. Joseph encouraged the child to tell his father he was sleeping over at friends' homes when he was actually spending nights with Joseph at his home out of state and also in a local motel. While the child admitted to spending time with Joseph, saying that they slept in the same bed and that Joseph wanted them to "take their relationship to the next level," he would never disclose sexual abuse. However, the grooming behavior and taking the child overnight without parental permission met the criteria for interference with custody and kidnapping.

Upon his arrest, Joseph agreed to an interview. Initially, he lied about his contact with the minor, but he ultimately admitted to trying to groom the child for sexual activity. Joseph talked about his prior convictions and how he built the trust of the children, groomed them, manipulated them, and bought them gifts and meals in order to sexually abuse them. Joseph admitted that he preferred younger males but that he resorted to a victim who he had ready access to in the absence of his preferred type. These admissions of his prior acts and of his deliberate grooming and manipulation of children for his sexual purposes, coupled with his prior convictions for those acts, allowed for his indictment on charges of attempted sexual assault on a minor. A search warrant resulted in the discovery of Joseph's sex offender treatment writings and plan.

The Incest Offender

Incest refers to overt sexual activity between related persons and is considered illegal. Incest may be cross-generational (between an adult and a child) or it can occur between agemates. The focus of this chapter is upon the most prominent type, parent–child incest. Incest can involve sexual activity between an adoptive parent, a stepparent, a common-law partner, or a foster parent. These types of offenders are found in all socioeconomic classes.

The 1997 Survey of State Inmates found that in inmates convicted of a sex crime against a child, the child was their own child or stepchild in one-third of the cases. When the victim was younger than 18 years of age, he or she was the prisoner's own child (16%), stepchild (16%), sibling or stepsibling (2%), or other relative (13%). When the sex crime involved an adult victim, only 11% of these cases involved a relative (Langan, Schmitt, & Durose, 2003).

Groth (1985) has created a typology of two basic offenders in terms of their primary sexual orientation and sociosexual development (Groth, 1985; Groth, Hobson, & Gary, 1985). There are the fixated offenders, whose primary sexual orientation is to children; their pedophilic interests begin in adolescence. And there are the regressed offenders, whose primary sexual orientation is to agemates; their pedophilic interests emerge in adulthood. Precipitating stress is usually evident with the regressed offenders. Larry, in Case Study 6, demonstrates traits of both the situational offender and the regressed offender.

Assessing the incest offender can be extremely difficult. Specifically, developmental traumas need to be assessed in the life history, especially sexual trauma. Sexual offenders have a higher incidence of having been sexually victimized as children (Groth, 1985). Wagemaker, a psychiatrist, suggests that pedophilia runs in families (Child Predatory Statistics, 2010). Case Study 9 illustrates that incestuous offences can run within family generations.

CASE STUDY 9: BILLY

Billy, a 39-year-old man serving in the military, was not directly referred for an evaluation. His 18-month-old daughter, Karen, was brought in for an assessment of developmental issues and an intense fear reaction to males. Her pediatrician could not approach her or examine her. Karen had two older brothers, Tom, 8 years old, and John, 10 years old. Karen's mother worked at night on the base to help support the family. Both parents came to the evaluation, and Karen sat on her father's lap the entire time. Recommendations were made to help her motor skills, and soon after the family was relocated to a southern state. About 3 years later, the mother returned with her daughter and sons but without her husband. Her husband was in prison for sexually abusing the children. Karen's mother had come downstairs one morning to find her husband fondling Karen and holding her down. Her sons were watching. As the details came out, the father actively engaged his two sons in the sexual abuse of his daughter, hitting her with sticks and fondling her. The father confessed, was convicted, and was imprisoned.

When asked about his activities, Billy reported that his uncle had sexually assaulted him when he was a young boy and continued to do so throughout adolescence. When Karen's mother was interviewed, it was revealed that both she and her sister were impregnated by their father while still in their early teens. The babies were given up for adoption. Ongoing therapy was recommended for Karen; however, when her oldest brothers were teenagers, they sexually assaulted her individually. Both were removed from the home.

REHABILITATION

In a review of the literature, Trowbridge (2009) identified the difficulties when evaluating the effectiveness of sex offender treatment. For ethical reasons, it is extremely difficult to have either a control or comparison group. Psychiatric diagnoses can also affect outcome, as with psychopathy as the underlying personality disorder. In addition, results vary based upon whether the offender is undergoing outpatient treatment or compulsory treatment while incarcerated. According to Trowbridge, recidivism rates may actually be lower for outpatient high-risk offenders than for other types of offenders. The recidivism rate must be put within the context of how few sex offenders are reported, arrested, or incarcerated (Trowbridge, 2009).

When treatment occurs with involuntary sex offenders, treatment is generally compulsory. The offender has three choices: serve the entire sentence, remain incarcerated until undergoing treatment, or accept treatment initially. A cognitive-behavioral approach is generally used. Expectations in treatment are that offenders recognize their problems, admit to their behavior, see it as inappropriate and in need of control, accept responsibility, and alter their behaviors. Consequently, treatment can be confrontational and is often in a group setting. Treatment may also involve a combination of medication and cognitive-behavioral therapy. Some medications are discussed in a moment.

When assessing offenders for treatment, several circumstances about the offense are reviewed to determine receptiveness for rehabilitation, including the harm or physical force that was used in the offense, the involvement of bizarre or ritualistic acts, whether the offense was one of many antisocial behaviors, whether the offense was secondary to serious psychopathology, whether the offense demonstrated a chronic fixation on children, and whether the offender denies the offense or regards his or her behavior as inappropriate (Groth et al., 1985). When some or most of these conditions exist, the treatment of choice is in an institutional setting. In addition, whatever treatment started should be continued on an outpatient basis after the offender's release (Groth et al., 1985). Institutional placements can include prisons, mental hospitals, residential treatment programs, and community treatment services.

Adult offenders with child victims generally victimize multiple children. Many of these offenders are not treated in prison and are inadequately treated. A variety of treatments have been utilized, such as Depo-Provera (medroxyprogesterone), a medication that blocks the hormone progesterone. Several other drugs have provided moderate success in some cases, including Celexa (citalopram), Luvox (fluvoxamine), Lexapro (escitalopram), Paxil (paroxetine), Prozac (fluoxetine), and Zoloft (sertraline). A combination of drug treatment with therapy has shown some success (Sex Offender Statistics, 2010). Behavior modification is another approach used with offenders of children, focusing upon specific behaviors with a series of conditioning exercises to diminish sexual arousal to children. Physiological measurements of erection responses are used to measure the effectiveness of the treatment. Psychosocial education involves a combination of reeducation, resocialization, and counseling. The aim is to help the offender to self-observe and recognize early warning signs of recidivism (Groth et al., 1985).

Child molesters are among the most difficult sex offenders to rehabilitate, and an effective treatment to prevent recidivism has not been established. Drug treatment holds promise, as long as the offender remains on the medication. Once off, there is no guarantee that the individual will not reoffend. As Groth et al. (1985) indicate, the chronicity of the problem requires that the offender work every day, and there must be support services—e.g., professional agencies and self-help groups. Unfortunately, many social service or mental health agencies are reluctant to work with sex offenders. Those agencies willing to provide treatment may use traditional psychotherapeutic approaches that are not appropriate for this type of client.

RECIDIVISM

As mentioned earlier, Trowbridge (2009) suggests that recidivism rates may actually be lower for outpatient high-risk sex offenders than for other types of offenders. We suggest that this be viewed with caution because of the underreporting of sexual assaults and the difficulties with convicting sex offenders (covered in the next section). Also, an offender may undergo treatment while not being rehabilitated. Returning to Billy (Case Study 9), this becomes clear.

CASE STUDY 9: BILLY (CONTINUED)

While incarcerated, Billy underwent group therapy and became the chaplain's assistant. He went up for early parole on two separate occasions. For both hearings, the agency treating his children was notified. Letters were sent requesting that Billy serve his entire sentence. He remained in prison for his entire sentence and was released on probation for 1 year. When released, the conditions were that he remain in the state where imprisoned and routinely check in with his parole officer. Within 10 days, Billy left the state, traveled to his ex-wife's house, and attempted to set it on fire. A restraining order was obtained by the facility treating his children. He was able to escape with the assistance of his sister and has not been apprehended.

Langan et al. (2003) examined the recidivism rates of 9691 male sex offenders who were released from 15 prisons in 1994. Four different categories were analyzed: released rapists, released sexual assaulters, released child molesters, and released statutory rapists. The initial analysis reviewed rearrest for a new sex crime. Compared to nonsex offenders released from the state prisons, "released sex offenders were four times more likely to be rearrested for a sex crime." During the first 12 months, 40% of sex crimes were committed by the released offenders. The study did not find that the older the prisoner when released, the lower the rate of recidivism.

The researchers also analyzed "rearrest for a sex crime against a child." Out of the 9691 released offenders, 4295 men had been in prison for child molesting. Of the victims, 60% were 13 years of age or younger, and half of the molesters were 20 years older than the child they were molesting. Compared, of all the sex offenders, as well as released nonsex offenders, released child molesters were the most likely to be rearrested for another sex crime against a child (Langan et al., 2003).

DIFFICULTIES WITH CONVICTING SEX OFFENDERS

To be a registered sex offender, an individual must have been convicted of a sex offense against an adult or child, which can include computer-initiated sex crimes and possession of images depicting sexual assault of a child. To be convicted, the individual must have been caught and prosecuted. Unfortunately, many offenders do not get caught because sexual assault cases are underreported to law enforcement. Thus, rape victims may never see their attackers apprehended, convicted, or incarcerated. It is estimated that fewer than half, 48%, of all rapes and sexual assaults are actually reported to the police (Rennison, 2002). Reporting rates, however, have improved, according the Clay-Warner and Burt (2005). These researchers investigated the effects of legal reforms during two time periods, 1975–1989 and 1990–present. Rape occurring between 1990 and 1996 was 86% more likely to be reported. Aggravated rapes involving a stranger, a weapon, or physical injury were significantly more likely to be reported during both time periods. The researchers also found that victims were significantly less likely to report to the police when they had consumed drugs or alcohol (Clay-Warner & Burt, 2005).

Sexual assault cases are dropped for various reasons, frequently because the victim did not want to pursue the case. A case may be dismissed because the witness cannot testify, either because he or she is too young or because the process is terribly traumatizing to the victim. When the offender is known to the victim, there is often resistance to press charges. For example, marital rape survivors are less likely than survivors of acquaintance and stranger rapes to seek medical, police, or agency assistance (Bergen, 1996; Mahoney, 1999). Marital rape victims have been found to minimize the sexually abuse perpetrated by their husbands (Basile, 1999; Bergen, 1995, 1996; Kelly, 1988). Campbell and Soeken (1999) found that women sexually assaulted by their husbands are most at risk of being killed by their husbands. In addition, family members may question the victim about what she did wrong to anger her spouse, indirectly suggesting that she is equally responsible for the assault.

The circumstances of a case continue to play a major factor throughout the criminal system. Lord and Rassel (2002) researched nine law enforcement counties in North Carolina. All the counties continued to focus on consent as well as the victim's behavior. Many required physical evidence to proceed with a case. Furthermore, many counties required victims to take a polygraph test, something that is rarely seen for other offenses. In addition, prosecutorial screening of sexual assault cases has been found to rest upon the victim's discredibility, specifically the potential that the victim is filing a false report (Frohmann, 1991). Spohn, Beichner, and Davis-Frenzel (2001) found that the victim's character and reputation, and the time of the incident formed the basis for accepting or rejecting rape cases.

The prosecutor's office takes a case based upon the probability that it will result in a conviction. Cases involving sex offenses are still commonly pled out to crimes that may not even fall into sex offense statutes, such as an aggravated sexual assault (rape) being pled out to a second-degree assault. This plea to a nonsexual offense results in the convicted party not being required to register as a sex offender.

If a sexual assault case proceeds, conviction is uncertain. A study of judges found that judges based their decisions on whether the victim was a "real" rape victim or a "risk takers." Risk takers were women who hitchhiked, walked alone late at night, went to a bar alone, or used alcohol or drugs. These women were less likely to have their cases result in a conviction (Spohn & Spears, 1996). Rape trials seem more concerned with the victim's than the offender's accountability. One study found that the defendant's criminal history did not affect the likelihood of a conviction, though the victim's criminal history significantly affected whether the offender was convicted (Williams, 1981).

Legal reforms have occurred that both limit and provide ways to investigate sexual crimes. The invalidation of the Violence Against Women Act of 1994 by the U.S. Supreme court in 2000 (Bernat, 2002) could result in fewer sexual assault cases going to trial or the offender being placed in the registry, as occurred in the case of the Virginia Polytechnic Institute female student who reported being raped by two male students in 1994. In this case, the charges were dropped on one student because of a lack of evidence. The other student was found guilty of sexual assault; however, after appealing to the university's committee, his charges were lowered from sexual assault to "using abusive language" (Bernat, 2002). In this ruling, it was determined that only states could enact such legislation. And few states, other than Illinois and California, have defined gender-based violence—e.g., rape and domestic violence—as sex discrimination, allowing the victim to sue in a civil court (feminist.com, 2008).

However, the Adam Walsh Child Protection and Safety Act of 2006 (H.R. 4472 EAS, July 20, 2006) has given the criminal justice system more options for investigations. The act includes several key sections—namely, the Sex Offender Registration and Notification Act, Federal Criminal Law Enhancements needed to protect children from sexual attacks and other violent crimes, Child Pornography Prevention, and the Internet Safety Act. In addition, funding was provided to improve public access via the Internet and web sites. Sex offenders are organized into three tiers, based upon the seriousness of an offender's act, and specific requirements for the sex offender accountability are mandated.

THE INTERNET AND CHILDHOOD SEXUAL OFFENDING

Many years ago, the sex offender was forced to lurk in public, looking for the right victim. Access to children or even adult victims required public exposure, with the suspect having to find activities or groups where he or she could find the right victim or having to spend time in public places such as playgrounds, parks, or shopping areas to connect with prey. There was great risk for the predator in locating prey in a public setting.

Sexual deviance was socially unacceptable, and therefore the predator was required to seek acceptance underground. Twenty years ago, men who preferred young boys could subscribe to the secret North American Man/Boy Love Association (NAMBLA) newsletter. Law enforcement investigators subscribed to the mail order publication in an undercover capacity. Now anyone can log onto the NAMBLA web site or join the many newsgroups and sites that accept deviant behavior. Many years ago, the predator sat at home hiding his or her behavioral preferences, believing that no one would understand. Now, however, the perpetrator can jump online and immediately find acceptance from many across the globe, thus justifying the deviance and making the offender feel as though he or she has support in those behavioral tendencies.

This fear about the effects of the Internet has raised the question of whether the Internet would affect the prevalence of sex crimes against children. It has been suggested that child sexual assault images, online sex slavery, minor children using the computer and other technology, and dating and social networking sites make for a target-rich environment for the sexual deviant. Relationships are formed online, false trust is built, and the grooming process begins well before the offender and victim meet in person. The process that once began and culminated in person can now be expedited online. The Internet has changed the way that sex offenders operate and has even resulted in a different type of offender in our prison system.

Child pornography laws have led to many convicted sex offenders who rather than being convicted of actually molesting a live child have been convicted of sharing the digital imagery of children. However, Wolak, Finkelhor, and Mitchell (2008) looked at the trends of arrested online predators, finding that few of those individuals who were arrested for online predation were actually registered sex offenders. In 2006, 33% of crimes between arrested offenders and victims occurred at the victims' networking site, suggesting that networking sites can be an outlet for deviant activity, though as Wolak et al. state, the sites are not a "risk promoter."

In reviewing the trends of arrests for online predation, overall the number increased from 644 estimated arrests in 2000 to 3100 arrests in 2006. The authors suggest that law enforcement has been successful in investigating, arresting, and prosecuting these offenders using the Internet. The authors note, however, that there was a decline in the number of reports of overall sex offenses against children and adolescents in the same period and a decrease in arrests (Wolak et al., 2008). These results suggest that it should not be assumed that convicted sex offenders are using the Internet for a new source of victims and that the Internet should be the major focus of investigations. Rather, law enforcement should continue to make extensive efforts to combat sexual abuse of children online and offline.

CHAPTER 5

Cyber "Pedophiles:" A Behavioral Perspective

Kenneth V. Lanning

Caution: This chapter will focus on insight into the behavioral patterns of offenders in sexual exploitation of children cases involving computers. The information and its application are based on my education, training, and more than 27 years of experience studying the criminal aspects of deviant sexual behavior and interacting with investigators and prosecutors. Although I have great confidence in its behavioral accuracy and reliability, its legal acceptance and application must be evaluated by prosecutors based on agency policy, rules of evidence, and current case law. The use of terms in this chapter, which are also utilized in the mental health field (e.g., impulsive, compulsive, pedophilia), is not meant to imply a psychiatric diagnosis or lack of legal responsibility. The sexual victimization of children involves varied and diverse dynamics. It can range from one-on-one intrafamilial abuse to multioffender/multivictim extrafamilial sex rings and from stranger abduction of toddlers to prostitution of teenagers.

PARAPHILIAS AND SEXUAL RITUAL BEHAVIOR

Paraphilias are psychosexual disorders defined for clinical and research purposes in the *Diagnostic and Statistical Manual of Mental Disorders*, Fourth Edition, Text Revision, commonly referred to as the DSM-IV-TR (American Psychiatric Association, 2000). They are defined as recurrent, intense, sexually arousing fantasies, urges, or behaviors that generally involve (1) nonhuman objects, (2) the suffering or humiliation of oneself or one's partner, or (3) children or other nonconsenting persons, and that occur over a period of at least 6 months. Better known and more common paraphilias include the following: exhibitionism (exposure), fetishism (objects), frotteurism (rubbing), pedophilia (children), sexual masochism (self-pain), sexual sadism (partner pain), and voyeurism (looking). Less known and less common paraphilias include the following: scatologia (talk), necrophilia (corpses), partialism (body parts), zoophilia (animals), coprophilia (feces), klismaphilia (enemas), urophilia (urine), infantilism (babies), hebephilia (female youth), ephebophilia (male youth), and many others.[3]

In the real world, each of the paraphilias typically has the following:

1. Slang names (e.g., big baby, golden showers, S&M)
2. An industry that sells related paraphernalia and props (e.g., restraining devices, gags, adult-size baby clothing)
3. A support network (e.g., North American Man/Boy Love Association [NAMBLA], Diaper Pail Fraternity)
4. A body of literature (e.g., pornography)

In fact, the paraphilias are the organizational framework or the "Dewey Decimal System" of pornography, obscenity, adult bookstores, and Internet sex chat rooms.

Paraphilias are psychosexual disorders and not types of sex crimes. They may or may not involve criminal activity. Individuals suffering from one or more of these paraphilias can just engage in fantasy and masturbate, they can act out their fantasies legally (e.g., consenting adult partners, objects), or they can act out their fantasies illegally (e.g., nonconsenting partners, underage partners). It is their choice.

Although any of the paraphilias could become elements of a computer child sexual exploitation case, pedophilia is the most obvious and the one best known to prosecutors dealing with these cases. It is important for prosecutors to understand that the diagnostic criteria for pedophilia require that there be recurrent, intense, and sexually

---

[3] Adapted from "Cyber Pedophile: A Behavioral Perspective," in *Prosecuting Online Child Exploitation Cases*, by James S. Peters (Ed.), U.S. Department of Justice, USA Books (2002).

arousing fantasies, urges, or behaviors involving *prepubescent* children, generally age13 years or younger. The absence of *any* of the key criteria could eliminate the diagnosis. For example, an individual with a strong preference for and repeatedly engaging in sex with large numbers of 14-year-olds could correctly be evaluated by a mental health professional as *not* being a pedophile. Nonetheless, some mental health professionals continue to apply the term to those with a sexual preference for pubescent teenagers.

The terms hebephilia and ephebophilia are not specifically mentioned in the *DSM-IV-TR* and are rarely used, even by mental health professionals. They are, however, being increasingly used in forensic evaluations submitted to the court by defendants attempting to minimize their sexual behavior. Although sexual attraction to pubescent children by adults has the obvious potential for criminal activity, it does not necessarily constitute a sexual perversion as defined by psychiatry.

On an investigative level, the presence of paraphilias often means highly repetitive and predictable behavior, focused on specific sexual interests, that goes well beyond a modis operandi or "method of operation" (MO). The concept of an MO—a strategy used by an offender because it works and will help him or her get away with the crime—is well known to most investigators. An MO is fueled by thought and deliberation. Most offenders change and improve their MO over time and with experience.

The repetitive behavior patterns of some sex offenders do involve an MO, but are likely to also involve the less-known concept of sexual ritual. Sexual ritual is the repeated engaging in an act or series of acts in a certain manner because of a sexual need; that is, in order to become aroused and/or gratified, a person must engage in the act in a certain way. Some aspects of the MO of sex offenders can, if repeated often enough during sexual activity, become part of the sexual ritual. Other types of ritual behavior can be motivated by psychological, cultural, or spiritual needs. Unlike an MO, ritual is necessary to the offender but not to the successful commission of the crime. In fact, instead of facilitating the crime, ritual often increases the odds of identification, apprehension, and conviction because it causes the offender to make need-driven mistakes.

Ritual and its resultant behavior are fueled by erotic imagery and fantasy and can be bizarre in nature. Most important to investigators, offenders find it difficult to change and modify ritual, even when their experience tells them they should or they suspect law enforcement scrutiny. The ritual patterns of sex offenders have far more significance than the MO of other types of offenders. Understanding sexual ritual is the key to investigating certain sex offenders. The courts in this country have, however, been slow to recognize and understand the difference between MO and ritual.

THE DISTINCTION BETWEEN A "PEDOPHILE" AND A CHILD MOLESTER ——

The general public, the media, and many child abuse professionals sometimes simplistically refer to all those who sexually victimize children as pedophiles. As discussed in Chapter 4, there is no single or uniform definition for the word "pedophile." As previously stated, for mental health professionals, it is a diagnostic term referring to persons with recurrent, intense sexually arousing fantasies, urges, or behaviors involving *prepubescent* children. Technically, pedophilia is a psychiatric diagnosis that can only be made by qualified psychologists or psychiatrists. Therefore, for many, the word is a diagnostic term, not a legal one.

What, then, is the difference between a child molester and a pedophile? For many, the terms have become synonymous. For them, the word pedophile is just a fancy term for a child molester. The media frequently make no distinction and use the terms interchangeably. The term pedophilia is being used more and more by law enforcement and prosecutors, especially in cases involving the use of computers. It has even entered their slang usage—with some talking about investigating a "pedo case" or being assigned to a "pedo squad." Although Americans most often pronounce the "ped" in "pedophilia" as ped, as in "pedestrian" (from the Latin for foot), the correct pronunciation is ped, as in "pediatrician" (from the Greek for child).

Not all pedophiles are child molesters. A person suffering from any paraphilia can legally engage in it simply by fantasizing and masturbating. A child molester is an individual who sexually molests children. A pedophile might have a sexual preference for children and fantasize about having sex with them, but if he does not act this fantasy out, he is not a child molester. Some pedophiles might act out their fantasies in legal ways by simply talking to or watching children and later masturbating. Some might have sex with dolls and mannequins that resemble children. Some pedophiles might act out their fantasies in legal ways by engaging in sexual activity with adults who look like children (small stature, flat chest, no body hair), dress like children, or act like children (immature, baby talk). Others may act out child fantasy games with adult prostitutes.

A difficult problem to detect and address is that of individuals who act out their sexual fantasies by socially interacting with children (e.g., in person or online) or by interjecting themselves into the child sexual abuse or exploitation "problem" as over-zealous child advocates (e.g., cyber vigilantes). It is almost impossible to estimate how many pedophiles exist who have never molested a child. What society can, or should, do with regard to such individuals is an interesting area for discussion but beyond the role of prosecutors. People cannot be arrested for their fantasies.

Conversely, not all child molesters are pedophiles. A pedophile is an individual who *prefers* to have sex with children. A person who prefers to have sex with an adult partner may, for any number of reasons, decide to have sex with a child. Such reasons might include simple availability, curiosity, or a desire to hurt a loved one of the molested child. Because the sexual fantasies of such individuals do not necessarily focus on children, they are not pedophiles.

Are child molesters with adolescent victims pedophiles? Are individuals who collect both child and adult pornography pedophiles? Is everyone using a computer to facilitate having sex with children, or trafficking in child pornography, a pedophile? Many child molesters are, in fact, pedophiles, and many pedophiles are child molesters. But they are not necessarily one and the same. Labeling all child molesters as pedophiles can be confusing. Often, it may be unclear whether the term is being applied with its diagnostic definition or with some other definition. Most investigators and prosecutors are not qualified to apply the term with its diagnostic meaning.

I recommend that investigators and prosecutors minimize the use of the term pedophile. For the purposes of this discussion, the term pedophile, when used, will be defined as a significantly older individual who prefers to have sex with individuals legally considered children. Pedophiles are individuals whose erotic imagery and sexual fantasies focus on children. Rather than simply settling for child victims, they prefer to have sex with children. The law, not puberty, determines who is a child. A pedophile is just one example or subcategory of what I refer to as a "preferential sex offender." The term preferential sex offender is merely a descriptive label used to identify, for investigative and prosecutive purposes, a certain type of offender. The term does not appear in the *DSM-IV-TR*, and it is not intended to imply or to be used for clinical diagnosis.

It is important to realize that to refer to someone as a pedophile is to say only that the individual has a sexual preference for children. It says little or nothing about the other aspects of the person's character and personality. To assume that someone is not a pedophile simply because he or she is nice, goes to church, works hard, is kind to animals, and so on, is absurd. Pedophiles span the full spectrum in regard to public perception, from saints to monsters. Nonetheless, over and over again, pedophiles are not recognized, investigated, charged, convicted, or sent to prison simply because they are "nice guys."

TYPOLOGY OF SEX OFFENDERS

When distinctions between types of offenders need to be made, I recommend theuse of a descriptive typology developed for criminal justice purposes. This discussion will set forth such a typology.

My original typology of child molesters was developed in the mid-1980s and was published and widely disseminated by the National Center for Missing and Exploited

Children (NCMEC) in a monograph entitled *Child Molesters: A Behavioral Analysis*. It was revised in April 1987 (2nd edition) and again in December 1992 (3rd edition). It divided child molesters into two categories (situational or preferential) and into seven patterns of behavior. Although still useful, this old typology has several limitations and has been updated by a new typology that places sex offenders, not just child molesters, along a motivational continuum (situational to preferential) instead of into one of two categories. Although motivation can often be difficult to determine, it is best evaluated by documenting behavior patterns. A detailed discussion of this newer typology was published by the NCMEC in September 2001.

At one end of the continuum are the more *situational* sex offenders. They tend to be less intelligent and are overrepresented in lower socioeconomic groups. Their criminal sexual behavior tends to be in the service of basic sexual needs or nonsexual needs such as power and anger. Their behavior is often opportunistic and impulsive, but primarily thought-driven. They are more likely to consider the risks involved in their behavior but often make stupid or sloppy mistakes. If they collect pornography, it is often violent in nature, reflecting their power and anger needs. Their patterns of behavior are more likely to involve the previously discussed concept of the MO.

Situational-type sex offenders victimizing children do not have a true sexual preference for children. They may molest them, however, for a wide variety of situational reasons. They are more likely to view and be aroused by adult pornography but might engage in sex with children in certain situations. Situational sex offenders frequently molest readily available children whom they have easy access to, such as their own children or those they may live with or have control over. Pubescent teenagers are high-risk, viable sexual targets. Younger children may also be targeted because they are weak, vulnerable, or available. Psychopathic situational offenders may select children, especially adolescents, simply because they have the opportunity and think they can get away with it. Social misfits may select children out of insecurity and curiosity. Others may have low self-esteem and use children as substitutes for preferred adults.

At the other end of the motivation continuum are the more preferential sex offenders. They tend to be more intelligent and are overrepresented in higher socioeconomic groups. Their criminal sexual behavior tends to be in the service of deviant sexual needs known as paraphilias. This behavior is often scripted and compulsive and is primarily fantasy-driven. Repeated fantasy over time creates need. They are more likely to consider their needs and therefore make "needy" mistakes that often seem almost stupid. When they collect pornography and related paraphernalia, it usually focuses on the themes of their paraphiliac preferences. Their patterns of behavior are more likely to involve the previously discussed concept of ritual.

THE MOTIVATION CONTINUUM

As this descriptive term implies, preferential-type sex offenders have specific sexual preferences or paraphilias (see Table 5.1). Those with a preference for children could be called pedophiles, those with a preference for peeping could be called voyeurs, those with a preference for suffering could be called sadists, etc. But one of the purposes of this typology is to avoid these diagnostic terms. Preferential sex offenders are more likely to view, be aroused by, and collect theme pornography. Some preferential sex offenders without a preference for children do molest children in order to carry out their bizarre sexual fantasies and preferences with young, less threatening, less judgmental, and highly vulnerable victims. Some of these offenders' sexual activity with children may involve acts they are embarrassed or ashamed to request or do with a preferred adult partner. Such offenders, even if they do not have a sexual preference for children, would still be preferential sex offenders and therefore engage in similar patterns of behavior.

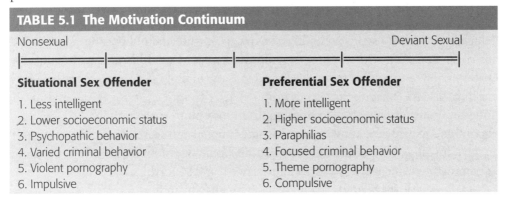

TABLE 5.1 The Motivation Continuum

Nonsexual ——————————————————————— Deviant Sexual

Situational Sex Offender	**Preferential Sex Offender**
1. Less intelligent	1. More intelligent
2. Lower socioeconomic status	2. Higher socioeconomic status
3. Psychopathic behavior	3. Paraphilias
4. Varied criminal behavior	4. Focused criminal behavior
5. Violent pornography	5. Theme pornography
6. Impulsive	6. Compulsive

There are many advantages to using this criminal justice descriptive typology. If there is a need to distinguish a certain type of sex offender, this typology provides a name or label instead of just calling them "these guys." The label is professional in contrast to referring to them as "perverts" or "sickos" or worse. Because the terms are descriptive, not diagnostic, and probative, not prejudicial, they may be more acceptable in reports, search warrants, and testimony by criminal justice professionals. For example, the currently popular term "predator" might be considered too prejudicial for court testimony. The continuum concept also better addresses the complexity of and changes in human behavior. Using the term "preferential sex offender" instead of "preferential child molester" addresses the issue of applying it to offenders who collect child pornography without physically molesting children. The one term, preferential sex offender, eliminates the need for investigators and prosecutors to distinguish between child pornography collectors and child molesters, between pedophiles and hebephiles, and among numerous other paraphilias. How to recognize and identify such offenders will be discussed shortly.

Prosecutors might argue that it is their job to prosecute individuals who violate the law and that whether or not that offender is a pedophile or a preferential sex offender is of little importance to them. There is no legal requirement to determine that a subject or suspect in a case is a pedophile or preferential sex offender. Often it is irrelevant to the investigation or prosecution. There are, however, clear differences between the types of individuals who sexually victimize children, and prosecutors handling these cases sometimes need to make such distinctions. Although there is not a single "profile" that will determine if someone is a child molester, preferential sex offenders tend to engage in highly predictable and recognizable behavior patterns. The potential evidence available as a result of the long-term, persistent, and ritualized behavior patterns of many sexual exploiters of children make these cases almost a prosecutor's heaven.

Need-driven behavior leads to bewildering mistakes. Why would a reasonably intelligent individual use his computer at work to download child pornography, deliver his computer filled with child pornography for repair, send his film with child pornography on it to a store to be developed, appear in child pornography images he is making, discuss engaging in serious criminal activity with a "stranger" he met on the Internet, transmit identifiable photographs of himself to such an individual, maintain incriminating evidence knowing investigators might soon search his home or computer, give investigators permission to search his home or computer knowing it contains incriminating evidence, agree to be interviewed, and so forth?

Defense attorneys might argue that such behavior indicates that their clients are innocent, lack criminal intent, or are not criminally responsible. Why else would an intelligent individual do something so obviously stupid? Such behavior does not necessarily mean the offender is insane or not criminally responsible. Another explanation is much more probable—the behavior is need-driven. The fantasy- or need-driven behavior of preferential sex offenders has little to do with thinking. As a father cautioned his son in the movie *A Bronx Tale*, it is more a matter of the "little head" telling the "big head" what to do. Their need is what makes preferential sex offenders so vulnerable to proactive investigations even though the techniques used have been well publicized. If necessary, an expert could be used to educate the court concerning certain patterns of behavior. The use of such an expert was upheld in *United States v. Romero*, 189 F.3d 576 (7th Cir. 1999).

Prosecutors should be aware of a "Cautionary Statement" that appears on page xxxvii of the DSM-IV-TR and reads in part as follows:

It is to be understood that inclusion here, for clinical and research purposes, of a diagnostic category such as Pathological Gambling or Pedophilia (emphasis added) does not imply that the condition meets legal or other nonmedical criteria for what constitutes mental disease, mental disorder, or mental disability. The clinical and scientific considerations involved in categorization of these conditions as mental disorders may not be wholly relevant to legal judgments, for example, that take into account such issues as individual responsibility, disability determination, and competency.

COMPUTER OFFENDERS

Offenders using computers to sexually exploit children tend to fall into three broad categories:

1. Situational offenders:
   a. *"Normal" adolescent/adult*: Usually a typical adolescent searching online for pornography and sex or an impulsive/curious adult with newly found access to a wide range of pornography and sexual opportunities.
   b. *Morally indiscriminate offender*: Usually a power/anger-motivated sex offender with a history of varied violent offenses. Parents, especially mothers, who make their children available for sex with individuals on the Internet would also most likely fit in this category.
   c. *Profiteer*: The criminal just trying to make easy money. With the lowered risk of identification and increased potential for profit, these individuals have returned to trafficking in child pornography.

When situational offenders break the law, they can obviously be investigated and prosecuted, but their behavior is not as long-term, persistent, and predictable as that of preferential offenders. They are a more varied group.

2. Preferential offenders:
   a. *Pedophile:* Offender, as previously discussed, with a definite preference for children.
   b. *Diverse offender:* Offender with a wide variety of paraphiliac or deviant sexual interests, but no strong sexual preference for children. This offender was previously referred to in my typology as the sexually indiscriminate.

c. *Latent offender:* Individual with potentially illegal but previously latent sexual preferences who has more recently begun to criminally act out when inhibitions are weakened after arousal patterns are fueled and validated through online computer communication.

The essential difference between the pedophile type and the diverse type of preferential offender is the strength of the individual's *sexual* preference for children. The pedophile type is primarily interested in sex with children that might, in some cases, involve other sexual deviations or paraphilias. The diverse type is primarily interested in a variety of sexual deviations that might, in some cases, involve children. For example, the pornography and erotica collection of the diverse preferential offender will be more varied, usually with a focus on the individual's particular sexual preferences or paraphilias (sometimes involving children), whereas a pedophile's collection will focus predominately on children (sometimes involving paraphilias). If children are being victimized, the diverse offender is more likely to directly molest pubescent children. More naive prepubescent children, however, are sometimes selected to minimize possible challenges to, or embarrassment over, the offender's deviant sexual interests. With an absence of prior criminal sexual activity, latent offenders present problems in determining the appropriate prosecution and sentence. A thorough investigation and a good forensic psychological evaluation, possibly aided by the use of the polygraph or other deception assessment devices, are helpful in evaluating such apparent "latent" offenders.

1. Miscellaneous "offenders:"
   a. *Media reporters:* Individuals who erroneously believe they can go online and traffic in child pornography and arrange meetings with suspected child molesters as part of an authorized and valid news exposé.
   b. *Pranksters:* Individuals who disseminate false or incriminating information to embarrass the targets of their "dirty tricks."
   c. *Older "boyfriends:"* Individuals in their late teens or early 20s attempting to sexually interact with adolescent girls or boys.
   d. *Overzealous citizens:* Individuals who go overboard doing their own private investigations into this problem. As will be discussed, investigators must be cautious of all overzealous citizens offering their services in these cases.

Although these miscellaneous "offenders" may be breaking the law, they are obviously less likely to be prosecuted. This category includes media reporters breaking the law as part of a bona fide news story. It does *not* include reporters, or any other professionals, who engage in such activity to hide or rationalize the fact that they have a personal interest in child pornography. They would be situational or preferential offenders.

Overzealous citizens could also include sex offender therapists and researchers engaging in this type of activity. *Only* law enforcement officers, as part of official, authorized investigations, should be conducting proactive investigation or downloading child pornography on a computer. It should be noted that federal law does allow an affirmative defense for the possession of child pornography, but *only* if (1) *less than three* items are possessed and (2) the material is *promptly* and in good faith, and without retaining or allowing access to any person, destroyed or reported to a law enforcement agency that is afforded access to each depiction (18 U.S.C.A. § 2252(c)). The test for those claiming professional use for child pornography should be twofold: First, do they have a professional use for the material? Second, were they using it professionally? Both standards must be met in order to seriously consider the claim.

Although a variety of individuals sexually victimize children, preferential sex offenders, for now, are the primary sexual exploiters of children. They tend to be serial offenders who prey on children through the operation of child sex rings and/or the collection, creation, or distribution of child pornography. Using a computer to fuel and validate interests and behavior, to facilitate interacting with child victims, or to possess and traffic in child pornography usually requires the above-average intelligence and economic means more typical of preferential sex offenders. The computer sex offenders discussed here have tended to be white males from a middle-class or higher socioeconomic background. As computers and use of the Internet have become more commonplace, however, there are now increasing numbers of the more varied situational sex offenders.

RECOGNIZING PREFERENTIAL SEX OFFENDERS

An important step in investigating sexual exploitation of children is to recognize and utilize, if present, the highly predictable sexual behavior patterns of these preferential sex offenders. If the investigation identifies enough of these patterns, many of the remaining ones can be assumed. However, no particular number constitutes "enough." A few may be enough if they are especially significant. Most of these indicators mean little by themselves, but as they are identified and accumulated through investigation, they can constitute reason to believe a suspect is a preferential sex offender.

You cannot determine the type of offender with whom you are dealing unless you have the most complete, detailed, and accurate information possible. The investigator must understand that doing a background investigation on a suspect means more than obtaining the date and place of birth and credit and criminal checks. School, juvenile, military, medical, driving, employment, bank, sex offender and child abuse registry, sex offender assessment, computer, and prior investigative records can all be valuable sources of information about an offender.

A preferential sex offender can usually be identified by the following characteristics:

1. Long-term and persistent pattern of behavior
   a. Begins pattern in early adolescence
   b. Is willing to commit time, money, and energy
   c. Commits multiple offenses
   d. Makes ritual or need-driven mistakes

2. Specific sexual interests
   a. Manifests paraphiliac preferences (may be multiple)
   b. Focuses on defined sexual interests and victim characteristics
   c. Centers life around preferences
   d. Rationalizes sexual interests

3. Well-developed techniques
   a. Evaluates experiences
   b. Lies and manipulates, often skillfully
   c. Has method of access to victims
   d. Is quick to use modern technology (e.g., computer, video) for sexual needs and purposes

4. Fantasy-driven behavior
   a. Collects theme pornography
   b. Collects paraphernalia, souvenirs, videotapes, etc.
   c. Records fantasies
   d. Acts to turn fantasy into reality

Prosecutors must not over- or underreact to reported allegations. They must understand that not all computer offenders are stereotypical "pedophiles" who fit some common profile. Keeping an open mind and objectively attempting to determine the type of offender involved can be useful in minimizing embarrassing errors in judgment and developing appropriate interview, investigative, and prosecutive strategies. For example, knowing that preferential offenders as part of sexual ritual are more likely to commit similar offenses, make need-driven mistakes, and compulsively collect pornography and other offense-related paraphernalia could be used to build a stronger case.

In computer cases, especially those involving proactive investigative techniques, it is often easier to determine the type of offender than in other kinds of child sexual exploitation cases. When attempting to make this determination, it is important to evaluate all available background information. The following information from the online computer activity can be valuable in this assessment. This information can often be ascertained from the online service provider and through undercover communication, pretext contacts, informants, record checks, and other investigative techniques (e.g., mail cover, pen register, trash run, surveillance).

- Screen name
- Number of files originated
- Screen profile
- Number of files forwarded
- Accuracy of profile
- Number of files received
- Length of time active
- Number of recipients
- Amount of time spent online
- Site of communication
- Number of transmissions
- Theme of messages and chat
- Number of files
- Theme of pornography

A common problem in these cases is that it is often easier to determine the computer being used than to determine who is using the computer. It is obviously harder to do a background investigation when multiple people have access to the computer. Pretext phone calls can be very useful in such situations.

CASE STUDY: AN EXAGGERATED EXAMPLE OF COMPUTER PORNOGRAPHY

An investigation determines that a suspect is a 50-year-old single male who does volunteer work with troubled boys. He has two prior convictions for sexually molesting young boys in 1974 and 1986, has an expensive state-of-the-art home computer, has a main screen name of "Boylover," and one screen profile that describes him as a 14 year old. For the last 5 years he has daily spent many hours online in chat rooms and in the "alt.sex.preteen" newsgroup justifying and graphically describing his sexual preference for and involvement with young boys and brags about his extensive pornography collection. Furthermore, he uploads hundreds of child pornography files, all focusing on preteen boys in bondage. If such a determination were relevant to the case, these facts would constitute more than sufficient probable cause to believe this suspect is a preferential sex offender.

Knowing the kind of offender with whom you are dealing can go a long way in determining investigative and prosecutive strategy. For example, this knowledge might be useful in:

1. Anticipating and understanding need-driven mistakes
2. Evaluating the consistency of victim statements
3. Developing offender and victim interview strategies
4. Determining the existence, age, and number of victims
5. Recognizing where and what kind of corroborative evidence might be found
6. Proving intent
7. Determining appropriate charging and sentencing
8. Assessing the admissibility of prior like acts
9. Evaluating dangerousness at a bond hearing, etc.
10. Explaining behavior patterns to a jury
11. Determining suitability for treatment options
12. Addressing staleness
13. Utilizing an expert search warrant

"EXPERT" SEARCH WARRANTS

Most computer exploitation cases involve searching homes, offices, and computers for child pornography and other related evidence. One controversial and misunderstood application of an offender typology is its use in so-called "expert" search warrants. In such search warrants, an expert's opinion is included in the affidavit to address a particular deficiency. The expert's opinion is usually intended for any of the following reasons:

1. Addressing legal staleness problems
2. Expanding the nature and scope of the search (e.g., for erotica-type material or for more than one location)
3. Adding to the probable cause

Addressing staleness and expanding the scope of the search are probably the most legally defensible uses of such opinions. Using the expert's opinion as part of the probable cause, however, is much more legally questionable and should only be done in full awareness of the potential judicial consequences. Despite the legal uncertainties of its application, there is little behavioral doubt that probable cause to believe that a given individual is a preferential sex offender is, by itself, probable cause to believe that the individual collects some type of pornography *or* paraphernalia related to his or her preferences (which may or may not include child pornography). If it is used, the expert's opinion should be the smallest possible percentage of the probable cause. As the portion of the probable cause based upon the expert's opinion increases, the expectation of a much more closely scrutinized, critical review should increase.

The affidavit should set forth *only* those offender characteristics necessary to address a specific deficiency. For example, if the expert opinion is needed only to address staleness, the only trait that matters is the tendency to add to and the unlikeliness to discard collected pornography and erotica. The expert's opinion concerning other behavioral traits could be used to justify searching a storage locker or a computer at work or searching for related paraphernalia or videos.

Not all offenders who might use a computer to traffic in child pornography have these traits. Therefore, the affidavit *must* set forth the reasons for the expert's conclusion that the subject of the search is among the particular group of offenders with the stated characteristics. The informational basis for the expert's opinion must be reliable, sufficient, and documented. The information must be from reliable sources and in sufficient quantity and quality to support the belief. Details concerning the information must be meticulously recorded and retrievable, especially if it is the basis for a warrant sought by another agency or department.

As stated earlier, it is useful to have a name for "these guys" with these distinctive characteristics. Although investigators have frequently called them "pedophiles" or "child pornography collectors," the term preferential sex offender is recommended.

Expert search warrants describing highly predictable offender characteristics should only be used for subjects exhibiting preferential sexual behavior patterns. The characteristics, dynamics, and techniques (e.g., expert search warrant) discussed concerning preferential sex offenders should be considered with any of the preferential types of computer offenders (e.g., pedophile, diverse, or latent). It is usually unnecessary to distinguish which type of preferential offender is involved.

Whenever possible, affidavits for search warrants should be based on reliable, case-specific facts. Because of legal uncertainties, expert search warrants should be used only when absolutely necessary. They should not be a replacement for reasonable investigation. When such warrants are used, the affidavit must reflect the specific facts and details of the case in question. Boilerplate warrants, or "go-bys," should be avoided. It is also best if the expert used is part of the investigation or from the local area. Regional or national experts should be used only when a local expert is unavailable.

STALENESS OF PROBABLE CAUSE

Because of delays in communicating details from proactive investigations, staleness is a common problem in computer exploitation cases. It may take weeks or months for the details learned from an undercover Internet investigation in one part of the country to be disseminated to investigators with jurisdiction over the target computer in another part of the country. Obviously, the best way to address the staleness of probable cause is to "freshen" it up with current investigation and information.

As stated previously, staleness can also be addressed with an "expert" search warrant. Before doing so, prosecutors should do legal research and be aware of appellate decisions that support this approach. They should also be aware of Congressional Finding 12 in the Child Pornography Prevention Act of 1996 that states, "prohibiting the possession and viewing of child pornography will encourage the possessors of such material to rid themselves of or destroy the material." I am not sure what this "finding" is based on, but it is contrary to my many years of experience studying preferential sex offenders and contrary to what is usually stated in such expert search warrants.

Another way to address staleness is to recognize that the information in question may not be stale. It is a matter of differing opinion as to when the informational basis for probable cause becomes stale. Some prosecutors say in days, others say weeks, but most say months. I believe that the time interval varies based on the type of information. Because of characteristics of technology and human behavior, probable cause about information on a computer should not be considered stale for at least 1 year. It is not easy to effectively delete the information on a computer, even when you try. Furthermore, most people do not delete the information on a regular basis. Such editing of a computer is likely to occur less often than cleaning out the garage, attic, or basement. Because this is a common human characteristic, it should not require the opinion of an expert.

"CONCERNED CITIZENS" ASSISTING LAW ENFORCEMENT

Many individuals who report information to the authorities about deviant sexual activity that they have discovered on the Internet must invent clever excuses for how and why they came upon such material. They often start out pursuing their own sexual/deviant interests but then decide to report to the police either because it went too far because they are afraid they might have been monitored by authorities or because they need to rationalize their perversions as having some higher purpose or value. Rather than honestly admitting their own deviant interests, they make up elaborate explanations to justify finding the material. Some claim to be journalists, researchers, or outraged, concerned citizens trying to protect a child or help the police. In any case, what they find may need to be investigated. If information from such "concerned citizens" is part of the basis for an expert's opinion in the warrant, there could be questions about its reliability.

Investigators must consider the following when these "concerned citizens" report such activity:

1. The reporters, motivated by a need to rationalize or deny their deviant sexual interests, have embellished and falsified an elaborate tale of perversion and criminal activity on the Internet.
2. The reporters, regardless of their true motivations, have uncovered others who are using the Internet to validate and reinforce bizarre, perverted sexual fantasies and interests (a common occurrence) but who are not engaged in criminal activity.
3. The reporters, regardless of their true motivations, have uncovered others involved in criminal activity.

One especially sensitive area for investigators is the possibility of preferential sex offenders who present themselves as concerned citizens reporting what they "inadvertently discovered" in cyberspace or requesting to work with law enforcement to search for child pornography and to protect children. Other than the obvious benefit of legal justification for their past or future activity, most do this as part of their need to rationalize their behavior as worthwhile and to gain access to children. When these offenders are caught, instead of recognizing this activity as part of their preferential pattern of behavior, the courts sometimes give them leniency because of their "good deeds." Preferential sex offenders who are also law enforcement officers sometimes claim their activity was part of some well-intentioned but unauthorized investigation.

CHAPTER 6

The Status of Serial Stalking: Persons, Processes, and Palliatives

Brian H. Spitzberg, Leila B. Dutton, and Charles Wesley Kim, Jr.

A CASE STUDY IN OBSTINATE PERSISTENCE AND UNWANTED PURSUIT

In March 1998, Jane commenced a brief dating relationship (four dates over 3 weeks) with Jim, a corporate executive. The parties met through an online dating service. On their second date, Jane told Jim that she was "the most sane person in her family." She also revealed to him that a court had recently (in December 1997) issued a 3-year civil harassment restraining order against her in favor of a former boyfriend, Tom, and his wife.

The harassment leading to issuance of Tom's civil harassment restraining order against Jane occurred 7 years *after* her relationship with Tom had ended. As with Jim, the relationship with Tom was a brief dating relationship (four times in 1 month). After Tom tried to break off the relationship, Jane made repeated attempts to contact him by letter and phone. Tom repeatedly told her to stop. He had her phone number blocked by the phone company and refused to accept her "emergency calls," in which Jane tricked the operator into connecting them under the guise of an "emergency" and by giving the operator a phony name.

Tom changed his address several times, changed his phone number repeatedly, changed jobs several times, had both his address and telephone number unlisted, and did not disclose any of these changes to Jane.

Somehow, Jane managed to track Tom down each time and contact him. Tom described her surprise contacts as "completely unnerving and unsettling to [him]," adding, "but they are also terrifying to my wife. Our peace of mind is being completely shattered." In court papers, Tom detailed repeated hang-up phone calls, phone calls in which the unidentified caller made a kissing sound, phone calls in which Jane identified herself and left long messages on his home answering machine, phone messages consisting only of music, a phone call in which the caller interrogated Tom's wife as to who she was, a call to Tom's workplace from a woman claiming that Tom's wife had called her (of course, Tom's wife could not call Jane as she had neither a way of knowing how nor any desire to contact her), and a letter from Jane admitting that she was the unidentified caller on a previous instance. The specific pattern of behavior resulting in the restraining order occurred within a 2-month time frame in 1997.

Jane's pattern of behavior that led to Tom's civil harassment restraining order against her was repeated with eerie similarity in her subsequent relationship with Jim. During the 3 weeks Jane and Jim dated, she constantly begged to have sex and tried to find out if he was dating someone else; if she thought he was dating someone else, she would threaten him. She also lied about her financial situation, claiming a six-figure income. Jim later discovered that she did not have a job, did not have a car, and had been evicted from her prior residence. By the fourth date, Jim decided it was time to break off the relationship with Jane. She began making repeated unwanted and harassing telephone calls to Jim's workplace, home, and hotels while he was traveling on business. Her calls were alternately friendly one time and abusive and threatening the next. Jane also began showing up uninvited at Jim's work and home, despite his requests that she not do so.

In an attempt to maintain the relationship, Jane claimed that their one sexual encounter 3 days before had resulted in her becoming pregnant, although she refused to provide any information about the alleged pregnancy. Jane also "ordered" Jim to not have sex with anyone else. While Jim was on a business trip out of state, Jane called his hotel repeatedly after midnight and hung up when he answered. When he refused to answer the phone, he received a knock on his hotel room door. It was someone from the front desk. Jane had called and said it was an emergency and that she needed to speak to Jim immediately.

The following day, Jane faxed Jim. In the fax, which was full of underlined obscenities and capital letters, Jane complained of how Jim was "disrespecting" her and "pissing [her] off," threatened to cut off future contact with their unborn child, and threatened to "ring [the] fucking neck" of the "bitch" who she claimed had called her. Of course, Jim did not have anyone call her; in fact, he had not discussed the situation with anyone at this point. Jane also threatened in the fax to "gladly take every cent your [former] wife does not already have."

Upon Jim's return, he met with Jane to inform her that if she were pregnant, he would take responsibility for the child but that he was not going to have a romantic relationship with her. Jane's response was that it was impossible to not have a romantic relationship if they were going to have a child together. The next day, Jane made repeated hang-up phone calls to Jim's home phone, intended to prevent him from being able to use his phone. Jane subsequently admitted that she had been making the hang-up calls, apologized, and said she would not do it again. Not surprisingly, she continued to make harassing phone calls.

After several other dramatic but failed attempts to reinvolve Jim in her life, Jane wrote the first of many harassing letters. Many were multipage and alternated between claiming she was a victim, apologizing, and attacking Jim. All contained multiple underlined words, and one included an obscene drawing. She then tracked him down with harassing phone calls during another of his business trips. Two days later, Jane again called and left a series of telephone messages. The tone was chatty—a complete change from the late-night calls a couple of days before. Jim did not return her calls. The following day, Jane's tone was again hostile and accusatory, threatening that if he did not get back to her, she would have to make a "decision" that would impact him and saying that joint custody "was out of the question." Jim did not return her call. Three days later, Jane sent him flowers and a card.

Throughout this ordeal, Jane had repeatedly made excuses for why she could not get a pregnancy test. Jim arranged for an appointment at Planned Parenthood to get a pregnancy test. Jim, suspecting Jane might try to alter the test in some way, asked that she leave her purse in the car while they went for the test. Jane refused. They left and Jim took her back to her work. Before exiting the car, Jane asked Jim if he wanted to have sex. He refused. While Jim was out of town on business, Jane went to Planned Parenthood and obtained a pregnancy test that showed she was pregnant. Jim did not know, and never learned, whether he was the father.

A few days later, Jim logged in to his online dating account and discovered that Jane was sending him messages. He responded that he did not want further contact. Jane responded with an insulting and harassing message.

A few days after that, Jane and Jim spoke over the telephone about the pregnancy. He agreed that if the child were his, he would pay child support and provide life insurance to secure the child support. Jane demanded that she have primary custody and said that if Jim did not agree, she would have an abortion. After this discussion, Jane demanded to know if anyone was at Jim's house. Jim told her it was none of her business. Jane became angry and hung up. Later that day, Jane arrived at Jim's home uninvited. She tried to find out if anyone were there and tried to look into his place. Jim asked her to leave.

The next day, Jane left 13 messages on Jim's voicemail consisting of illegally taped conversations between Jane and Jim (surprisingly, the court did not take any action in response to the illegal wiretap). Three days later, Jim logged in to his dating account and discovered that Jane had recorded over the greeting message on his account making derogatory remarks about Jim and telling other women to call her. At 1:52 AM, Jane called and left a message of herself laughing. At 2:00 AM, Jane called again and left another harassing message calling him a "freak" but ending with a cheery, "I hope you have a nice life!" When Jim logged on again, he discovered that she had again logged in using his password and altered his greeting. It appeared she was trying to recover his messages as well. She then proceeded to leave a series of seven harassing messages in her own name. Two days later, Jane reversed course yet again, calling and faxing apologies. She demanded that Jim "forgive her" and said things should "be the way they were before."

Three days after that, Jane called Jim and said she was "over" the relationship, but added that it was "very important" that he call her right back. He did not call her. Two days later, when Jim logged in to his account, he discovered that Jane had again impersonated him and posted a response to a dating inquiry in which Jane (impersonating Jim) called the dating inquirer a "fat bitch."

The next day, Jane called and left a message demanding that Jim call back in the next couple of hours. She said that if he did not, he was "going to be very sorry," adding, "If you're just not there this morning, then tough luck, because I'm going to do what I need to do." When Jim got this message, he became concerned that Jane would fly out to where he was engaged in business and try to physically injure him. He changed hotel rooms and the name under which he was registered.

After a couple of weeks during which Jane harassed and attempted to locate Jim during his business trips, she engaged in subsequent communications in which she threatened to have an abortion if they did not resume their relationship. When Jim then filed a paternity action, Jane responded by claiming that she had had an abortion but refused to disclose any information that would allow him to confirm the alleged pregnancy or alleged abortion.

In reviewing the pattern of conduct, it is remarkable how similar Jane's behaviors were in both Tom's and Jim's cases. Unfortunately for Jim, Jane decided that she wanted to engage him in a much more destructive way when he obtained a domestic violence temporary restraining order (DV-TRO). Jane initially opposed the DV-TRO on the ground that they did not date for long enough to have a "dating relationship"—a position rejected out of hand by the court. She then proceeded to engage in protracted litigation intended to bleed Jim financially.

Although Jane claimed to have no money, she managed to hire well-known counsel to defend her case, which they did with vigor. For example, at her initial deposition, she would only give her name. She then proceeded, on the advice of counsel, to take the Fifth Amendment over 500 times, refusing to answer questions like her birth date. It took three depositions (and two court hearings) before Jane would answer questions. She then proceeded to invoke her right to privacy to refuse to answer a number of questions, and her responses were characterized by a distinct inability to recall anything she had done to Jim but perfect memory as to what she perceived Jim had done to her.

Jane also embarked on a campaign intended to destroy Jim's professional relationships by sending "anonymous" letters to his workplace and customers. All of these communications from "third parties" using aliases were generated in the same font, with the same misspelled address, and sent out on the same paper using the same envelopes. None contained any fingerprints, which curiously coincided with the fact that none of Jane's known letters or court papers contained any fingerprints either. It took a motion and several contested court hearings to get Jane to submit a set of her fingerprints. During her depositions, she wore gloves or had her counsel handle all of the papers. She would only pick up a glass of water using a paper napkin, which she took with her. It was never possible to get a good set of prints off of any documents she handled.

To protect himself, Jim implemented company-wide security measures intended to prevent the disclosure of any information regarding his whereabouts when in San Diego or traveling, met with the District Attorney's Stalking Unit, and implemented personal safety protocols. These were insufficient to prevent someone from gaining access to his residence and putting a fishhook (cut off from fishing gear in his house) in his bed or to prevent Jane from sending letters in her own name to his customers falsely alleging that he had committed perjury in the domestic violence action.

In an attempt to expand the engagement (even as Jane claimed she could not be stalking Jim because she was trying to "disengage"), Jane filed a bogus perjury complaint against Jim in the District Attorney's Office. Jane's perjury complaint against him ironically wound up on the desk of the same investigator who was handling the stalking allegation by Jim against Jane. The investigator reported that Jane seemed reasonable and rational for about the first 30 minutes of the interview, but the more she talked the more it became apparent that something was not right about her and her story.

When the District Attorney's Office declined to press perjury charges against Jim, Jane directed some of her ire at the investigator by filing a complaint against him. It apparently mattered not to her that by this time the family court had already issued a no-contact order against her that essentially confirmed what Jim had been saying all along.

After a couple of years, Jane apparently tired of the chase. Jim was glad to be rid of her harassment and chose not to pursue the action further for fear of inciting her to refocus on him. Not surprisingly, Jane began obsessing about someone else. The court records reflect that in December 2005, she was the defendant in yet another civil harassment restraining order case.

Like any hunter, Jane pursued her prey with obstinate persistence, overcoming the dodges and detours the prey engaged to avoid being caught. She demonstrated the ability to give up the hunt for a given target but not the process of the hunt itself. When one target escaped or demonstrated too much capacity for resistance, she moved on to another target. The hunt itself, rather than the capture of the prey, obviously became part of the *sine qua non* of survival for her.

WHAT IS STALKING?

Stalking clearly evokes some specific sense of urgency and cultural concern. Part of the cultural concern is the somewhat natural association between stalking and the abject fear (and fascination) the public has in the exploits of serial killers (Carlisle, 1998; Godwin, 2000; Holmes, 1998a). Serial killers, given the need to continue a crime across times and targets, often must be sufficiently strategic to gain the advantages of stealth, surprise, and tactical advantage. Serial killers often stalk their prey, and the fact that celebrity and relational stalkers alike may employ tactics similar to those of serial killers is likely to have provided a significant psychological impetus to the passage of antistalking legislation (Holmes, 1998b; Petherick, 2006).

In the 1980s after celebrities sometimes suffered tragic fates at the hands of their fanatical or obsessed devotees and citizens were sometimes tracked, harassed, threatened, and injured by former intimate partners, the state of California passed the world's first law explicitly regulating a process referred to as stalking, although statutes with relevance to stalking have existed in some jurisdictions for almost a century (Modena Group on Stalking, 2007). Within a little more than a decade after the California statute was passed into law, all 50 U.S. states, Australia, Canada, the United Kingdom, the Netherlands, Germany, Austria, Japan, Italy, and a number of other jurisdictions passed some form of antistalking legislation (De Fazio, 2009; Finch, 2001; Miller, 2001; Miller & Nugent, 2001; Tjaden, 2009).

Most legislation, however, identifies some subset of the following features in proscribing stalking: (1) a pattern (2) of explicitly unwanted or dispreferred (3) pursuit, intrusion, or harassment (4) that is intentional (*mens rea*), (5) threatening or causes the victim (or a reasonable person) fear, apprehension, or anxiety, and (6) that serves no other legitimate purpose or is not an otherwise legally protected form of speech (Tjaden, 2009). Legislation sometimes specifies particular types of behaviors that are proscribed and sometimes simply delineates some set of these defining features. The challenge of legislating against stalking is suggested by Jane's case. It would be difficult for legislation to anticipate a fishhook in a bed or a "threat" of alleged pregnancy or abortion.

Serial Stalking

In Western cultures, there is now a fairly solid scientific understanding of what stalking is, who stalks, and how they stalk. There are even relatively advanced insights into why stalkers stalk. There are other vexing aspects of stalking that are yet almost completely unexplored. Among these seriously underexplored areas is the nature of serial stalking (Lloyd-Goldstein, 2000; Petherick, 2006).

There are relatively few theoretically or empirically grounded bases upon which to formulate a conceptual definition of serial stalking. According to Lloyd-Goldstein, "No standards or criteria have been established or recognized as authoritative to define serial stalking" (2000, p. 177). One relevant dimension, however, seems structurally obvious— the *spatiotemporal* relationship of the objects of pursuit relative to the stalking activities. Specifically, stalking can involve multiple *concurrent* targets, or *sequential* (e.g., *ad seriatim*) targets (Lloyd-Goldstein, 2000; Petherick, 2006). Stalkers may be pursuing multiple objects, as when a fan-obsessed stalker happens to be fixated upon multiple celebrities simultaneously. Another example is a stalker who pursues a relationship with one object and extends that stalking concurrently to an affiliate of that object (e.g., a new romantic partner, family member, friend), as appears strategically necessary to the stalker.

Another important dimension is the nature of the *relationship of targets* to one another. For example, Jane might have pursued the executive and then the executive's attorney. Or, a stalker might pursue a former dating partner and then that dating partner's new girlfriend or boyfriend. In such cases, regardless of whether the stalking occurs concurrently or sequentially, the interrelationship of the targets would seem a relevant basis upon which to consider the nature of the stalking and the stalker. In contrast, the more traditional conception of "serial" crimes would consider stalkers who pursue one target, cease this stalking at some point, and initiate a new campaign of stalking on a new target, unrelated to the previous target, at some point in the future.

A third dimension is the victim's *relationship to the pursuer* (Mohandie, Meloy, McGowan, & Williams, 2006). In their analysis of more than 1000 clinical or forensic stalking cases, Mohandie et al. (2006) found that types of stalkers and stalker activities could be significantly differentiated by whether the stalker had a prior relationship with the target. They further differentiated these relationship types. Prior relationships were classified as either intimate (e.g., marital, dating) or nonintimate (e.g., work colleagues, friends). Those stalkers with no prior relationship to their targets were classified as either public (e.g., celebrity, politician) or private (e.g., person encountered in everyday activity).

Serial stalking in this scheme is therefore distinct from *stalking recidivism* as it has been studied previously. In the two studies currently available on stalking recidivism, both samples were primarily or entirely populated by stalkers who committed the same type of crime against the *same target victim*, in which the offenses were separated by substantial time or legal interventions such as issuance of a restraining order, arrest, imprisonment, or conviction. In a study of 40 stalking cases in San Diego, Huffhines (2001) identified a reoffending rate of 57.5% (71% of female stalkers, 54.5% of male stalkers), although in some of these cases the reoffense could not be confirmed to have stalking elements. The average amount of time between the legal resolution of the index offense and the reoffense was 9 months. In this sample, 45% had a prior criminal history.

In a study of 7 years of records of stalkers in New York City, Rosenfeld (2003) identified a 49% rate of recidivism. Some percentage of these may have met the criteria of serial stalkers, but the author indicates that the rate of stalkers subsequently harassing different victims was probably "quite low" (personal communication, September 30, 2009). The average time between the index offense and reoffense was 12 months, and 80% of those who reoffended did so within a year. In this sample, 54% had a prior criminal history.

Three other studies provide potential recidivism estimates, although this terminology was not used. Melton (2004) studied domestic violence cases that had been closed in the criminal justice system (time 1) and followed the cases up at time 2 (6 months) and time 3 (1 year). Stalking by the former partner was fairly prominent from time 1 (92%) to time 2 (56%) and time 3 (58%). In this approach to recidivism, however, it is not always clear how to distinguish recidivism from simple *persistence* in one continuous process of stalking (see also Bell, Cattaneo, Goodman, & Dutton, 2008). Johnson and Spitzberg (2006) examined 63 closed stalking case files from a family justice center and found that 30% of the accused stalkers had a previous restraining order against them. In a study of state stalking arrest cases in Delaware, Scocas, O'Connell, Huenke, Nold, and Zoelker (1996) found that 73% were rearrested within a year, and 17% had been charged with stalking more than once.

The problem with the concept of serial stalking arises in distinguishing stalking of multiple sequential victims from stalking persistence and recidivism in their more common criminological uses. Stalking by its nature is a form of recidivism. Thus, *serial stalking* requires multiple victims separated in sequence as well as time, *concurrent* stalking involves stalking multiple victims within the same time frame, and stalking *recidivism* should ideally be marked operationally by some specific time of inactivity or some form of legal intervention that marks a point at which the system has ordered or taken actions to make it stop. Stalking *persistence*, then, simply becomes briefly punctuated or continuous unwanted pursuit. These four types of stalking are not consistently differentiated in the stalking literature, and there are likely to be some ambiguous cases in which these distinctions overlap, thus making generalizations from existing research problematic.

These findings on stalkers can be compared to recidivism research of intimate partner violence, which has revealed rates of reoffense, rearrest, or recidivism of 15% (Kingsnorth, 2006), 16% (Wooldredge & Thistlethwaite, 2005), 23% (Maxwell, Garner, & Fagan, 2002), 30% (McCarroll et al., 2000), 44% (Ménard, Anderson, & Godboldt, 2009), and 68% (Mele, 2009). Thus, although the evidence is still meager, at this point there is little evidentiary basis to conclude that the prevalence of serial and recidivist stalking among all stalking cases is substantially greater or lesser than the rate of serial or recidivist intimate partner violence in general.

These three dimensions are visually displayed in Figure 6.1. At this point, this description is merely intended as a heuristic typology. It serves to identify three relatively obvious dimensions of interest, but these dimensions may be highly correlated. For example, the vast majority of serial stalkers, when narrowly defined as pursuing sequential targets only, may involve unrelated targets. Regardless, each of the cells of this typology represents a potentially distinct type of *multiple-victim* stalking case. From the perspective of these dimensions, *serial stalking can be defined as an unwanted pattern of fearful or threatening behavior that extends sequentially over distinct times and targets of pursuit. Recidivist* stalking refers to an unwanted pattern of fearful or threatening behavior that is punctuated or interrupted, extending sequentially over distinct times toward a given target of pursuit. *Concurrent* stalking involves an unwanted pattern of fearful or threatening behavior that extends across targets of pursuit during the same episode of time. *Persistent* stalking refers to an unwanted pattern of fearful or threatening behavior that extends relatively continuously over time with a given target of pursuit.

THE NATURE OF STALKING

A full understanding of stalking requires consideration of the nature of stalkers, victims, the stalking process, and the ways in which victims and law enforcement cope with the crime. These topics will be examined with an eye toward three concerns. First, a selective review and interpretation is made of scholarship on each topic. Second, this selective review is bolstered by the results of an analysis of an ongoing descriptive meta-analytic database maintained by Brian Spitzberg (see the note at the end of the chapter for a description of the analytic method, as well as Appendix I). Third, wher-

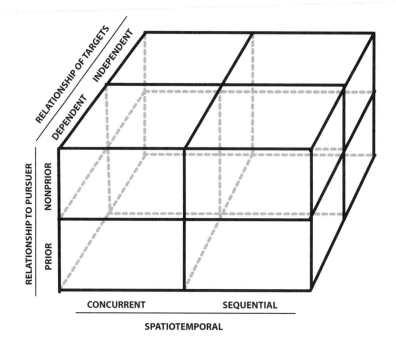

TABLE 6.1   Strategies and Exemplary Tactics of Stalking
Source: Adapted from Cupach & Spitzberg, 2004; Dutton & Spitzberg, 2007; Spitzberg & Cupach, 2007.

ever possible, available research findings and speculations regarding the serial nature of stalking or stalkers are considered.

Stereotypes of stalkers may focus upon notions of obsessive celebrity fan(atic)s or murderous strangers lurking constantly in the shadows of a person's everyday spatial periphery. Such stalkers exist, to be sure (see Meloy, Sheridan, & Hoffman, 2008), but they are not typical of the phenomenon. Celebrities and public figures may bear significantly elevated individual risks for lifetime likelihood of stalking victimization, simply as a cost of coming into contact with so many people and of serving both as a high-status figure and as a figure who may well symbolize actions or policy decisions that evoke strong emotional investments in others. Despite the elevated individual risk of celebrities and public figures, across the entire population, the vast majority of stalking occurs among relatively "normal" people. A full understanding of stalking requires a consideration of the nature of stalkers, victims, the stalking process, and the ways in which victims and law enforcement cope with the crime.

Prevalence of Stalking

The vast majority of stalking emerges out of preexisting relationships of some sort. Across 73 studies in the database, 81% of stalking victims or stalkers claim some prior acquaintanceship, and of the 63 studies providing a separate estimate for the percentage emerging from a prior relationship as "strangers," the complementary statistic is 21%. Of the types of relationships coded, 44% represent prior romantically involved relationships, 28% are considered "acquaintances," 24% involved "service-related" relationships (e.g., counselor, instructor, police), 79% involved intimate but nonromantic relations (e.g., close friend, family member), 14% were colleagues of some sort (e.g., classmate, coworker), and 13% were neighbors.

There are at least two significant implications of these findings. First, most stalkers emerge from existing social and relational network members. Second, as a consequence, stalkers appear "normal" enough to "fly in under people's relational radar." If these stalkers were particularly deviant, aberrant, abnormal, neurotic, or otherwise disturbed, it did not seem to prevent some form of preliminary, and most often serious, relationship development from occurring before the stalking behavior emerged. In the case study involving Jane, it did not take long (a month or so) for each of the victims to figure out that there was something wrong with her. At first, they each considered her intelligent, attractive, vivacious, and engaging.

According to one assessment, in general "it appears that exposure to multiple stalking episodes is a phenomenon with an exceedingly low base rate" (Nobles, Fox, Piquero, & Piquero, 2009, p. 499). Past research has not clearly differentiated stalking recidivism, persistence, or concurrent stalking from serial stalking, and it is impossible from current descriptions in most studies to determine what their estimates of prevalence represent. Understanding the many limitations of the data, therefore, if they are quantitatively summarized, an average of 26% of stalking cases involve some form of concurrent, recidivist, or serial stalking. This estimate reveals a wide range (2% to 75%), but is a summary of almost 10,000 cases or participants. These estimates are not exactly suggestive of a "low base rate" of serial stalking, although the rate of "exposure" to serial stalking in the general population is almost certainly a rare event.

Heterosexual Stalking

The vast majority of research indicates that females are far more likely to be victimized by stalking, and males are more likely to be the victimizer. This sex difference is in line with general intimate partner violence recidivism research (e.g., Renauer & Henning, 2005). Most larger-scale representative studies provide population prevalence estimates among Western populations ranging from approximately 8% to 20% for women and 2% to 12% for men (e.g., Basile, Swahn, Chen, & Saltzman, 2006; Budd & Mattinson, 2000; Baum, Catalano, Rand, & Rose, 2009; Dressing, Küehner, & Gass, 2005; Kohn, Flood, Chase, & McMahon, 2000; McLennan, 1996; Morris, Anderson, & Murray, 2002; Purcell, Pathé, & Mullen, 2002; Steiger, Burger, & Schild, 2008; Tjaden & Thoennes, 1998; Walby & Allen, 2004). Thus, a female stalking a male, as in the chapter opening case, represents a relatively unusual occurrence.

Same-Sex Stalking

Because women are more likely to be stalked by men and because domestic stalking has received much scholarly and public attention in recent years, little research has examined same-sex stalking, although there is evidence that it occurs (Meloy & Boyd, 2003; Mullen, Pathé, & Purcell, 2008; Purcell, Pathé, & Mullen, 2001; Tjaden & Thoennes, 1998). Meloy and Boyd (2003) conducted an archival study of mental health and law enforcement professionals and, with a sample of 82 female stalkers, found that 8% of the perpetrators were lesbian and 12% were bisexual.

In the National Violence Against Women (NVAW) study of 16,000 U.S. adults, Tjaden and Thoennes (1998) found that male respondents who had ever lived with another man as a couple were more likely to report being stalked, suggesting that gay males may be more at risk for stalking victimization than heterosexual males (they did not report on stalking of women who had lived with another woman as a couple). They did not collect data on the circumstances surrounding the same-sex stalking and did not assess the type of relationship between the victim and perpetrator (e.g., current/former intimate, acquaintance, stranger). Indeed, it is likely that some stalking of gay men by men is motivated by homonegativity as well as reasons unrelated to their sexual orientation. Similarly, females who stalk other women are likely to have a variety of motivations that may or may not be related to sexual or romantic interest. Although lesbian, gay, and bisexual individuals are vulnerable to being stalked, one study with undergraduate women indicated that being a lesbian or bisexual is not a significant risk factor for stalking victimization (Mustaine & Tewksbury, 1999).

CHARACTERISTICS OF STALKER BEHAVIOR

Stalkers

The research literature indicates that typical stalking cases tend to involve multiple categories of behavior. That is, the vast majority of stalking victims experience a broad cross-section of these actions. Jane employed many of these tactics such as sending flowers, communicating through faxes, showing up at Jim's home and work, (presumably) breaking and entering to leave a fishhook in his bed, making frequent unwanted contacts, and making threats about the alleged unborn child. Cupach and Spitzberg (2004) identified eight strategies, within which these tactics can be categorized (Table 6.1). Serial stalkers may be expected to replay a standard repertoire of strategies, adapting their tactics to their target's perceived vulnerabilities.

The potential importance of the breadth of stalking activities is suggested by the typical duration of stalking cases. Across 30 studies in the meta-analysis, the average was almost 1.5 years. Thus, every day, month after month, with no known end in sight, stalking victims attempt to endure the prospect that in any given day or moment they may encounter unexpected and unwanted contact, invasion, harassment, threats, or violence. They may not know whom to trust (e.g., due to stalking by proxy), and they may have no real insight into how to free themselves from such onslaught. Even without explicit threats or violence, it is obvious that a collective and enduring pattern of such unwanted activities could accumulate into an exhausting, debilitating, and ultimately traumatizing experience.

In the event there are threats and violence, the case is potentially much worse yet. According to those studies offering estimates in the meta-analysis, 44% of stalking cases involve threats, one-third involve physical violence, and 11.85% involve sexual aggression or violence. Across studies, the percentage of threats correlates significantly with the percentage of physical violence in that sample, and the amount of physical violence in a sample relates positively with the percentage of the sample in which

TABLE 6.1	
Hyperintimacy: Inappropriate behavior masking as courtship, flirtation, or efforts to ingratiate target and/or pursue greater intimacy. Examples: sending gifts or symbols of affections	
Mediated contact: Use of technologies to establish or maintain contact and engage in communication. Examples: faxes, instant messaging, social network sites	
Interactional contact: Efforts to engage in face-to-face communication. Examples: showing up at places, entering into conversation target is having with another person, joining common clubs or organizations	
Surveillance: Efforts to obtain information about the target's life, location, or activities. Examples: driving by the target's home or work, following, using of technologies (e.g., GPS, computer Trojan horses), coverting monitoring	*Proxy pursuit:* Use of third parties to facilitate any of these strategies or tactics. Examples: pursuer uses relatives or acquaintances, hires private detectives, inveigles unwitting associates of the target
Invasion: Unwarranted intrusions into the property or personal space of the target. Examples: trespassing, breaking and entering target's property, soliciting information from target's acquaintances	
Harassment/intimidation: Efforts to influence target through infliction of minor irritants or costs. Examples: extraordinary persistence of contact, regulatory harassment, interference with everyday routines	
Coercion/threat: Use of implicitly or explicitly threatening actions or objects to influence target reactions. Examples: issuing verbal warnings, leaving startling objects in startling places, sending threatening images or messages.	
Aggression/violence: Use of physical force in the form of contact that has the potential to harm or injure the target, target's property, or associates. Examples: kidnapping, physical assault, driving dangerously with or at target	

the prior relationship was romantic. This finding is consistent with multiple studies indicating that violence is most likely in stalking cases in which the prior relationship involved sexual intimacy, and less likely when the stalker was a stranger or had a diagnosed psychological or personality disorder (Mohandie et al., 2006; Rosenfeld, 2004; Rosenfeld & Lewis, 2005). It appears that the former lover is not only the most likely to stalk, but is also the most likely to engage in violence.

Serial Stalkers

While the dynamics of stalking suggest that stalking often emerges out of a relatively normal relationship and is perpetrated by relatively normal people, this does not seem quite as plausible for serial stalkers. While highly speculative, it seems likely that serial and recidivist stalkers are indeed a relatively different breed than most of the typical stalking cases identified in the research.

Because serial stalkers demonstrate both a consistency and deviance of their behavior across situations, there is clearly something distinctive about them. Any given stalking case can be attributed to the unique dynamics of that particular *relationship*, but a person who stalks across different relationships seems more likely to have personal issues, whether a personality disorder or mental illness. Perhaps anyone can be "crazy in love" once in their life, but twice?

Serial stalking also implies much greater stalker investment of time and resources, and the realization of substantially elevated risks of legal interventions or victim retaliation. Stalkers may be able to evade serious repercussions from one victim, but to victimize multiple parties significantly increases both the risks and the stakes that one or more of these victims is "not going to take it anymore" and will be willing to retaliate with dire consequences for the stalker. Jane's willingness to interfere in destructive ways with the lives of each of her victims, to repeatedly persist in pursuing failed relationships, and to engage in protracted litigation, including drawing in law enforcement, illustrates the willingness to absorb and inflict costs upon self and others.

As an analogue, a study of serial batterers in Massachusetts found that 91% had a prior criminal or delinquent arraignment on record (Adams, 1999). Not only may serial stalkers be particularly prone to law enforcement intervention, but they may be more criminal in their very nature. Thus, it seems reasonable to suggest that serial stalkers may be more likely than the typical stalker to have significant personality or psychological disorders, attachment disorders, serious interpersonal and social skill deficits, and elevated levels of criminality or exposure to the criminal justice system.

WHY DO STALKERS STALK?

Speculation regarding the underlying pathology of stalkers necessarily raises issues of why stalkers engage in such abnormal patterns of behavior. There are at least three approaches to addressing this question: motivational, nosological, and typological. Motivational approaches tend to employ folk psychological or common language approaches to attributing motives to stalker behavior. *Nosological* approaches seek an underlying disease, personality disorder, or diagnosis of disturbance. Such approaches tend to rely on the standardized nomenclature of the *DSM* or other relatively common theoretical distinctions. *Typological* approaches tend to formulate dimensional or multidimensional classificatory schemes for identifying groups of stalkers who differ in ways that provide valuable clinical, legal, or practical distinctions.

Motivational research has spanned dozens of studies. According to one review, there are four basic clusters of motivation: intimacy, aggression, disability, and task (Spitzberg & Cupach, 2007). Intimacy motives include break-up distress, jealousy, loneliness, grief, dependency, infatuation, love, obsession, reconciliation, relational escalation, and sexual issues. Aggression motives include anger, control, possession, intimidation, harassment, and revenge issues. Disability-based motives include drug, mental illness, or severe social incompetence issues. Finally, some stalkers engage in campaigns of harassment because they have a specific topic or task they seek to bring to the attention of their target, such as business or neighborhood disputes, political agendas, or specific legal concessions. A potential category often overlooked for its motivational implications is life or attachment trauma. Many studies identify a recent trauma, such as a break-up, death of a family member, loss of children in a custody battle, unemployment, or other significant life disturbance as a common precursor of stalking (Brewster, 2002; Coleman, 1999; Meloy & Boyd, 2003; Morrison, 2001). Other studies have identified childhood or developmental traumas, such as child abuse victimization, parental divorce, or other attachment losses, as significantly related to the onset of stalking (Blackburn, 1999; Gentile, Asamen, Harmell, & Weathers, 2002; Hall, 1998; Kienlen, Birmingham, Solberg, O'Regan, & Meloy, 1997; cf., Langhin-richsen-Rohling, Palarea, Cohen, & Rohling, 2000).

Nosological research seeks to identify various underlying personality or psychological conditions that might contribute to the stalking activity. In their study of more than 1000 stalking cases, Mohandie et al. (2006) found that 46% of stalkers had some "clear or probable diagnosis," of which 14% had a form of psychosis, 32% had some form of substance abuse problem, and 25% had some degree of diagnosable suicidality. A number of specific disorders have been identified as potentially elevated among stalkers, including borderline personality disorder, antisocial personality disorder, narcissistic personality disorder, mood disorder, and schizophrenia (Galeazzi, Elkins, & Curci, 2005; Gentile et al, 2002; Gill & Brockman, 1996; Hall, 1998; Harmon, Rosner, & Owens, 1995; Harmon, Rosner, & Owens, 1998; Huffhines, 2001; Kienlen et al., 1997; Lewis, Fremouw, Del Ben, & Farr, 2001; Morrison, 2001; Mustaine & Tewksbury, 1999; Pathé, Mullen, & Purcell, 2000; Romans, Hays, & White, 1996; Sandberg, McNiel, & Binder, 1998). A syndrome closely associated with stalking is erotomania, or the pursuer's delusional belief that another person is in love with her or him (Berrios & Kennedy, 2002; Harmon, Rosner, & Owens, 1995; Lloyd-Goldstein,

1998; Meloy, 1999; Mullen, 2000; Zona, Sharma, & Lane, 1993). Insecurely attached persons, and in particular preoccupied attached persons, may also be more prone to engage in stalking (Del Ben, 2000; Dutton & Winstead, 2006; Eke, 1999; Langhin-richsen-Rohling, 2006; Langhinrichsen-Rohling et al., 2000; Lewis et al., 2001; Mc-Cutcheon, Scott, Aruguete, & Parker, 2006; Tonin, 2004; cf., Davis, Ace, & Andra, 2000; Montero, 2003).

Spitzberg and Cupach (2007) identified 24 separate typologies that have been proffered for the classification of stalkers. Only a few of these typologies have received any extensive empirical validation (Holmes, 2001; Mohandie et al., 2006; Mullen, 2003; Mullen, Pathé & Purcell, 2009; Sheridan & Boon, 2002). Spitzberg (2010) noted that all of these typologies represent distinctions among four sets of characteristics: type of disorder (e.g., personality, physical, behavioral), type of primary motivation (e.g., aggression, intimacy, task), type of relationship or context (e.g., prior relationship, no prior relationship, public or private), and type of behavior (e.g., affectionate, covert, electronic, harassment, violence). He further noted that some of these typologies are simple (i.e., unidimensional), whereas others are complex (i.e., multidimensional), resulting in categories of multiple intersecting features. For the sake of understanding why stalkers stalk, the very existence of these typologies indicates that stalking motivations are heterogeneous across stalkers. Further, a given stalker may experience multiple simultaneous motivations (e.g., desire for reconciliation and retaliation) or an evolution of motivation over the course of a stalking relationship (e.g., a desire for reconciliation that becomes a desire for retaliation when it becomes clear that reconciliation is not possible). There are some stalkers who clearly act out a fundamentally disturbed or disordered personality, reflecting severe deficits of mental or social ability, or inappropriately enacting a range of relatively "normal" emotional or strategic interests.

THE CHARACTERISTICS OF STALKERS AND THEIR VICTIMS

Who Are the Victims?

Anyone can become a victim of stalking (Pathé & Mullen, 2002). Research, however, indicates that some individuals are more likely to be stalked than others. Women are more likely to be stalked (as discussed earlier), but there exist numerous other characteristics and victim circumstances that place individuals at greater risk.

Ethnicity/race. Research suggests that some ethnic and racial groups are more likely to be stalked than others. In the Supplemental Victimization Study (SVS) of over 65,000 U.S. adults, Baum et al. (2009) found that non-Hispanics were more likely to report stalking victimization than Hispanics. Baum et al. (2009), Tjaden and Thoennes (1998), and Fisher, Cullen, and Turner (2000) found that Asian/Pacific Islanders were the least likely to report stalking victimization among all ethnic/racial groups. Tjaden and Thoennes (1998) found that a significantly larger percentage of American Indian/Alaskan Native women (17%) and men (4.8%) reported being stalked in their lifetime than individuals of other races/ethnicities. Similarly, with a national sample of college women, Fisher et al. (2000) found that American Indian/Alaskan Native women were more likely to report stalking. As with the Baum et al. (2009) study, there were few American Indian/Alaskan Native women in Fisher et al.'s (2000) study. Thus, despite the small subsamples, the findings across these three large-scale studies are consistent. One study with female college students, however, did not find race to be a risk factor for stalking victimization (Mustaine & Tewksbury, 1999).

Age. Although individuals of all ages can be victims, research indicates that younger people are at greater risk for stalking victimization (Baum et al., 2009; Nobles et al., 2009; Tjaden & Thoennes, 1998). Baum et al. (2009) found that approximately 58% of victims were between 18 and 24 years of age, whereas 14% were 50 years or older. Similarly, Tjaden and Thoennes (1998) found that 64% of victims were 29 years of age or younger when the stalking commenced, whereas 15% were 40 years or older. Nobles et al. (2009) found that the earliest age of onset of victimization was age 10 years, with about a quarter of stalking victimization occurring prior to age 18 years, and a mean victimization onset of age 20 years. Very little research has examined stalking in older populations. In a reanalysis of the NVAWS data for victims aged 55 year or older, Jasinski and Dietz (2003) found a stalking prevalence estimate of 2.7% of women and 2.3% of men.

Income. General population studies indicate that those with lower income are at increased risk of stalking victimization. Baum et al. (2009) found that almost 60% of victims reported a household income below $15,000, whereas 22% of the victims had a household income of $50,000 or more. Similarly, Budd and Mattinson (2000) found that women and men who were poor were more likely to be stalking victims. Fisher et al. (2000), however, found that female college students who came from an affluent family were more likely to be stalked. Thus, there may be differences between sample types (e.g., general population, criminal justice/forensic, college student) regarding the relationship of socioeconomic status and victimization risk, which need to be further investigated.

Previous and concurrent victimization. Previous victimization at any point in a person's life appears to place that person at greater risk for stalking. For example, Fischer et al. (2000) found that female college students with a history of sexual victimization prior to the current academic year were more likely to report stalking victimization. Among women especially, a prior history of physical abuse was associated with stalking victimization. Tjaden and Thoennes (1998) found a link between stalking and other forms of intimate violence. Over 80% of the women stalked by a current or former husband or cohabiting partner were also physically abused, and 31% were sexually assaulted by that partner (Tjaden & Thoennes, 1998).

Victim circumstances. Budd and Mattinson (2000) found that women who were single and living in privately rented housing were more likely to be stalking victims. Similarly, other research has found that female college students who lived alone or who lived off campus were at increased risk of victimization (Fischer et al., 2000; Mustaine & Tewksbury, 1999).

Victim attachment style. One study found that, as with stalkers, targets of relational stalking were more likely to have an anxious attachment style (Dutton & Winstead, 2006). Thus, it is possible that when individuals with an anxious attachment style become romantically involved with another individual with an anxious attachment style, the relationship will be tumultuous from early on. These relationships may be characterized by more instances of breaking up and getting back together, which is a predictor of stalking (Davis et al., 2000).

Victim behaviors. Research suggests that female college students who frequently go to places where alcohol is consumed, drink at home, and buy drugs are at greater risk for being stalked (Fischer et al., 2000; Mustaine & Tewksbury, 1999). In addition, dating and shopping at malls increases victimization risk (Mustaine & Tewksbury, 1999). In these cases, women are easier targets for stalking because they are out more in public, interacting with more potential perpetrators, and/or engaging in behaviors that make them vulnerable. Contrary to prediction, Mustaine and Tewksbury (1999) found that college women who carry mace or pocketknives for protection are at increased risk for being stalked. They suggest, however, that stalking victimization may have preceded the carrying of such self-protective devices rather than the reverse (Mustaine & Tewksbury, 1999). It may also be the case that the kinds of women who choose to carry such protection do so because of a riskier social network.

Relationship with the primary victim. In addition to the primary victims of stalking, others known to the victim can be stalked as well. These individuals are those the stalker perceives as interfering with or blocking access to the victim and can include parents, friends, children, potential or current relationship partners, roommates, and work colleagues (Meloy, 2007; Pathé & Mullen, 1997). In the opening case example, an examination of the court file in Tom's case revealed to Jim that Jane had contacted Tom's wife to interrogate her. Even if the stalker does not directly target those associated with the victim, individuals close to the victim (e.g., parents, friends, children, partners) can be affected psychologically simply because they are involved with the victim. For example, some children of stalking victims suffer from anxiety and depression (Pathé & Mullen, 2002). It is likely that those close to the victim may experience social and financial effects, as well (Dutton & Spitzberg, 2007; Logan, Shannon, Cole, & Swanberg, 2007).

Who Are the Stalkers?

Stalkers are a heterogeneous group (Sheridan, Blaauw, & Davies, 2003). Women and men of all ethnicities/races, ages, income levels, and life circumstances engage in stalking. Research indicates, however, that certain demographic characteristics are associated with an increased likelihood of stalking perpetration.

Ethnicity/race. Baum et al. (2009) state that "stalking is primarily intraracial in nature" (p. 4). They found that 83% of white victims perceived their perpetrators to also be white, and 66% of black victims perceived them to be black. Individuals of other ethnicities/races, however, were equally likely to report that their stalker was white, black, or of another race (Baum et al., 2009). Jane was multiracial (African American and white) and Tom was white, providing an example of a case that does not represent a typical case on this dimension.

Age. With a sample of 187 women who had been stalked by a former intimate partner, Brewster (1998) found that stalkers were slightly younger than victims. The average age of stalkers was 31 years, and the average age of victims was 35 years. Results from the British Crime Survey revealed that 49% of male stalkers and 60% of female stalkers were between the ages of 20 and 39 years, and a substantial percentage (29%) of male stalkers were between the ages of 16 and 19 years (Budd & Mattinson, 2000). The case study is consistent with these findings in that Jane fell within the most frequent age ranges, and Jim was somewhat older. In one of the few "career"-based studies of stalking, Nobles et al. (2009) found an age of onset for stalkers in a college sample of 12 years, and about a quarter of stalking was initiated before the age of 18 years. The mean age of onset for stalking was 20 years. It is possible that individuals who stalk at a particularly early age are at increased risk of becoming serial stalkers.

Employment status. Baum et al. (2009) found that, according to victims, nearly a quarter of stalkers were unemployed, and approximately 6% were underemployed or sometimes employed (15% of the victims did not know the employment status of their stalkers). Based on an analysis of stalking cases in the United States., Mohandie et al. (2006) similarly found that 29% of the stalkers were unemployed. Among a sample of 187 females who were recent victims of intimate partner stalking, 23% of the victims reported that their perpetrators were unemployed (Brewster, 1998). Thus, many stalkers have ample time to engage in stalking activities, including stalking more than one victim at a time. This was certainly the situation in Jane's case, where despite being unemployed, she managed to finance protracted litigation intended to justify her actions and had the time to contact the victims' coworkers, employees, customers, and wife.

OUTCOMES OF STALKING

What Are the Effects on Victims?

Individuals can experience a variety of effects as a result of being stalked. Cupach and Spitzberg (2004) analyzed data from 35 studies that assessed the consequences of stalking on victims. They developed a typology that identified 11 types of effects. Although research has focused primarily on the negative effects, there can also be positive ones, as noted in the following discussion.

Cupach and Spitzberg (2004) describe the first two types, general effects and behavioral effects, as those that are "vague or broad-based" (p. 123). General effects include stress, psychological or emotional injury, personality change, and emotional or psychological injury. Behavioral effects include a variety of ways that victims alter their regular activities in response to being stalked. Examples include changing jobs or schools, altering interpersonal behaviors (e.g., avoiding interactions with others, becoming more aggressive), and avoiding the place where the person was victimized.

Affective effects involve changes in the quality of the victim's emotional well-being. The more common emotional effects include anger, annoyance, anxiety, depression, fear/terror, and distress/frustration. Cupach and Spitzberg (2004) identified some affective effects that they collectively labeled as attractiveness. Examples include feeling admired, loved, cared for, and flattered. Research indicates that the psychological effects of stalking are not the same across victims. In some cases, the effects have little to do with the types of behaviors to which they are being subjected. Some victims experience severe levels of stalking behaviors but few psychological effects (Davis, Coker, & Sanderson, 2002). On the other hand, victims who are targets of minor forms of stalking experience negative effects (Cupach & Spitzberg, 2004; Dutton & Spitzberg, 2007). Research indicates that women experience more fear when stalked by a man than men do when stalked by a woman (Davis, Coker, & Sanderson, 2002). They also feel more threatened by unwanted pursuit than men (Cupach & Spitzberg, 2004). For example, women are more likely to report fear than men even when they experience the same behaviors (Bjerregaard, 2000).

Many victims experience changes in the quality of their mental and analytical life, which Cupach and Spitzberg (2004) label *cognitive effects*. The most common are a general loss of faith, loss of faith in others, loss of faith in institutions, a sense of isolation, a sense of apprehension and cautiousness, and distraction or confusion. Potentially positive cognitive effects include improved safety awareness, a sense of direction or purpose, and a strengthened self-concept. Victims report various *physical/physiological effects*, as well, and these can include sleep problems, physical injuries, self-injury, physical illness (e.g., fatigue), eating/digestive problems, addictions (e.g., to alcohol), and headaches. Victims' social lives are often impacted. Such *social effects* can include avoiding certain places, going out less, loss or deterioration of a romantic relationship, and loss or worsening of family relationships. One positive effect reported by some participants is the strengthening of family and/or romantic relationships. Individuals close to the victim may be affected by the experience for many reasons, including the stress of feeling unable to help the victim and/or to stop the stalking as well as being targeted by the stalker themselves.

Other identified effects include *resource effects* that can impact the financial well-being of the victim, including expenses related to the case (e.g., increasing home security, moving), losing a job, taking time off from work, being less productive at work, and loss of property (Cupach & Spitzberg, 2004; Logan, Shannon, Cole, et al., 2007). Victims may also experience *spiritual effects*, sometimes reporting a loss of faith in God (Cupach and Spitzberg, 2004). Stalking can have negative *societal effects*, including development of an inaccurate public assessment of the likelihood of being stalked, which may results in excessive expenditure of resources (e.g., law enforcement, security) to prevent and punish stalking. Victims may experience ambivalence. Such *ambivalent effects* include feeling both relieved and nervous at the time the stalking ended. Some victims report *minimal effects*, meaning that they experience little-to-no negative consequences of being stalked (Cupach & Spitzberg, 2004).

How Do Victims Respond?

Just as there is a wide variety of behaviors in which stalkers engage, there are numerous ways that stalking victims respond to being stalked. Cupach and Spitzberg (2004; Spitzberg, 2002; Spitzberg & Cupach, 2003) developed a typology of five coping strategies based on 59 studies that yielded 491 victim coping tactics. The five types are *moving with*, *moving against*, *moving away*, *moving inward*, and *moving outward*.

Targets often engage in direct interactions with the stalker, which can be either negative (e.g., yelling at the person) or positive (e.g., engaging in friendly negotiation). There are a number of subtypes of *moving with* tactics. Acceptance/reconciliation includes responses such as accepting phone calls from the stalker, meeting the stalker somewhere, initiating contact with the stalker, and showing greater affection toward the stalker. Victims may make up excuses such as saying they already have plans or are already in a relationship. They can derogate the stalker by verbally or physically attacking the person, yelling at the person, and ignoring the person's feelings. Disconfirmation involves disengagement such as treating the stalker like a stranger and considering the stalker to be not taken seriously. Targets engage in boundary setting when they demand to be left alone, state that they do not want to see the person, and tell the stalker that what she or he is doing is wrong. Victims often attempt to rationalize with the stalker by politely talking to and reasoning with her or him and trying to persuade the stalker to change her or his behavior. Victims may negotiate the relationship with the stalker by defining it. They may end the relationship or tell the pursuer they just want to be friends. Victims may threaten to harm the stalker, call the police, or tell others. They may seek sympathy by pleading with the stalker. Jim engaged in numerous moving with tactics (e.g., taking Jane's calls, trying to reason with her, driving her home from Planned Parenthood, repeatedly telling her to stop her behaviors). His erroneous assumption was that Jane would respond to reasoning.

Moving against tactics aim to inflict some form of harm on the stalker. Victims may seek legal redress by filing charges, insisting on arrest, and initiating a lawsuit. Some victims respond in physical ways, such as inflicting physical harm by assaulting the stalker, hurting the stalker through self-defense tactics, and acting in a hostile manner toward the stalker. After determining that reasoning would not work with Jane, both Tom and Jim engaged in *moving against* tactics by filing charges.

The goal of engaging in *moving away* tactics is to avoid contact with the stalker (Cupach & Spitzberg, 2004). Types of *moving away* behaviors in which victims engage include limiting the stalker's proximity. Victims report a wide range of methods to limit the stalker's proximity to them with respect to communicative access (e.g., screening telephone calls, getting an unlisted telephone number, obtaining caller ID), information control (e.g., not answering the doorbell or phone, changing their name), and physical availability (e.g., avoiding one-on-one interactions, hiding). Victims also may isolate themselves in response to being stalked by withdrawing socially and/or not leaving their home. Some victims change jobs, schools, and/or residences in response to their victimization. Many change their daily routines such as taking different routes to work or school. Some engage in what Cupach and Spitzberg (2004) term "target hardening" (p. 254), which involves techniques to make it more difficult for stalkers to gain access to the victim such as increasing security at home and/or the workplace.

Tom, one of Jane's victims, engaged in numerous *moving against* tactics, which were often ineffective in stopping Jane's stalking. He did not return telephone calls, did not accept her "emergency" calls, changed his phone number, had her number blocked by the phone company, moved, changed jobs, and got his telephone numbers and home addresses unlisted. He involved his employer in preventing her from knowing his whereabouts. Being highly resourceful, as many stalkers are, Jane still managed to find out where he worked and lived and to obtain his phone number.

Moving inward responses involve efforts "to repair, empower, enrich, or merely focus on self as a source of managing" the stalking (Cupach & Spitzberg, 2004, p. 254). Some responses may be considered adaptive (e.g., seeking counseling, sharing feelings with someone, looking for something good in what was happening, using stress reduction techniques). Included in this type of response are acts in which victims engage in preparation for future interactions with the stalker such as taking a self-defense class, purchasing/carrying a weapon, and carrying pepper spray. Other responses are maladaptive such as using alcohol or drugs to cope, denying that a problem exists, and attempting suicide. Jim engaged in at least one *moving inward* response when he attended counseling to reduce the stress he was experiencing.

Moving outward responses are those that entail the victim seeking help from others in an attempt to stop or curb the stalker's behavior (Cupach & Spitzberg, 2004). Victims may seek advice and assistance from a variety of sources, including the police, religious leaders, friends and family, and victim's advocates. Such responses can include disclosing the stalking to someone, asking someone to confront the stalker, contacting the police, obtaining a restraining or protective order, and getting someone to escort them to their car. Both Jim and Tom sought restraining orders against Jane and yet another person applied for one in 2005.

With respect to these five response types, it is likely that moving inward responses are the least likely to affect the stalker's behaviors because the victim's actions are directed toward the self and not the stalker (Cupach & Spitzberg, 2004). Cupach and Spitzberg (2004) assert that moving away responses are likely to be the most effective because they render the victim inaccessible to the stalker. *Moving outward* responses can be effective, if utilized competently, because the victim is mobilizing a variety of resources that essentially serve to insulate the victim (Cupach & Spitzberg, 2004). Research reveals that some victims' responses work some of the time but no particular response is effective all or most of the time. In fact, one study found that none of four types of responses was associated with a reduction in stalker's behaviors (Cupach & Spitzberg, 2000). Thus, the effectiveness of stalking responses is undoubtedly affected by numerous factors, including characteristics of the victim, the perpetrator, and the unique situation (Truman & Mustaine, 2009). In Jane's case, her victims engaged in numerous efforts to deter her pursuits and harassment, but they also made certain mistakes in continuing certain forms of contact. The pursuit ran its extensive course despite extensive efforts to stop it.

SYSTEM RESPONSES

One of the ways in which many survivors of stalking cope is by seeking the intervention of law enforcement and the services available in the network of societal resources designed to assist victims. Relatively little is known about the extent to which stalking victims avail themselves of victim service resources, such as victim's advocates, counseling, shelters, or family justice centers. In the large-scale NVAW survey, 4% of stalking victims claimed to have moved to a shelter (Tjaden & Thoennes, 1998). In the larger SVS survey, about 12% of stalking victims contacted a mental health professional, 9% contacted clergy or a faith leader, 9% contacted a health professional, and 7% contacted victim services, a shelter, or a help line. In all, 30% claimed to have sought no help at all (Baum et al., 2009). An online survey of stalking victims in Belgium, Italy, and Slovenia found that 25% sought assistance from a general practitioner, 20% from mental health professionals, 15% from victim support groups, and 10% from social services (Galeazzi, Bu ar-Ru man, De Fazio, & Groenen, 2009). Victims reported feeling moderately supported by most of these sources.

Victim Service Agencies

In a survey of victim service agencies in Florida and California, 15% reported no services for stalking victims, whereas 83% reported offering some services for domestic stalking victims (Spence-Diehl & Potocky-Tripodi, 2001). Spence-Diehl and Potocky-Tripodi (2001) found that services offered by one or more agencies ranged from community referrals, information about the crime or the criminal justice system, legal advocacy programs, personal safety planning, restraining order assistance, and filing claims for a variety of services ranging from transportation to support groups. The highest ranked needs were restraining order assistance, face-to-face crisis counseling, information about the criminal justice system, legal advocacy, and emergency shelters. In a European survey of general practitioners and police, there were wide variations across countries (Belgium, Italy, the Netherlands, the United Kingdom) in perceived adequacy of training and awareness regarding stalking issues (Modena Group on Stalking, 2005). Online services are becoming increasingly available, but there are numerous risks involved with such services (e.g., inability to verify the identity of the source of the counseling, or the possibility that such communications are being covertly monitored by the pursuer), and their efficacy is difficult to demonstrate (Finn & Banach, 2000).

A study of victim service and justice system professionals asked how they believe stalking victims cope with their situation (Logan, Walker, Stewart, & Allen, 2006). Of the institutional responses listed, the most common were receiving protective orders (21.5–38.9%), filing or applying for protective orders (13.9–34.7%), calling the police (12.7–29.2%), talking to a victim's advocate (12.5–16.5%), going to a shelter (7.0–13.9%), seeking mental health treatment (4.2–10.1%), attending couples or family counseling (3.8–8.6%), and seeking assistance from a healthcare professional (2.9–6.4%).

Marital status affected the recommendations. Three of the most common forms of advice offered to married female stalking victims involved criminal justice responses (protective orders, 48.1–54.8%; law enforcement, 45.6–52.1%; criminal charges, 38.0–49.3%), whereas safety planning (12.3–43.0%), shelter (12.2–35.4%), and mental health treatment (1.4–11.4%) were less frequently recommended. The recommendations for women being stalked by a dating partner were similar in ranking, but different in proportions: criminal court (63.3–93.1%), law enforcement (25.0–34.2%), restraining order (18.1–22.8%), safety planning (4.5–25.3%), victim services advocate (2.8–20.3%), shelter (4.2–10.1%), and mental health treatment (0.0–6.3%) (Logan, Walker, et al., 2006).

Justice System Agencies

There are innovative programs, such as the Los Angeles Threat Management Unit (Boles, 2001) or San Diego's Stalking Case Assessment Team (Maxey, 2002). Expertise is slowly emerging in regard to other approaches, such as crisis intervention in potentially severe cases (e.g., Knox & Roberts, 2003; Mohandie, 2004; Roberts & Dziegielewski, 1996). These approaches bring together cross-functional, cross-departmental, and cross-disciplinary expertise to assess cases in a vertical manner and facilitate the coordination of services or recommendations for victims. The efficacy of these approaches has not been systematically evaluated, although they appear relatively advanced efforts relative to most of the status quo.

One of the most vexing problems of stalking is that even though the law characterizes it as a course of conduct, this is quite different from indicating the precise point in such a course of conduct at which formal intervention is warranted. The warrant for intervention could be either the victim's safety or the prospect of successful legal intervention. These concerns are related but not identical. There may well be times when the individual seems obviously a victim of stalking or in imminent danger, but there is insufficient evidence that would stand in a court of law. There may be other times when a case clearly rises to meet the legal standards of stalking, even though the victim may not seem to be in imminent danger. Furthermore, it is possible that formal intervention could function to escalate the severity or risks of the stalking relationship. It is precisely the complexities of these issues that have led to comprehensive case assessment groups such as threat management units or case assessment teams.

Cases tend to come to the attention of such units and teams if and when they are reported to law enforcement. In the large-scale NVAW study, 53% of stalking cases were claimed to have been reported to the police, and 82% of these were claimed to have been reported by the victims themselves (Tjaden & Thoennes, 1998). In the SVS study, 37% of stalking cases involving male victims and 41% of cases involving female victims were reported to the police, 83% of which were reported by the victim (Baum et al., 2009). In the three-country European study, almost 43% of stalking victims reported their situation to the police (Galeazzi et al., 2009). Across 42 studies in the meta-analysis, 45% of victims claim reporting the stalking to police (SE = 4.32, SD = 28.01, range = 7–97%).

Police Response

The efficacy of the police response appears to be somewhat inconsistent across victims. In the NVAW study, 19% of victims who reported to the police claimed that the police did nothing, and 50% claimed to have been satisfied with the police response, with 54% claiming the situation got better after reporting the situation (Tjaden & Thoennes, 1998). In the SVS study, 20% claimed the "police took no action when contacted" (p. 9), 50% thought the situation improved after contacting the police, and 46% were satisfied with the police response (Baum et al., 2009). In the European study (Modena Stalking Group, 2007), the police were perceived as the least supportive (a mean of 2 on a 5-point scale) of any sources of assistance and as not being particularly effective (a mean of 2 on a 5-point scale). A little-noticed finding regarding police is the possibility that they are part of the problem. When victims who elected not to report to police were asked their reason, 8% of stalking victims in the NVAW study indicated that the attacker was a police officer (Tjaden & Thoennes, 2000, Exhibit 17). In the SVS survey, 6% of those who did not report the stalking to the police said the reason was that the perpetrator was a police officer (Baum et al., 2009, Appendix 12).

Protective Orders

Once reported, several traditional criminal justice responses are possible, depending on the severity of the case and the credibility of the victim (Logan, Cole, Shannon, & Walker, 2006; Maxey, 2001; Morewitz, 2003; Mossman, 2007; Roberts, 2006). One of the more common types of advice offered to stalking victims is to seek a restraining or protective order (PO), which may serve a deterrent function and often provides greater prosecutorial options for future violations (Logan, Cole, et al., 2006). In the study of more than 1000 stalking case files, Mohandie et al. (2006) found that 14% were "subject to a restraining order" (and 15% were on probation or parole; p. 149). In a study of males charged with stalking, 60% had a restraining order against them at some point (Logan, Nigoff, Walker, & Jordan, 2002). Logan et al. (2002) found that a protective order appeared to index a higher degree of risk of perpetrator violence. This may account for why at least two studies of intimate partner violence have found that victims with POs experience elevated risks of subsequent violence (Kingsnorth, 2006), in less time (Mele, 2009), than victims without POs. The type of perpetrator who motivates a victim to seek a PO may represent a particularly recidivistic type of perpetrator (as would be the case with Jane). On the other hand, POs increase the face threat of the pursuer and increase the stakes of a situation that previously may have been seen as a "private" matter by making a "relationship problem" public and subject to adjudication.

Evidence of PO efficacy in the context of stalking is somewhat limited. Logan and Cole (2007) found in a longitudinal study that 34% of women with a protective order against a former partner reported stalking both before and after the order, and another 11.6% reported stalking only after the order had been obtained. In contrast, in a Finnish sample of stalkers with restraining orders, assaults dropped to zero after the order had been issued, although 28% of victims reported receiving death threats from the stalker after the order (Häkkänen, Hagelstam, & Santtila, 2003). Studies of restraining orders, however, show mixed results of their efficacy (Cupach & Spitzberg, 2004; Logan, Shannon, Walker, & Faragher, 2006). Professionals identify a host of barriers and challenges associated with protective orders, including fear of the perpetrator, lack of knowledge of the criminal justice system, lack of proof or evidence, lack of access to the justice system, lack of social or system support, unresponsiveness of the system, and even political corruptness, such as the protection of those with higher status or resources (Logan, Walker, et al., 2006). The case study shows that even when a victim has the sophistication and financial wherewithal to litigate the case fully, determined stalkers will find a way to circumvent the scope of the orders issued to pursue their prey through the justice system and extrajudicial channels.

Prosecution

Legal prosecution of stalking cases appears to be the exception rather than the rule. In the NVAW sample, only 12% of stalking victims indicated the perpetrator was prosecuted, and among those cases, 54% indicated that a conviction was sustained (Tjaden & Thoennes, 1998). In the SVS sample, 21% reported that charges had been filed, but only 12% indicated that the perpetrator was convicted or found guilty (Baum et al., 2009, Appendix 18). In a more detailed study of 390 persons charged with stalking, almost two-thirds (64%) were charged with misdemeanor stalking rather than felony stalking (36%), over half (55%) were dismissed by final disposition, with final conviction rates approximating 30% (Jordan, Logan, Walker, & Nigoff, 2003). Stalking cases tend to be evidence-intensive and challenging to police investigators. Stalking is often a challenge to investigate because of the nature of the crime as a course of conduct over time, the fact that victims often engage in compromising actions such as permitting ongoing interaction in various forms (e.g., Jim gave Jane a ride home after he had told her to leave him alone), and the difficulty of demonstrating reasonable victim fear or threat (Maxey, 2001; Wells, 2001). In the case study, Jim explored the possibility of having Jane criminally prosecuted, but the circumstantial nature of the evidence and potential adverse publicity operated as a deterrent to pursuing a criminal case. Furthermore, given that stalking was only made illegal in most jurisdictions within the past 2 decades, there is still a relative paucity of case law, and many prosecutors may seek to deal stalking charges away in exchange for pleas or charges on other more traditional crimes often associated with stalking, such as harassment, trespass, fraud, theft, threat, and assault.

CONCLUSION

There are various reasons to consider recidivist, concurrent, and serial stalkers as distinct categories of stalkers. Most research to date has not. What research has provided some designation of seriality has performed little or no further elaboration or investigation of whether or how such stalkers (or victims) differ from other types of stalking cases. Unlike serial killers or rapists, stalkers in general are often not prosecuted even when they are identified and found; and when they are prosecuted, they are often not prosecuted for the crime of stalking; and when they are prosecuted for stalking, they are not always convicted; and when they are convicted, they do not always receive long sentences. Thus, unlike some prototypical serial criminals, serial stalkers remain a bit of a mystery, for lack of exposure and lack of inquiry in the lens of scholarship.

Serial stalking is inherently counterintuitive and paradoxical. In a cultural context of increasingly temporary and unstable relationships, one of the defining features of stalking is an "unyielding fixation on a single love object who is pursued. . . . The stalker stands out as a paragon of absolute fidelity, single-mindedly and relentlessly devoted to his or her 'loved one'" (Lloyd-Goldstein, 2000, p. 177). Yet, within such fixated devotion, the category of "serial stalking" seems almost tautological, as stalking "is by its very nature a crime prone to repetition" (Petherick, 2006, p. 132). Thus, the behavior of stalking is intrinsically predicated on an ongoing course of conduct, which generally takes the form of repeated activities and routines. The tendency of stalkers to focus such efforts on one object of fixation suggests a reluctance to betray this fixation by extending the gaze of the stalking process across multiple objects over time. These apparent paradoxes seem to resolve for a small proportion of stalkers, who find ways of enacting repetition both within and across relationship objects of attention. For example, the fact that Jane repeated her aberrant behaviors in two (possibly three) consecutive relationships illustrates that some stalkers are able to simply shift their obsessions sequentially, repeating the same patterns with minor variations adapted to their victim's vulnerabilities. What drives a person to straddle such paradoxes remains a relative mystery and, therefore, a significant research question.

Note: Our review of the research on serial stalking is based on the results of an analysis of an ongoing descriptive meta-analytic database maintained by Brian Spitzberg. The meta-analysis includes 50 variables coded for any given study (although typically any given study only reports data useful for a small number of these variables), and for the purposes of this study, the data set from September 29, 2009, was employed, constrained only to "Western" samples (i.e., Australia, Canada, Europe, the United Kingdom, the United States). A total of 260 stalking samples were analyzed, representing over 274,000 cases. Not all of these cases are stalking cases; these are people who are surveyed, interviewed, or otherwise observed in regard to some stalking variable. To be included, a study had to include some data point that was interpreted as constituting "stalking." Because operationalizations vary considerably, from holistic (e.g., "I have been stalked") to behavioral (e.g., has experienced X intrusive or harassing behaviors across Y situations) to legalistic (e.g., "I have been persistently pursued in an unwanted way in a manner I found threatening or fearful"), there is a wide variety of studies included.

Certain coding biases are *a priori*, including that estimates that would be a product of the sampling design are excluded. For example, if the participants were selected because they had been victims of domestic violence at the hands of their stalker, then there is no estimate entered for the percentage of stalking victims in the sample that have experienced violence at the hands of their stalker. Another example of an *a priori* coding bias is that in the event multiple estimates are offered for threats, physical violence, or sexual violence, the highest estimate is accepted. In contrast, in the event that multiple operational definitions and estimates are provided for the prevalence of stalking, the more conservative estimate is entered for that study.

CHAPTER 7

Serial Arson

Richard Parenteau

DEFINING ARSON

According to Mavromatis (2000), arson is defined as a "deliberate act of firesetting" (p. 69). Douglas, Burgess, Burgess, and Ressler stated that "arson is the willful and malicious burning of property" (as cited in Sapp, huff, Gary, & Icove, 1994, p.1). Although these definitions are vague, they do have some merit. In classifying arson, the Uniform Crime Report (UCR) only includes those acts of arson that are "willfully or maliciously set" (FBI, 2001, p. 56). Mostly, this definition is accepted because it creates a legal foundation for courts to process individuals who engage in fire setting. By including the term *willfully*, the definition indicates that the perpetrator was sane, an element needed to process a court case. *Malicious* indicates that the perpetrator intended to cause harm and intentionally engaged in the act, showing that the individual was sane at the time of the arson.

The key element hidden in the terms malicious and *willfully* is centered upon intent and having the mental capacity to comprehend the severity and danger of one's personal actions. In particular, Crossley and Guzman state that arsonists have the ability to control their impulses but disregard their better judgment. They *willfully* decide to set fires and are driven by *malicious* alternative motives such as money, revenge, and vandalism (Crossley & Guzman, 1985).

Those unable to block these impulses fall into a separate category. The 1980 *Comprehensive Textbook of Psychiatry* and the *DSM-III* (as cited in Crossley & Guzman, 1985) describe these impulse-driven fire starters as *pyromaniacs* who have a constant and extreme infatuation with setting fires and receive intense excitement from watching the burning process. There is a clear difference between the motives and mental capacities of these two types of individuals, which can ultimately lead to different personality labels as well as various types of sentencing and punishment.

Examining the mental state of the offender is crucial in arson cases because it can ultimately play a pivotal role in the types of sanctions handed out to offenders. For example, an offender who is determined to be sane may receive a prison sentence, while someone who is considered mentally unstable or has an intellectual disability might be placed in a treatment facility. Yet, a problem that lies beyond distinguishing between "sane" or "insane" deals with pinpointing an offender in the first place, which is supported by the relatively low arrest rate among arson offenses.

Hall (as cited in Davis & Lauber, 1999) notes that in 1989, 15% of arson cases resulted in the arrest of an alleged offender and only 3% of all arson cases actually led to a conviction. More recently, UCR data from 2008 indicated that 17.8% of all arsons were considered cleared (person arrested, charged, and prosecuted for the offense). Only burglaries (12.5%), motor vehicle thefts (12%), and property crimes (17.4%) had lower clearance rates (FBI, 2009). This is a seemingly low success rate for law enforcement agencies considering the vast nature of the crime.

Annually, arson accounts for roughly $1.4 billion of damage to property and people (Phoenix Business Group, 1996), and departments such as the U.S. Fire Administration (USFA) provide an annual budget of $2 billion to "develop anti-arson programs" ("U.S. Fire Administration Combat's Nations Arson Problem," 1996). In 1970, Title XI of the Organized Crime Control Act was instituted and allowed the Bureau of Alcohol, Tobacco, Firearms and Explosives (ATF) to assist in bombing and arson investigations on a state level.

In 2008, 14,011 law enforcement agencies reported 62,807 offenses (FBI, 2009). While this is a significant number, the exact amount of fires may be underrepresented.

TABLE 7.1 Arson Characteristics by Type of Property, 2008 (13,980 agencies; 2008 estimated population: 250,243,947)

Property Classification	Number of Offenses	Distribution (%)[1]	Not in Use (%)	Average Damage ($)	Total Clearances	Offenses Cleared (%)[2]	Clearances Under Age 18 Years (%)
Total	56,972	100.0		16,015	10,277	18.0	37.4
Total structure	24,750	43.4	19.0	29,701	5,520	22.3	35.2
Single occupancy residential	11,435	20.1	21.4	28,788	2389	20.9	25.7
Other residential	4062	7.1	13.6	29,343	983	24.2	25.0
Storage	1629	2.9	20.7	18,021	298	18.3	48.7
Industrial/manufacturing	251	0.4	22.3	212,388	48	19.1	41.7
Other commercial	2331	4.1	15.7	55,531	450	19.3	28.0
Community/public	2667	4.7	16.2	15,799	857	32.1	65.3
Other structure	2375	4.2	21.4	13,668	495	20.8	47.1
Total mobile	16,454	28.9		8766	1461	8.9	20.3
Motor vehicles	15,572	27.3		8186	1314	8.4	18.7
Other mobile	882	1.5		18,991	147	16.7	34.7
Other mobile	15,768	27.7		2099	3296	20.9	48.7

[1] Because of rounding, the percentages may not add to 100.0.
[2] Includes offenses cleared by arrest or exceptional means.

Source: 2008 Crime in the United States.

Information that is reported by the UCR is sometimes unreliable because of gaps in reporting from agency to agency.

The UCR records the data in several categories, including characteristics, rates, clearance rates, and arrests.

Characteristics

Arson characteristics are broken down into two main classifications: type of arson and dollar loss. Type of arson is divided into three main categories: structure, mobile, and other. Structural arson is the most frequent type, accounting for 43.4%. It involves residential, commercial, and industrial buildings, with an average loss per structural offense in 2008 of $29,701 dollars. Mobile properties (cars, trucks, mobile homes, and trailers), which averaged $8,766 dollars per act, were second in frequency, totaling 28.9% of arsons. Other arsons (e.g., crops, timbers), which accounted for 27.7% of all arsons, had an average loss of $2099 (FBI, 2009). See Table 7.1.

Rates

In 2008, arson rates dropped nationally by a rate of 3.6% from 2007. In large cities with over 250,000 people, arson decreased a total of 4.3% from the previous year. Data in suburbs also registered a decline of 3.4% from 2007 rates. The UCR program also calculates an arson rate. Because populations differ in size, these rates are based on an average population of 100,000. The national arson rate was 24.1 per 100,000 people. Cities (250,000 people or more) averaged 39.2 per 100,000; cities with populations ranging from 10,000 to 24,999 had a lower rate of 17.9 per 100,000 (FBI, 2009). Metropolitan areas had a rate of 20.1 per 100,000, and nonmetropolitan (rural) areas had the smallest arson rate with 15.4 per 100,000 people. See Table 7.2.

Clearance Rates

The UCR definition for a clearance is:

when an arrest is made and charges have been brought against the arrestee. A clearance by exceptional means can also be made when the offender has been identified and located and there is enough evidence to support an arrest, but conditions beyond the control of law enforcement personnel preclude the arrest, charging, and prosecuting the offender. (FBI, 2003, p. 58)

The UCR provides in-depth data on clearance rates by breaking down statistics in a variety of ways. Clearances, which are arranged by population size, are further broken down by age. Therefore, total rates for all arson clearances are shown, as well as statistics on only those under 18 years of age. Furthermore, in the UCR, clearance rates vary by geographic area. Data are organized by region (Northeast, Midwest, South,

TABLE 7.2 Arson Rate by Population Group, 2008 (11,729 agencies; 2008 estimated population: 244,628,024; rate per 100,000 inhabitants)	
Population Group	Rate
Total	24.1
Total cities	26.5
Group I (cities 250,000 or more)	39.2
(cities 250,000 to 499,999)	45.0
(cities 500,000 to 999,999)	35.9
(cities 1,000,000 or more)	37.8
Group II (cities 100,000 to 249,999)	26.0
Group III (cities 50,000 to 99,999)	23.4
Group IV (cities 25,000 to 49,999)	19.6
Group V (cities 10,000 to 24,999)	17.9
Group VI (cities under 10,000)	21.0
Metropolitan counties	20.1
Nonmetropolitan counties	15.4
Suburban area[1]	18.4

[1] Suburban area includes law enforcement agencies in cities with less than 50,000 inhabitants and county law enforcement agencies that are within a metropolitan statistical area. Suburban areas exclude all metropolitan agencies associated with a principal city. The agencies associated with suburban areas also appear in other groups within this table.

Source: 2008 Crime in the United States.

and West) and further classified by geographic location (New England, South Atlantic, Mountain, etc.) (FBI, 2009). Clearance rates by geographic area are as follows (FBI, 2009):

- Northeast: 23.6%
- South: 19.1%
- Midwest: 15.9%
- West: 15.5%

Clearance rates for arson in the United States are nearly the complete opposite of those in other countries. For instance, in 1996 Japan had a clearance rate of 95% for all arson cases. While in 2004 this rate was found to have dropped to 70%, it still overshadowed the U.S. number of 17.1% for that same year (FBI, 2005; Wachi et al., 2007). Ueno (as cited in Wachi et al., 2007) attributed this decrease in Japan's clearances to a shift in arson style and location. More offenses were found to have been committed in cities than in suburban-type areas, and offenders were motivated by trouble with daily life more so than by conflict with others. These two factors make the investigation process much more difficult for authorities. Cities are more compact and offenders do not stand out as much as in suburban areas. Also, when motivated by personal issues instead of through relationships with others, offenders leave less incriminating evidence that others could have otherwise provided.

The same rationalization may also explain the relatively low clearance rates that exist in the United States. Nationally, the clearance rate is 17.8% of all arson cases. Rural areas had the highest clearance rate of arson activities at 22.1%; suburban areas had a 19.8% clearing rate; and cities had the lowest rate at 17% (FBI, 2009). Cities have higher arson rates, which means there are more cases to be solved and perhaps not enough resources to spread around. Therefore, offenders slip through the cracks and escape detection.

Also, suburban areas are more secluded, people are recognizable (or even personally known) by others, and citizens have a heightened awareness for strange or unusual loitering and activities. Arsonists do not stick out, are quiet in nature, and their actions are difficult to anticipate (Martinez, 2004). Therefore, the suburban public can become an asset to the investigation if they suspect or notice anything, while in cities, officials may have to rely more on evidence found at the scene that did not get destroyed by the fire.

Often, these cases are hard because communities in general have limited resources available to dedicate to such in-depth fire investigations. Moreover, many smaller departments only employ volunteer fire personnel and must call in outside sources for assistance. To add to the difficulty, arsonists do not have to bring weapons with them and evidence linking them to the crime is rarely left behind. These factors, coupled with offenders having an unlimited number of available and potential targets (communities, houses, vehicles, boats, etc.), make apprehension extremely difficult (Martinez, 2004). There is also a portion of fires that go unreported to authorities due to apathy, distrust of law enforcement, or fear of the offender. These factors can play a role in the disparity between city and suburban rates.

Low clearance rates may also be due to an oversight in the investigation process. The public often views arson as a crime masterminded and committed by a sole offender. Yet, depending on the motive, there may be multiple perpetrators. A study done by the FBI's National Center for the Analysis of Violent Crime, using the Prince George's County,

Maryland, Fire Department Fire Investigation Division's research on 1016 fire offenders, indicated that 74% of offenders who committed arson-related vandalism had at least one other person with them. Those using arson to cover up other crimes had at least one accomplice 50% of the time, while 47% of excitement-driven offenders received assistance (Icove & Estepp, 1987). Investigators should not assume that the offender acted alone and should never dismiss a search for witnesses and potential accessories.

While clearance rates vary depending upon geography and residency, the one constant in fire setting is that juveniles account for roughly 48–50% of all arsonist activity. Nationwide in 2008, 38.2% of arson offenses cleared by arrest or exceptional means involved juveniles (persons under 18 years of age), which was the highest juvenile clearance rate among all offenses. The next highest juvenile clearance rate was larceny-theft, at 19% (FBI, 2009).

In 2004, the National Volunteer Fire Council estimated that 55% of all arson arrests were of children younger than 18 years of age. Furthermore, of those juveniles who are arrested, almost half are younger than 15 years of age (National Volunteer Fire Council, 2004). With that in mind, we need to turn to what motivates an individual to commit arsonist activities.

SERIAL ARSON

While regular arson can be a one-off crime, serial arson must be done repeatedly. Although both local and federal agencies such as the FBI and the USFA track arson rates in the United States, most do not keep specific records for serial arson.

There are specific characteristics assigned to serial arson that are used to help distinguish it from other arson offenses that also possess a repetitive nature. As cited in the study A Motive-Based Offender Analysis of Serial Arsonists (Sapp, Huff, Gary, & Icove, 1994), Douglas et al. explain that serial arson is a separate act altogether from offenses such as double arson, triple arson, spree arson, and mass arson. An offender falls into one of these categories depending on the number of fires set, the quantity of sites used, and the amount of time between events.

Serial arson differs from these other categories in that the fire setter takes time off between each offense. Douglas et al. (1997) define serial arson as the act of repeatedly setting fires "in three or more separate fire setting episodes, with a characteristic emotional cooling-off between fires. This period may last days, weeks, or even years" (pp. 186–187). While double and triple arson cases involve multiple offenses that can take place at different sites, the perpetrators in these cases set the fires during one single event, with no respite between fires (Sapp et al., 1994).

Douglas et al. (1997) extend the definition of serial arson by stating that it can be further broken down into two additional groups: spree and mass. A spree arsonist is someone who "sets fires at three or more separate locations with no emotional cooling off period between them" (p. 189). A mass arsonist "involves one offender who sets three or more fires at the same location during a limited period of time" (p. 189). The key element that separates serial arson from these other categories is the presence of intervals or breaks between each fire that is set.

The FBI and ATF have conducted several studies to develop arson typologies. In the latest study utilizing arson statistics (Sapp et al., 1994; Wright & Gary, 1995), researchers "examined 83 convicted serial arsonists responsible for 2611 arsons (an average of 31.5 fires per arsonist), and 7 deaths by fire" (Rossmo, 1999, p. 45). According to the FBI and ATF, the archetypal serial arsonist is:

> *male (94%), white (81.9%), young (most fires are set by juveniles), single (65.9%), nocturnal, and of average to above average intelligence. Over half were laborers. Two-thirds described themselves as middle class and one-third as lower middle class. About half indicated they came from dysfunctional families. Only 16.3% of this group lived alone, but most lacked stability in their interpersonal relationships. Approximately 255 reported they were homosexual or bisexual. Accomplices to the arsons were involved in 20.3% of the cases. (FBI as cited in Rossmo, 1999, pp. 46–47)*

The FBI/ATF study reports that serial arsonists frequently had previous involvement with the law, stating "most . . . had prior felony arrest (86.6%, 23.9% involving arson), many with multiple felony arrests (63.4%)" (Rossmo, 1999, p. 47). Like the one-off arsonist, the serial arsonist begins his or her career as a teenager. According to Rossmo (1999), the mean age of a serial arsonist is 15 years, and the recidivism rate is 28% (p. 47). The vast majority have spent time in juvenile facilities (54.2%) with more than two-thirds (67.5%) of offenders spending time in the county jail system. The study also reports that "over half of these offenders had psychological histories, over one third with multiple psychological problems. One quarter had attempted suicide" (Rossmo, 1999, p. 47).

Planning patterns also differ among serial arsonists. As Rossmo reports, "Many responded that their fires were premeditated and planned (46.2%), others said impulsive (35%), and a few opportunistic (12.8%)." Targets also varied among the population under study: "reported reasons included random selection (17.6), prior knowledge (14.6%), convenience (11.8%), within walking distance (5.9%), and multiple reasons (32.4%)" (Rossmo, 1999, p. 47). Like most crimes, a large percentage of offenders used alcohol (almost half) and drugs (one-third) before the commission of the crime (Rossmo, 1999, p. 48). Contrary to media portrayals of arsonists, most leave the scene of the fire altogether (40%). However, many serial arsonists do remain at the scene (31.4%), and a smaller percentage leave the scene to watch from another location (28.6%). According to Rossmo, "Of those who left the scene, over half (52.9%) returned to the crime scene later, the majority within 1 hour (54%) and almost all (97.3%) within 24 hours" (p. 48).

Other researchers have described serial arsonists in similar ways to what was found in the FBI/ATF study. Martinez (2004) explains that most serial arsonists are white males between 18 and 49 years of age who have poor social skills. Fritzon (2000) states that serial arsonists usually live within a mile of the scene of the crime and either stay or return to watch the blaze. Furthermore, Fritzon reports, "The typical serial arsonist is usually an unemployed or erratically employed male, and possibly a juvenile, with a history of substance abuse and police involvement for minor nuisance offenses. He will be minimally educated, . . . will have poor interpersonal relationships, and [will] be socially inadequate" (p. 170).

Some of these characteristics are common not only in male serial arsonists, but in females as well. Although women have consistently been the minority participant in all forms of arson, researchers Lewis and Yarnell state that in the 19th century arson was considered to be a crime committed mainly by young females (as cited in Mavromatis, 2000). Still, recent research has shown that they do share some of the same characteristics as male offenders.

Lewis and Yarnell's study of female fire setters indicates that women are quite similar to men with respect to motivation. Locations are typically close to home or familiar to the offenders. However, females usually plan their actions and do not act on a whim or out of pure instinct. They are driven by motives and tend to experience intense emotions and release when setting the fire and watching it burn (Mavromatis, 2000).

A study of female serial arsonists in Japan explored how qualities reported by Rossmo (1999) are present in the lives of female fire setters. While nearly the entire sample of 83 serial arsonists were adults at the time of the study, 5% were younger than 20 years (some of whom were as young as 14 years). Most females were in their 20s (30%). Nearly half of the arsonists were married (49%), while 25% lived alone and 29% lived with their parents. The majority of the women (43%) were unemployed, and 19% held unskilled jobs. Of all the female participants studied, 22% had at least one prior arrest, most frequently for theft crimes. In only 5% of cases was the prior offense arson related. Finally, 28% of the sample was found to have some type of mental problem (Wachi et al., 2007).

The women were also more likely to commit their arson offenses near their homes. In terms of their targets, 83% of the sample was considered to be opportunistic and impulsive in their acts. On the contrary, 17% planned their actions and had specific goals in mind when setting their fires (Wachi et al., 2007).

Relatively few studies have been done on female arsonists, making it difficult to draw comparisons to males. Specifically, this female study had a much smaller sample and took place in an entirely different country. Yet, the presence of certain variables such as criminal history and psychological issues provides a strong foundation to generate predictors of serial arson. The fact that most of the female serial offenders were in their 20s during the time of the study suggests that they were most likely juveniles when they first started engaging in arson crimes, which would be very comparable to males. More in-depth research on target preparation and goals, or the lack thereof, may also show similarities among the sexes.

MOTIVATIONS

In the past, researchers have used several descriptive terms to encapsulate the array of motivations experienced by arsonists and serial arsonists. Douglas et al. (1997) report six main motivational typologies:

- Revenge
- Excitement
- Vandalism
- Profit
- Crime concealment
- Extremism

A revenge arsonist is someone who sets a fire "for some injustice, real or imagined, perceived by the offender" (Douglas et al., 1997, p. 173). The emotional need for vengeance and retaliation is a significant factor in arson-related crimes. Rice and Harris (as cited in Davis & Lauber, 1999) estimate that roughly 40% of arson cases are driven by revenge. Offenders seek revenge as a result of various internal emotions such as anger, jealousy, and sadness. These psychological issues are a common part of everyday life, and they provide offenders with many opportunities to achieve revenge through fire-setting activities.

An offender motivated by excitement is "prompted to set fires because he craves excitement that is satisfied by fire setting. This offender rarely intends to harm people" (Douglas et al., 1997, p. 170). Excitement can be generated from setting the fire and watching the flames or be associated with the response and operations of the fire department (Sapp et al., 1994). Offenders look to stimulate themselves and satisfy needs that other, more conventional activities are unable to fulfill. Icove and Estepp (1987) found that the vast majority of excitement arsonists in their study on arson motives were juveniles (69%), whereas mainly adults (81%) were driven by revenge (Icove & Estepp, 1987).

Vandalism offenders commit arson "due to malicious and mischievous motivation that results in destruction or damage" (Douglas et al., 1997, p. 167). The Insurance Information Institute claims that vandalism is the most common type of arson committed across the country (Insurance Information Institute, 2009a). This motive is common among younger offenders and carries little to no purpose other than to show a complete lack of value and respect for other people's property. These offenders are simply looking to cause trouble or gain status among their peers (Kocsis, 2002). Common areas targeted by arson vandals include school properties and residential areas (Fritzon, 2000). This would support the claim that arson vandals tend to be younger. The vast majority (96%) of those responsible for vandalism-related arson in Icove and Estepp's study (1987) were in fact juveniles.

Profit-motivated arson "is a fire set for the purpose of achieving material gain, either directly or indirectly" (Douglas et al., 1997, p. 180). The USFA (2009) states that arson for profit is used by businesses or individuals "to reduce financial losses, recoup initial investments, or dispose of depreciated assets usually for a payout from insurance companies" (p. 1). Data collected by the Insurance Research Council estimated that 14% of all alleged arsonists commit the offense as a way to cheat insurance companies, though this rate fluctuates depending on the source (USFA, 2009).

With the recent slump in the economy and more people facing financial issues, insurance companies have seen an increase in arson crimes on cars and homes. The National Insurance Crime Bureau released statistics showing that when comparing rates between the first quarter of 2008 and the first quarter of 2009, the number of fire and arson claims rose by 76% (Insurance Information Institute, 2009b). A lack of money and options can lead people to crime as a last resort. In Detroit in particular, where the recession has hit extremely hard, city fire officials have stated that arson rates increased 27.8% between 2004 and 2008. Furthermore, the city experiences an average of 18 arsons every single day (Esparza, 2009).

Author David J. Icove (as cited in United States Fire Administration, 2009) explains that arson for profit can take the form of collecting insurance, liquidating property, clearing property, reducing competition, or gaining employment. The fires set for profit are not limited to just homes or owned land. Targeted objects of offenders include vehicles, boats, businesses, and abandoned buildings. Recently, according to a

Coalition Against Insurance Fraud survey (as cited in Insurance Information Institute, 2009b), vehicle "give-ups" have been on the rise in many states such as New York and Florida. In these cases, owners falsely report their cars as stolen and then often use fire to destroy evidence and hide the vehicle's identification. Overall, a leading insurance company recently found that vehicle arson claims rose by 6% from 2007 to 2008 (USFA, 2009).

This crime can involve multiple offenders as well. A business owner may develop the plan but might hire a "torch," or accomplice, to physically set the fire (Fritzon, 2000). All of these targets of arson for profit combined to decimate roughly $900 million in insured property and kill 295 civilians in 2007, according to the Insurance Information Institute (2009b).

Crime concealment arson "is a secondary or collateral criminal activity, perpetrated for the purpose of covering up a primary criminal activity, of some nature" (Douglas et al., 1997, p. 176). In theory, the fire incinerates any evidence and covers up any tracks that could lead authorities to the offender. Someone who steals a car (primary crime) may burn the stolen vehicle (secondary crime) after it has served its purpose as a way to destroy traces of DNA or fingerprints (Kocsis, 2002).

Extremist arson "is committed to further a social, political, or religious cause" (Douglas et al., 1997, p. 184). The offenders use arson to express themselves and prove a point about their beliefs, whether they are conventional or unconventional (Fritzon, 2000). Extremist arson is used as a form of violent protest against the perceived opposition, and it is common for multiple offenders to play a role. Examples of extremist offenses are groups who use arson to follow through with terrorist acts, attack abortion clinics, or burn down buildings associated with specific races or religions (Sapp et al., 1994).

Inciardi's study (1970) on paroled fire setters looked at specific characteristics within these same arson motivations and how the groups differed. Of the 138 fire setters in his sample, 96% were male and the median age was 27 years. Specifically, the vast majority (58%) fell into the revenge category, while 18% were motivated by excitement. Vandalism accounted for only 4.1% of the sample. Inciardi found that the majority of the fire setters studied grew up in single-parent homes located in urban areas and were likely to have contact with the police as juveniles. Furthermore, the sample was comprised mainly of unskilled laborers who were not married. Heavy drinking was also found to be associated with fire setters who were motivated by revenge and excitement, while those driven by profit and crime concealment had higher intelligence levels (Inciardi, 1970).

Many times, investigators can determine which motive the offender was following without even apprehending the suspect. Determining whether the arson was organized or disorganized can tell the investigator a lot about a potential suspect. Organized acts are clean, leave no evidence, and often utilize special devices. These types of arson crimes suggest that the offender is an intelligent adult who premeditated the attack. They are also typical of arson for profit or hired torches. Disorganized scenes usually have traces of evidence that were not destroyed by the fire. The offender uses whatever is readily available to light the fire, and his or her crime is motivated by vandalism or is pathologic in nature (Mavromatis, 2000).

In some instances, juvenile is considered a classification. For example, investigators in Massachusetts use the following seven motives to process a crime scene:

- Revenge
- Financial
- Crime concealment
- Civil disobedience
- Juvenile
- Hero/vanity
- Serial/pathologic

While both Douglas et al.'s (1997) typologies and those used by Massachusetts investigators include revenge, profit/financial, crime concealment, and extremist/civil disobedience, the Massachusetts list also includes the categories of juvenile, serial/pathologic, and hero/vanity.

Although age is one means for classifying an arsonist, being a juvenile does not capture the arsonist's motivation. One juvenile offender may be a pyromaniac, while another juvenile may be a vandal. By focusing on the age of the arsonist, other important characteristics may be overlooked when trying to identify possible suspects, such as gender, race, or motivation. For example, two juvenile offenders may commit the same crime, arson, for very different reasons. The classification of juvenile or financial, are not necessarily distinct motivations; they are more in line with penal classifications. Penal classifications are primarily a system for describing offender characteristics. By focusing on personal characteristics, the investigator can lose track of what the criminal motivation may be in the case.

PYROMANIA

Bennett and Hess (as cited in Davis & Lauber, 1999) define pyromaniacs as those who lack any real motivation to set fires and receive no physical or intrinsic gain from committing the crime. Pyromaniacs lack emotion on several different levels, which sets them apart from other arsonists. They are unable to manage or resist their impulses to light fires. Their obsession with fire is uncontrollable and far from comparable to those motivated by revenge, excitement, or any other arson-related motives. Also, pyromaniacs feel no shame or regret for their actions, do not recognize the severity of damage they cause, and overlook the danger they put people's lives in (Australian Institute of Criminology, 2005).

The accepted definition of pyromania has changed repeatedly over time. Early researchers, who were some of the first to look at pyromania, first labeled it as a psychiatric disorder. This definition was later rejected due to thoughts that a mental disorder absolved the offender of blame and responsibility. However, many of the aspects attributed to pyromania today were developed starting in the 1900s. Issues looking at impulse control, childhood growth, and sexual development all became important in discussing pyromania (Geller, McDermeit, & Brown, 1997).

In Lewis and Yarnel's 1951 study (cited in Mavromatis, 2000), they classify pyromaniacs as impulse driven, lacking a clear motive, and easily fascinated by watching the flames. They assert that the offenders' inability to control their urges also suggests a lack of concern for potential injuries or death that may result. They further explain that although the goal is not to destroy property (only to watch something burn), over time destruction and devastation may become part of the offender's overall fascination.

Today, in the *DSM*, the APA reverts to the definition that points to a lack of impulse control in offenders. As Geller et al. (1997) point out, there are five criteria established by the *DSM* that an offender must display to be labeled as a pyromaniac.

- Deliberate fire setting on multiple occasions
- Tension or arousal before setting the fire
- Feelings of relief or pleasure while setting the fire or watching afterward
- An intense interest or obsession with fire and/or its associated characteristics
- Absence of any other motivating factors (e.g., money, revenge) for setting the fire

Pyromania is disputed in recent social science research (Doley, 2003; Davis & Lauber, 1999; Geller et al, 1997), with some social scientists concluding that pyromania is a concept that is poorly understood by the psychiatric and criminal justice community (Doley, 2003; Geller et al, 1997) and misrepresented by the fire scene investigative community. FBI research supports this notion. In 1994, the FBI conducted a study to gauge the level of understanding of pyromania. Of the 548 participants, over 86% were either members of fire services or law enforcement agencies. The study measured how many of the five criteria presented by the *DSM* the respondents used in their own definitions of pyromania. By far, the only part of the *DSM* definition that respondents correctly identified was the first criterion involving repeated and deliberate fire setting (81.9%) (Geller et al., 1997).

Tension or arousal before the setting of the fire was mentioned by less than half of the participants (45.3%), and feelings of pleasure or arousal were referenced by 45.4%. Respondents' answers were far less consistent with the *DSM* definition in regard to the last two criteria. Only 15.9% identified pyromania as involving an infatuation or deep interest with fire or fire-related characteristics. Furthermore, only 1.5% correctly mentioned that pyromaniacs lack motives that are commonly associated with other arson crimes (Geller et al., 1997).

This study shows that there is still widespread confusion surrounding the application of the term pyromaniac, even among law enforcement and fire department officials. In some cases, the classification and labeling of a pyromaniac may be unjust and unwarranted because of an inadequate understanding or education. For example, when a motive is lacking in an arson case, investigators tend to fall back on labeling the offender a pyromaniac, without putting forth a more in-depth analysis (Mavromatis, 2000). This rush to judgment can skew actual rates of pyromania.

Likewise, research done on arson in the past has faced similar trends. Different criminologists have applied diverse definitions of pyromania in their research. While some researchers may incorporate sexually driven fire setters into their test group of pyromaniacs, others may not (Mavromatis, 2000). This inconsistency in defining pyromania produces an unpredictable database on which to refer and rely.

While the sample plays a role in the type of data received, research has proven that these factors have produced great disparities in the number of pyromaniacs found in different studies. For instance, Mavromatis and Lion (as cited in Davis & Lauber, 1999) found a pyromania rate of 40% in their 1977 research. Leong (1992) found no pyromaniacs in a study examining the element of psychosis. Lewis and Yarnell's 1951 study on fire setters shows how delicate the definition can be. About 40% of their sample showed no concrete motive for setting fires. They acted purely out of impulse and could be viewed as pyromaniacs. However, when eliminating other factors, such as mental retardation, psychiatric illnesses, and alcoholism, this number went down to roughly 4% of their entire sample (Mavromatis, 2000). These varying rates show that along with the sample involved, the knowledge of the researchers and the methods they apply can also affect the data.

OTHER FACTORS

Researchers have also examined other elements concerning the mental state and capacity of fire setters. Internal issues such as intellectual disabilities and psychiatric disorders may affect the mental state of fire setters. Davis and Lauber (1999) stated that overall, mental illness is not a significant factor in fire-setting behavior. They cited Baker's 1994 study, which found that roughly 10% of arsonists are mentally ill. This finding is similar to that of Lewis and Yarnell, who concluded that roughly 13.5% of the males in their study were considered psychotic when they set their fires (as cited in Mavromatis, 2000).

However, Leong (1992) found considerably more individuals who were diagnosed as psychotic. Using the DSM, Leong found instances of schizophrenia, bipolar disorder, substance abuse, schizoaffective disorder, and other disorders. While the sample consisted of only 29 court-referred fire setters who were charged with arson, about 79% had significant psychiatric histories involving stays in psychiatric hospitals or treatment centers. Over half of those in the sample (51.7%) were found to be psychotic at the time of their respective arsons. Yet, the number of those found to be incompetent to stand trial was significantly high, suggesting that the court's participant referrals may have been predetermined and therefore distorted the data (Leong, 1992).

Regardless of possible biases, Leong's study shows the degree to which psychological issues can affect fire setters. These disorders may be playing a role in their decisions to set fires and their inability to control impulses, which may go hand in hand with the rate at which pyromania is found. When a motive is lacking, there may be underlying issues involved, such as a psychological disorder. Pyromania may not be the correct diagnosis, and researchers need to expand their work to take other issues into consideration.

JUVENILES

In a sense, arson all starts with young children. One of the main differences between children and adults is the factor of curiosity. Playing with matches, lighters, and other forms of fire out of curiosity and entertainment is considered a common part of childhood development in young males (Kocsis, 2002). In addition, our society tends to glamorize fire in almost subliminal ways in popular culture. Fire is often designated as a symbol for love, passion, and other positive aspects of life. It is used in music, art, entertainment, and everyday speech in attractive and noncondemning ways (Sakheim, Vigdor, Gordon, & Helprin, 1985). It surrounds children starting at early ages and only fuels their fascination. While the vast majority of juvenile fire setters are young teens or preteens, children as young as 2 or 3 years have been found to play with fire (Zipper & Wilcox, 2005).

Gaynor and Hatcher (1987) (as cited in Kocsis, 2002) explain that children's lack of education and knowledge about fire and its threats allows them to give in to their curiosity. As they grow older and gain an understanding of the potential dangers, most children express more caution when using fire or even grow out of the fire-playing phase altogether. Those who do not grow out of it tend to be antisocial and aggressive, and often express their anger in alternative and hidden ways, such as through fire setting (Slavkin, as cited in Virginia Commission on Youth, 2003). Zipper and Wilcox (2005) attribute this behavior in part to the finding that "these young arsonists tend to act impulsively and in externalizing fashion when confronted with situations that provoke intense reactions, rather than thinking first about the consequences of their behavior" (p. 3).

Other factors such as emotional vulnerability, inability to develop close relationships with peers, and persistent family problems are also very common in juvenile fire setters (Virginia Commission on Youth, 2003). The USFA suggested that family problems and issues within the home are significant predictors for recidivism of juvenile arsonists. Lewis and Yarnell (1951) were among the first researchers to examine juvenile arson risk factors. According to Sakheim and Osborn (1999), "They noted a high incidence of family dysfunction, including alcoholism, psychosis, criminality, and illegitimacy" (p. 414).

Kolko and Kazdin (1986) (as cited in Pollinger, Samuels, & Stadolnik, 2005) describe similar potential risk factors that make certain children more likely to participate in fire-setting activities. They stated that the family unit, and parents especially, have a significant impact. In particular, the amount of supervision, parental involvement, and conflict or stress present in the family can lead children to grow comfortable with setting fires. Karchmer (1984) is more specific in his explanation, stating that an absent father is a frequent characteristic of juvenile fire setters. This finding touches upon a simple fact of childhood development. If no one is around watching a child and telling him or her what to do and not do, the juvenile will simply act out of impulse and fulfill curiosity. Also, with more alone time to experiment with assessable goods such as matches and lighters, fire setting becomes easy to perform and acts almost as a hobby for children.

Two other elements that Kolko and Kazdin put forth are personal repertoire and modeling. Personality traits such as cognitive and behavioral skills affect the decisions children make and their education (as cited in Pollinger et al., 2005). Also, modeling, or mimicking what they see, is a significant part of children's lives, especially if they do not understand the potential consequences of the action. Behavioral problems and a history of delinquency are also persistent with juvenile fire setting (Devapriam, Raju, Singh, Collacott, & Bhaumik, 2007). Crime can snowball for any offender. Minor deviant behaviors can quickly turn into major crimes, especially when associating with other delinquents.

Karchmer (1984) argues that juvenile arson motivational factors do not receive the same in-depth investigation and research as the motivational factors of adults. He argues that because those under 18 years of age are more likely to receive treatment or other alternatives to prison time, investigators spend less time and resources getting to the root cause of the problem. They do not search high and wide for personal or family problems that may have driven the child to start the fire in the first place, thus making it harder to explain future cases involving juveniles because there is little precedent to go by. Also, it hurts the planning and development of treatment options because authorities do not know what specific problems to target in the child's life.

One element that explains why juvenile arson may receive less attention is that juveniles tend to start out by setting smaller fires that cause less destruction. Only after gaining experience in the crime do they set out to destroy larger and more costly areas (Schwartzman, Stambaugh, & Kimball, 1998). Investigators may be less inclined to use valuable and sparse resources on small fires with little destruction.

While curiosity plays a significant role in child fire setting, juveniles are driven by some of the same motives that are found in adults. Revenge, crime concealment, vandalism, and profit are factors in juvenile arson. Burning school property or striking back at parents through setting things on fire shows the juvenile's inability to cope with stress or resolve issues in conventional ways (Karchmer, 1984). Gangs often use arson as a way to strike back at rivals or the community that rejects them, or they may even use arson as a way to cover up drug crimes or murders (Schwartzman et al., 1998).

Karchmer explains that juveniles have been used in crime concealment offenses in cities such as Boston and Seattle, receiving money or goods (such as alcohol) to torch property for insurance or extortion purposes. Juveniles are ideal hired torches because they work for cheap and have relatively clean criminal records (Karchmer, 1984).

One of the main concerns with any juvenile offender is the likelihood of the individual becoming a career criminal and continuing delinquent activities into his or her adult years. However, certain juvenile fire setters are at more of a risk of recidivism than others. Obviously, those surrounded by the aforementioned risk factors are more likely to continue fire-setting behaviors if their personal and behavioral issues go untreated and are left to evolve. Kolko and Kazdin (as cited in Slavkin & Fineman, 2000) point out that those who are not disciplined for their actions, face constant family conflict, are ignored by their parents, and feel disconnected to their families are more likely to continue setting fires. Some type of positive change is needed to thwart their urges to express their emotions through fire.

A study by Sakheim and Osborn (1999) specifically addresses some of the predictors that put children at risk of becoming repeat offenders. They built upon their earlier research that compared severe and nonsevere fire setters. Their updated study consisted of 180 children and adolescents who lived away from their parents in psychiatric hospitals, residential facilities, or group and foster homes. The sample was broken down into three groups consisting of severe fire setters (75), nonsevere fire setters (50), and non–fire setters (55). The sample was 90% males, and the mean age of the severe fire setters was 12.5 years, while the average age of the minor fire setters was 12 years. Significant differences were found when the severe sample was compared to the nonsevere fire setter and non–fire setter groups. Variables such as sexual excitement from fire, poor social judgment, attraction or preoccupation with fire, lack of empathy, cruelty to children and animals, history of fire play, anger at parental rejection/abandonment, and fantasies of revenge/retaliation were all found more frequently in severe fire setters (Sakheim & Osborn, 1999). Also, inadequate superego, early exposure to fire, rage at insults/humiliation, a history of physical violence, and anger at parental rejection, abuse, neglect, and abandonment were all more characteristic of those in the severe fire setters group.

Other important data from the study came from those variables that were more common in the nonsevere fire setter and non–fire setter groups. More children in these two groups were found to want a reunion with an absent father (Sakheim & Osborn, 1999). This finding shows a sense of care and forgiveness that may overpower their urges to strike back with fire. Also, these children were found to have greater levels of verbal aggression (Sakheim & Osborn, 1999), which may indicate that they use alternative avenues to fire setting to express their anger and frustration. Yelling or screaming when they are mad may relieve tension and frustration, which could eliminate the need to express these feelings through fire. The data in this study provide considerable insight into the differences between those who are repeat offenders and those who have little risk of becoming career fire setters.

Sakheim, Osborn, and Abrams offer four different classifications of juvenile arson risk, which help to determine and predict recidivism (as cited in Fritzon, 2000). Children who are considered to be low risk are those who use fire out of curiosity but lose their fascination with it due to education, supervision, and other forms of conventional and developmental intervention. The juveniles in the cry for help category face a moderate risk because they set fires out of some type of psychological or emotional void. There is a good chance that they will continue to set fires unless parents or peers intervene and respond to their cry and their needs. Those considered to have a definite risk of continued fire-setting behavior are those who have conduct, behavioral, and/or family issues and use fire setting to express their anger. These fire setters have already grown accustomed to using fire as a form of expression and therefore would require serious intervention from parents and trained professionals. Finally, children with an extreme risk of continued fire setting are those who are labeled pyromaniacs and have psychological issues that hinder their ability to resist impulses (Fritzon, 2000). Simple punishment will not change their behaviors. These children require professional rehabilitation from psychologists such as in residential treatment centers.

Slavkin and Fineman (2000) classify the different levels and sublevels of juvenile arson, which helps characterize the severity of their behavior, the possibility of it becoming serial in nature, and the potential for rehabilitation. The first level is composed of fire setters who are considered *nonpathologic*. Their fire-setting activities are experimental in nature and are motivated by curiosity. These acts are typical of children who find matches in their house or "teenagers playing scientist." These juveniles are typically one-time offenders and do not carry on this behavior beyond their experimentation (Slavkin & Fineman, 2000). Fineman states that roughly 60% of all juvenile arsons fit into this category (as cited in Fritzon, 2000).

The second level includes *pathologic* fire setters. Five different types fall into this category. First, there is the *cry for help* type. These juveniles use fire as a way to attract attention as a result of some negative feeling or experience. Intervening and answering this cry can put a stop to the child's fire-setting behavior (Slavkin & Fineman, 2000). Once these juveniles see the response from others, their emotional needs are fulfilled and their fire-setting urges cease.

Next is the *delinquent* type. These juveniles tend to be older. Their fire-related activities are due to conduct and aggression issues, and they are more likely to set fires as a means to destroy property more so than to harm others. As with the *cry for help* type, early intervention and treatment can put a stop to their delinquent behaviors.

Another type of juvenile fire setters consists of those who are *severely disturbed*. They have an obsession with lighting fires and doing so frequently. These juveniles are described as psychotic and often as pyromaniacs. Injury to others and to themselves may occur as a result of their fire setting. They require immediate and intense treatment due to their engrossed passion for fire, which is reinforced by the burning flame (Slavkin & Fineman, 2000).

The final two types are defined as *cognitively impaired* and *sociocultural*. The *cognitively impaired* fire setters consist of those who are also developmentally disabled, the learning disabled, and the organically impaired. They do not intend to harm others and can be aided by therapy and treatment. The juveniles who fit in the *sociocultural* category set fires to gain popularity or attention for a certain cause. They focus on property damage, and their activities can be thwarted by treatment (Slavkin & Fineman, 2000).

Fineman's model maps out which types of juvenile offenders are most at risk for continuing their fire-setting behaviors into adulthood. With early recognition, intervention, and treatment, most juveniles may cease their actions as they grow into adulthood.

CONCLUSION

Arson is a broad topic, the scope and magnitude of which are still relatively unexplored. Many areas of arson—serial arson in particular—have been untouched by criminology research. However, the excuse for this inadequacy cannot focus on the silent and rare nature of the crime. This is far from the case. The crime of arson is truly a paradox of criminal research when one compares the frequency at which it occurs to the amount of study and analysis performed on it by criminologists.

In Fritzon's criticism of arson research, she presents a reason for the lack of in-depth examination. She starts with the lack of a universal typology set that researchers can use in their research. For example, the *cry for help* type of arsonist may be present in one study but absent from another. Similarly, a researcher may include other motives that are not used in research done by the FBI. Vreeland and Waller (as cited in Fritzon, 2000) recognize this same problem in their 1979 study on arson. Fritzon maintains that one classification system is needed that encompasses all motives, but that is also open to integrating future typologies that have not been extracted by researchers yet (Fritzon, 2000). In a sense, if everyone is doing their own thing, how is progress going to be made? A uniform classification system would provide order and assist researchers in comparing their data to results from other studies. This comparison would help pinpoint possible lapses and ways to improve future studies to generate more answers and, ultimately, create possible solutions.

Fritzon is also more concerned about answering the question of *why* offenders choose to set fires. She argues, "For example, with the revenge motive that is commonly cited as one of the most frequent motives for firesetting, merely identifying it as a category of arson does not explain why individuals use this particular form revenge" (Fritzon, 2000, p. 170). Developmental or family problems may cause delinquency, but they do not directly explain why the offender chooses to use fire as a weapon. What makes one person use fire when other people in the same exact situation do not? This is the question Fritzon wishes to answer.

However, this same question can be asked of any crime. Why do some economically deprived and poorly educated youths turn to gangs, drugs, and violence while others in similar situations go on to live successful lives? Or why do those from the middle and upper classes, with strong educations and favorable upbringings, turn to crime while others with no support, education, or money avoid delinquency? Arson has many facets, many of which have not been studied in depth, if at all. The various motivations, risk factors, and types of arson must all be examined to gain a stronger understanding of *why* arson occurs. Thus far, all reported data concerning arson indicate that it is a severe problem and perhaps even more serious and common for those younger than 18 years old. To combat this issue, provide authorities and professionals with greater knowledge of the problem, and develop proactive treatment and care for those at risk further research needs to be done that builds upon existing data and provides more influential analysis for the field.

CHAPTER 8

Muti Murder: Murder for Human Body Parts

Gerard Labuschagne

Bewitchment beliefs remain part of black South African beliefs despite the influence of Western rational-scientific explanatory frameworks (Ivey & Myers, 2008). However, supernatural beliefs are not confined to African cultures; indeed, many modern-day Westerners believe in the existence of good and evil spiritual entities. A number of anthropologic, legal, and forensic reports (Ashton, 1943; Chavunduka, 2001; Minaar, 1998; Minaar, 2001; Minaar, Offringa, & Payze, 1991; Nel, Verschoor, Calitz, & van Rensburg, 1992; Ngubane, 1986; Prinsloo & Du Plessis, 1989; Schapera, 1952; Scholtz, Phillips, & Knobel, 1997) indicate that muti murder, an element of bewitchment beliefs, has been practiced as part of a subculture of traditional African beliefs for centuries. With the arrival of Western criminal justice systems and beliefs, such practices have become illegal. Because little is known about muti murder, modern law enforcement agencies lack guidance in investigating these cases.

A few studies of muti murder were conducted earlier in the 20th century (Ashton, 1943; Grové, 1950; Schapera, 1952), but many questions have been left unanswered, especially with regard to appropriate strategies for the investigation of muti murder. Scholtz, Phillips, and Knobel (1997) have argued that political issues are partly responsible for there being little empirical literature available. Scholtz et al. (1997) state that there are persistent rumours linking top political and law enforcement officials with such practices, leading some to consider the topic too politically sensitive to investigate. However, Scholtz et al. (1997) do not elaborate on their sources for these rumours.

For law enforcement agencies, it is imperative to be able to distinguish between muti murders, cult-related murders, sadistic murders, serial murders, and other types of murder that may involve mutilation, but that may require different approaches when conducting an investigation. Each one of these crimes has a different context. Some are group related, such as a cult murder; others are part of a broader belief system, such as muti murder and honour killings; and others are unique to the offender's own psyche, such as a sadistic murder. People not knowledgeable about muti murders could launch an inappropriate investigative process focused on the incorrect type of offender. People tasked to assist law enforcement from a behavioral perspective, such as criminologists and psychologists (broadly referred to as behavioral analysts), in such circumstances might make signature interpretations, compile offender profiles, or give investigative inputs that could prove to be extremely misleading for investigators (cf., Keppel & Birnes, 2003).

TYPES OF TRADITIONAL HEALERS IN SOUTH AFRICA

There are two main types of traditional healers in South Africa—the sangomas who consult with ancestors to determine the cause of a person's problems, and the inyangas who are herbalists. On a day-to-day basis, these practitioners intend no harm to the people they assist or to others. Lambrecht (1998) claims that 84% of black South Africans seek treatment from traditional healers. It is the mungome or vhuloi/baloyi who is associated with harmful practices. It is important to emphasize that most traditional healers play a vital role in African society, often fulfilling the combined role of medical practitioner, spiritual guide, and psychologist.

Traditional healers such as sangomas oppose referring to those practitioners involved in muti murder as "traditional healers" and suggest that such individuals be referred to as "witches." Traditional healers state that their form of assistance is aimed at helping people, whereas those who use their skills to bring harm to others (such as wanting someone dead) or who directly harm others in executing their duties (as in muti murder) should not be classified under the same term "traditional healer." Based on this request, the term "witches" will be used in this chapter.

DEFINING MUTI MURDER

"Muti" is a Zulu word meaning medicine. It is therefore a mistake to assume that whenever the word muti is used, crime is involved. Even medicine prescribed by a doctor in a hospital is called muti. "Muti murder" may be loosely defined as a murder where the intention is to gather human body parts for use in traditional African medicine (Minaar, 2001). The purpose is usually to improve an individual's or a community's circumstances. A witch usually advocates the act after being consulted by a client. A third party carries out the actual murder. The witch is rarely involved in the murder.

Human body parts are used because they are considered more powerful than the usual ingredients (e.g., roots, herbs, other plant material, animal parts, seawater) or methods used in traditional medicine. Namely, the human body parts are believed to contain the person's "life essence." They therefore are a fast track to achieving what the person who uses the muti wants to achieve. Characteristically, the witch consults the ancestors to determine the cause of the problem and then prescribes the treatment. The victim usually dies from the injuries sustained during the removal of the body parts. Traditionally, the victim must be alive when the body parts are removed because the body parts then retain the person's life essence, thereby increasing the power of the muti.

SACRIFICIAL MURDER OR MUTI MURDER?

There are important differences between muti murder and sacrificial murder. While the muti murder may be *ritualized* in that it is done in a certain way, it is not, in itself, a sacrificial act in that the act is not performed to appease a god or deity. The aim is solely to obtain body parts for ingredients. A sacrificial murder, which can occur in a wide variety of belief systems, such as satanism, voodoo, or other African beliefs, is intended as a sacrifice (Minaar, 1998; Olivier, 1990; Prinsloo & Du Plessis, 1989). In other words, the aim is to offer the life of an individual to appease or win favor with a deity. For example, a sacrificial murder in the South African context might include the myths referring to Venda virgins who were sacrificed to the crocodiles in the Fundudzi Lake or thrown into the Tshatshingo Whirlpools as offerings to ancestral spirits for the good of the community (Minaar, 1998; Prinsloo & Du Plessis, 1989). In the case of muti murders, some feel that to use the term "murder" is incorrect because it is "far from just an act of wanton wickedness" (Ngubane, 1986, p. 191) and the death of the victim is not the intention in muti attacks, although it is a likely outcome.

HISTORIC CONTEXT

As mentioned, belief in the supernatural remains a part of modern African society. As Ivey and Myers (2008) explain, "Psychological and psychiatric explanations have less currency in these communities where traditional supernatural belief systems provide established and culturally accessible understandings. This is particularly so when individuals in these communities are confronted by adverse or apparently inexplicable events" (p. 55).

In terms of the "African worldview" (Makwe, 1985), there are certain key elements central to the understanding of witchcraft:

- *The belief that there is constant interaction between the spiritual and human worlds.* Deceased family members become ancestral spirits and continue to play a role in the lives of the living.
- *The emphasis on "intuitive knowledge."* Subjective experience and personal knowledge are more highly valued means to obtain truth than scientific deductive or empirical methods. Therefore, communal acceptance of a belief outweighs scientific validity.
- *The African understanding of causality, which is linear and personal.* When misfortune arises, its origins are believed to stem from the actions or intentions of others with hostile intent.
- *The belief in magical powers.* Good magic is associated with the use of mystical or supernatural powers for the benefit of people. In contrast, evil magic involves sorcery, which is the employment of supernatural powers to inflict harm on others (Ivey & Myers, 2008).

In traditional African beliefs, it is assumed that there is only a certain amount of luck or good fortune in society, with each individual receiving a portion of that good fortune. It is therefore believed that if another person is successful, then that person has obtained an extra portion of luck, often through the intervention of ancestors, or with the intervention of the supernatural. It is also traditionally believed that setbacks or calamities, such as drought or illness, are signs that the natural and social order has been disturbed (Minaar, 2001). One means of obtaining this extra portion of luck or restoring the natural order is through the use of strong muti. It is with this strong muti that muti murders are often associated. Muti made from human body parts is considered to be exceptionally powerful. The witch will determine which specific body parts are necessary, as guided by the client's aims.

It should, however, not be assumed that in modern times such practices are sanctioned by the larger community or by most traditional healers. The majority of Africans and traditional healers do not condone such behavior and associate it with charlatans and "evil" traditional healers—or, as they call them, "witches." It is not uncommon for community members to seek out witches, usually after a calamity has befallen an individual (such as ill health, accident, or death) or community, and kill the person whom they suspect to be a witch. This practice led to legislation in 1957 and further amendments in 1970 known as the Witchcraft Suppression Act, which made it a crime to accuse anyone of being a witch. This piece of early legislation has come under fire as being Eurocentric and lacking in appreciation of the role that traditional beliefs play in society. As Petrus (2007) states, "What may be considered a ritual crime in one context may be viewed as an acceptable expression of belief in another" (p. 123).

EPIDEMIOLOGY

Currently, crime statistics in South Africa only record muti murder within the general crime category of murder. It is therefore difficult to determine the extent of such crimes. It has been estimated as occurring between 15 and 300 times each year (Jonker, personal communication, 2002). Times of political unrest, periods of competition for resources, and conditions of a power vacuum have all been associated with increased incidence of muti murder, and the general use of witchcraft (Geshiere, 2000). The Limpopo Province and KwaZulu-Natal Province tend to have a high incidence of muti-related crime, although instances of muti murder have occurred all over South Africa in rural areas and in urban areas such as Soweto, near Johannesburg.

Estimates of these murders are complicated by a number of factors. The murders often occur in rural areas and may go unreported to the police. Also, with the high temperatures in South Africa, bodies rapidly decompose, making it difficult to determine precisely what injuries to the body were inflicted. Furthermore, animal predatory activity leads to the damaging or complete destruction of wound sites, thereby making it difficult to determine the original cause of the wound. The timing of a wound is also important. Muti mutilation is typically premortem; therefore, the wound site shows an indication of a vital reaction and bleeding. While it is often possible to see if there was a vital reaction by looking at the wound at the crime scene, the forensic pathologist's report should clarify any uncertainty.

Police may also not recognize the bodily injuries to be muti in origin and may assume them to be the actions of a "crazed" killer. Serial murder victims sometimes have mutilated bodies or removed body parts. For example, serial murderer Stewart Wilken in South Africa cut off the nipples and external genitals of one of his black victims. Samuel Jacques Coetzee removed the penis and scrotum of one his black male victims, and the Cape Town Serial Killer disemboweled one of his female victims. Additionally, sadistic murderers may inflict seemingly comparable wounds to their victims premortem.

Some members of law enforcement may adhere to more traditional belief systems and thus be unwilling to define a murder as being a muti murder for fear of retribution from the witch involved. Also, because certain high-ranking politicians, business people, and other civil servants have allegedly participated in such dealings, some members of the police may be cautious about their involvement in such cases. Consequently, media, community, and politics all play a part in the investigation of these cases.

Cases of grave robbing and thefts from mortuaries have occurred in order to obtain body parts. Other authors (Chavunduka, 2001; Minaar, 2001; Schapera, 1952) report similar incidents.

THE OFFENDERS

In muti murders, there are typically three parties involved in perpetrating the crime: the client, the witch, and the murderer(s).

The Client

The client who approaches the witch is usually someone who wants to achieve a measure of personal gain. Motives may include financial gain for a businessperson, fertility assistance for someone trying to conceive, power for a politician, or protection for a criminal. There are numerous instances in which cash-in-transit vehicle robberies were foiled and the suspects apprehended all had muti on their persons. They had first consulted with a witch regarding their criminal intention, and the witch had provided them with muti for purposes such as making them bullet-proof or invisible to prevent arrest by the police. Other investigators of similar crimes have reported similar findings. At this point, however, it is not clear if the muti used by criminals, such as cash-in-transit robbers, has human body parts as an ingredient. Clients may be either male of female.

Large sums of money are involved for muti involving human body parts. Prices for body parts can vary depending on the body part and on the witch. The client is typically not involved in the murder and would only approach the witch to explain his or her need, provide the money, and collect the muti once prepared. It would not usually be the client who suggests the use of human body parts, as is discussed in the next section; the witch decides what ingredients would be necessary to meet the client's needs. This makes it difficult to convict the client in instances of muti murder, as it is difficult to prove that the client knowingly paid for muti that would eventually require the murder of an individual.

The Witch

These traditional healers are not included among mainstream traditional healers, and such practices are rejected by other healers. While they are trained as traditional healers, they have chosen a path that involves harming others and are therefore referred to as "witches" by traditional healers. These witches may be of either sex.

Once approached by the client, the witch decides whether the request from the client will require herbs and roots, animal body parts, or human body parts. If the muti that the witch wishes to prepare requires a human body part, the witch will then instruct a third person, the murderer(s), to collect the specific body parts and describe how to carry out the removal of those body parts. The witch is not typically involved in the removal of the body parts. Once the body parts are obtained, they are often mixed with herbs, roots, and even animal parts to make the final muti.

Depending on the client's need, he or she will be instructed on how to use the muti. Businesspersons may be instructed to bury a hand under or near the front door of their business, as a hand is symbolically what attracts customers and takes their money, or they may be instructed to smear a small amount of the muti on the products they sell. Criminals might be instructed to smear some of the muti on their weapon or bullets, or to bath themselves in a certain concoction to aid in their criminal endeavours (e.g., to make them bullet-proof or invisible). The body parts are usually obtained on request when there is a need and are not "stockpiled" for future use.

The Murderer

The murderer is approached, usually by the witch, to obtain the body parts. The author has only encountered one instance in which a suspect acted on his own initiative to obtain a human head and then seek a buyer. This led to an informer contacting the police. With the aid of a local traditional healer, the police set up a trap, pretending to be interested in purchasing the head, and subsequently arrested the suspect.

The murderer is carefully instructed in how to remove the body parts and told that the victim must be alive when they are removed. The murderer will then take the body parts directly to the witch. This is the only apparent role the murderer has. The murderer must also make sure that the victim possesses the qualities that the client needs and may therefore know the victim to a greater or lesser degree. For example, if the client's need is to be luckier at gambling, then the murderer might be instructed to seek out a victim who is known to be a "lucky" person. It is even rumoured that the murderer may select victims from within his or her own family.

There are two general categories of individuals who commit the actual murder. It may be a person who seeks the financial reward offered for the body parts (Minaar, 2001). It is the author's experience that the murderer can also be a trainee of the witch making the muti.

The weapons used tend to be everyday items such as pocketknives, sharp kitchen knives, or even in one instance a sharpened putty spatula used for tiling and inserting panes of glass.

Although the three perpetrator roles are usually taken by different people, two cases are known in which an individual decided on his own to use muti made of human body parts (witch role), harvest the parts (murderer role), and use the body parts (client role). In both cases, the offender was diagnosed as psychotic (i.e., experiencing hallucinations and delusions). These cases suggest that, as in other areas of psychosis, individuals can absorb beliefs from their culture and internalize them. There is thus a question in these two cases of whether they should really be considered muti murders or an aspect of psychosis.

THE VICTIMS

The victims tend to be selected because they satisfy the criteria required for the necessary body parts (Nel et al., 1992). Victims tend to be healthy (Minaar et al., 1991) and of either sex. The victim (Scholtz et al., 1997) may be known to the murderer, perhaps as a friend or relative. The author has encountered a case in which a father, who was a self-styled traditional healer, used his infant son for muti purposes. Victims tend to be strangers in the majority of muti murders. Victims can range in age from a newborn infant to an adult.

It is not completely clear why one person is chosen as a victim instead of another, but some determining factors are obvious. If the muti requires a penis, for example, then the victim would have to be male. The elderly are perhaps the only age group not targeted in muti murder, presumably because any muti made from an older person would be considered weak and ineffective or because the elderly, by virtue of their advanced age, are closer to the ancestors, and using a body part from such a person would offend the ancestors.

Almost all victims are black, with the author having experienced very few muti murders involving victims who are white or of other ethnicities. One such case involved the desecration of a deceased white person's grave to obtain his skull, which was then buried in a small altar outside the witch's house. In another case, a mortuary worker removed the breast and hand of a deceased white female from the mortuary where he worked. In another case, as reported by Steyn (2005), an adult white male was hijacked, and his body parts were removed while he was alive for muti purposes.

BODY PARTS AND THEIR USES

Experience and literature indicate that typically the genitalia and certain other body parts are removed, but any body part can potentially be used, depending on the muti required. The stomach may be slit open from the sternum down to the hip region, and it is not uncommon for the head to be removed. The author has been involved in at least 10 instances in which the head was removed from a muti victim. As mentioned, for the muti to be effective, the body parts must be removed while the victim is still alive (Nel et al., 1992; Scholtz et al., 1997). However, the author has experienced a number of cases in which body parts were removed from mortuaries or graves for muti purposes. Scholtz et al. (1997) state that the body parts may be wrapped in specifically colored material, with red and white being associated with "good" medicine, and blue and black being associated with "evil" medicine. This, however, has not been experienced by the author, who has more typically encountered body parts inside plastic bags, newspaper, or even an old coffee tin.

The body is usually not buried and is often left near running water. Nel et al. (1992) state that the body is characteristically not hidden or buried because the discovery of the body contributes to the efficacy of the medicine. In a few reported incidents, the victims of such muti-motivated attacks survived after certain body parts, such as breasts or the scrotum, were removed. This finding highlights the difference between muti attacks and ritual/sacrificial murders. The goal of the ritual/sacrificial murder is the death of the individual; in muti attacks, the goal is to obtain body parts.

It must be pointed out that people who commit muti murders, or the witches who advocate such murders, do not all work from the same "textbook." These beliefs are passed down from one generation to another by word of mouth and in secrecy. Therefore, the finer details, such as the basis for determining which body parts are used for what purposes and the process involved in the removal of the body parts, may differ from witch to witch and region to region. No hard and fast assumptions can be made about which missing body parts will be significant in any given murder. It has, however, been said that for every human body part there is an animal equivalent and that true traditional healers would use the animal equivalent; only witches would use the human body part. Because human body parts are believed to have more power than the animal equivalent, they speed up the process or help ensure that the user of the muti achieves his or her aims.

The following is a description of some of the typical body parts used:

- *Hand:* Used by business owners to improve their business
- *Genitalia:* Used for people with fertility problems
- *Lips or tongue:* Used to silence a critic or witness in a court case
- *Brains:* Used to improve intelligence
- *Body fat:* Used as a common ingredient
- *Skull:* Buried on another person's property to bring the person misfortune; or buried in the foundations of a new building to ensure good business
- *Eyes:* Used to symbolize vision
- *Blood:* Used to give vitality, protection, and longevity

Again, keep in mind that such skills and knowledge are passed down by word of mouth, and the purposes of a body part may vary from witch to witch.

CASE STUDY 1: MISTAKEN MUTI MURDER?

In September 2001, the torso of a young boy was discovered floating in the Thames River near Tower Bridge in London. The boy, who was black and approximately 5 years old, was christened "Adam" by the London Metropolitan Police. His head and neck had been removed along with both his arms and legs. He had died from massive blood loss. The skin and underlying tissue had been carefully cut with a sharp instrument, and both his femur and humerus bones had been bisected with an instrument similar to a cleaver or machete. Approximately 24 hours after death, a pair of bright orange shorts had been placed on him, and approximately 24 hours later, his body was placed in the river. His arms, legs, and head were never discovered.

No one reported a child of that age missing, and no one has come forward with information as to his identity. Nelson Mandela was even approached to use his status as a public figure to advertise the appeal for information to assist with the investigation. Candles and a white sheet with an African name on it were also found nearby, and this aroused initial fears that Adam had been the victim of an African ritual. Police later showed that these items were not connected to Adam's case (O'Reilly, personal communication, 2002).

Forensic tests revealed that Adam's stomach contents indicated meals similar to those prepared in Western Africa, and the pollen spores on the food were also indicative of a West African origin. Tests revealed that Adam had been given a cough syrup approximately 24 hours prior to his death and that he appeared to have been in good health prior to his attack.

Initially, muti murder was suspected. Detectives from the London Metropolitan Police Service contacted the Investigative Psychology Unit of the South African Police Service for assistance. This unit assists in the investigation of crimes such as serial murder, serial rape, muti murder, and murders with bizarre circumstances. The Investigative Psychology Unit provided the investigation team with information from their own experience with muti murders and also consulted a traditional healer, Credo Mutwa, for further advice on the nature of the murder. The information was passed on to the London Metropolitan investigation team. The Investigative Psychology Unit believed Adam was not the victim of a muti murder as defined by the author. The reasons for this were as follows:

1. It is not common for all limbs to be removed in muti murder. It may occur that a hand or forearm is removed.

2. Usually the genitals of the victim are removed. Adam's genitals were intact.

3. Usually the stomach is opened and certain organs removed. Adam's stomach was intact.

4. Adam died of massive blood loss from a cut to the throat prior to decapitation and dismemberment. This is more indicative of a sacrificial murder.

Further information from the traditional healer indicated that the orange shorts were meaningful in that the color indicates resurrection. The intention of putting them on Adam was to allow his soul to be resurrected. Also, dressing the victim can indicate a sense of respect for the body. The traditional healer suggested that based on the information available, the circumstances appeared to be similar to a ritual practiced in Western Africa called "Obeh" (Mutwa, personal communication, 2002). It should also be pointed out that Adam might have died as a result of a sacrifice or ritual, yet the dismemberment and decapitation might still have been of the type intended to delay identification or to help with disposal of his body.

CASE STUDY 2: PROTOTYPICAL MUTI MURDER

On Sunday, May 30, 1999, 11-year-old Tsepo Molemohi left his mother's house at approximately 1:00 PM to play soccer nearby. By 6:00 PM, he had not returned and his mother sent neighborhood boys to try to locate him. Shortly thereafter, it was reported that the body of a small boy was found in a nearby field. The body was identified to be that of Tsepo.

Tsepo had been decapitated and his scrotum and penis had been removed with a sharp implement. He was fully clothed, with only the area around his genitals exposed. The following day his head was found in a plastic bag on the roof of a building at a nearby tennis court. Within 4 days, a suspect had been arrested. Seventeen-year-old Jimmy Bongani Mokolobate was seen walking with a bloody knife and with blood on his clothing on the day in question. He admitted to police that he had killed the young boy.

Jimmy's account of events in a confession before a magistrate indicated that 2 days prior to the murder he had been approached by two sangomas, one male and one female, who had offered him money to obtain a male head, tongue, eyes, and genitals. His first attempt to find a suitable victim was unsuccessful on the Saturday. On Sunday he found Tsepo and proceeded to decapitate him and remove his genitals. He took the genitals with him but placed the head on a roof to be collected the next day. He used an okapi knife, which is a simple folding pocketknife, with a blade about 13 cm long and a wooden handle. On Monday, he took the genitals to the sangomas after hearing that the head had been discovered. The sangomas were disappointed that he had failed to bring the other parts and asked if he would be able to try again to obtain those parts from another victim. Jimmy claims that at the time of the murder he had been smoking a mixture of marijuana and crushed methaqualone tablets, a practice that appears to be unique to South Africa. Jimmy was found fit to stand trial and was subsequently found guilty. The two sangomas were also charged but later had the charges withdrawn when Jimmy refused to testify against the sangomas for fear of retribution. The scrotum and penis he handed over to the sangomas were never found.

This case has many of the common characteristics found in a muti murder. The offender was not the traditional healer but had been approached to obtain the body parts for a fee. The traditional healers had specified which body parts were to be obtained (head, tongue, eyes, and genitals) and the type of victim (male). The victim was a stranger to the offender. The victim was left clothed, with only the genitals exposed, and there was no evidence of sexual activity or rape. The victim's body was not hidden but left where the murder took place. There were also few wounds. The victim had been stabbed in the neck three times, and the head and the genitals were removed. There was no fantasy expressed by the offender concerning the murder. Finally, the body parts were found neither in the offender's possession, nor where he lived with his parents. Those that were found (the head) were discovered at the nearby tennis court, and those that were not found by the police were handed over to the two sangomas, according to the offender's confession.

CASE STUDY 3: MUTI MURDER OF A FAMILY MEMBER

On August 13, 2009, police were called to a murder scene in the Winterveld area near the capital city of Pretoria, South Africa. The body of a 12-year-old girl had been found in the yard of her home. The body was completely naked, and the victim had a long incised wound from her sternum down to the pubic region. She was lying on her stomach, and some of her intestines were protruding.

Her body had been discovered by her mother, a sangoma, who had reportedly gone looking for her daughter in the backyard in the morning after realizing she was not in the house.

Police at the scene searched the house and the yard for evidence. Outside in an empty oil drum, an old blanket was found with possible human blood on it. Three more items that possibly contained blood were found inside the mother's traditional healer practice. All four items were sent for forensic analysis. Once police had finished processing the crime scene, detectives decided to bring the mother in for questioning at the local police station due to their suspicion that she, despite being the mother, could be the suspect.

Shortly after beginning questioning, the mother confessed. She said that since she had qualified as a traditional healer the year before, her practice had not been financially successful. She decided to murder her daughter for body parts to make her practice flourish. In the early hours of the morning, she had carried her daughter from her bed, taken her outside to the same location where the body was found, and stabbed her in the chest and neck. She then made the long incision with the intention of removing the necessary body parts, such as the gallbladder. However, she became confused as to which body parts to take and ultimately did not remove anything. She also stated that she washed the body. The mother confirmed that the exhibits seized by the police were involved in the crime. She made a written confession before an independent officer of the South African Police Service who was not involved in the investigation. She also made a formal pointing-out of the crime scene. A "pointing-out" is a formal police procedure in which the offender agrees to point out any desired locations to an independent member of the police who is a commissioned officer and who was not involved in the investigation. All locations indicated by the offender are photographed, and what is said during this procedure is also written down and regarded as a formal confession. During the pointing-out, she identified the weapon used, a kitchen knife, and another exhibit used during the commission of the crime that the police had not discovered during their initial processing of the crime scene.

This case illustrates that muti victims can include the very young and even be family members of the offender. Also consistent with other muti cases was that the body was left where the murder took place and not hidden, and the offender used water to wash the body afterward. What was different from most instances was that the actual murderer was the traditional healer, as opposed to another person. Most likely, the reason for this was that the offender's business was flagging, and she therefore could not afford to pay someone to commit the crime. Furthermore, the muti was intended for herself as opposed to a paying client, and she was too newly qualified to have her own apprentice. Another difference was that the body was found completely naked, most likely due to the fact that the incised wound began at the sternum and ended just above the vaginal area, requiring the offender to remove all the clothing. The success of the investigation was undoubtedly aided by the specialized detectives and crime scene investigators, with knowledge of muti murder cases, who were called to the crime scene to assist the local detective branch.

WHAT CRIMES CAN THE OFFENDERS BE CHARGED WITH?

There are various crimes with which a person involved in such a scenario can be charged. Murder is defined in the common law of South Africa as the unlawful and intentional causing of the death of another human being. Therefore the person(s) who actually physically commits the act of murder, as well as the person who instigates or initiates the murder (the witch), would be charged with murder. If the client knows that the money he or she is paying for the muti will go toward the murder of another person, then he or she will also most likely be charged with murder.

Other crimes include transgressions under the Human Tissue Act 65 of 1983. This act, which is soon to be replaced by Chapter 8 of the National Health Act 61 of 2003, states the following at section 34 under the heading *Offenses and Penalties*:

> *Any person who (a) except in so far as it may be permitted by or under any other law, acquires, uses or supplies a body of a deceased person or any tissue, blood or gamete of a living or deceased person in any other manner or for any other purpose than that permitted by this Act . . . shall be guilty of an offense and liable on conviction to a fine not exceeding R2 000 or to imprisonment for a period not exceeding one year or to both that fine and that imprisonment.*

The National Health Act at Chapter 8 at 60(4)(b) states that it is an offense "to sell or trade in tissue, gametes, blood or blood products, except as provided for in this Chapter."

However, unlike the Human Tissue Act, the National Health Act only refers to *selling* or *trading* and not *acquiring* or *using*. It is therefore unclear how the crime of being found in possession of human body parts would be treated by the law. The punishment prescribed for selling or trading is a fine or imprisonment for a period not exceeding 5 years or both a fine and such imprisonment.

CONCLUSION

The use of muti is a part of some mainstream traditional African beliefs. In many respects, traditional African muti is no different from herbal or naturopathic remedies used by people throughout the world. The use of human body parts as an ingredient for medicines or potions, however, is practiced by a minority of individuals and is rejected by the majority of traditional healers and members of society.

Bodily mutilation can occur for various reasons other than the desire to obtain human body parts for use in traditional African medicines. Determining the reason for the mutilation is an important step when analyzing the crime scene. An experienced forensic pathologist is instrumental in helping determine the process by which the mutilation occurred. This report can then help to generate hypotheses regarding the motive and ultimately the suspect. The designation of a crime as a muti murder will have a significant impact on how the investigator will approach the investigation.

While not a new phenomenon, little empirical research has investigated this type of crime. Suspending one's own belief system and attempting to understand another is imperative for any person trying to solve such crimes. This is often the most difficult hurdle to overcome.

CHAPTER 9

Criminal Profiling

Gerard Labuschagne and Kevin Borgeson

O riginally, the term offender profiling involved solely the process of predicting offender characteristics based on crime scene information (Beauregard, 2010; Labuschagne, 2003). However, over recent years the term has expanded to include a wide range of services that behavioral science advisers, such as psychologists, psychiatrists, and criminologists offer to investigations. Thus, what was originally a specific activity (developing an offender profile of an unknown offender) became a term applied to a whole field. This broad definition has led to much confusion in the profession. As will be discussed, Canter prefers to term the field "investigative psychology," under which the activity of offender profiling is but one service provided. Similarly, Almond, Alison, and Porter (2007) refer to "behavioral investigative advisors," who provide services that include offender profiling, risk assessments, DNA-intelligence–led screening, linkage analysis, and geographic analysis. These approaches are supported by the authors here.

This chapter will examine the history and different types of criminal profiling and will offer a snapshot of the profiling unit for the South African Police Service. A history of profiling is needed because it establishes that profiling is not a new tool for criminal justice agencies but one that has been used over a period of time under various circumstances. An emphasis on the different types of profiling is warranted so the public has an understanding that there are several types of profiling, which are more complex than the glorified renditions of this tool that are shown in television and movies. Lastly, a look at the Investigative Psychology Unit of the Criminal Records and Forensic Science Division of the South African Police Service will allow the reader to see two important things: how a profiling unit is set up and the cross-cultural analysis of how profiling is used (see Chapter 10 on case linkage for a more in-depth discussion of profiling tools).

HISTORY

Over the last 2 decades, criminal profiling has become a tool used by many law enforcement agencies in investigating cold cases and cases involving unknown offenders. During this time, different terms have been used to describe profiling: offender profiling, behavioral profiling, psychological profiling, criminal profiling, and crime scene profiling. Although these terms are not synonymous and have different stages and processes, one thing they do have in common is that they all deduce characteristics of the offender from the evidence this individual leaves behind.

The use of profiling in the social sciences can be traced back to the 1870s with the work of Cesare Lombroso (Keppel, 2006). According to Keppel, Lombroso believed that different criminals had certain atavistic characteristics, and based on these characteristics, each type of offender would have various physical and psychological differences that made up his or her unique profile (p. 7). Keppel states, "In 1872, Lombroso created a typology of criminals that included four classes: born criminals, criminals by passion, insane criminals, and occasional criminals, and identified eighteen characteristics that indicated a born criminal" (p. 7). Lombroso believed that physical characteristics would differentiate criminal types. One of the classifications he developed was on murderers. Lombroso, as stated by Keppel (pp. 7–8), believed the profile of a murderer consisted of:

- An aquiline beak of a nose
- Fleshy, swollen, and protruding lips
- Small, receding chin

- Dark hair and bushy eyebrows that meet across the nose
- Little or no beard
- An abundance of wrinkles, even in those younger than 30 years of age
- Four to five times greater taste sensibility than the average person
- A cynical attitude, completely lacking remorse
- Most likely to bare a tattoo
- Attaches no importance to dress and is frequently dirty and shabby

Lombroso was not the only social scientist who attempted to link physical characteristics to crime types. According to Sheldon (as cited in Vold, 1981), there were three distinct body types—endomorph, mesomorph, and ectomorph—and each was associated with personality characteristics that could tell investigators something about an individual's possible involvement in criminal activity.

The endomorph was a person whose body was soft and round, and whose muscles were not fully developed. This person, whose personality Sheldon referred to as viscerotonic, was tolerant, not emotional, and social (Vold, 1981, p. 66).

The mesomorph, by contrast, had a hard muscular body. This individual, whose personality Sheldon referred to as somotonic, was courageous, assertive, and aggressive (Vold, 1981, p. 67).

The ectomorph was thin, tall, fragile, and young in appearance. This individual, whose personality Sheldon referred to as cerebrotonic, was introverted and sensitive to noise (Vold, 1981, p. 67).

According to Sheldon, the mesomorph possessed the characteristics most associated with committing crimes because this body type had desire and power and was always looking for adventures. This, however, did not mean that others could not commit crimes. What was important about Sheldon's research was that he believed physical characteristics would reveal something about a person's future criminal activities. Although this type of criminology had its followers, it soon fell out of favor with social scientists and was discredited by those who were trying to advance the field of criminology. Although we disregard this theory today as invalid, it was the beginning of an era in which social scientists believed that a positivistic methodology could be used to determine social behavior.

JACK THE RIPPER

In the late 1800s, one of the earliest criminal profiles was constructed on the Jack the Ripper murders (Canter, 2004a). Dr. Thomas Bond was hired to compile a report on the types of person who would commit the murders of prostitutes that were taking place in London. According to Keppel (2006, pp. 10–11), Bond was able to make the following statements about the crime scene and victims:

- All five murders were most likely committed by the same person.
- Victims were lying down when murdered.
- The time of death could not be easily determined.
- No evidence of struggling was present.
- The direction the attacker approached the victims was evident.
- The attacker's hands and clothing would be covered in blood.
- Mutilation was a part of all the crimes.
- The person committing the crime had no medical or surgical knowledge.
- The instrument used in the crimes was a knife.

It is interesting to note that this profile introduced the concept of case linkage based on crime scene behavior.

Bond also came up with physical and psychological characteristics of the killer (Innes, 2003, p. 22):

- Middle aged
- Well groomed
- Wore coat to hide possible blood on hands
- Unemployed
- Loner
- Eccentric habits
- Might have some occupational experience in cutting meat

Even with Bond's assistance, the murderer was never apprehended and murders continued throughout London for several years. To this day, the debate has gone on about who the real Ripper was, and profiles have been done to determine who the perpetrator may be.

THE LINDBERGH KIDNAPPING

One of the most high-profile crimes of the 20th century was the kidnapping of national hero Charles A. Lindbergh's son Charles A. Lindbergh, Jr., on the night of March 1, 1932. An unknown offender(s) took Charles Lindbergh, Jr., from his nursery and left a note demanding Lindbergh pay a $50,000 ransom or he and his family would never see the baby again. The ransom was paid, but the Lindbergh's never received their son back. It was not until May 12, 1932, that Charles Lindbergh, Jr., was found in an unmarked grave a mile from the Lindbergh home.

Due to the seriousness of the crime, and a lack of leads in finding the kidnapper, New York City psychiatrist Dudley Shoenfeld (1936, pp. 29–36) was asked to look at all the evidence—including the numerous ransom notes—and come up with a profile of the assailant. According to Schoenfeld, the perpetrator:

- Was in his 40s
- Had German ancestry
- Lived nearby
- Had been hospitalized for mental illnesses
- Was confident
- Was skilled
- Would be spending the ransom in proximity to his residence
- Would be defiant about his involvement when caught

The case went unsolved for more than 2 years. Finally, a lead came in regarding a person who was using treasury bills used in the ransom. That person, Bruno Hauptmann, was a German carpenter who was living in New York. The profile drawn up by Shoenfeld was very consistent with Hauptmann's characteristics. For example, Hauptmann:

- Was in his 30s
- Was German
- Had little education
- Was skilled in carpentry
- Had been diagnosed with what is now called schizophrenia
- Spent money in the area near his residency
- Denied any involvement in the crime

The focus on proximity, which is used today by those in the field of investigative psychology, was one of the most important aspects of the profile. Schoenfeld drew a triangle around the area of the crime and stated that the perpetrator would live within the area of the triangle, which turned out to be where Hauptmann lived. Although the Lindbergh baby kidnapping is still seen as controversial (some believe Haupman was innocent), it was one of the first modern profiles to be done in which an attempt was made to understand the makeup of an unknown offender, and also included an element of what we now refer to as a geographic profile.

ADOLPH HITLER

During World War II, the Office of Strategic Services in Washington, D.C., asked Walter Langer to construct a psychological analysis of Adolph Hitler. The aim was to develop a better understanding of Hitler's way of thinking and his future actions depending on the outcome of the war. The report on Hitler was to be divided into four main parts:

- Hitler as he believes himself to be
- Hitler as the German people know him
- Hitler as his associates know him
- Hitler as he knows himself

Part of the report was a psychological analysis of Hitler to assess the effect his mental condition would have on the German people and the possibility of winning the war. The profile predicted the possibility of the following outcomes (Langer, n.d., pp. 243–249):

- *Hitler may die of natural causes.* This prediction was seen as unlikely but important to consider due to the psychological importance Hitler had on the German people. If they believed he was dying or that his mental capacity was diminishing, doubt could rise over his actions.
- *Hitler might seek refuge in a neutral country.* This action was also seen as improbable but needed to be considered because Hitler had "escaped from other unpleasant situations" in his past.
- *Hitler might get killed in battle.* This action was seen as a "real possibility. If he is convinced that he cannot win, he may lead his troops into battle and expose himself as fearless."
- *Hitler might be assassinated.* This situation was seen as highly probable because Hitler developed an extreme paranoia over someone wanting to kill him. Due to the paranoia, Hitler always had someone around to make sure no one would be able to carry out such an act.
- *Hitler might go insane.* This was also seen as highly probable. Langer believed that Hitler had what we would today consider schizophrenia.
- *The German military might revolt and seize him.* This was seen as unlikely because Hitler held a Godlike status with most of the German people and was seen by some as immortal.
- *Hitler may fall into the hands of Allied forces.* The report suggests that this was the most unlikely scenario of all. Because Hitler believed he was a divine leader among the German people, he would do everything in his power to prevent this from happening.

- *Hitler might commit suicide.* According to Langer, this was the most likely out-come of Hitler's future behavior. Langer believed that Hitler would commit suicide in a dramatic effect due to being a "hysteric." Langer also believed that Hitler may not be able to commit the act himself and may engage someone else to commit the act in a dramatic fashion.

In the end, Langer's assessment of Hitler was true. When forces closed in on him while he was hiding in his bunker, he took his own life so no one else would be able to claim they had gotten the upper hand on him.

THE MAD BOMBER

Probably the most written-about profile has been that of the Mad Bomber of New York. The bombings first started on November 16, 1940. A crude bomb was placed in a wooden toolbox in the Con Edison building in New York City. The bomb never went off because the bomber never wound the clock that served as the detonation de-vice. Roughly a year later, a second bomb was found (which also never went off) near the site of the first attempted bombing. Although the crime was serious, investigators did not feel the two crimes were related and investigated them as separate incidents. A few months after the second event, the bomber, most likely feeling slighted from the lack of coverage of his crimes due to the ongoing war, left a note telling the public of his future endeavors.

Over time, several letters were sent to Con Edison warning them of impending doom. As time went on, the bomber became bolder with his actions and began to mail more letters to various agencies and people. Frustrated by the lack of leads, the police asked a psychiatrist, James Brussel, to construct a profile on the person who would commit such a crime (Madden, n.d.).

According to Madden, Brussel's profile consisted of the following characteristics:

- Male
- Paranoid
- Neither thin nor fat
- Foreign born
- Unmarried and a loner
- Slavic
- Living in Connecticut
- When found, will be wearing a double-breasted suit

After much investigation, the police eventually arrested a man named George Metesky for the crimes. Upon his arrest, Metesky was found to have some of the characteristics predicted by Brussel's profile:

- Male
- Paranoid
- Neither fat nor slim
- Slavic
- Unmarried and living with his sisters

The profiles on Jack the Ripper, the Lindberg kidnapper, and the Mad Bomber were rudimentary in their construction because they lacked a solid base in methodology and social science theory. It was not until the early 1980s that profilers began to adopt a methodology of inductive or deductive analysis to apply to their field of profiling and began to use psychology, sociology, geography, and forensics to assist in developing a better tool assisting investigations.

INDUCTIVE/DEDUCTIVE ANALYSIS

Most types of profiling have at their premise an inductive or deductive approach. According to Holmes and Holmes (2002), an inductive criminal profile "rests on the assumption that if certain crimes committed by different offenders are similar, then the offenders must also share some common personality traits" (p. 5). Such a profile is strongly based on previous quantitative research on similar offenders. These characteristics are then generalized to one suspect. For example, in profiling a pedophile, the type of logic would be represented in the following statement: "A study of 100 incarcerated pedophiles found that the average age when apprehended is 24 years, the average type of occupation is white collar, and 80% are married with children. Therefore, the suspect in this case must be approximately 24 years old, is probably a white collar worker, and is most likely married."

Computer databases have proven to be a valuable source of information for investigators. Such databases would often be referred to when compiling an inductive profile. In a further attempt to consolidate information to assist in creating links between crimes, the National Center for the Analysis of Violent Crime (NCAVC) in the United States became operational in 1984, designed to be a "clearing house" of information regarding violent crimes. It is a law enforcement–oriented behavioral science and computerized resource center that consolidates research, training, and operational support functions.

The NCAVC consists of four programs: Research and Development, Training, Profiling and Consultation, and the Violent Criminal Apprehension Program (VICAP). The Profiling and Consultation program conducts analyzes of violent crimes on a case-by-case basis in order to construct profiles of unknown offenders so the focus of the investigation can be narrowed to concentrate more readily on the most likely suspects. Consultation also includes planning case strategies, furnishing information for search warrant preparation, conducting personality assessments, defining interview techniques, and coaching prosecutors of violent criminals (Brooks, Devine, Green, Hart, & Moore, 1987). Other computer databases include the Homicide Investigation Tracking System (HITS) in Washington State, the Homicide Assessment and Lead Tracking (HALT) in New York, and the Violent Crime Linkage Analysis System (ViCLAS) in Canada (Hickey, 2002).

According to Holmes and Holmes (2002), the advantages of an inductive approach to profiling are that it is quick and inexpensive and the profiler need not "special skill or knowledge of human behavior" (p. 5). Furthermore, such profiles can be compiled in a relatively short time. The disadvantage to such an analysis is that it can become too general, making the profile applicable to so many people that it becomes useless.

Holmes and Holmes (2002) go on to state deductive profiling, is "a thorough analysis of the crime scene and the evidence left at the scene, [allowing] the profiler . . . to construct a mental picture of the unknown offender (p. 5). Such profiling is also more useful for developing a thorough victimology of the offender and considering whether the case could be linked to other cases.

Holmes and Holmes (2002, pp. 6–7) believe that this type of profiling is slow and cumbersome due to the "examination of forensic reports and victimology" that must be conducted to complete the profile. This type of profiling does not work well on cases in which evidence is destroyed at the scene. The perfect type of profiling would include the use of both inductive and deductive analysis to construct a profile. Holmes and Holmes point out: "One may be quicker to develop where the other takes more time but can more thoroughly evaluate the unknown offender, thereby differentiating him or her from the other offenders who have committed similar crimes" (pp. 6–7).

Some authors, such as Almond, Alison, and Porter (2007), have suggested a "Toulminian" approach to the evaluation process involved in offender profiling (see Toulmin, 1958). This approach involves six interrelated components:

1. *The claim*—for example, "the suspect is under the age of 30 years"
2. *The strength*, which reflects the extent to which the investigators must rely on the claim—for example, "87% likelihood"
3. *The grounds*, which are the support for the claim—for example, "Because this is a murder of a 25-year-old woman"

4. *The warrant*, which is the reason the profiler has made a specific claim—for example, "The majority of offenders who murder women younger than 25 years old are themselves younger than 30 years old."

5. *The backing*, which is the formal support for the warrant—for example, "Research by X (date)"

6. *The rebuttal*, which is a condition under which the assumption may need to be adjusted

By following this process, these researchers believe that the offender-profiling process can overcome many of the current criticisms against it.

TYPES OF PROFILING

Crime Scene Analysis

The best-known method of profiling is crime scene analysis. The FBI invented this type of profiling in the late 1970s, but it was not until the early 1980s that it began to catch on and agencies from all around the United States began asking for assistance from the FBI to help apprehend serial offenders. In the 1980s, the Behavioral Science Unit was interested in creating a tool that could be used at crime scenes to determine offender characteristics, which in the end would help the agency create a pool of suspects. The result of that eff ort was the organized/disorganized dichotomy that is still in use today. An organized offender is an offender who is psychopathic in nature and is meticulous about committing his or her crime. The disorganized offender is also psychotic but is not interested in concealing evidence at the scene.

According to the Behavioral Science Unit (as cited in Holmes & Holmes, 2009, pp. 81–88), the organized crime scene would reflect the following characteristics:

- Offense is planned.
- Victim is a targeted stranger.
- Offender personalizes victim.
- Conversation is controlled.
- Crime scene reflects control.
- Offender demands submissive victim.
- Restraints are used.
- Aggressive acts are performed prior to victim's death.
- Victim's body is hidden.
- Weapon/evidence is absent.

- Offender transports victim.

In contrast, the disorganized crime scene would reflect these characteristics:

- Offense is spontaneous.
- Victim or location is known to offender.
- Offender depersonalizes victim.
- Conversation is minimal.
- Crime scene is random and sloppy.
- Sudden violence is involved.
- No restraints are used.
- Offender performs sexual acts after victim's death.
- Victim's body is not moved.
- Weapon is left.
- Physical evidence is found.

Based on the evidence left, or taken, from the crime scene, the Behavioral Science Unit's study (as cited in Holmes & Holmes, 2009, pp. 81–84) stated that characteristics of the offender could be predicted. Given an organized crime scene, the offender would most likely have some of the following characteristics:

- Average to above average intelligence
- Socially competent
- Skilled work preference
- High birth order status
- Father's work stable
- Inconsistent childhood discipline
- Controlled mood during crime
- Use of alcohol with crime
- Precipitating situational stress
- Lives with partner
- Mobility with car in good condition
- Follows crime in the news media
- May change job or leave town

Given a disorganized crime scene, the offender would have these characteristics:

- Below average intelligence
- Socially inadequate
- Unskilled work

- Sexually incompetent
- Low birth order
- Father's work unstable
- Harsh discipline as a child
- Anxious mood during crime
- Minimal use of alcohol
- Minimal situational stress
- Lives alone
- Lives/works near crime scene
- Minimal interest in news media
- Significant behavioral change

While this type of profiling is the most common, it has not been proven accurate statistically. Part of the problem lies in the sample technique used by the FBI to develop this typology. In the original study, the sample size was only 36 imprisoned offenders. From a social science perspective, this sample size is not significant and would be considered exploratory in its results rather than explanatory. The study has never been duplicated by the agency; because behaviors change over time, the FBI should complete another study with a larger sample and make sure the results are significant. Various academics draw attention to the misrepresentation of established psychological theory within the ideas of these FBI agents, the weaknesses of their methodologies, and the lack of empirical evidence for their assertions (Alison & Canter, 1999; Canter, 2004a; Coleman & Norris, 2000; Muller, 2000). (See the work of David Canter, who has severely criticized this approach.)

Furthermore, the FBI approach sees profiling as more of an art dependent on the individual than a science, as illustrated by the following statement:

> *Successful profilers are experienced in criminal investigations and research and possess common sense, intuition, and the ability to isolate their feelings about the crime, the criminal, and the victim. They have the ability to evaluate analytically the behaviour exhibited in a crime and to think very much like the criminal responsible. (Hazelwood, Ressler, Depue, & Douglas, 1987)*

However, it is perhaps unfair to state that the FBI's approach made no contribution to the field of profiling. They can undoubtedly be credited for placing offender profiling on the map and initiating scientific interest in the field. There have also been recent initiatives to reanalyze the data from their original study. Furthermore, their earlier training programs for U.S. and foreign law enforcement agencies have helped establish the concept of behavioral advisers throughout the world.

Geographic Profiling

From the time of the Chicago School, geography has played a role in crime investigation. Many television programs depict police officers standing around a map into which pins have been inserted to indicate areas where a series of crimes has occurred. It is only recently that a more rigid scientific approach, with the aid of computers, has been applied to understanding geography and crime (Ainsworth, 2002).

The 1990s saw the reemergence of the early works by Shaw and McKay (1942). This revival was referred to as the "New Chicago School." While adopting an ecologic approach, it also was spurned by computerized mapping and spatial analysis techniques. Geographic information systems allowed for the measurement of spatial aggregation and thereby opened up a host of possibilities with regard to the ecology of crime (Ainsworth, 2002).

Canter and Rossmo are two figures who stand out when it comes to geographic profiling. Canter (1994), for example, states that offenders rarely travel long distances to commit their crime(s) and are more likely to offend in a relatively small geographic area, based around their home address. Similarly, Rossmo (1995, 1997) suggests that examining the exact locations of a series of crimes can be helpful in identifying the most likely area in which an offender lives or works, and all represent some type of mental map to the offender (Canter, 2000). The basis of geographic profiling is the distance decay function (Palermo & Kocsis, 2005, p. 238), which suggests that patterns exist in the association of a criminal event and that the event decreases "as distance away from the activity spaces increases" (Rossmo, 2000, p. 119). While the system is based on mathematic formulas, it is useful under certain circumstances. Computer programs that were developed include RIGEL, DRAGNET, and Crimestat (Paulsen, 2006).

Earlier models for inferring the location of offenders, focusing on offenders traveling around their "anchor point" according to distance decay probabilities, can be improved by additional information about where offenders who commit crimes in a particular area tend to be based. This Bayesian approach, adding new, increasingly localized information, is seen as an improvement upon the more generalized earlier models of geographic profiling (Canter, 2009). In essence, a Bayesian approach is a process for deriving patterns in geographically specific data sets, where the earlier center-of-gravity–orientated approaches sought to establish general theories and principles independent of any given locality. Canter (2009) states that while earlier this was referred to as "geographic offender profiling," it may have been more accurate to refer to it as "geometric offender profiling" because the algorithms used took no account at all of the actual geography of the crime scene locations.

The advantage of geographic profiling is that the data required are more quantitative in nature—for example, an address of a crime scene or coordinates on a map. Other forms of profiling, such as offender profiling, are more open to qualitative interpretation. The result is that the efficacy of geographic profiling inputs is easier to determine.

According to Palermo and Kocsis (2005), geographic profiling has five main uses: suspect prioritization, patrol saturation, database trawling, peak of tension polygraphy, and bloodings.

- *Suspect prioritization* is used to predict the area in which a perpetrator resides. As Palermo and Kocsis state, "This information can be interpreted as a sorting or vetting tool to prioritize the investigation of identified suspects based on their known residence, for example, relative to the predicted area" (p. 227).
- *Patrol saturation* is when the "geographic profile is used to determine the general domain where an offender is prepared to commit offenses. This information can be used by investigators to employ saturation tactics within a given area by increasing police patrol or conducting stakeouts aimed at apprehending the offender" (p. 228).
- *Database trawling* is when "the prediction area from a geographic profile can be cross-referenced with information contained in other databases or archives to either prioritize or identify potential suspects for investigation" (p. 228).
- *Peak of tension polygraphy* is a novel way of using geographic profiling. Instead of focusing on locating offenders, or those suspected of being the offender, this approach focuses on eliciting information from offenders through polygraph testing. This is done by focussing questions "on various locations identified by a geographic profile of being of possible relevance to the offender. A suspect's polygraph responses to questions concerning these areas can be interpreted as potentially assisting an investigation by indirectly eliciting further information from the suspect which may assist police in their inquiries" (p. 228).
- *Blooding* is the use of geographic profiling to assist in the collection of DNA evidence of possible suspects in a given area. Police do this by engaging in "large scale surveys of DNA samples from individuals within a certain area in the hope of securing a match between a surveyed DNA sample and DNA found at a crime scene" (p. 228).

Canter later extended geographic profiling by coming up with two main types of offenders: the commuter and the marauder. The commuter hypothesis "describes a movement pattern where an offender travels from their base or residence to another area to commit offenses that [are] not necessarily constrained by the extent of their home range" (Palermo & Kocsis, 2005, p. 232). The marauder hypothesis "describes a movement pattern where the offender's base acts as a centralized point of orientation from which the offender moves out to commit crime and then returns" (p. 232).

One concern of such a method is that if inaccurate information is recorded or if information is missing, such as if certain crimes are not included in the series because they were not reported or if crimes not committed by the suspect are included, it can skew the geographic profile. However, this is the same criticism for any other form of profiling. Furthermore, this method has so far only been tested in Europe and the United States, not in other parts of the world. Consider, for example, the following discussion of geographic profiling in South Africa.

While the generic suggestion that offenders will offend in an area in which they feel comfortable, such as near their home or work place, has been correct for some instances of serial offenses in South Africa, there are also many examples in which this has not been the case. South Africa's socioeconomic circumstances can be one reason why geographic profiling is not as useful. A large portion of the population travels great distances to and from work and uses informal transport such as taxis. Also, due to the high rate of unemployment, people are often quite willing to go with a stranger if it may mean the promise of employment; thus, victims are easily lured to out-of-the-way areas where the crime is committed. In offender profiles compiled by the Investigative Psychology Unit of the South African Police Service, commentary is always made regarding the geography and environment of the crime scenes. While offenders often may not live near the area where they offend, serial offenders in South Africa do often like to group their crime scenes in close geographic proximity.

When these principles are communicated to investigators, it can lead to rapid success in an investigation. An example would be the so-called Sasolburg Serial Rapist in South Africa. When a previous victim spotted the suspect again in her neighbourhood with a young girl, she alerted the detectives who had been warned by the Investigative Psychology Unit that the suspect would continue to take his victims to the same deserted area. The detectives then headed straight to the rapist's "comfort zone" and arrested him walking with his next victim.

To further challenge the utility of complex geographic profiling techniques, Paulsen (2006) compared the predictions made by humans using simple heuristics to predictions made by complex algorithm-based methods such as RIGEL, DRAGNET, and Crimestat. The outcome of his study was that humans performed as well as the complex algorithm-based methods. This finding was also reflected by other researchers (e.g., Levine, 2002; Snook, Zito, Bennell, & Taylor, 2005). The question that then begs answering is whether such advanced software systems, which require extensive training, investigative experience, and experience in the use of advanced algorithms, are actually necessary?

Investigative Psychology

Investigative psychology is a relatively new field of psychology. It focuses on the contributions that psychology can make to police investigations, as opposed to the more umbrella-like term of forensic psychology, which can encompass anything from offender rehabilitation to custody evaluations to expert evidence in courtrooms. This field has its origins in environmental psychology and made significant contributions to geographic profiling. Investigative psychology has developed to further the effective use of police information, the study of police investigations, and decision support systems. In essence, it has become an umbrella term for various tools and techniques that have psychological underpinnings and support investigations.

Although this field is fairly well established in the United Kingdom, it does not seem to get as much coverage as it should in the United States. Part of the reason is that FBI profiling is so dominant in the United States. However, John Jay College of Criminal Justice at the City University of New York has employed well-known academic Professor Gabrielle Salfati who was trained by David Canter. Furthermore, with the development of the *Journal of Investigative Psychology and Offender Profiling*, the field has found a medium through which much of its ideas are communicated.

Canter developed investigative psychology in the 1980s when he was asked to assist with a serial rape case in which police had no leads. Canter, who is trained as an environmental psychologist, took on the case believing that psychological concepts from his discipline could be applied to the practice of profiling. After looking at the profiling techniques of the FBI, Canter believed that the FBI's type of profiling lacked psychological rigor and that a better method needed to be developed that would include a more thorough analysis of criminal behavior to go beyond what was considered at that time as profiling (Ainsworth, 2001).

By introducing a scientific method to the analysis of criminal behavior, and crime scene characteristics, Canter was able to merge the fields of applied psychology, criminology, and profiling, developing what he would later call investigative psychology. Canter believed investigators would be able to "establish whether the way in which an offender's behavior while committing a crime mirrored their behavior in everyday life" (Ainsworth, 2001, p. 118). He further believed that the perpetrator may select victims who are similar to others, or those who remind the perpetrator of someone who plays a significant part in his or her life.

In the United States, Canter's concepts were most notably seen in the Ted Bundy case. Bundy selected victims who fit a certain physical description. Only after his apprehension did officials learn that the victims' characteristics were similar to those of his ex-fiancé. Ainsworth (2001) points out that this finding is supported by most serial offenders who "target victims within their own ethnic group" (p. 119). It is also shown to be true in one-off violent crimes where offenders choose victims intraracially.

With environmental cues taken into account, Canter's approach has five main components: "residential location, criminal biography, domestic/social characteristics, personal characteristics, and occupational/educational history" (Ainsworth, 2001, pp. 199–120):

- *Residential location* accounts for the likelihood that an offender will commit crimes in places with which he or she is familiar. The Green River serial murderer, for example, positioned his victims' bodies on the banks of the Green River. The offender spent most of his time frequenting areas where prostitutes operated and was able to move in and out of the area without being caught due to his familiarity with the area and the people who lived there. This component has been seen most recently in a case in the United States in which an offender mutilated three prostitutes and left their bodies in construction sites. After apprehension of the offender, it was discovered that he was a construction worker who had frequented these sites and was able to move with ease in the area without anyone finding his presence suspicious.
- *Criminal biography*, according to Ainsworth (2001), is the belief that "careful study of the ways in which an individual committed a crime might prove valuable clues as to their criminal history" (p. 119). Offenders who do not have previous experience in their crime may show an unorthodox manner in how they treat the crime scene or victim. With this lack of criminal knowledge, perpetrators may leave evidence, which could lead to their apprehension.
- *Domestic/social characteristics* refer to the idea that criminals have varied social backgrounds that and these backgrounds may influence the crime they will commit. As Ainsworth (2001) explains, "For example, one rapist might appear to be sexually naïve, suggesting that he has little sexual experience and is not involved in a sexual relationship currently. By contrast, a rapist who appears to be sexually sophisticated yet demands one particular form of sexual gratification from his victim, might be more likely to be currently living with a sexual partner" (p. 119).
- *Personal characteristics*, Canter believed, are like everyday behaviors that are performed "within a familiar environment and [signify] that the way in which individuals interact with others is so well rehearsed and ingrained that it will influence all their interactions with others, including the interaction between perpetrator and victim" (Ainsworth, 2001, p. 118). Canter believes that there is "some central theme, core or objective to a series of crimes that represents

the criminal's way of dealing with other people. A man who rapes many women then starts deliberately to kill his victims shows a central violent nature" (Canter, 2000, p. 51).

- *Occupational/educational history*, Canter believed, are significant in that "a careful study of offense behavior could sometimes reveal clues as to the perpetrator's background. Thus offenses which showed evidence of careful, sophisticated and detailed planning might be more likely to have been committed by someone with high intelligence" (Ainsworth, 2001, p. 120).

As demonstrated, coming up with a definition of criminal profiling is hard due to the various types of profiling used within the criminal justice and academic community. The remainder of this chapter will attempt to define criminal profiling and give a snapshot of what the Investigative Psychology Unit of the Criminal Records and Forensic Science Division of the South African Police Service looks like.

OFFENDER PROFILING: A PROPOSED DEFINITION

The definition constructed by the Investigative Psychology Unit of the Criminal Records and Forensic Science Division of the South African Police Service is as follows:

Any activity specifically undertaken with the intent of assisting an investigator to determine the most likely type of individual to have committed a specific crime. The process would usually involve an assessment of the crime scene, attending the autopsy, examining all available docket material such as statements, photographs, forensic reports and investigative decisions. This information is then compared to any available research. Finally hypotheses are formulated regarding the type of suspect who committed the crime. These hypotheses might be verbally communicated to the investigator but would normally also be formulated in a structured written report. The aim is to assist the investigator to focus his investigation on the most likely type of suspect. (Labuschagne, 2003, p. 67)

Five important features can be identified in this definition:

- The aim is to assist the investigating officer. In other words, the person compiling the offender profile is not the person leading the investigation. A myth perpetuated by the media is that the "profiler" is the one who leads or solves the case.
- The offender profile is intended to indicate the type of person who could have committed such a crime. The profile cannot be used to highlight an individual

as a suspect. The profile is intended to be compared to available suspects in an investigation. Those suspects that fit the characteristics indicated in the profile are prioritized above other suspects who fit the profile to a lesser degree. Evidence is still needed to link a suspect to a crime and lead to a conviction.

- The process would usually involve an assessment of the crime scene, attending the autopsy, and examining all available docket material such as statements, photographs, forensic reports, and investigative decisions. This component implies that the person compiling the offender profile must have access to confidential investigative information. Ideally, the person attends the crime scenes and autopsy. If unable to, the person should revisit the crime scene and compare it to crime scene and autopsy photographs. Furthermore, the person should have access to reports relevant to the investigation such as autopsy reports, ballistic reports, fingerprint reports, and statements made by relevant witnesses.

- The information must be compared to available research. With the popular media influencing the concept of offender profiling, even professionally, there are growing efforts to make the concept more scientific. It is therefore essential that available, relevant research be used to support the statements made in any offender profile. It should be emphasized that research is contextually bound in that results from a study from one part of the world are not necessarily transplantable to another part of the world.

- Finally, hypotheses are made that can be communicated verbally but should be followed up in a structured, written report. Investigations proceed rapidly; information is often given verbally as certain hypotheses are made by the person compiling the offender profile. Because a profile is often up to 20 pages or more in a serial offense, it can take a long time to compile. However, to prevent misunderstandings, and to protect oneself in a legal environment, these hypotheses must be formulated into a structured, written report, the actual offender profile.

This definition is the current working definition used by the Investigative Psychology Unit of the South African Police Service.

THE USE OF CRIMINAL PROFILING IN SOUTH AFRICA

Despite the image created in the media, not all law enforcement agencies have units similar to the FBI's original Behavioral Science Unit. In Europe, some of the German states have Operational Case Analysis Units, and within the Netherlands National Police Agency there is a similar unit. The Investigative Psychology Unit has been in existence since 1996 and is currently stationed under the Criminal Records and Forensic Science Division of the South African Police Service (SAPS). It is a national unit, which can be called upon to provide investigative support throughout the country and has also assisted in the neighboring countries of Swaziland and Namibia. The unit has also interacted with foreign law enforcement agencies such as the London Metropolitan Police (on the "Adam" murder discussed in Chapter 8) and the Central Bureau of Investigation in New Delhi, India, for a serial murder investigation. The SAPS is one of the few police services in the world that has a full-time unit devoted to investigative psychology.

The unit's function is to assist with any psychologically motivated crimes. These crimes include serial murder, serial rape, sexual murder, muti murders, infant rape, spree and mass murders, extortion, intimate partner murders, blackmail and death threats, and one-off murders with bizarre circumstances. Some of the well-known cases the unit has assisted on are the Wemmerpan Serial Murderer; Moses Sithole, South Africa's most notorious serial murderer to date; the rape of 9-month-old baby Tshepang in Upington; the "Adam" murder in the Thames River, London; the quarry serial murderer Richard Nyauza; the Capital Park serial murderer Samuel Sydino; the Phoenix serial murderer Sipho Twala; and the "Highwayman" serial murderer Elais Chauke. The unit also has a coordinator in each province to monitor and coordinate any investigations that would require the unit's services.

The Investigative Psychology Unit's Structure

The unit currently has four members: a Colonel, who is the unit commander and a clinical psychologist; a Lieutenant Colonel, who is the second in command and has an investigator background; and two Captains, one with a psychology background and one with an investigator background.

The unit has found it extremely beneficial to combine investigators with other members who have a social sciences background, predominantly psychology. This does not mean that there is a clear division in terms of input—e.g., psychological versus investigative. Instead, each person develops knowledge in the other's field, and members usually give input of both a psychological and investigative nature. However, like many units in the SAPS, this unit is understaffed and, for the workload, should be much larger. In 2009, the unit dealt with 105 investigative assistance requests. Among those requests were 27 murder series and 60 rape series. The total number of victims in those 105 requests was 327. Ideally, besides having a larger staff component, the unit seeks to develop a larger in-house research capacity, requiring the skills of an adequately trained social sciences researcher.

Besides these full-time members, the unit also has a Provincial Coordinator for Psychologically Motivated Crimes in each of the nine provinces of the country. This person's role is to facilitate communication between the unit and the respective province regarding such cases and to coordinate serial investigations in his or her province.

Roles of the Unit

The unit has three overlapping roles within its mandate of providing support to investigating officers:

- Investigative support
- Training of detectives
- Research

Investigative support: The unit provides investigative support nationally to investigating officers by means of consultations, reports, crime scene analysis, and offender profiles as defined previously. The members also assist in interrogating suspects and interviewing witnesses. The unit provides "witness handling guidelines" for sensitive witnesses. The unit's members are also often called on to testify in court for the cases on which they have assisted. They are all functional police officers, and this unique position allows them access to crime scenes, autopsies, and the interrogation of witnesses and suspects. They are literally involved from crime scene to courtroom. Many professionals doing similar work in other countries are appointed as civilian personnel and are therefore prevented from such access.

The members can also be called upon after an investigation has taken place, should the need arise, to act as expert witnesses. This function helps the SAPS by reducing the need to contact outside professionals who would require payment.

Training of detectives: The Investigative Psychology Unit has a world-renowned, distinguished reputation when it comes to the field of serial murder. Over the past 19 years, approximately 80 serial murderers have been active in South Africa, the majority of them having been apprehended and convicted. Numerous serial murderers have been apprehended within 6 weeks of a task team being assigned to the case, and the unit has received praise from retired FBI agent and serial murder expert Colonel Robert Ressler for the speed of its successes. This highly successful rate of apprehension of serial murderers is in part due to the training programs offered by the Investigative Psychology Unit. The unit assists in the training of detectives as part of various detective training courses offered by the SAPS and also offers a specialized 3-week course known as the Psychologically Motivated Crimes Course. This course is a prerequisite for someone to be allowed to investigate a serial murder case.

Almost 350 detectives have undergone the Psychologically Motivated Crimes Course. This course focuses on investigative psychology issues unique to serial murder investigation and furthermore focuses on issues related to serial rape, child molestation, sadism, sexual murder, muti murder, and certain paraphilias. Previously known as the Investigative Psychology Course, in 2002 the course was renamed the Psychologically Motivated Crimes Course. The focus is on the investigation of such crimes and the practical application of research and experience. In 2002, the unit also expanded its training function to include courses for crime scene photographers, who often cover areas that include the jurisdiction of numerous detective units that would be investigating murders and who are therefore ideally placed to help link serial crimes. Furthermore, crime scene photographers are called out to all crimes, not just murder, and can therefore also help link incidents of sexual burglary, serial rape, and other crimes that can be associated with serial murder. The unit also provides training to prosecutors.

Research: Besides the investigative support and training roles, the Investigative Psychology Unit also has a research role and is currently involved in research focusing on muti murder and serial murder. Other research projects include criminal mutilation, foreign object insertion in sexual murder, spree murders, and infant rapes. These research efforts are aimed at supporting the investigative support function and training function of the unit. Due to limited resources, such research is often undertaken in collaboration with local and international universities, such as John Jay College of Criminal Justice in New York.

CONCLUSION

Offender profiling has taken on a life of its own, partly due to the popular representation of people providing such a service. This image is a powerful one, which has also influenced the academic opinion of offender profiling. This chapter has attempted to provide an understanding of three important areas: the history of profiling, types of profiling, and the definition of offender profiling as used by the Investigative Psychology Unit of the SAPS.

The profiling unit discussed in this chapter is the only unit in the SAPS mandated to provide such a service for investigating officers. Furthermore, the chapter has given brief definitions as to the other uses of the word "profiling" in a cross-cultural context. As discussed, individuals providing such a service have a greater role to play in investigations, and the Investigative Psychology Unit offers a model for these individuals to follow. Hopefully, a cross-cultural analysis can promote discussion and facilitate understanding of this service and the role that forensic professionals can provide in investigations.

Note: Due to the fascination of serial killer movies, which use the oversimplified methodology of FBI profiling, the general public sees profiling as only FBI-style profiling. Other types of profiling are never used, giving a lack of exposure to the various methodologies used in the field.

CHAPTER 10

The Use of a Linkage Analysis as an Investigative Tool and Evidential Material in Serial Offenses

Gerard Labuschagne

For as long as investigators have been investigating crimes of a serial nature, whether murders, rapes, bank robberies, or burglaries, they have had to deal with the problem of deciding which cases are linked to the same offender(s). With the development of the forensic sciences, this task has become easier for the investigator. Fingerprints, DNA, fiber comparison, closed-circuit television, tool marks, ballistics, soil profiles, shoe and tire imprints, and bite marks are just some of the ways in which an offender can be linked to one or more crimes, or in which crimes can be linked to each other. A more recent method of linking crimes to one offender has been the use of a linkage analysis, which focuses not on the hard forensic sciences but instead on the behavior of the offender when committing a crime or series of crimes.

A linkage analysis, sometimes referred to as comparative case analysis (Bennell & Canter, 2002; Merry, 2000), is useful in two regards. First, during the investigation phase of a crime, it helps investigators decide which crimes to include or exclude from an investigation into the series, or how to focus their search for other similar crimes previously committed, possibly in neighboring areas. Second, the analysis can be presented as evidence in court to demonstrate that a single offender is responsible for the commission of a number of crimes when hard forensic evidence may be lacking in certain instances of those crimes.

WHAT IS LINKAGE ANALYSIS?

Hazelwood and Warren (2003) describe linkage analysis as a form of behavioral analysis used to determine whether a series of crimes was committed by one offender. The analysis integrates information from various aspects of the offender's crime pattern, including the modus operandi (MO), the ritual or fantasy-based behaviors exhibited, and the signature or unique combination of behaviors exhibited by the offender during the crimes. The individual(s) performing the linkage analysis engages in five assessment procedures: (1) obtaining data from multiple sources, (2) reviewing the data and identifying significant features of each crime across the series, (3) classifying the significant features as either MO and/or ritualistic, (4) comparing the combination of MO and ritual/fantasy-based features across the series to determine if a signature exists, and (5) compiling a written report highlighting the findings.

However, Hazelwood and Warren (2003) do not include another valuable aspect of an offender's behavior that can be useful in its own right for linking cases, that of geographic behavior. Various authors (e.g., Canter, 2003, 2004b; Rossmo, 1995, 1997, 2000) have written about the geographic behavior of serial criminals, albeit serial murderers, serial rapists, or serial house burglars. Besides the implications for determining the offender's anchor point, such as a place of residence or employment, the close proximity of crime scenes to each other can also be used as a linkage factor (see Keppel, 1995). It is the author's experience that many of the assumptions about geographic patterns of behavior hold true in the South African context. This sentiment is shared by Hodgskiss (2004) in his research into South African serial murder. It is also not clear from Hazelwood and Warren (2003) the part that victimology plays in a linkage analysis.

Keppel (1995, 2000a; Keppel & Birnes, 2009; Keppel & Weis, 2004) refers to a signature analysis. Signature is seen by Keppel as the offender's unique personal expression on the crime scene, the actions that go beyond what is necessary to commit a crime (Douglas & Munn, 1992b; Geberth, 2003; Keppel, 1995). Keppel (2000b) further describes the signature as the offender's personal expression, or an imprint that he or she feels psychologically compelled to leave at a crime scene. Examples he lists are mutilation, overkill, carving on the body, leaving messages, positioning the body, postmortem activity, or forcing the victim to respond verbally in a specific fashion (Keppel, 2000b). Keppel regards MO as the behaviors that allow the offender to commit the crime successfully and escape detection. Hazelwood and Warren (2003) seem to echo the sentiment on MO, but see signature as being made up of MO behaviors (if the combination is unique enough) *and/or* the ritual/fantasy behavior. Perhaps a shortcoming of a signature analysis as proposed by Keppel, as opposed to a linkage analysis (proposed by Hazelwood and Warren, 2003) that encompasses signature commentary, is that a signature analysis requires behaviors "over and above" what is necessary to commit the crime. The implication is that it does not assess common MO behavior for linkage purposes (Keppel, 1995) that are perhaps unique *in combination* with each other.

Irrespective of which approach is used, case linkage rests upon two main assumptions: (1) the assumption that an offender will display some consistency in his or her behavior across a series of offenses and (2) the assumption that there is sufficient variation between offenders, allowing them to be distinguished from each other (Bateman & Salfati, 2007; Woodhams & Grant, 2006). Grubin, Kelly, and Brundson (2001) state that for any case comparison procedure to be successful, techniques are required that will reliably recognize when similarities between cases are more than coincidental. Establishing similarities necessitates:

- The identification of relevant offenses features
- A valid procedure to compare offenses based on these features to determine the degree of similarity between them
- A means to calculate the likelihood that any similarity is more than a mere random event

Once similarities have been identified, it is essential to determine if they are due to coincidence or other factors. For example, murder victims being found on their backs is most likely not a unique-enough finding to use as a linkage factor. Grubin et al. (2001) go on to state that once a linkage analysis has been done based on similarities, further methods can be used to improve specificity. They advocate using temporal and geographic information to improve accuracy. For example, if two similar offenses have been committed at almost the same time but hundreds of miles apart, then it is not likely that the same offender was involved, regardless of how similar the crimes.

It is essential to have enough knowledge of the crime being assessed to determine if the behavior, or combination of behaviors, is unique enough for it to have relevance for linkage purposes. Linking of cases is therefore not a generic skill that can be applied to any crime that the analyst is faced with. Expert knowledge of the crime is regarded as a prerequisite. This is especially relevant if the linkage analysis is to be presented in court as evidence.

WHY USE LINKAGE ANALYSIS?

A linkage analysis can have various uses depending upon the stage of the criminal justice system in which it is used. In initial phases, it can be used as a stand-alone report aimed at helping investigators sift through cases to determine if a series exists and which past and new cases should be assigned to a task team to investigate the series. While this could be a stand-alone report, it is often, in South Africa, the first section of a broader offender profile (Labuschagne, 2003). Secondly, it can be used at the trial phase during the presentation of the prosecution's case to suggest that certain crimes are the work of one individual. This application may help link the accused to other cases for which he or she is on trial if some of the cases lack eyewitness and forensic evidence, despite the strikingly similar and unique manners in which the crimes were committed. In South African courts, the presiding officer at a trial can decide for himself or herself, without expert evidence being presented, that certain crimes are unique and similar enough in nature and circumstance that the reasonable, logical conclusion is that one offender was responsible. A linkage analysis is aimed at assisting the presiding officer to come to such a conclusion.

The linking of cases allows law enforcement agencies to act more proactively in the investigation and identification of serial crimes, thus allowing limited resources to be more effectively allocated. As Woodhams, Hollin, and Bull (2007) state, the linking of a series is useful in three ways. First, linking increases the amount of evidence against the offender. Each case might have limited evidentially relevant information that, in isolation, might have little impact on the investigation; however, when put together, like a jigsaw puzzle, these findings could amount to vital information that can help identify and convict an offender.

Second, if crimes are suspected to have been committed by one offender, they can be investigated together, rather than separately, allowing police resources to be allocated more efficiently. For example, suppose there are five offenses committed by one offender, and each case is being investigated by a different investigator. Once the offender is arrested, each investigator has to charge the offender on his or her case, which means five court appearances and court dates running independently. This takes up the time of five, instead of one, investigator.

Third, after arrest, a linkage analysis can be used as similar fact evidence (discussed later in this chapter) to help convict a serial offender. Some cases in a series may lack physical evidence (e.g., DNA or fingerprints) or eyewitness evidence to link the suspect to the specific crime(s); however, due to an overwhelming similarity of all of the offenses, the only logical conclusion that can be drawn by the court is that the same offender was responsible for all of the offenses. It is most logical that such evidence be presented at the end of the prosecution's case, once all of the facts are before the court. The linkage analysis forms a sort of "web" over the existing evidence that has been presented, which may (depending on each case) include DNA, fingerprints, and other traditional linking factors in a trial. It must be remembered that the linkage analysis itself should not mention other nonbehavioral evidence.

The use of a linkage analysis during an investigation should be seen as an ongoing and not static process. Invariably, investigators will not have all the information about a case at the early stages after a crime has been reported. For example, in a sexual murder scenario, investigators may wait weeks if not months for DNA results, autopsy reports, and other forensic results such as toxicology. In the South African situation, this leaves investigators to make linkage decisions based on less information than is ideal. Investigators tend to "cast the net" wider than might be expected in search for other old, current, or future cases that could be related. Cases are often tentatively included, the current case file contents are reviewed for further details that might indicate a linkage, and ultimately some cases may be excluded when further information becomes available, or confirmed if results such as DNA become available and confirm that the same offender's DNA is present.

It must be remembered that not every action taken by investigators will lead to positive results. Certain lines of inquiry may be investigated that turn out to be dead ends. It is often creativity or initiative that leads to investigative success, and academic researchers should be wary of creating a situation in which investigators believe that no investigative decisions can be made unless extensive research exists to back up the decision. Therefore the context in which the linkage analysis is being used is very relevant.

Nonetheless, when a linkage analysis is used as evidence in court, it must be able to stand up to the requirements for admissibility. Linkage reports have been presented as similar fact evidence in courts in South Africa, including *State v. Sukude*, 2006, the Newcastle Serial Murderer; State v. van Rooyen, 2007, the Knysna Serial Murderer; and State v. Nyauza, 2007, the Quarry Serial Murderer. In all of these South African cases, the linkage analysis evidence was accepted and the accused was found guilty of all of the murders for which he was charged. In one case (*State v. Stander*, 2008, the Port Elizabeth Prostitute Serial Murderer), the linkage analysis was provided to the defense before the author's testimony, which, nearing the end of the trial, in part led to the accused deciding to make formal admissions to the court that he had indeed murdered the two victims for which he was charged, with the provision that the linkage analysis then not to be presented to the court as evidence.

Keppel (2000a) refers to at least five instances in the United States in which a signature analysis was admitted in murder trials, and their appeals, as evidence that certain cases were linked. Keppel and Birnes (2009) also refer to a case in Canada (*Regina v. Burlingham*, 1986) in which case linkage evidence in the form of similar fact evidence was used as evidence in a double murder trial. He further states that signature analysis is "the only crime scene assessment technique that is accepted in court testimony and appellate decisions" (Keppel, Weis, Brown, & Welch, 2005, p. 14). Keppel and Birnes (2009) list the following cases in which evidence was presented regarding the similarities of cases:

- *California v. Bogard*, 1996. Evidence was offered that the same person was responsible for a series of six rapes.
- *New Jersey v. Fortini*, 2000. Evidence was presented regarding the similarities across a series of offenses.
- *South Dakota v. Anderson*, 1998. A review of the signature aspects of two murders was offered at a hearing to determine if they would be joined for prosecution.

They also list a number of murder cases where linkage testimony was admitted at trial and upheld under appellate scrutiny in the United States:

- *Louisiana v. Code*, 1994
- *Delaware v. Pennel*, 1989
- *California v. Prince*, 1992
- *Washington v. Russel*, 1994
- *Washington v. Parker*, 2000

The legal principles and expert evidence used in some of these cases will be discussed in the following sections.

WHAT DOES THE RESEARCH SAY? IS LINKING POSSIBLE?

So far, activities or techniques that fall within the realm of behavioral analysis, such as offender profiling, have often lacked a solid research-based foundation to support the assumptions underlying these techniques. Linkage analysis, however, seems to have a slowly growing body of empirical support for its claims. One field that has proven to be an asset in studying this process is that of personality psychology (Woodhams, Hollin, & Bull, 2007). For many years, this field of psychology has been studying the consistency of people's behavior in nonforensic settings. Researchers in this field have discovered that people have stable but distinctive ways of reacting to situations, so-called "if-then" contingencies (Mischel, 1999). This field acknowledges that while people are consistent because of their personality traits, situational aspects also have an impact on people's behavior and, therefore, consistency.

Much of the focus in linkage analysis is on similarities across different cases in a series. This approach is based on the assumption from personality psychology that offenders are consistent in the way they behave across their criminal activities and that the behavior of one offender can be distinguished from the behavior of another. While similarities are undoubtedly important in this process and can perhaps be regarded as the "bread and butter" of linkage analysis, the author has experienced that changes in offender behavior across offenses can also be vital linkage factors. This finding is echoed by Keppel and Birnes (2009), who regard behaviors such as "increasing number of death-producing wounds from the first case to the last case" and "decreasing number of defensive wounds from the first case to the last case" (p. 11). Grubin et al. (2001) similarly found that evolution across a series occurs and that such evolution can provide valuable information about whether an offender is in the early, middle, or advanced stages of a series, an insight that could be factored into a linking algorithm. This finding was also noted by De Wet (2008) regarding the sexual behavior of South African serial rapists. Similarly, Wentink (2001), who analyzed the first three offenses of a sample of North American serial murderers, discovered that there was an evolution in the form of thematic differentiation; in other words, the offense behaviors became more thematically specific. Hodskiss (2001), who studied the offenses of 13 South African serial murderers, found that offense behaviors evolve as the series progresses, with an MO developing and becoming more thematically distinct.

This evolution in behavior is often due to the progression of an offender's behavior across a series of offenses as more of the fantasy gets enacted upon subsequent victims, or as the offender becomes more effective in committing the crimes due to experience and confidence. It is incorrect to describe these findings purely as changes in behavior, but rather as the acting out of more of the offender's original intention as the offender "settles in" to his or her crime with each subsequent offense. Also, it is important to note that changes do not occur in all aspects; for example, victimology may remain the same, but specific behaviors may become embellished. These "changes" can be important linkage factors. They can indicate "trial runs," as illustrated by the following example that occurred in South Africa.

An offender, who eventually murdered an interior decorator in his home by means of multiple axe and hammer blows to the head and kept her body in his bathtub for a few days before finally leaving her nearly naked body along a busy highway, first engaged in trial runs. His first potential victims, to whom he inflicted no injury, were estate agents. Using a false name and a different cell phone number, he would make appointments with them at houses they were selling. He would meet with them, pretend to be interested in buying an expensive house, enjoy the treatment he received from them, then leave without harming them or giving them any indication that they were in danger. Just prior to the murder of the interior decorator, he met with his first interior decorator, who came to his house to give him a quote for work he wanted done to his house. She cut her consultation short after seeing a hammer in the bathroom, which made her feel uncomfortable. This was the same bathroom where the murder victim was finally attacked and murdered.

On the surface, there are many "changes" in the offender's behavior. For example, he initially met estate agents at houses they were selling but later focused on interior decorators who would come to his house. He did not hurt the first few people he contacted; only the final victim, the second interior decorator who came to his home, was attacked and murdered.

As Grubin et al. (2001) state, if behavior is to provide a means for linking offenses committed by one offender, it must be assumed that at least some behaviors remain consistent across the series of offenses, or evolve in a predictable way. This raises the question, how similar must the behaviors be? And on what level must there be similarity? "Micro" or "macro"? The offender in the preceding example changed in certain aspects on a superficial, microlevel (e.g., from real estate agents to interior decorators) and remained the same in other ways (e.g., female victims). However, he remained the same on a thematic, macrolevel, using a con story to lure female victims in occupations that required them to meet with potential clients in isolated circumstances. Also, he only harmed one victim, the final victim.

In another example from South Africa, during a series of five murders, in two cases the offender made a small fire on the vagina of the victim. In another two cases, the offender inserted objects into the victim's vagina; the first insertion was a small bag of marijuana, and the second insertion was the investigating officer's business card, rolled up and tied with a piece of the victim's hair. For the fifth victim, what the offender did to the vagina differed (i.e., did not involve fire or insertion), but the theme remained constant—tampering with the victim's genitals—and this was the offender's signature. Also, in that particular series, the victims were from three different racial groups, but were all prostitutes, which was also part of the offender's signature. Keppel and Birnes

(2009) note that in their experience the serial prostitute murderers tend to be racially indiscriminate in their victim selection.

Keppel and Birnes (2009) also refer to the case of William Heirens in 1945 who murdered two adult women and a 6-year-old child, and committed 26 additional crimes including burglaries, assaults, and robberies. In the case of one of the adult victims, he wrote on a mirror in the victim's home, "For heaven's sake, catch me before I kill more; I cannot control myself," and in the home of the 6-year-old girl, he left a "ransom" note (p. 22). Regarding the written notes, Keppel and Birnes state, "The messages he scrawled were the visual representations of his attempt to manipulate others, even though the wording was different in each note. It was not the actual wording of the notes or the writing medium, but his compulsion to leave notes that was the signature" (p. 23).

Bateman and Salfati (2007) refer to two different approaches—consistency in individual behaviors and consistency in themes of behaviors. Consistency in individual behaviors looks for more unique, signature types of behaviors. Their critique of this approach is that much of the literature on signatures is not supported by empirical studies. However, other studies, focusing on aspects such as geographic linking have found consistent behavior in this regard (Lundrigan & Canter, 2001; Tonkin, Grant, & Bond, 2008). Others (Grubin et al., 2001) examined consistency in serial sexual offenses and statistically developed four offense domains of behaviors relating to control methods employed by the offender, sexual aspects of the offenses, escape mechanisms used by the offender to avoid detection, and the offender's offense style. Grubin et al. (2001) found that the control and escape domains proved to be more useful for linking purposes due to their consistency. Criticism of the individual behaviors approach highlights reasons such as the situationally dependent nature of such behaviors (Bennel & Canter, 2002), the victim–offender interaction in contact crimes (Salfati & Bateman, 2005), and the offender's ability to learn from previous experience (Grubin et al., 2001).

The other approach is the consistency of themes. In this approach, investigators examine "pools," or groups, of offender behaviors that all encompass the same psychological meaning, instead of individual behaviors displayed throughout the commission of a crime (Bateman & Salfati, 2007). This approach partially negates the impact of the criticisms leveled against the individual behaviors approach. Bateman and Salfati's (2007) research states that there is no evidence to suggest that it is better to use one approach above the other when linking murders.

Woodhams and Grant (2006) examined the use of a categorization system for rapists' speech as a means for linking rapes. They discovered that the system demonstrated a satisfactory inter-rater reliability and could classify the majority (91%) of the rapists' utterances in the sample, with positive implications for linkage. Other earlier researchers also focused on speech profiles of offenders (Canter, Heritage, & King-Johannessen, 1989; Dale, Davies, & Wei, 1997).

Other studies that indicate a measure of success for the field of linkage analysis include those by Bennell and Canter (2002) and Green, Booth, and Biderman (1976). Tonkin et al. (2008) found that in serial car theft spatial behavior, specifically the distance between theft locations and dump locations, is consistent and distinctive. Woodhams, Grant, and Price (2007) found support that linked offenses were significantly more similar than unlinked offenses. Woodhams et al. (2007) found support for two of the assumptions underlying the practice of linking crimes, those of behavioral consistency and inter-individual variation. Woodhams and Toye (2007) found support for the hypotheses of offender behavioral consistency and offender behavioral distinctiveness.

De Wet (2008) analyzed the MO of nine South African serial rapists who had a total of 75 victims. This research revealed that offenders were consistent in their method of approaching their victim. For example, five offenders always used a con story when approaching their victims, and another two offenders used a con story almost every time (94% and 89% of incidents). One offender used a surprise approach in 75% of his attacks, while only one offender varied his methods of approach. Regarding crime location, five of the nine offenders raped all their victims (in total 48) outside. Three of the others were consistent in rape location (90%, 86%, and 75% of incidents). Five offenders were consistent in only attacking victims during the day, no offenders took precautions to hide their identity from the victims, and only one used a condom (once) during his series.

Other literature dealing with linkage analysis is provided by Hazelwood and Warren (2003), who describe the processes involved in linkage analysis; however, their findings are based on investigative experience, not on a formal study. Similarly, the publications of Keppel (1995, 2000a), Keppel and Weis (2004), and Keppel and Birnes (2009) are based on experience, while Labuschagne (2006) describes the process of linkage analysis and its use as similar fact evidence in the conviction of a serial murderer in the form of a case study.

INFORMATION REQUIRED TO COMPILE A LINKAGE ANALYSIS ──────

Keppel (1995) lists the following as sources of information when compiling a signature analysis: police reports from the initial investigation of the crime scene, victim background, crime scene diagrams, evidence reports, laboratory reports, autopsy reports, and photographs. Hazelwood and Warren (2003) refer to the gathering of "detailed, varied, multi source documentation" (p. 587) and state that for a series of rapes this documentation would be victim statements, police and medical reports, and, if possible, a commercial map depicting all the significant locations featured in the process of the crime. For murder cases, they state that the following should be included: police, autopsy, and toxicology reports; crime scene and autopsy photographs; and, if appropriate, a commercial map depicting all the significant locations featured in the process of the crime.

Another tool that can be used when doing a linkage assessment is electronic databases such as the Homicide Investigation Tracking System (HITS) in use in Washington State and Oregon, which also contains murder cases from other states and Canadian provinces (Keppel & Birnes, 2009); the Violent Criminal Apprehension Program (VICAP); and the Violent Crime Linkage Analysis System (ViCLAS) used in Canada and in certain European countries. When certain unique features are noted at a crime scene, investigators can search these databases for cases with similar features for linkage purposes, or, when at trial, to indicate how rare those features are, thus supporting the evidence that the cases were most likely committed by one offender. This process is in essence similar to investigators comparing crime scene fingerprints or DNA to similar databases for a "hit" and then stating statistically in court what the likelihood is of someone other than the offender having the same fingerprint or DNA. Granted, linkage analysis is far from having the same statistical reliability of fingerprinting or DNA. As Grubin et al. (2001) state:

> *Unlike the matching of DNA samples where comparison parameters are well established, we have only a limited understanding of which variables to compare, and of what counts as a good match between them, when searching for relevant offence behaviors. Just as important, we do not have population base rates that will allow estimates of how frequently specific behaviors, or combinations of behaviors, occur. In the absence of such base rates it is not possible to estimate the likelihood that a particular behavioral pattern relates to a single source. (p. 4)*

However, if such databases are available and can be made use of either in the investigation phase or trial phase, then they should be. In the absence of these applications, the databases are still of great value if used to request murder cases in the surrounding area for a set time frame before and after the murder, and to compare the characteristics of those cases to the cases under review. This is an activity often done by the author in intimate partner murders where the crimes have been staged as a house robbery. The author reviews house robbery cases before and after the incident in question, compares those features to the case under review, and comments on the similarity or difference thereof.

FACTORS THAT CAN INFLUENCE A SIGNATURE OR LINKAGE ANALYSIS ——

Hazelwood and Warren (2003) highlight factors that can influence crime scene behavior and, therefore, what the analyst will see when making an analysis. They refer to six observations:

1. A crime scene analyst will often identify more MO behaviors than ritual behaviors.
2. All aspects of the ritual may not be present in every crime, depending on the time available, mood of the offender, and external circumstances beyond the control of the offender.
3. Some ritual aspects may not be recognized as such and may be attributed to MO; they may only be determined as ritual upon interviewing the offender after apprehension.
4. Some elements may function as both MO and ritual. Tying up a victim, for example, may allow the offender to commit the crime and flee the scene, but the offender may also be sexually aroused by bondage.
5. Ritualistic behaviors may remain known only to the offender.
6. An impulsive offender may be devoid of ritualistic behaviors or even a clear MO.

In South Africa, due to high temperatures, bodies decompose quickly, and animal predatory activity is common in bodies not quickly discovered. It is the author's experience that most murder series occur outside, thus increasing the problems regarding a speedy discovery of the body and the activity of predators. Keppel (1995) echoes this sentiment regarding decomposition and also comments that crime scene contamination will also affect the linkage analysis. One example of crime scene contamination is when members of the public or even police officials cover up the face or whole body of a sexual murder victim. If it is not made known to either the profiler or the person compiling the linkage or signature analysis that the body was covered by someone other than the offender, then faulty interpretations can be made regarding the relevance of the covering.

Certain types of crimes can also compound the difficulties associated with signature or linkage analysis. One example would be a muti (medicine) murder, common to South

Africa (Labuschagne, 2004). As discussed in Chapter 8, in this situation, a person is instructed by a traditional healer to obtain a particular human body part, which is then to be used as an ingredient in the concoction of a "potion" used to allow the user to achieve a particular aim. The mutilation is enacted upon the instruction of the traditional healer and is not due to the inner psychology of the person committing the murder.

In crimes such as rape or other sexual offenses, the absence of a behavior could be a positive linkage factor (Woodhams et al., 2007); however, the absence of a behavior in a victim's statement might be due to memory lapse. The behavior may not have seemed significant to mention or the interviewer may have failed to ask questions to elicit the information or may have failed to record the information.

It must also be taken into account that interpersonal crimes are an interaction between an offender and a victim. Depending on how the victim reacts, passively or aggressively, the offender might not be able to exhibit or act out all of his or her desired behaviors. Other situational factors, such as the presence of passersby or witnesses, might cause the offender to the prematurely terminate the crime. Such factors may complicate linkage in that a crime that started out with the intent of being a rape-murder might only end up being a rape or an assault with intent to do grievous bodily harm. As a result of this alternative crime classification, investigators searching for similar murder cases might overlook an assault case that could be the work of the same offender. Similarly, an intended rape might end up being only an assault case if for various reasons the offender did not go through with the crime.

Unreported crimes can leave "gaps" in the offender's behavior. For example, in a rape series, a victim may not come forward to the police to open a case. These gaps might lead cases to appear very different; yet, if all cases were reported, then a logical progression in behavior could be clearly seen.

Finally, certain information may not be available at the time of the linkage analysis, or might not be made known to the person compiling the linkage analysis, either intentionally or unintentionally.

Similar to this discussion is the concept of "linkage blindness," a term coined by Steven Egger (1984). He says linkage blindness occurs when law enforcement agencies are prevented from seeing, or make little attempt to see, beyond their jurisdictional areas of responsibility. He states that this concept is applicable to all types of "mobile" crimes, including serial murders (Egger, 2002). As a result of linkage blindness, similar crime patterns or MOs are not noted across geographic areas of responsibility. This problem is heightened when these areas are managed by different law enforcement agencies, but it is also seen in a single law enforcement agency that is very large, such as the South African Police Service, which is a national law enforcement agency that is divided up into different management areas within a province, and between provinces. As a result, certain cases that fall into the jurisdictions of different police stations might not all be identified as being the work of one individual.

Grubin et al. (2001) highlight certain practical difficulties in developing a linkage system. These include consistent but extremely common behaviors, consistent but extremely uncommon or idiosyncratic behaviors, variations in consistency, precision of the description, victim response, the weighting of behaviors, evolution of behaviors, and the interpretation of behaviors.

LEGAL PRINCIPLES UNDER WHICH LINKAGE EVIDENCE IS ADMISSIBLE —

Ormerod (1999) comments on the use of "psychological profiling" as evidence in court, and some of the concerns expressed in that regard are relevant to the use of linkage analysis in court. He refers to the use of a psychological profile as an aid for the prosecutor to conduct a more effective cross-examination of the accused, in which event, it is not playing an evidential role but rather a strategic role. He further states that a psychological profile may, albeit problematically, be used to highlight to the court how the accused fits the profile compiled during the investigation. The difficulties of its use in a trial would be to overcome two laws of evidence: relevance and admissibility. However, while psychological or offender profiles may have difficulty standing up to cross-examination in court because of a lack of supporting research and their non-specificity, it must be remembered that they are created primarily as an investigative tool (Gudjonsson & Haward, 1999; Labuschagne, 2003), not as evidential material. This is similar perhaps to the use of a polygraph or Layered Voice Analysis during an investigation to aid investigators in deciding on which possible suspects to focus, but the results of which will not be introduced as evidence in trial proceedings.

The United States (on both the state and the federal levels) and countries throughout the world have their own legal systems with their own rules for the admissibility of evidence and requirements for expert or opinion evidence. In the United States, some states use the *Daubert* (1993) standard, others the *Frye* (1923), and others the *Kumbo* (1999). There are also the *Federal Rules of Evidence* for federal cases. Under the Daubert standard, unless the testimony rests on a reliable foundation and is based on scientifically valid principles, the judge may deem such testimony inadmissible. Under the Frye standard, unless the testimony offered reflects either a principle or discovery that has gained general acceptance in a particular field, it should be excluded by the judge. The Frye test is usually reserved for testimony involving new methods or new scientific principles from which conclusions are drawn. This was the test in the cases

Delaware v. Pennel and *Washington v. Russel* mentioned previously. Under the Kumho standard, "expertise that is fausse and science that is junky" may be excluded by the judge as part of his or her gatekeeping function; thus, it is up to the judge to decide if it is true science or not.

The Federal Rules of Evidence, specifically rule number 702, states:

If scientific, technical, or other specialized knowledge will assist the trier of fact to understand the evidence or to determine a fact in issue, a witness qualified as an expert by knowledge, skill, experience, training, or education, may testify thereto in the form of an opinion or otherwise, if (1) the testimony is based upon sufficient facts or data, (2) the testimony is the product of reliable principles and methods, and (3) the witness has applied the principles and methods reliably to the facts of the case.

These different requirements would undoubtedly affect whether certain techniques, such as a linkage analysis, would be admissible. It is therefore essential to determine what those requirements would be before applying any technique, or appearing as an expert, in a court of law.

An expert witness has primarily one role in the court: to provide the court with expertise not typically within the knowledge framework of the court or jury. If accepted, the court adopts the expert's opinion as its own, as the court may not delegate its responsibilities to another—e.g., the expert witness (van der Berg & van der Merwe, 2002). For this expert testimony to happen, a person must be qualified as an expert by the court because, as a general rule, opinion evidence is not admissible except when the witness is in a better position than the presiding officer or jury to form an opinion. The opinion of an expert is admissible if it has evidential value and relevance. A person is qualified as an expert by the presiding officer based on knowledge and experience, and ultimately the presiding officer decides whether to accept or reject the expert evidence, or in a jury system, to allow it to be used as evidence during the trial. It is imperative in the linkage analysis situation that the witness be not only an expert in the process of compiling linkage analyses and the supporting literature, but also an expert in the type of crime under investigation (e.g., serial murder or serial rape).

The other principle involved regarding the use of a linkage analysis in court is that of "similar fact" evidence, sometimes referred to as "other crimes" evidence. Other crimes evidence was used in the cases *Louisiana v. Code, New Jersey v. Fortini*, and *Washington v. Russel* mentioned earlier, and similar fact evidence was used in *R v. B* (a sexual assault trial) and *R v. Burlingham* (two murder cases) in Canada. Generally, the courts will not admit similar fact evidence because the evidence is irrelevant to the facts at hand. An example of this is the use of previous convictions to try to convince the court that an accused is guilty of the current similar charges, due to his or her character. It is regarded as irrelevant, as it cannot prove or disprove the facts at hand for the current trial.

The exception to the rule is if the evidence can contribute to the facts in issue. There must be a logical connection or nexus between the similar facts and the facts in issue. The greater the correspondence and the closer the evidence and facts in issue are in time, place, manner, and nature, the easier it is to conclude that the required nexus exists (Schwikkard, 2002). The relevance of the similar fact evidence will also be determined by the strength of the other evidence available (Hoffmann & Zeffertt, 1988). Similar fact evidence is often used when an accused is charged with numerous crimes that are of a similar nature and unique in their MO (Petherick, Field, Lowe, & Fry, 2005), such as serial murder or serial rape where there is strong evidence of guilt, as evidenced by DNA or identity parade, in some but not necessarily all of the instances. Based on other similarities, the court may conclude that the suspect was responsible for the other charges also, even without there having been expert evidence regarding linkage during the trial. For other crimes evidence, findings that the accused had committed a similar, unique, crime in the past can be introduced as evidence. In *Louisiana v. Code* (1994), the court stated the following:

> *Several factors must be met for evidence to be considered as evidence of modus operandi: (1) there must be clear and convincing evidence of the commission of the other crimes and the defendant's connection therewith; (2) the modus operandi employed by the defendant in both the charged and the uncharged offenses must be so peculiarly distinctive that one must logically say they are the work of the same person; (3) the other crimes evidence must be substantially relevant for some other purpose than to show a probability that the defendant committed the crime on trial because he is a man of criminal character; (4) the other crimes evidence must tend to prove a material fact genuinely at issue; (5) the probative value of the extraneous crimes evidence must outweigh its prejudicial effect. (p. 11)*

Invariably, for someone to be indicted on a crime(s), he or she must have been linked to the crimes in some or other manner, such as by DNA, fingerprints, or any of the other traditional means by which an offender is identified. Without such evidence, a prosecutor would most likely have declined to prosecute in the first place. A linkage analysis is typically presented at the end of state's case (in adversarial systems), once all the evidence is before the court. In that sense, the linkage analysis presents the final, overarching piece of evidence, or the final "layer" of evidence. Ideally, the trial would proceed in the order that the offenses occurred, allowing the court to follow in the footsteps of the offender's series. To present linkage analysis too early might result in much of the information being regarded as hearsay, as the witness would be testifying about facts that have not yet been presented to the court and were not personally experienced by the witness.

CASE EXAMPLE: THE NEWCASTLE SERIAL MURDERS

The First Incident

At 6 pm on Saturday, February 14, 2004, a young black couple walked to a park bordering the town of Newcastle in the KwaZulu-Natal province of South Africa. After drinking a few beers, they decided to engage in sexual intercourse. While they were engaged in intercourse, the offender crept up to them and struck the male on the head with a large rock and killed him. He pushed the male victim off the female victim and slapped the female with an open hand while she tried to keep him at bay. The offender then hit the male victim with the rock a second time before dragging the female victim away. When the female victim screamed, the offender displayed a knife, threatened to stab her, and dragged her to a nearby ditch approximately 10 meters from where the initial attack occurred, where he raped her once. After the rape, he told her to dress and leave.

The male died at the scene at the same location where he was struck. The cause of death was determined to be blunt force trauma to the head. There were no other wounds inflicted on the murder victim. The bloodied rock was found at the scene, approximately 1 meter from the head of the deceased, who was lying on his back. He was clothed, but his pants were unzipped and his belt undone. Nothing was stolen from either victim.

The Second Incident

At approximately 11 pm on Wednesday, October 27, 2004, at the same park as the first incident, a young black couple decided to engage in sexual intercourse. The male victim, a minibus taxi driver, parked his taxi in an open space. While engaging in intercourse on a blanket next to the minibus taxi, the offender crept up to them and struck the male on the head with a large rock and killed him. The offender told the female victim not to dress, displayed a knife, and took the female victim to the nearby river, approximately 20 meters from the minibus taxi, where he raped her once. Afterward, he returned to the deceased's vehicle with the female victim, took the keys from the deceased's pocket, and removed two cell phones from the vehicle. The victim asked for money from her purse for transport, which the offender agreed to give to her. Thereafter, the offender set fire to the vehicle and fled the scene without giving the victim the promised money. The female victim then also fled the scene. The fire quickly burnt itself out and did not cause any significant damage to the vehicle, leaving only a burnt patch approximately half a meter in diameter in front of the first row of passenger seats.

The cause of death of the male victim was determined to be blunt force trauma to the head. There were no other wounds inflicted on the murder victim. The male died at the scene at the same location where he was struck by the offender. The bloodied rock was found at the scene approximately 1 meter from the deceased's head. The deceased was found lying on his back, next to the blanket he had placed on the ground. His shirt and shoes were on, and his pants were around his ankles. His underwear was in place, with his penis sticking out of the top of his underwear.

The Third Incident

In the early hours of Friday, November 26, 2004, near the scene mentioned in the second incident, the body of an adult black male was found along a footpath by a passerby. He was wearing only his underwear and a shirt. A shoe was found approximately half a meter from his body. The pants and the other shoe were not found at the scene. At the scene, a large bloodied rock was found approximately 1 meter from the deceased's head. The cause of death was blunt force trauma to the head. No female victim came forward to report any rape or assault.

The Fourth Incident

At approximately 9 pm on Friday, January 7, 2005, an adult Indian male left his relative's residence with his sports bag containing his personal belongings. He proceeded to the park mentioned in the previous incidents. In the early hours of Saturday, January 8, 2005, he was found unconscious with severe blunt force trauma to the head and a large bloodied rock nearby, approximately 8 meters away, down a small embankment next to where the victim was discovered. He was found wearing a yellow t-shirt and black jeans but no shoes. One shoe was found near the body. This scene was near the second incident, between the locations of the first and second incidents. A large roll of money belonging to the victim was found next to his body. He was taken to a hospital by ambulance and died 2 days later without ever recovering consciousness. His sports bag was missing from the scene. No female victim came forward to report any rape or assault.

The State's Evidence

The state's evidence was strongest on the first two incidents. Both the rape victims had pointed the offender out at either an identity parade (lineup) or a photographic identity parade. Unfortunately, there was no DNA evidence although a sexual assault crime kit was taken for each victim. The state also had a member of the public to whom the accused had mentioned that he had murdered people in the park. This member of the public alerted the police who then arrested the offender.

During interrogation, the offender admitted to murdering the men in the first two incidents but refused to do a pointing-out of the crime scenes or to make a formal confession to an independent officer or magistrate. (Recall from Chapter 8 that a pointing-out is a formal police procedure in which the offender agrees to disclose information relevant to the crime scene.) In South Africa, a confession to a noncommissioned officer of the South African Police Service (SAPS) is not admissible as evidence. However, the accused's informal confession to a member of the public that he was responsible for the murders in the park was admissible.

In the last two incidents, there were no eyewitnesses, surviving victims, or physical evidence linking the offender to the crimes. It was here that the decision was made, in consultation with the Director of Public Prosecutions, to charge the accused on the third and fourth counts of murder, relying on similar fact evidence. A linkage analysis was then compiled in support of similar fact evidence.

Methods Used in the Linkage Analysis

In this instance, the author was contacted shortly prior to the arrest of the offender by the investigating officer for assistance in the investigation. The author is responsible for assisting in all serial murder investigations conducted by the SAPS, which is a national police service. The investigating officer, attached to a Serious and Violent Crime Unit of the SAPS, had identified the series. The author traveled to consult with the investigator once the offender had been arrested. Later, the author submitted a brief report to the Director of Public Prosecutions suggesting that the offender be charged for all four murders and that the author would be able to testify in this regard. Once it was agreed to follow such a route, the author compiled the linkage analysis report for trial purposes. The following data sources were used to compile the linkage analysis:

1. Consultations with the investigating officer
2. Post-fact visits to the crime scenes
3. Plotting of the crime scenes on a handheld global positioning system (GPS)

4. Overlay of the crime scene GPS readings in a high-altitude photograph of the area
5. Examination of the police dockets, which included:
    a. Crime scene photographs
    b. Autopsy photographs
    c. Sworn statements taken by the police
    d. Autopsy reports

6. Interview with the rape victim who was involved in the first incident
7. Experience with the research and investigation of serial murders
8. Scientific literature regarding serial murder, linkage analysis, and signature analysis

Interviews were held with the offender but were not included as part of the data sources for the linkage analysis for two reasons: (1) the accused denied the accusations and, more importantly, (2) it was not the intention of the author to say that the accused committed the crimes but rather to give an opinion as to whether the crimes were committed by one offender, irrespective of who the court found guilty of the crimes. This sentiment is echoed by Keppel (1995) in his analysis of three females murdered by George W. Russell. Keppel states, "The analysis could not include any information about Mr. Russell or evidence about why he was connected to any one case" (p. 671). The steps followed were similar to those suggested by Hazelwood and Warren (2003).

The Linkage Analysis

The linkage analysis report was structured under the following headings:

1. Aim of the report
2. Information sources
3. Key terms
4. Linkage analysis
5. Conclusion

The actual linkage analysis was based on the manner in which the crimes were committed and the circumstances of the crimes.

Manner in Which the Crimes Were Committed

Tools Used to Commit the Crime

The offender displayed a weapon brought to the crime scene and used a weapon of opportunity (rock).

In the first two incidents, the offender displayed a weapon (knife) to the female victims; however, he used a weapon of opportunity from the crime scene, a rock, to kill the male companion. In all four incidents, the offender used a weapon of opportunity (rock) to murder the male victims. In each case, the rock was found near the deceased with blood stains on it.

Cause of Death: Traumatic Head Injury

In all four incidents, the cause of death was traumatic head injury leading to brain hemorrhage. Serial murderers tend to keep to one method of murdering.

Method of Obtaining Victims: Blitz/Sudden Attack

Serial murderers typically stick to one main method of obtaining their victims. In this particular instance, the offender surprised his unsuspecting victims and attacked them. All deceased died as a result of traumatic head injury leading to brain hemorrhage. The postmortem reports did not indicate any significant injuries to the limbs, which would have indicated an escalation of violence or a physical altercation between the offender and the victims.

Sexual Theme

In the first two incidents, the offender engaged in involuntary sexual intercourse with his victims. In the third incident, the deceased was found without his pants on.

Signature

Signature refers to a unique combination of events and behaviors exhibited by the offender. This is often referred to as a "calling card." In these instances, it can be said that the sudden lethal attack of adult males with a rock is the signature of the offender. Further, the lack of theft of opportunistic items of value appears to be a signature of the offender.

Circumstances of the Crimes

Time of Crimes: Nighttime

In these crimes, the offender targeted victims during the nighttime. Serial offenders often remain consistent in the manner in which they commit their crimes.

Geographic Pattern of Crime Scenes

These crimes were committed in close geographic proximity to each other. The distance between the location of the first incident and the location of the third incident (the two crime scenes farthest apart) was 1.2 kilometers. The distance between the second incident and the fourth incident was 50 meters.

Victimology

The offender targeted two types of victims. His rape victims were black adult females, and his murder victims were adult males (three black, one Indian). Serial murderers tend to be consistent with their victimology. Of serial murderers in South Africa, 40% include victims of multiple races in their series, and 34% include victims of both genders.

Findings of the Court

The court found the accused guilty on all charges. The court referred to the testimony presented to the court by the author and accepted it. The court concurred that the crimes were similar and unique enough for it to conclude that the accused was responsible for all the murders. The accused received five life sentences (four for murder and one for the rape of a minor child), 10 years for the rape of an adult female, 30 years for two incidents of robbery with aggravating circumstances, and 12 months for malicious injury to property. In South Africa, an accused is charged with each crime committed, not just the most serious crime. While the offenses were committed in four separate incidents, the sentences are served concurrently.

CASE EXAMPLE: THE QUARRY SERIAL MURDERS

Background of the Cases

From January to September 2002, the bodies of five unidentified adult black females were found along a small river near a highway just outside the city of Pretoria in South Africa, near a township known as Olievenhoutbos. These five cases were initially investigated as part of another series of bodies found along highways, known as the Highwayman series; however, when the Highwayman suspect, Elias Chauke, was arrested, it was found that he was in jail for an unrelated crime during the time of these five murders. Chauke was subsequently convicted for five other murders. These remaining cases that occurred during Chauke's imprisonment were eventually closed off as unsolved. Then in early January 2006, two bodies of adult black females were found approximately 2.8 kilometers from the nearest 2002 body. This discovery sparked concerns that the same offender was again committing murders after a 4-year hiatus. The 2002 task team was reformulated with the author as the head of the team. This series was labeled the "Quarry" murder series due to the bodies being found in close proximity to a nearby quarry. From January to September 2006, a total of 11 adult black females were murdered, and a 12th case, that of attempted murder, also took place. To date, only 6 of the 16 murder victims have been identified, a common problem experienced in South Africa.

The State's Evidence

In 8 of the 16 murder cases, there was evidence linking that offender to the crimes. This evidence was in the form of either cell phone evidence in two cases (the offender was in the possession of two victims' cell phones), DNA in four cases (from vaginal swabs), or a formal pointing-out of the crime scene in seven cases. Only one case had all three of these evidential aspects. In the other eight murders, there was neither physical nor eyewitness evidence linking the Quarry suspect, Richard Nyauza, to those murders.

Initially, the state prosecutor only wanted to indict the offender on the eight murder cases for which there was one of the three evidential aspects, and on the attempted murder for which there was eyewitness evidence and circumstantial evidence to link the offender to the offense. Negotiations were held between the task team and the prosecutor about charging the offender on all cases. Eventually, the prosecutor agreed to do so.

The Linkage Evidence

This linkage analysis differed slightly from the preceding Newcastle example in that firstly a linkage analysis was done on the five 2002 cases, then an analysis was done on the eleven 2006 murders, and finally an overall analysis of the 2002 and 2006 cases was done in one report. This approach was due to the 4-year gap between the first part of the series and the second part of the series.

Linkage Analysis: 2002 Murders

The linkage analysis was based on the manner in which the crimes were committed and the circumstances of the crimes.

Manner in Which the Crimes Were Committed

Tools Used to Commit the Crime

The tools used were objects that can cause blunt force, but not penetrative, trauma. No weapons were found at the scenes.

Cause of Death: Traumatic Injury

In three of the five murders from 2002, the cause of death was blunt force to the victim's body (head and torso). In the other two cases, the cause of death could not be determined by the pathologist at the postmortem examination.

Method of Obtaining Victims

It is unknown how the suspect obtained his victims, as none have been identified. Most South African serial murderers use a con story to lure victims away. It is highly likely that this MO was used in these cases.

Sexual Behavior

In none of the cases could it be determined by medical examination that the victims had been raped. There was, however, a sexual theme in four of the five murders, either in the form of nakedness of the victims or semen found.

Signature

In these instances, the suspect's signature can be described as targeting adult black females and leaving their bodies out in the open, usually in or near water, in close proximity to each other.

Circumstances of the Crimes

Time of Day of the Crimes

This could not be determined because none of the victims were identified and their last movements were therefore unknown.

Geographic Pattern of Crime Scenes

The crime scenes were all extremely close to each other. The greatest distance between any two crime scenes was 1.3 kilometers. The closest distance between any two scenes was 51 meters (the last two scenes of 2002).

Serial murderers tend to cluster their crime scenes together. The first two scenes of 2002 were slightly farther out, with the final three scenes being extremely close together.

Victimology

All victims were adult black females. Serial murderers often tend to keep to a particular victimology.

Linkage Analysis: 2006 Murders

As before, the linkage analysis was based on the manner in which the crimes were committed and the circumstances of the crimes.

Manner in Which the Crimes Were Committed

Tools Used to Commit the Crime

In most of the cases, the suspect used weapons that were not left at the scene.

Cause of Death: Strangulation

The predominant cause of death was strangulation (5 out of 11 cases). In five cases, the cause of death could not be determined at autopsy. One incident toward the end of the series involved stabbing the victim. Strangulation is typically the most common cause of death in serial murder cases. South African serial murderers have been known to alter their method of killing during a series. This inconsistency is either due to experimentation, unforeseen events that take place during the actual murder (such as victim resistance or the presence of passersby), or a change in MO that leads to a change in the method of murdering.

Method of Obtaining Victims: Con Story

Most South African serial murderers use a con story to lure unsuspecting victims. The most common con story is the offer of employment. Both Evelyn Dube and Molline Gunduza had come to Olievenhoutbos to sell metal pots and containers on the day of their respective disappearances. They were subsequently found near Rossway Quarry with their wares near them. Selina Mahlangu had traveled from KwaMhlanga (Mpumalanga Province) to meet with the suspect, who had offered her employment. Rosina Mosvana last had contact with her sister informing her that she was in Olievenhoutbos and that someone had offered her employment.

Sexual Behavior

Ten of the eleven 2006 murders had a sexual theme based on the crime scene, as indicated by nakedness or partial nakedness, rape, or semen. Most serial murderers in South Africa commit sexual serial murders.

Signature

The suspect's signature in the 2006 series was the targeting of adult black females for sexual murders by means of strangulation and leaving their bodies in or around the Rossway Quarry.

Circumstances of the Crimes

Time of Day of the Crimes

In the cases where the victims have been identified, they all went missing during the daytime.

Geographic Patterns of the Crime Scenes

The crime scenes from the 2006 cases were all close to each other, again, consistent with the behavior of serial murderers in South Africa and elsewhere. As with the 2002 cases, some of the bodies were found in or next to the Riet River—victims 6 and 8, both unidentified, and victim 10, Evelyn Dube.

Five of the eleven 2006 bodies were found among the rocks on the perimeter of the Rossway Quarry: victim 11, Molline Gunduza; victim 12, unidentified; victim 13, Selina Mahlangu; victim 14, unidentified; and victim 15, Elizabeth Mabasa. Victims 14 and 15 were found at the exact same location.

The following victims were found in the field near the quarry, in close proximity to each other: victim 7, unidentified; victim 9, unidentified; and victim 16, Rosina Mosvana.

Victimology

All victims were adult black females. Serial murderers often tend to keep to a particular victimology.

Overall Report

Across both series, the suspect preferred adult black females. Serial murderers tend to have an ideal victim. A category of victim (e.g., black adult females) is selected because it has some relevance to the offender. Often, hatred is developed within the individual for the victim group as a result of his or her own life experiences. Usually, perceived maltreatment by women is the main reason for targeting this group.

In the 2002 cases, the offender committed his first two murders outlying, then moved toward a central point, with the last three murders being within a very close proximity to the Riet River (Table 10.1). In the 2006 cases, the offender moved from the river and field to a central point, Rossway Quarry. He therefore exhibited the same pattern of movement in both the 2002 and 2006 series. The offender had three main crime scene groupings: (1) near the N14 highway where the Riet River intersects; (2) at the Rossway Quarry; and (3) near the golf estate.

In the 2002 series, the offender seemed to prefer using blunt force to murder his victims. In the 2006 series, the offender seemed to have developed and preferred strangulation, although there was one incident of stabbing and one incident of strangulation and blunt force trauma. This pattern of having more than one cause of death is not uncommon in South African serial murderers. An offender may begin using one dominant method and later use another, more satisfying method of murdering victims. There was a hiatus of 3 years between the 2002 and 2006 series in which the events in the offender's life could have led to his preferring a new method of murdering his victims.

In all except the last murder, there was a sexual theme, as described previously. A sexual theme tends to be consistent in a series where the murders are sexual in nature, as this has to do with the offender's inner motive for targeting his victims. In cases where no sexual theme is observed at the crime scene, it is often due to a disruption in the crime process, such as victim resistance or behavior, presence of passersby, or the mood or temperament of the offender.

The signature in both instances tended to be the suspect targeting adult black females and then leaving their bodies out in the open, usually in or near water, in close proximity to each other.

Conclusions of the Report

It is the opinion of the author of this report that the offenses referred to in this report were committed by the same offender. The uniqueness of the behaviors and circumstances accompanying these crimes are indicative of one offender and are unlikely to be imitated by another offender in such a similar fashion, due to the psychological motivation of such offenders. To date, the author has not come across copycat offenders in the serial crime investigations that he has assisted on.

Findings of the Court

The trial was held in the High Court in Pretoria, South Africa. South Africa has an adversarial system but no jury. Hence it is up to the judge, and his or her assessor(s), to deliver a verdict and impose a sentence. The trial lasted 5 court days from start to finish. In the end, the judge and his assessor (a magistrate) convicted on all counts for which the accused was indicted. In the eight cases where there was no direct evidence, the accused was found guilty based on the evidence tendered by the author, with the judge and his assessor relying on the legal principle of similar fact evidence.

In his judgment, Judge Murphy stated the following:

> *The last issue then is whether the linkages are sufficient to establish that the accused is the perpetrator of the crimes of the remaining 8 counts . . . where there*

is no other evidence linking the accused. We believe that such evidence is indeed sufficient. Were we to reject it as insufficient we would in effect be concluding, despite the strikingly similar geographic, signature and method evidence, that these victims landed in the two series by sheer coincidence or their killings were the work of a copycat killer with insider information regarding the geographic profiling, signature and modus operandi. The possibility of such a coincidence is remote in the extreme and we accept the evidence of Dr. Labuschagne that a copycat killer can be safely ruled out. In the result, therefore, I find the accused guilty of all the charges proffered against him in counts 1–24. (State v. Nyauza, 2007, p. 49)

TABLE 10.1 Similarities Across the 2002 and 2006 Cases				
Case Number	**Victimology**	**Location**	**Sexual Theme**	**Cause of Death**
289/01/2002	Adult black female	Field near the N14 highway	Yes	Undetermined
502/04/2002	Adult black female	Riet River	Yes	Blunt force
293/06/2002	Adult black female	Riet River	Yes	Blunt force
442/06/2002	Adult black female	Riet River	No	Blunt force
46/09/2002	Adult black female	Riet River	Yes	Undetermined
285/01/2006	Adult black female	Riet River	Yes	Strangulation
168/01/2006	Adult black female	Field near golf estate	Yes	Undetermined
911/02/2006	Adult black female	Riet River	Yes	Drowning and strangulation
705/04/2006	Adult black female	Field near golf estate	Yes	Undetermined
851/04/2006	Adult black female	Field near Rossway Quarry	Yes	Undetermined
1005/04/2006	Adult black female	Rossway Quarry	Yes	Strangulation
1041/05/2006	Adult black female	Rossway Quarry	Yes	Undetermined
994/07/2006	Adult black female	Rossway Quarry	Yes	Undetermined
995/07/2006	Adult black female	Rossway Quarry	Yes	Stab wounds
22/09/2006	Adult black female	Rossway Quarry	Yes	Blunt force and strangulation
463/09/2006	Adult black female	Field near golf estate	No	Strangulation

CONCLUSION

Linkage analysis has proven to not only be a valuable tool for investigators of serial offenses but also a useful tool during a trial as evidence. A growing body of research is finding support for the hypotheses underlying linkage analysis. While the concept of a linkage analysis has been understood and put into practice for investigative purposes for decades, its application to trial proceedings is relatively new. The rules of evidence will determine if such an analysis is admissible, along with the author of the analysis being qualified as an expert in court, depending on local legal requirements. In the future, it might be more relevant for behavioral analysts to focus on presenting linkage analysis testimony as opposed to profile evidence in the courtroom.

CHAPTER 11

The Missing Missing: Toward a Quantification of Serial Murder Victimization in the United States

Kenna Quinet

Early attempts to estimate the annual number of serial murder victims in the United States greatly varied (Fox & Levin, 1985; Holmes & DeBurger, 1988; Kiger, 1990). Kiger (1990) noted that the most extreme estimates of the number of serial murder victims were as high as 6000 victims per year, with claims of as many as 500 active annual killers during the mid to late 1980s. By 1990, scholars suggested that the incidence of serial murder was overestimated and that the United States was spending an extraordinary amount of money and attention on what may have constituted as little as 1% of total annual homicides (Kiger, 1990).

Jenkins (2005) suggests that the exaggerated magnitude of serial murders in the United States resulted from several factors. When apprehended, serial killers (e.g., Henry Lee Lucas) claimed to have hundreds of victims, when in fact they had far fewer (Egger, 2002; Fox & Levin, 2005).[4] There was also confusion about differences between stranger homicides in which the killer was known to have been a stranger to the victim and unknown homicides in which the identity of the offender, and thus the relationship with the victim, was unknown (Kiger, 1990). It was believed that most stranger homicides were committed by serial murderers and that many, if not most, of the unknown offender homicides might be serial murders. There was no evidence to suggest that either was the case (Kiger, 1990).

Political agendas also may have influenced the exaggeration of serial murder: The FBI wanted its Behavioral Science Unit to have authority over serial murders and wanted to expand federal authority to other serial crimes such as arson and rape; feminists drew on serial murder to highlight the victimization of women; get-tough-on-crime and death-penalty advocates used the heinous nature of serial murder to call for stricter sentences; religious groups used serial homicides as a warning about the evils of satanism; and all forms of media made money from the public's interest in the crime (Jenkins, 2005).

More recent research suggests far fewer serial murder offenders and victims. Hickey (2004) estimates there may be 30 to 40 active and unapprehended serial killers at any given time (though it is unclear whether this estimate includes cases carried over from previous years or only newly discovered cases). Although exaggerated estimates from the 1980s have tempered, there is still variation in estimated annual numbers of offenders and victims. Some of the divergence reflects a lack of clarity regarding whether estimates refer to apprehended killers, known but unapprehended killers, or suspected but unapprehended serial killers. The discovery of serial killers who have been active over a number of years does not typically result in additions to Uniform Crime Reports or Supplementary Homicide Reports from years or decades past (see Kiger, 1990). The detection of a nurse who has murdered a patient, for example, generally does not result in a review of the hundreds of past patient deaths under her care. In addition, how do we count an unidentified dead body whose cause of death may be homicide? How do we categorize a missing person whose disappearance is likely attributed to foul play? The true number of serial murder victims in the United States is a function of what we know (apprehended killers and strongly suspected serial murder

---

[4] Lucas claimed more than 300 victims and, although Fox and Levin (2005) suggest that at some point he may have claimed to have as many as 600 victims, in all likelihood, he had approximately 10 victims.

cases) as well as what we do not know (serial murder cases that for one reason or another are off the radar of police, coroners, medical examiners, and other officials).

The exaggeration and hype of the 1980s have been replaced by more reasonable estimates, but we may yet be undercounting the number of serial murder victims in the United States by discounting what we do not know. Virtually all estimates neglect the types of killers and victims that are always partially discounted: the serial killer who murders victims who have never been reported missing; the serial killer who disposes of bodies in such a way that when discovered the cause of death and victim identity are unknown; and killers who choose marginal victim populations such as illegal aliens, prostitutes, and the homeless (populations known as the less-dead; see Egger, 2002). Estimates also neglect deaths we do not realize as homicides, much less as part of a series.

As Ritter (2002) reminds us, it is important to establish the number of active serial killers and their victims so we do not just publish the estimates, have the debate about how many exist, and walk away. Our primary goal in quantifying this phenomenon should be to aid the police in prevention and intervention. Improved surveillance of a phenomenon is one of the first steps toward effective public policy. This chapter argues that by neglecting certain types of homicides (and other deaths) and ignoring some victim pools, we may be underestimating the number of serial murder victims in the United States and masking an even darker figure of serial murder. The argument is not that the phenomenon of serial murder is increasing; rather, it is that we have always missed some victims in our counts.

This chapter will review previous estimates of the number of serial murder victims in the United States; analyze missing persons, unidentified dead, and misidentified dead data for possible serial murder victims; and provide a methodology for creating a more valid estimate of the number of serial murder victims in the United States, paying particular attention to overlooked, special populations. The purpose of this endeavor is to examine the various sources of data where serial murder victims may be concealed and provide estimates of the annual numbers of possible uncounted victims. Careful examination of these populations suggests that there may be hundreds of uncounted serial murder victims each year in the United States. Some of the assumptions and extrapolations that constitute the contribution of this discussion may be subject to debate, but the intent is to spur expanded research on the number of serial murder victims in the United States.

DOING THE MATH

To establish a reliable number of annual serial murder victims in the United States, some scholars have attempted to establish the average active period for a serial killer and how many victims they have in a year, a month, or a week. Hickey (2004) suggests that the average contemporary female serial killer kills for 9 years and averages seven to nine total victims. However, the variation in the length of the active period is significant. For example, Hickey describes one female who killed for 34 years and others who were active for only a few months. Male serial killers averaged 6 to 11 victims over a similar period (9 years). Based on Hickey's (2004) estimates, 40 active killers per year averaging less than 1 victim per year would generate a victim count of less than 40 victims per year; this average is used as Hickey's lower estimate, with 63 victims per year (based on known serial murder offenders from 1975 to 2004) as the upper estimate of the number of serial murder victims per year. Using the FBI serial killer database covering the years 1977 to 1992, Egger (2003) finds an average of 13 known serial killers per year and an average of 67 victims per year. Fox and Levin (2005) count the number of killers by decade. For the 1980s, they count 150 serial killers, with 1100 to 1700 total victims for an average of about 120 to 180 known serial murder victims in the United States each year.

The variation in victim counts is significant, and given the relatively small base numbers of 40 or even 180 victims per year, missing cases with large victim counts could have a significant proportionate impact. Contrary to Hickey's findings (2004), several cases illustrate a significant trend toward more than one victim annually. From 1979 to 1981, Wayne Williams, who was active approximately 22 months, likely had as many as 30 victims, or 1.4 victims per month; Eileen Wuornos was active a little over a year and had seven victims, or one victim approximately every 2 months; and Orville Lynn Majors was active approximately 24 months and had a minimum of 70 victims and possibly as many as 160 victims (three to seven victims per month).[5] John Wayne Gacy killed 33 victims in 6 years, approximately five victims annually. Guillen (2007) notes that, at his peak, Gary Ridgway, the "Green River Killer," was killing four to five women per month. Moreover, recent research suggests that many U.S. medical murderers average two victims per month (Fox, Levin, & Quinet, 2005).

Recent lists of U.S. serial killers find that as many as 17% are nurses (Stark, Paterson, Henderson, Kidd, & Godwin, 1997). In contrast to male killers, Hickey notes that approximately one-third of female killers are place-specific.[6] Given the discovery of significant medical victim counts. it is possible we are underestimating the occurrence of place-specific, institutional killers. In addition, focusing heavily on serial homicides known to have large counts of certain types of victims, such as prostitutes, creates an

---

[5] Interview of prosecutors Gregory Carter and Nina Alexander in the case against Orville Lynn Majors, Vermillion County, Indiana, February 4, 2005.

[6] Place-specific refers to homicides that occur in one location (e.g., a hospital, home, prison, nursing home).

overemphasis on the male sexual serial killer—not the female serial killers who choose victims less likely to be detected as homicides (children, spouses, and patients) or the serial killer, male or female, who chooses victims who are never found, never missed, or never recognized as homicide victims.

The number of active killers is, in part, a function of the average length of activity until detection (e.g., finding the body). But what if no one finds the body? And what if no one is looking because no one ever reported the victim missing? What if we find bodies in clusters that may have been put there over a long period of time (such as in the case of Gary Ridgway)? Do we attribute all of those homicides to the year of body discovery? Recent media coverage about serial murder cases involving significant numbers of missing persons and unidentified dead, the detection of killers who were active for decades, and Ritter's (2002) challenge to conduct policy-relevant research suggest that we should revisit current estimates to more accurately estimate the annual numbers of serial homicide victims and offenders. Although early myths contributed to exaggerations of the risk of being a victim of serial murder, more recent myths may contribute to an underestimate of the risk for certain populations. To accurately re-evaluate annual serial homicide numbers, we must first look for the hidden victims.

MISSING PERSONS AS UNCOUNTED SERIAL MURDER VICTIMS ————

The important link between missing persons and serial murder victimization can be illustrated by a number of cases. Herbert Baumeister of Indiana killed at least 16 victims in 16 years. Most of his victims were reported as missing. Although this case was eventually solved by police diligence, there was an initial reticence to create a task force and declare a possible serial killer at large. This reticence was in part because missing victims were gay males, many of whom were known hustlers (and consequently more transient). The delay was not because these victims were any less of a priority but rather because of the impression that "these guys come up missing all of the time . . . same as with prostitutes" (Indianapolis Police Department [IPD], interviews of missing persons detectives, personal communication, June 2005). Research suggests that, indeed, prostitutes are a more transient population. A survey of prostitutes found that many prostitutes do not have households; 34% to 46% of prostitutes surveyed did not live in a household but rather stayed in hotels, motels, halfway houses, and homeless shelters (Potterat et al., 2004). Police who work missing persons cases suggest the reasons for the transient lifestyle of prostitutes and hustlers are numerous—eluding pimps and court dates, time in jail, and multiple-city work circuits (e.g., Indianapolis prostitutes will also work in Cincinnati and Louisville; IPD, 2005).

Potterat and colleagues (2004) note that the leading cause of death for prostitutes is homicide, with a homicide rate for prostitutes at 229 per 100,000. Most prostitute murders (64%) were committed by clients, as illustrated by the cases of some serial killers such as Gary Ridgway, Robert Pickton, and Robert Lee Yates. They demonstrate that one client can kill many women, thereby accounting for a significant portion of the homicides in a cohort. Depending on the cohort and decade, murder accounted for 29% to 100% of all prostitute deaths (Potterat et al., 2004). Although most prostitute homicides are not serial killer homicides, there are many serial murder cases documented in the literature with prostitute victims. Egger (2003) suggests that as many as 78% of all female serial murder victims are prostitutes. Although Egger documented several active serial murder cases with prostitute victims, there are no other claims in the serial murder research that three-fourths of female victims are prostitutes. Until there is replication of this finding, it should be treated with some caution.[7]

A recent interview of serial killer Keith Hunter Jesperson, the "Happy Face Killer," suggests that it is not only a transient victim pool that makes these murders difficult to trace. As Jesperson states, "I had a transient lifestyle—they were victimized because they were in my lifestyle" (Kamb, 2003). Jesperson, a long-haul truck driver, provided great detail about the extent to which he selected certain types of victims and hid their bodies in remote places so as to remain undetected—he understood the nature of missing persons and unidentified dead investigations and took pride in the fact he had been killing for a year before any of his bodies were discovered. Jesperson claimed to have 160 victims in multiple states and was legally tied to eight murders in five states (Kamb, 2003). Part of the risk for transient populations such as prostitutes, hustlers, runaways, and the homeless is their exposure to transient lifestyles.

In addition to the evidence that certain populations of people are more transient and therefore less likely to be missed, interviews with police and recent research indicate several reasons for reluctance to initiate missing persons cases (IPD, 2005). First, a missing persons case is not a criminal case (Olsen & Kamb, 2003). Because the majority of missing persons investigations are eventually resolved (e.g., the missing person comes home or is found), these cases may not be viewed as important assignments for police officers. Solving runaway cases is not the trajectory to promotion in a police department.

---

[7] In the book, *The Killers Among Us* by Steve Egger (2002, p. 89), the following appears: "In the United States, nearly 78% of female victims of serial murderers are female prostitutes (K. Egger, 2000)." The reference section of the book does not include a full reference for K. Egger, 2000, but rather only K. Egger, 1999, which is cited as an unpublished preliminary database of serial killers from 1900 to 1999. Aside from the citing confusion, it is not possible to deconstruct this claim because data are unpublished. This finding is cited by others (e.g., Hickey, 2004), but again, without any further explanation or documentation.

The politics of missing persons cases also affect their likelihood of investigation. Several cases illustrate a difference in the amount of time it takes to get a missing persons investigation initiated—although, in most jurisdictions, it is no longer true that you must wait 24 hours to file a missing adult report. In addition to delays in the initiation of missing persons (who are presumed to still be alive) investigations, jurisdictions are slow to initiate serial murder investigations, even when there are bodies discovered that should serve as catalysts. This reluctance is compounded by the ability of some serial killers to hide their victims. Gary Ridgway, for example, clustered bodies in burial sites that held as many as six victims (Guillen, 2007). Most of Ridgway's known victims (more than 60 women) were killed in and around Auburn, Washington, from 1983 to 2003 (Guillen, 2007; Rule, 2004). Many of these victims were not reported missing in a timely fashion or reported missing at all.

QUANTIFYING THE MISSING

How many missing persons are there? The answer depends on our definition of missing. Missing persons includes a number of different categories, including family abducted, stranger abducted, "thrownaway," kidnapped, voluntarily missing, involuntarily missing, and short- and long-term missing.

According to the FBI, all categories combined, there were 840,279 adult and child missing person reports filed in 2004. Of these cases, 85% to 90% were missing juveniles, and most cases were eventually resolved (National Crime Information Center [NCIC], 2005). Although more than 800,000 missing persons reports will be filed each year, only a subset of those are active cases at any given time. According to NCIC statistics, there are currently 106,097 (juvenile and adult) active (unresolved) missing persons cases in the United States (T. Matthews, personal communication, October 21, 2005). Of the 106,097 active missing persons cases, 47,633 (45%) are adults. Of these, 3,598 (8%) were missing less than 30 days, 2850 (6%) were missing from 30 to 60 days, 1850 (4%) were missing 61 to 90 days, 8743 (18%) were missing 91 to 364 days, and 30,622 (64%) adults were missing for 1 year or more (NCIC, 2004). Thus, the majority of active adult missing persons has been missing for more than 1 year.

The gender breakdown of missing persons statistics is also noteworthy; it looks more like the gender ratio of serial murder victims (65% female) as described by Egger (2003) than of overall homicide victims. Current statistics suggest an overall U.S. homicide victim gender split of 25% female and 75% male (Fox, 2004). The gender split for missing adults is nearly 50/50. Missing persons records for the state of Washington (long considered a model state for tracking unidentified dead and missing persons) were carefully scrutinized and analyzed by the *Seattle Post-Intelligencer* and showed a gender split of 40% male and 60% female (Olsen, 2003). Of the 47,633 missing adults in the NCIC database, 25,322 (53%) are males, and 22,338 (47%) are females. The NCIC gender ratio changes depending on the age group. Of missing adults ages 18 to 21 years, only 35% are male; for ages 22 to 29 years, 45% are male; for ages 30 to 39 years, 56% are male; and this trend continues. Essentially, the older the age group, the more likely the missing persons are to be male (NCIC, 2004). The overrepresentation of females as missing persons is in the age categories most associated with prostitution (Potterat, Woodhouse, Muth, & Muth, 1990). If long-term missing persons are a potential pool of serial murder victims and the missing are 47% to 60% female, then the "real" homicide victim gender ratio might not be 3 to 1.

There is much less detail available on the characteristics of missing juveniles in the United States. Of the 106,097 missing persons in the United States, 55,988 (53%) are juveniles, 60% of whom are female, similar to the adult gender ratio. Eighty-nine percent of the missing juveniles are 13 to 17 years of age (NCIC, 2004).

In the recent Washington State analysis of missing persons statistics, 130 (20%) of the 600 missing persons were presumed victims of homicide/foul play. Of the 130 suspected homicide/foul play cases, as many as 20 (15%) were suspected serial murder victims (Olsen & Kamb, 2003). Applying the Washington formula to national NCIC missing statistics, 20,000 (20%) of the 100,000 missing persons in the United States could actually be homicide victims yet to be found, with as many as 3000 (15%) of those being serial homicide victims.[8] More conservatively, if even 5% of the missing persons who may in fact be homicide victims are victims of serial murderers, this pool alone would generate an additional 100 to 200 serial murder victims each year. Table 11.1 presents reworked estimates using data transformations from various sources including missing persons.

Much has been written about the state of missing persons recordkeeping (Olsen & Kamb, 2003). Records are incomplete, closed without cause, and not closed when the person is found. Although Washington's (and most other states') law requires a dental records search if the person is missing for 30 days, the noncompliance rate with this law is greater than 60%. Many missing persons cases are not entered into any database, and most cases are cleared within a month. Some of these clearances are not because of face-to-face contact with the missing but rather public records, credit card use, or sightings

---

[8] The formula used for most estimates, with the exception of missing missing, which is only calculated for female prostitutes (see note 8), is to take the base number, multiply by 0.20 (because 20% are suspected homicides according to the Washington formula), and then multiply by 0.15, as the Washington findings suggest 15% of all homicides in the missing and unidentified dead categories may be the work of serial offenders.

TABLE 11.1 Annual Estimates of Uncounted Serial Murder Victims in the United States: Reworked Estimates from Data Transformations

Data Source	Lower Estimate	Upper Estimate	Formula—Sources of Data Transformations
Missing persons	100–200	300–600	Application of Washington findings—20% of missing as homicide 15% of those as serial murder victims (5% for lower estimate) divided by 5-year and 10-year accumulations
Missing missing persons	6 (Hickman, Hughes, Strom, and Ropero-Miller 2007) 11 (NCIC, 2005)	19–29 (Fox & Levin, 2005)	Extrapolating from known victim counts for female prostitutes only
Missing foster children	14	23	Application of Washington findings (70 by 3- and 5-year divisions)
Unidentified dead*			Washington formula applied to NCIC (2006) and BJS survey figures (Hickman et al., 2007) and NCIC extrapolations from Matthews (2006), by 10-year and 15-year divisions
NCIC	12	18	
BJS	27	40	
Matthews	24–36	120–180	
Misidentified dead*			500–1000 from Fox, Levin, and Quinet (2005), 10% (50–100) as very low lower estimate
Medical Murder	500–100	500–1000	
Total	182–361	860–1832	

NOTE: NCIC, National Crime Information Center; BJS, Bureau of Justice Statistics.

*Only one of these figures should be used in the total, as either the NCIC, BJS, or Matthews number is the most accurate.

by someone. The Washington investigation revealed that, over time, 1 in 10 cases is lost or destroyed (and 100 of the 700 cases still active with state police could not be accounted for in any local agency), suggesting that the numbers of the long-term missing may be underestimated by at least 10% (Olsen & Kamb, 2003). If all of these problems exist in a state recognized for its progressive missing persons system, one can only speculate about the condition of missing persons records in other states.

Given the number of high-profile, long-term serial murder cases (e.g., Gary Ridgway) in the state of Washington, some suggest that these state records may actually be some of the best in the United States. Using the state of Washington missing persons findings as the best available model for extrapolating to the United States may be a problem if there is something different about the number and type of missing persons in Washington as opposed to other states. Although each state's distribution of missing persons is likely a function of the race, gender, and age distribution of the population of that state, there is no evidence to suggest that the patterns of serial murder vary by state. Hickey (2004) asserts that the likelihood of serial murder is a function primarily of that state's population, and other research finds that, although there may be a western effect in the distribution of serial homicide (with those states having more cases than would be expected as a function of the population), there is nothing unique about the Northwest (Rossmo, 2004). So despite the Gary Ridgway, Ted Bundy, and other high-profile cases, no research thus far finds any unique properties in the state of Washington. Hickey ranked states according to the number of serial murder cases from 1800 to 2004 and found that the state of Washington had 6 to 19 cases of serial murder (as did 11 other states). California had 60 known cases during the same time period, and a second tier of states—Florida, Illinois, New York, and Texas—had 20 to 30 cases. Thus it appears that the number of serial murder cases in the state of Washington falls somewhere in the median range, meaning this state may provide a reasonable source from which to extrapolate conservatively.

THE MISSING MISSING

The most successful serial killers know to select the unmissed as victims if they intend to kill for an extended period of time. How many people are missing but have never been reported as missing? One way to get at this number may be to do an analysis of serial murder cases to determine how many of the victims were missing persons never reported as missing, or were reported as missing with the case having been prematurely or incorrectly closed or purged.

The case of Gary Ridgway in Washington is a suitable case example for analysis because the victims were female prostitutes who went missing. Of the 48 known victims, 4 women were reported as missing but were deleted from missing persons records by police personnel because of false rumors of sightings; another four cases were purged by accident from the missing persons database.[9] Additionally, after the identification of remains, it was discovered that two victims were never reported as missing, and one other was reported but not until five years after disappearing. Five of the victims are still unidentified (Guillen, 2007; Rule, 2004).

In the Rigdway case, 23% (11 of the 48, not including unidentified dead) of victims were missing missing—victims for whom there was no active missing person case. Had many of the bodies not been dumped together in clusters, many of the victims may not have been discovered at all. Unless the bodies are found, the missing missing do not exist. Moreover, approximately 10% (five victims) in the Ridgway case were unidentified dead. If these unidentified dead are also counted among the missing missing, the possible total of missing missing in just one case of a serial killer who preys on prostitutes would be 33%.

Applying Egger's (2003) claim that 65% of all serial murder victims are female and approximately 75% of known female serial murder victims are prostitutes to Hickey's (2004) lower estimate of 40 serial killer victims per year, 26 would be female and 20 of those would be prostitutes. Extrapolating from the Ridgway case, if we assume that this figure (20 prostitute serial killer victims per year) is underestimated by 33% because of missing missing victims, approximately six additional victims would be added to lower estimates of the number of female victims per year (see Table 11.1, lower estimate missing missing). Applying Egger's claim to Fox and Levin's (1985) upper estimates of 120 to 180 serial killer victims per year, 78 to 117 victims would be female and 59 to 88 of those would be prostitutes. If we have a missing missing pattern similar to the Ridway case (33%), there could be an additional 19 to 29 annual female prostitute serial murder victims that are never discovered (see Table 11.1, upper estimate missing missing).[10]

Foster children are another source of missing missing. Children in foster care in the United States are protected by confidentiality laws; their identity and the fact that they are in the foster care system is strictly private information. In most states, when foster children go missing, their names are not publicly released. With a few

---

[9] Ridgway remembered and confessed to 48 murders, but there is strong evidence to suggest he killed more than 60 women (Guillen, 2007). The current analysis uses 48 as the total victim count.

[10] The assumptions are that there are additional unfound, uncounted female prostitute victims each year. Using the Ridgway case as a basis for calculation, as many as 33% of his victims are missing missing or unidentified dead, which we know only because he buried his victims in clusters and we were able to find more bodies than we would in most cases. The way to calculate is to multiply the estimated total annual number of serial murder victims by 0.65 (because 65% of victims are female), then multiply by 0.75 (using Egger's approximate estimate that 75% of female victims are prostitutes), and then by 0.33 (the percentage of missing missing in the Ridgway case). These figures reflect only the missing missing that are female prostitutes; analysis of other cases involving male prostitutes could be used to further refine the estimates, but there has been no scientific attempt to establish the proportion of serial murder victims that are male prostitutes.

exceptions, there is no Amber Alert, no milk carton, no organized community search, and child protective services representatives will not speak to the public about these missing kids. In fact, in some states, biologic parents are not even allowed to go to the media if their child who has been placed in foster care goes missing ("Few Looking for Missing," 2002).

Of the 585,000 foster children in the United States, 20% (117,000) are missing at any given time, with 98% of those thought to be runaways (suggesting they are voluntarily missing) and 2% (2340 children) unaccounted for (Peterson, 2002). Applying the Washington formula, 468 of the 2340 unaccounted for missing children could be additional homicide victims, with 70 of those being additional serial murder victims. Dividing this total across 5 years would add an additional 14 annual serial murder victims, and dividing across 3 years would add an additional 23 victims (see Table 11.1, missing foster children).

These revised estimates do not take into account possible murder victims among another pool of missing missing kids—the so-called "thrownaways." Thrownaways are children who are forced out by their parents. Rarely do parents call police to report that they forced their child out; thus, there are virtually no statistics about this group. Even recent statistics from the National Incidence Studies of Missing, Abducted, Runaway, and Thrownaway Children do not specifically estimate the number of thrownaway kids each year in the United States. Instead they include this estimate within the runaway category (Sedlak, Finkelhor, Hammer, & Schultz, 2002). One organization, Families of Missing Loved Ones, suggests there may be as many as 127,000 thrownaway children at any given time in the United States (Families of Missing Loved Ones, 2002). This group of children would be particularly vulnerable to predators. By definition, no one cares enough about them to report them as missing, and no one knows where they are. Estimates of the number of thrownaway children come from only one source and are not included in the estimates in Table 11.1.

Further case studies of serial killers and their victims are needed to establish the number of victims, once discovered, who were never reported as missing. Unless the bodies are found, the missing missing do not exist.

UNIDENTIFIED DEAD

The unidentified dead are made up of persons who died from any number of causes, including natural deaths, although the cause of death is unknown. For this analysis, the concern is the extent to which those unidentified dead are victims of homicide and, more specifically, serial homicide. It should be noted that some of the persons listed as missing persons also may be entered into unidentified dead databases so there may be some double counting when using both of these sources. Thus, lower, more conservative estimates are provided for extrapolations presented here.

Identifying the unidentified dead is not an easy process, particularly if the individual had spent a lifetime trying to hide his or her identity—a reasonable assumption for drifters, prostitutes, and other transient populations. Davis (1996) describes a California case of an unidentified man killed in a stolen car in an accident. As the search for his identity unfolded, it turned out he had 25 different aliases, three social security numbers, and five different birthdates (all in different years). This man had not had any contact with family members for months but had never been reported as missing. Clearly, unidentified dead can be very challenging cases for law enforcement. Identification is even more remote when all that is discovered is a few bones. Many jurisdictions across the United States only keep unidentified remains for a year, after which they are either buried in unmarked graves, or as is the case in San Francisco, once a month, the unidentified dead are incinerated and the ashes taken out to sea (Davis, 1996). The likelihood of ever tying most of the unidentified remains across the United States to a single serial killer under these conditions is unlikely.

According to the NCIC, there are currently 6036 unidentified dead cases in their records (NCIC, 2006). Once a case is entered into NCIC (and it can only be entered by law enforcement), it has to be renewed annually by the originating agency to avoid having the records purged (Olsen & Kamb, 2003). Twenty-five percent of the unidentified dead in the NCIC system are female, and 71% are male (the gender of the remaining 4% is unknown; T. Matthews, personal communication, October 21, 2005). Findings for the state of Washington are similar. Of their unidentified dead, approximately 60% are male, 25% are female, and 15% are unknown. The proportion of NCIC unidentified dead who are female is similar to the proportion of female homicide victims in the United States.

A June 2007 Bureau of Justice Statistics (BJS) survey of medical examiners and coroners offices across the United States finds the NCIC statistics on unidentified dead to be significantly lacking (Hickman, Hughes, Strom, & Ropero-Miller, 2007). The total number of unidentified human remains reported in the BJS survey (13,486) is twice that of the NCIC figure of 6036. The nation's medical examiners and coroners report approximately 4400 new unidentified human remains each year, and 1000 of those cases remained cold/unidentified after a year. Only half of those offices surveyed reported having a policy for retaining records on unidentified remains (e.g., dental, DNA, fingerprints; Hickman et al., 2007). The BJS director, Jeffrey Sedgwick, suggests that a large number of the nearly 14,000 unidentified dead were likely homicide victims and that the true number of remains is likely even much higher than 14,000 (Willing, 2007).

Another source of unidentified dead statistics, the Doe Network, is a volunteer organization that works with law enforcement and medical examiners to solve missing persons and unidentified dead cases. The Doe Network maintains its own database/web site of unidentified dead cases and devotes significant effort toward finding matches between missing persons and unidentified dead records (Doe, 2006). Of the 1112 unidentified dead cases in the Doe database, there are 11 cases from 1800 to 1969 (bodies discovered during this time period), 50 cases from 1970 to 1979, 251 cases from 1980 to 1989, 469 cases from 1990 to 1999, and 331 cases from 2000 through July of 2006 (Doe, 2006). If Doe patterns prevail, the 6036 unidentified dead tracked by NCIC have accumulated primarily since 1970, with as many as 70% having accumulated since 1990 and more than 50% since 1996.

No public information is available at the national level through NCIC to indicate a typical cause of death for the thousands of unidentified bodies in morgues and other storage facilities, but we can look to other sources that track unidentified dead across the United States. The Network of Medicolegal Investigative Systems (NOMIS) is a death investigation web-based program for agency use. As of January 2004, NOMIS differs from NCIC, as cases may be entered by medical examiners and coroners, not just law enforcement. Of the approximately 473 unidentified dead entered into the NOMIS system, 36 died of homicide (8%), and an additional 41 died of undetermined (9%) causes (NOMIS, 2006). However, because NOMIS has been up and running for only 2 years and is used by only a limited number of agencies across the United States, it will not be used for establishing lower and upper estimates in this discussion.

As previously indicated, Washington state data contain 97 unidentified dead, 19 of which (20%) were homicides, with 3 (15%) of those likely serial homicides. Even in this model state, journalists for the *Seattle Post-Intelligencer* during a county-level investigation in Washington found another 21 cases of unidentified dead who had never been entered into the FBI-NCIC database (Olsen, 2003). Using the Washington unidentified dead findings to calculate likely causes of death for NCIC unidentified dead, 1200 (20%) of the 6000 NCIC unidentified dead would be homicide victims, and 15% of those (180) could be serial murder victims. If these 180 victims were the result of 10 years of accumulation (as are more than 50% of the Doe unidentified dead), then the annual number of unidentified dead that are likely serial murder victims is approximately 18. If they accumulated over a 15-year period (as did more than 70% of the Doe listings), then the annual number of serial murder victims would be 12 (see Table 11.1, NCIC).

Using the BJS estimates from the 2004 survey of coroners and medical examiners would suggest as many as 2697 (20%) of the 13,486 unidentified dead could be homicide victims, and 405 of those (15%) could be serial murder victims. If these unidentified remains accumulated over a 10-year period, we would have an additional 40 annual serial murder victims. If they accumulated over a 15-year period, then the annual number of serial murder victims in the BJS unidentified dead would be 27 (see Table 11.1, BJS).

Some experts feel that the NCIC unidentified dead number, 6036, reflects as little as 10% and only as much as 50% of actual unidentified dead numbers because many law enforcement agencies do not report to NCIC and coroners cannot use NCIC (Matthews, 2006). Hypothetically, there could therefore be as many as 12,000 to 60,000 unidentified dead in the United States (Matthews, 2006). If Matthews is correct, and there are 12,000 to 60,000 unidentified dead in the United States, then extrapolation from Washington state data suggests that 2400 to 12,000 (20%) could be homicide victims with 360 to 1800 (15%) of those being serial murder victims. Dividing this range (360 to 1800) across 10 and 15 years of accumulation would generate the lower range estimate of 24 to 36 and the upper range estimate of 120 to 180 shown in Table 11.1 (Matthews, 2006).

One would hope for a match/identification when information from missing persons and unidentified dead databases converge, but we know from recent research that if very specific information on a missing person is entered into NCIC and the same specific information on an unidentified dead person (the same missing person) is entered by another jurisdiction, there may be no match made. Haglund (1993) reported on a search in NCIC that included an exact dental match between an unidentified dead and a missing person, but because of the weight of matching requirements, the NCIC system did not find the match. Bell's (1993) critique of the NCIC missing and unidentified dead matching program describes the problem of inaccurate data input from the law enforcement agency. Haglund also notes extremely low national compliance (maybe as little as 2% for dental records entries), a lack of access by medical examiners and coroners, forms that need to be refined, and old cases that need to be updated or verified.

MISIDENTIFIED AND ELSEWHERE CLASSIFIED DEAD

The misidentified dead are comprised of deaths with unknown causes or deaths that are wrongly categorized as suicides, accidents, or natural causes, when in fact they are the result of homicide. Each year in the United States, approximately 2.5 million people die. For the National Vital Statistics System (NVSS) to classify a death as a homicide, it must be certified by a coroner, medical examiner, or prosecutor acting as coroner, and (almost always) autopsied. In most states, all homicides require an autopsy, but because they are often not affordable, potential homicides may be coded as a natural death, accidental death, or suicide to avoid incurring the costs of an autopsy (L. Smit, Deputy Coroner, Kitsap County, Washington, personal communication, November 4, 2005). In many jurisdictions, accidental deaths and suicides are also certified and require autopsies if there are questions or pending litigation.

The NVSS death certificates code the manner of death as natural, accidental, suicide, homicide, pending, or could not be determined (NVSS, 2006). The cause of death (e.g., gunshot, stabbing, car accident) is classified by state-level employees using International Classification of Diseases codes. In several instances, the discovery of a body, particularly if time has passed since death, may result in the cause of death as undetermined when the manner of death is homicide (F. Kelley, Marion County Deputy Coroner, personal correspondence, summer 2004). In a recent case, 10 female bodies were found at truck stops in Texas, Oklahoma, Arkansas, Missouri, Louisiana, and Tennessee. Of the 10 bodies, 1 is unidentified, and although the manner of death appears to be serial-related homicides, the specific cause of death is undetermined in 4 of the 10 cases (Lavendera, 2004; Ramirez, 2004).

Of the annual 2.5 million U.S. deaths, 32,000 (less than 1% of all deaths) deaths are coded as "something not elsewhere classified" (NVSS, 2006). In other words, the cause of death could not be determined. One of the populations most likely to be overlooked as the victims of serial murder are people at risk or expected to die (e.g., those who are in hospitals or nursing homes) and those killed by custodial killers (e.g., nurses, mothers, landladies). This trend is counterintuitive, as custodial or stationary killers would seem more likely to be detected because observers (e.g., other nurses and doctors, tenants, family members) would notice their actions; however, detection may actually be more difficult because these killers operate in settings where the opportunity is so significant. Custodial killers have distracted coworkers, a defenseless and vulnerable victim pool, and easy access to drugs and other homicide methods. As suggested by Stark, Paterson, Henderson, Kidd, and Godwin (2001), there are motivated offenders in all professions but the medical murder phenomenon may be a result of extraordinary opportunity combined with a lack of surveillance and detection.

There are nearly 6000 hospitals in the United States with nearly 1 million beds that serve an annual admission population in excess of 35 million people (American Hospital Association, 2003). In addition, according to the National Center for Health Statistics, 3 million people pass through 17,000 nursing homes each year. This amounts to a nursing home population of 1.8 million on any given day with more than 1.4 million employees (Schneider & O'Connor, 2002). Of the 2.5 million deaths in the United States each year, more than 860,000 occur in hospitals and over 500,000 occur in nursing homes. Thus, greater than 50% of all deaths each year occur in hospitals and nursing homes (Agency for Healthcare Research and Quality, 2003). The opportunities for foul play are staggering.

Research on pediatric deaths also suggests room for error in reliable cause of death information (McClain, Sacks, Froehlke, & Ewigman, 1993). One team reviewed medical and death records of children and found that many cases were likely homicide but coded as deaths as a result of SIDS or other injury. They suggest that the infant homicide death rate may be three times as high as previously reported, making it similar to the homicide rate of teens (McClain et al., 1993). Although the SIDS death rate has decreased from 5000–6000 deaths per year to 2100 deaths per year, it is still the third-leading cause of death for persons under 1 year of age (NVSS, 2006).

Many medical murderers (doctors, nurses, and other medical staff who murder patients) have used various poisons to cause cardiac arrest; the cause of death stops there without further investigation into what actually caused the cardiac arrest. The coroner in Little Rock, Arkansas, suggests that when it is reported that a patient's heart "just stopped beating," it is time for suspicion. This is an insufficient explanation of death; all hearts stop beating when we die. The real question is why. He suggests that 73% of death certificates from nursing home deaths list incorrect causes of death (Schneider & O'Connor, 2002).

Research on medical murderers/custodial killers has illustrated that many female serial killers use their workplace as their hunting and killing grounds; not only do they know their victims (dispelling the stranger myth) but they are often charged with their care. Recent focus on female serial killers finds that women have different hunting grounds and different killing opportunities than men. Their victims are both men and women, children, and the elderly. From faux-SIDS cases to nursing home and hospital deaths—female serial killers are cradle-to-grave, equal-opportunity killers (Fox et al., 2005). These types of homicide are not represented anywhere in the Uniform Crime Reports or Supplementary Homicide Reports data; they are classified as natural deaths or SIDS, or within other misidentified cause of death categories.

If we are overlooking female serial offenders, then we are overlooking their victims. Thus, the age/gender profile of serial murder victims is likely skewed as well. Fox and Levin (2005) note that known female serial killers were twice as likely to have patients or elderly persons as their primary target (17% of the time) as were male serial killers (8% of the time). Based on the gender distribution of people in hospitals and nursing homes (for age group gender distributions, see Safarik, Jarvis, & Nussbaum, 2000), those who target the elderly or hunt in hospitals and nursing homes should be even more likely to have female victims than are serial killers who choose younger victims. Thus, we may not only be overlooking female serial killers but undercounting female victims as well. Hickey (2004) notes that since 1975 the likelihood of serial murder cases involving elderly victims has risen rather dramatically.

As shown in Table 11.1, an examination of known cases suggests that a reasonable estimate of the number of medical murder victims annually could be 500 to 1000 (Fox et al., 2005). Known medical murderers appear to average two victims per month. In a small county in Indiana, Orville Lynn Majors killed as many as 130 patients in about 2 years, all of which were coded as natural deaths. Even after investigations revealed the true causes of death, the death certificates were never updated (G. Carter & N. Alexander, prosecutors in the Orville Lynn Majors case, personal communication, February 4, 2005).

Each year approximately 3175 inmates die in U.S. prisons. The bulk of the deaths, 2400 (75%), are coded as natural causes; of the others, approximately 1% (56) are due to homicide, 6% (198) to suicide, 10% (302) to AIDS, and the rest are considered "other," including executions and unspecified accidents or drug overdoses (Stephan & Karberg, 2003). There have been recent reports of jails and prisons hiring physicians who have lost their medical license (Skolnick, 1998). These doctors have either been convicted of some sort of crime or lost their license because of professional misconduct, but prisons and jails—filling with more prisoners every day and dealing with an aging population, AIDS, tuberculosis, mental illness, and other diseases—will still hire them. The idea that incompetent, possibly dangerous physicians are now turned loose on a captive jail and prison population has come under scrutiny, but the practice has not stopped (Skolnick, 1998).

Mott (1999) suggests that serial killers may remain undetected because of their transient, multijurisdictional, geographically mobile nature. However, research comparing solved serial killings to unsolved serial killings finds that solved serial killings were more likely to include the geographically mobile killer whereas the place-specific killer was more likely to be the culprit in unsolved cases. This finding seems counterintuitive, as it would appear to be easier to detect and apprehend a stationary killer, but that is not the case.

In addition to the mobility issue, research comparing solved serial killings to unsolved serial killings finds that unsolved serial killings have longer time periods between murders, and the bodies are more likely to be discarded outdoors (although our institutionally place-specific killers typically do not discard bodies outdoors). Place-specific killers are not necessarily harder to investigate or profile, but they are often not being investigated until the offender is already identified. It is also noteworthy that the unsolved serial murders were significantly more likely to have targeted vulnerable populations such as prostitutes or homeless (Mott, 1999).[11] Another possibility is that there are not actually longer time periods between unsolved murders of populations of prostitutes or the homeless but, rather, because the unsolved population is a more marginal and invisible group, the time periods between murders are not marked by telltale events such as victims reported missing, discovered bodies, significant media coverage, or official investigations.

There is no reason to suggest that opportunity patterns that exist for other crimes do not also apply to perpetrators of homicide. Assuming opportunity matters and as our institutionalized population numbers increase, we should expect to see an increase in the medical murder phenomenon in our prisons, nursing homes, hospitals, and hospice centers. A sick, trapped/incarcerated, vulnerable, weak victim pool makes for easy prey for serial killers. If potential offender pools include not only people who are motivated to kill but who also have opportunity (e.g., home healthcare providers, nurses, doctors, and prison staff) and access to means, then our victim pools—Egger's less-dead—will also include institutional populations.

CONCLUSION

This chapter provides extrapolation from existing databases including missing persons and unidentified dead to estimate uncounted serial murder. Results suggest we have overlooked a number of serial murder victims for years. In any given year, we can conservatively add hundreds of additional serial killer victims—missing persons who are actually dead, missing missing who are dead (unreported missing prostitutes and foster children), the unidentified dead who were murdered by serial killers, and serial murder victims from institutional settings (nursing homes, hospitals, and prisons) who were misclassified as natural deaths. The present research suggests that even if a small proportion of these deaths were serial homicides then our true serial murder victim count is and always has been low (excluding the exaggerated estimates of the 1980s). By counting potentially hidden serial murder victims, we add a minimum of 182 annual serial murder deaths (doubling the 2005 estimate of Fox and Levin) and as many as 1832 uncounted annual serial murder deaths (more than 10 times the estimate of Fox and Levin) to existing counts.

---

[11] Potterat et al. (1990) found that there were approximately 84,000 working prostitutes in the United States during the 1980s and that average career lengths were 4 to 5 years.

An inherent limitation of this study is the fuzzy nature of many of the data sources used for extrapolation. To the extent that official data on the numbers of missing persons, unidentified dead, the missing missing, and causes of death in institutional and other settings are invalid, the extrapolations and estimates from these sources are flawed, potentially in either direction. For example, if the state of Washington's missing persons data collection system and analyses of the number of missing who are dead and the number who were victims of serial homicide are not reflective of other states, the present estimates may require revision. Research is needed to determine the demography of missing persons and unidentified dead by state. The accuracy of revised estimates presented here is also dependent on the accuracy of current serial murder counts that serve as the baseline for extrapolations accounting for hidden victims. This study is a first step toward a more detailed attempt to quantify serial murder victimization in the United States, but much work is needed to improve the primary data sources on which it relies.

As researchers, we can do further serial murder case study analyses to better establish the possible number of missing missing among the victims. The present research most likely underestimates the missing missing in serial murder cases, as it only addresses missing missing female prostitutes. Cases where bodies are discovered buried together will shed the most light on the number of victims who were either never identified or never reported as missing. Additional research is needed to verify Egger's (2003) claim that approximately 75% of female serial murder victims are prostitutes and to quantify the proportion of serial murder cases that involve male prostitutes, runaways, homeless, and other vulnerable populations likely to account for the missing missing. Hickey's (2004) research suggests that the most likely category of victim selection for serial killers is young women alone, comprised of prostitutes and female college students (followed by children, boys, and girls). In all likelihood, missing college coeds who were slain by serial killers are well counted. It is the other dimension of this category—prostitutes—who are more likely undercounted as serial murder victims.

Statistics on the number of teenage runaways and children who are abandoned ("thrownaways") by parents and guardians are the least reliable. In fact, almost no entity is even trying to estimate the number of thrownaway kids. When teenage runaways turn 18 years old, they are no longer on the rosters of missing children, and almost no entity is scientifically estimating the number of thrownaway kids. These troubling patterns present room for policy change. Missing children who are thought to be runaways could be kept as active missing persons cases even when they are no longer juveniles; school systems could play a more active role in tracking children who slip through the cracks and may be thrownaway and in need of supervision; and the foster care system could be overhauled and repaired.

On the law enforcement side, there are a number of impediments to the investigation of the reports of missing persons. Warrants are required to access bank and credit card activity, and it is difficult, sometimes impossible, to get information from government entities including the Social Security Administration, the military, the Internal Revenue Service, public assistance, and the U.S. Postal Service. The Health Insurance Portability and Accountability Act of 1996 protects the release of medical information, even to law enforcement, regarding whether a person has been admitted to a hospital, mental hospital, or emergency room. Domestic violence shelters, understandably, will not tell police whether a woman is in their facility. In the event that police do locate a missing person 18 years of age or older, they are not required to disclose the person's location to those who reported him or her as missing (IPD, interviews of missing persons detectives, personal communication, June 2005). At a minimum, permitting law enforcement greater access to critical, timely information would aid in the investigation of missing persons cases.

Death surveillance systems in hospitals and nursing homes, greater control of lethal drugs and medications not currently classified as controlled substances, and increased scrutiny of nurses, doctors, and other medical personnel who hospital hop would help deter and detect medical murder. Although it may be popular to dedicate limited resources to enhancing safety on college campuses and in suburban neighborhoods, such initiatives are not likely to significantly impact the incidence of serial homicide. Wiser alternatives may include security cameras at truck stops frequented by transient offenders and less-missed victims, systems for tracking the missing homeless, and strategies for reporting and finding missing migrant workers and illegal immigrants.

Ritter's (2002) call for research that has policy and investigative implications challenges us to assess the ways we may begin to prevent serial homicide. Much has been written and speculated about the etiology of a serial murder. Potential victims and society may be better served if we think about monitoring the opportunities given to serial killers. A hot-spot approach to preventing serial murder might begin at truck stops and other areas frequented by prostitutes. A less punitive, more resource-based approach to dealing with prostitution (similar to the ways we have tried to track and care for the homeless) may encourage prostitutes to report other missing prostitutes or suspicious customers. With prostitution as the most dangerous job on record, a preventive focus and more resources could prevent the horrific prostitute body counts of one killer who has 60 to 70 victims.

We have a limited amount of resources to combat homicide, including serial homicide. The horrific loss of life, the fear engendered by serial murder, and the high cost of investigations make it critically important to establish reliable estimates of risks for certain populations. The present research suggests a paradigm shift in which missing persons cases and marginalized victims are prioritized rather than minimized will be necessary to effectively address this crime.

Although we exaggerated the prevalence of serial murder in the 1980s, we now may be underestimating the prevalence of serial murder victims and offenders in certain sectors of our society. Although it seems improbable that we underestimated a phenomenon as widely covered and as sensationalistic as serial murder, in many cases the victims we are overlooking are the marginalized—Egger's less-dead— those who are less-missed, less-guarded, and, as this research suggests, less-counted.

CHAPTER 12

Targeting the Serial Offender: Task Force Structuring and Organization

Mark W. Schmink

The serial offender has been and will be a constant source of a host of problems to potential victims and members of law enforcement. There are many types of serial offenders, but for the purposes of this chapter, we will focus primarily on the most serious crimes associated with this type of individual. A basic foundation will be laid on how serial offenders operate, whom they choose, the crimes they commit, and how they are caught and prosecuted.

This chapter will discuss the formation, structure, and organization of a task force. These entities have a unique distinction in law enforcement and are rarely used except in the most serious of crimes and situations. Background, purpose, and methodology of these task forces will be discussed to help you understand them throughout the investigative process.

Finally, we will look at previous studies conducted in the area of serial offenders and the utilization of task forces by various law enforcement agencies. Recommendations for future studies in a specific area for the gathering of data, interpretation, and statistical analysis will follow.

SERIAL OFFENDERS

Definition of a Serial Offender

A serial offender is an individual who engages in deviant behavior that violates prevailing norms (criminal acts) more than twice over a period of time. For the purposes of this chapter as pertains to the serial offender, these laws, *mala prohibita*, are crimes that violate these social norms to a higher degree.

Criminologists and researchers generally separate crimes into three types: public order crimes, property crimes, and violent crimes. A serial offender may engage in any one of these areas or all three types; however, this would be extremely rare. A serial crime is a classification, as is a federal, state, organized, or white collar crime, to name a few other classifications.

To better understand this chapter's topic, we will concentrate on violent crimes. These crimes are classified in the United States as Part I crimes under the Uniform Crime Reports collected and administered by the FBI. More specifically, serial murder and serial rape, focusing on the offender's choice of specific victims, will be discussed.

The apprehension and prosecution of a serial offender is paramount in today's society. Federal, state, and local agencies collaborate and expend all available resources to bring this individual to justice. Victims do not have the tools to investigate or seek legal recourse for their injuries. Many times, victims desire compensation for injuries; however, other associated penalties are of little importance (Polinsky, 1997). Fear of retaliation to both victims and witnesses can hinder an investigation. In the most serious of cases, the victims die and are therefore unable to seek redress. The federal, state, and local government, along with law enforcement, must proceed with due diligence. One of the most effective means to accomplish this goal is the formation and utilization of an organized task force.

Modus Operandi of Serial Offenders

Serial offenders choose their victims by various thought processes, which are unique to each individual. This psychological process may be conscious or subconscious and depends on the individual's basic needs and desires. The Behavioral Science Unit of the FBI (formerly the "profiling" section) has made great strides in understanding the criminal mind to aid law enforcement in targeting, locating, and catching a serial offender.

The victim may be chosen for a variety of reasons, including specific age, race, religion, physical attribute, external environment, geographic location, personality type, or other characteristics that fulfill the needs and expectations of the offender. Once the victim is chosen, the mechanics of how the crime is carried out become specific and unique to the offender. These mechanics constitute the modus operandi, which means "mode of operating." It should be noted at this point that there is also the possibility of choosing victims at random, "staging" scenes of the crime, enacting "copycat" crimes, and changing methods on purpose (e.g., organized vs. disorganized crimes). These elements can be a deliberate attempt to stall an investigation and mislead investigators, thereby evading detection. All of these factors determine the ability of law enforcement to identify, locate, and apprehend the offender.

Types of Serial Offenders

As previously discussed, the serial offender may commit different types of crimes. The most significant of these offenders for the purpose of concentrated efforts on behalf of law enforcement are violent criminal serial offenders. On this spectrum, serial rapists and serial murderers are the primary target population.

These two types of offenders require a significant amount of personnel and resources to identify, target (locate), and apprehend. This is especially significant if the offenses go unsolved, have no witnesses, and offer little if any forensic evidence, and if similar or identical crimes continue to occur over a period of time. Time as a variable in these cases can be described as anywhere from a period of days to many years. Some serial offenders of this nature go "dormant" for a period of time for a variety of reasons. This inactivity can stretch the time span and scope of the investigation significantly. Reasons for dormancy include incarceration for unrelated offenses, travel abroad, physical ailments, change in employment, and psychiatric counseling; dormancy may also be related to the modus operandi (such as the "Zodiac Killer," whose crimes depended upon specific dates and years).

Identifying and Targeting Serial Offenders

Once a crime of this magnitude is committed and a pattern emerges, the nature and scope of the investigation change significantly. An administrative decision is made to step up the level of the investigation to include other agencies and resources in a collaborative effort to solve the crime and apprehend the suspect, ending future incidents and protecting the public. Sometimes external pressure is exerted during this time, which may include media interest and local politics. This can quickly expand to national coverage, especially when dealing with a high-profile case associated with serial murder and rape.

In some instances, local protocol (policy and procedure) dictates the course of events from the outset of an investigation. For instance, in the case of a kidnapping for ransom or a felony crossing state lines, the FBI is immediately contacted and assumes lead in the investigation as this falls under federal jurisdiction. In other cases, the span of the investigation may be beyond the means of the local jurisdiction, therefore requiring outside assistance from an agency specializing in the type of crime committed. It is also likely that in smaller jurisdictions the local authorities do not have the education, training, and experience to deal with these types of crimes and must call in those who are more suited to the task.

One key resource for these types of cases that has a proven track record is the FBI's Behavioral Science Unit (BSU). This unit includes the specialized Child Abduction and Serial Murder Investigative Resources Center (CASMIRC). Also within the BSU is the Violent Criminal Apprehension Program (VICAP). This unit is comprised of highly trained, educated, and experienced investigators who have conducted research and interviews and accumulated data that assist all law enforcement agencies across the country. They provide criminal investigative analysis using these tools, review and assess case files, and interpret offender behavior based upon the facts surrounding the crime itself as it relates to the offender. They provide crime analysis, profiles of unknown offenders, threat analysis, interview strategies, expert testimony, investigative suggestions, and major case assessment. All of these techniques give clues to police that will assist in the identification of a criminal still at large.

Other resources that are sought and part of a collaboration may include the attorney general's office, the district attorney's office, members of the medical and psychiatric community, federal law enforcement (e.g., FBI; Drug Enforcement Agency [DEA]; Bureau of Alcohol, Tobacco, Firearms and Explosives [ATF]; and Secret Service), state police, academics, and others. This collaboration begins with the local jurisdiction and expands as the crime and evidence unfold. The involvement of these resources for the express purpose of aiding in an investigative process relating to a serial offender constitutes the formation of a task force.

TASK FORCES

Background of Task Forces

Task forces were originally established by the U.S. military to be used in conjunction with other units for maximum efficiency during times of war. This type of operational flexibility unit was used extensively around 1941 by the U.S. Navy. There are many different types of task forces used for a variety of purposes around the world by different countries, entities, and organizations. Today, the term is used in contextual terms for law enforcement to establish a temporary collaborative tasked with investigating a specific criminal activity. As mentioned previously in this chapter, the goal of the task force is to investigate, target, locate, and apprehend the serial offender.

In 1984, local police in King County, California, created a multi-agency group termed a "task force" to address the Green River murders committed by Gary Ridgway. In this instance, the police department had to deal with problems normally associated with these types of cases, including (1) limited resources; (2) frustrated parents and various victim types such as runaways and prostitutes; and (3) investigative limitations, missing persons, and filing problems (Guillen, 2007).

A task force in this respect should not be confused with other similar formations that are used to solve specific problems. There are formations of "work groups," "ad-hoc committees," and "initiatives" that address problems in law enforcement (such as domestic violence, elderly exploitation, and child abuse). Such entities represent legitimate and current methodologies for combating criminal activity, but are not synonymous with a "task force."

This chapter provides several examples of task forces used for law enforcement purposes that can be extremely useful to the serial offender task force. In Texas, a task force consisting of three teams of 62 members, from 48 fire, police, and emergency medical services, was set up to help respond to the terrorist attacks of September 11, 2001 ("Texas task force," 2001). This is an example of a known entity that was successful in their purpose. To overcome the denial that inevitably accompanies the beginning of a serial offender investigation, a group of select individuals within a law enforcement agency should meet to determine if the formation of a task force is necessary given the facts and circumstances of any particular incident. The size of the agency and the severity of the crimes are factors to consider when convening a work group set up for this purpose. The sooner this group is formed and a determination is made, the better the chances of success for a multi-agency task force.

Organization of Task Forces

Once law enforcement determines that a situation warrants the formation of a task force, a formal request for assistance will be made of each respective agency. The assignment of personnel from these agencies will be left to the discretion of the head administrator of that particular entity (e.g., chief of police, director, district attorney). An organizational hierarchy will be established, and the task force will meet to review and discuss the case and formulate a plan of action.

Many factors present challenges to consider during the investigation, including number of suspects, population size, vice crimes, and activity levels of the jurisdiction.

The requesting agency will normally take the lead role as they assume jurisdiction and have completed the preliminary investigation and case file to this point. This formation is a collaborative effort, which provides a diverse field of personnel and resources to increase the likelihood of a successful outcome. Sharing of ideas and suggestions, brainstorming, and determining assignments and investigative strategies occur prior to the action plan implementation.

Structure of Task Forces

Overall command of the task force is assumed by the lead agency; however, each of the members are equal in pursuit of the same goal. Standard operating procedures govern the body of the task force. Rigid investigative policy is followed, with a written timeline to distinguish past and present developments in the case. The unique aspect of the assignments that are distributed is the ability of the involved personnel and agencies to accomplish the goals over and above normal or "routine" duties. This is what establishes a higher success rate than other means of investigation.

Task force commanders need to provide a framework for confidence building, invigorate members consistently, renew case management, and assign tasks based upon suitability. Securing and processing a stable and reliable headquarters to work from is important for morale and support of members and staff assigned to the task force. Deeming a case "unsolvable" is demoralizing to task force members (Guillen, 2007).

The responsibilities of leaders are vast and ongoing. Some of the overlooked aspects of a task force investigation include the purchase of vehicles (use of cabs, in the case of the Green River investigation) and forensic (scientific?) tests (e.g., fingerprints, forensic lasers, spectrographs, microscopic collection and analysis, and comparisons). Politics and bickering as well as jurisdictional disputes often persist throughout the investigation. Sources of conflict include manpower, funding, oversight, budget, expenditures, state lines being crossed, and breakdowns in cooperation.

The reason this type of unit is not implemented on a regular basis is the cost involved. Personnel and equipment are expended at a much higher rate than would normally exist in the host organization. The responding or participating agencies also incur large expenses for the same reasons. Therefore, for lower-level crimes, task forces are not cost effective.

In the beginning of the formation of a task force involving serial offenders, there is jockeying for position surrounding jurisdictional boundaries. There are numerous personalities to contend with and varying investigative ideas; cohesiveness is slow in evolving. Many times there is bad faith; arguments ensue about the case and the way to proceed, which results in a disorganized structure. The Green River task force was disbanded after several months only to be restarted. In a case such as this one, there is an overwhelming number of tips, and the input of evidence to computer databases for analysis is slow and painstaking. Separating task force activities from "routine" activities is something that the task force leaders need to address and resolve prior to implementation.

A well-structured and organized task force involves a number of external resources and individuals in tracking the serial offender: odontologists, anthropologists, profilers, medical examiners, forensic pathologists, scientists, psychologists, and other "specialists" incorporated into the investigation. There are also virtual unknowns, and the number of personnel increases exponentially with each death. Resources utilized, although not readily apparent, include scouts, construction tools (e.g., backhoes), crime scene technicians, emergency medical services, fire department personnel, civilian search volunteers, entomologists, trackers, archaeologists, etc.

The politics of policing, basic human nature, jealousies, resentments, divisions in ranks, favoritism, loss of valuable resources to units, and other challenges make it difficult to maximize task force effectiveness and organization. It is extremely difficult to form and organize a task force from its inception. The methods associated with task force organization can often be disorganized, convoluted, and not methodical in their breakdown, composition, and dynamics. This is not an easy process, and future task forces and their formation are based upon previous cases—their successes and failures as well as research on methodology worldwide.

Different elements within the task force have responsibilities that are commensurate with their resource ability and expertise. Each of the members brings to the team unique attributes that are established at the outset. Personnel are used in a manner that maximizes their effectiveness, thus increasing their likelihood of successfully completing an assigned task.

Purpose of Task Forces

Once formed and established, the main purpose and objective of the task force is to investigate, target, locate, apprehend, and prosecute the individual responsible for the specific crime they were tasked to solve. Success leads to public trust and reliance on law enforcement to protect them from future crimes of the same nature. It also serves as deterrence to other offenders. This restores faith in the system, alleviates fear, and builds confidence within the community.

In 1986, a multi-agency investigative team made a task force recommendation that established a set of guidelines and procedures for how task forces should operate. All participants were experienced investigators who believed that "successful prosecution of serial predator cases depended on a strong case management system within the task force, [in] which each person in the chain of command knew his responsibility and relied on the system itself to provide support for the investigation" (Keppel, 2003, p. 170).

Methodology of Task Forces

The personnel within the task force analyze all of the data, records, photographs, interviews, forensics, and other aspects of the full investigation. With this knowledge, they apply their own ideas, philosophical assumptions, methods, and techniques. Specific assignments are divided among all personnel based upon their levels of training, experience, and education. Every resource is expended during this next phase of the investigation.

As this information is processed in this manner, a pattern begins to emerge and the most constructive path is followed. Further interviews are conducted, more forensic evidence is collected and compared with previous submissions, and other tests are reconducted using similar scientific methods. A profile is created including demographics, personal, and geographic data—all based upon the accumulation of information by the task force and tracked throughout the final stages of the investigation.

A task force forms and continues to work on all aspects related to the case until its conclusion. Not all cases end with the successful solving of the crime; sometimes there are no more leads or incidents, and the allocated funds are depleted. The case in effect turns "cold."

The scheduling of task force members should be meted out in such a way as to maximize organizational effectiveness. The bulk of the work and overload comes at the outset of a serial offender task force investigation, obtaining leads, collecting information, and staying on track to catch the offender as early as possible. This early prioritization pertains mainly to the 48- to 72-hour rule. If this approach proves to be unattainable for any reason, then a reasonable and constant scheduling process should be made and maintained throughout the course of the investigation. Preventing burnout and maintaining a high degree of morale is important. Disciplined leadership in this area should be a focus for administrators to accomplish their mission. This does not mean staffing a position arbitrarily; the same investigators should maintain the same assignments with a corresponding overlap of time schedules to complement each other.

Geographic location of the crime has a significant bearing on the outcome of a particular case. Another element to consider is the time frame between incidents and the number of crimes committed by the same offender. These are all elements critical to an investigation, whether the crimes were committed on the East Coast or West Coast, whether the population base is large or small, and whether the police department is large or smaller. These factors contribute to the formation of a task force and determine clearance rates of the crimes. Some crimes span large areas, involve numerous similar crimes by the same offender, and take place over many years. Other cases are in the same general vicinity, with the crimes taking place over several weeks. The former scenario is vastly more complicated and difficult to solve than the latter. However, there is no set standard or predictability in either case.

Serial offenders are notorious for interjecting themselves into an investigation, offering advice or innocuous information. In the case of the Green River investigation, Gary Ridgway's name and involvement showed up early in the investigation and continued throughout, establishing a pattern. The investigators concede that had they reviewed and analyzed data collection regularly over time, Ridgway may have been caught sooner.

The ultimate goal is the apprehension of the perpetrator of the crime as a result of the task force's collaborative effort using expanded resources and investigative imagination. Success is reliant upon the diverse nature of every aspect of the task force elements.

MEDIA RELATIONS AND TASK FORCE COMMUNICATION

A high-profile criminal investigation prompts more media interest, the creation of a task force, and a public outcry for justice and safety. Law enforcement personnel in these cases are more prone to secrecy. A serial offender's crimes are the most disruptive injection into a community, society, and the private lives of individuals associated with each case. Such crimes have a negative impact on the community as a whole, and damage is inflicted on families of the victims.

All forms of media should be used to the advantage of the task force and participating agencies. They are an important resource and tool for investigators. Freedom of press often hinders an investigation. When a public relation or media liaison is assigned to communicate with the media, an open and honest relationship is required.

Grieving is a private matter for families, who are living a horrific event that often leaves them traumatized. The media have been known to seek out victims and their families early on for a story by conducting interviews and making repeated phone calls (from numerous sources/news agencies). These acts constitute an invasion of privacy. In some high-profile cases, the media will make visits to the family members' residence and place of employment. They will attend the funeral and provide coverage, and call on victims and their family right after death or notification of death. If given the proper handling, training, and information early on, this type of behavior can be avoided.

An investigator assigned to the task force should be mindful of these facts during interviews and conversations; empathy is an important trait and characteristic of a good investigator in these interactions (Guillen, 2007).

The media liaison is designated the responsibility of coordinating and distributing all forms of communication to all levels of media and participating agencies. This person, approved by command staff, represents the task force as a whole, including all agencies and jurisdictions, and is solely accountable for the release of information. The media liaison is a resource that can be used by the task force to not only disseminate information but to control its release to maximize its impact; furthermore, this individual can receive feedback and information relative to the investigation. This function also contributes to the morale of the task force members themselves, as previously discussed.

The release of specific details is unnecessary and may be counterproductive to an investigation. For example, the presence of rocks in a victim's vagina, evidence of necrophilia (as in the Ridgway case), findings that victims were strangled with their own clothing, or evidence of animal activity with body remains provides catchy headlines and sensationalism, which is detrimental to the case, hurts the victims and their families, and thereby hinders the investigation due to lack of cooperation. Guillen (2007) notes that referring to victims in articles or on television as whores, prostitutes, or hookers is a form of character degradation and adds nothing positive to the investigation. Offering details or statements to the media that could encourage such reporting should be avoided.

If used properly and handled professionally, the media can act as a conduit between the police who are investigating the victims and the serial offenders themselves. This service can aid the investigation by securing leads, tips, and information that may not be attainable through other traditional means, ultimately leading to the identity of suspects and capture of the offender. (Offenders use the media to communicate with police and the public.)

It is just as important to provide summaries on a regular basis to the heads of the participating agencies. Doing so supports team efforts and avoids multiple statements and communication with the media, which could be self-serving and conflicting and could have adverse effects or thwart an investigation. The task force is the sole proprietor of all information regarding the investigation. Specific details, facts, leads, and other information should be kept within the task force. However, each agency should be briefed at roll call by the task force member or liaison from that particular agency. The briefing would provide the bare-bones minimum of the investigation and offer minimal details.

Keeping team members informed is important because the absence of information or lack of communication contributes to a sense of secrecy that breaks down morale, leads to resentment, and hinders cooperation. Line staff is an important resource and should not be disregarded. Numerous cases are solved by officers on patrol conducting routine traffic stops, issuing parking tickets, and interacting with the community. Information provided, in the broadest sense, by the task force could lead to a street officer making an observation or discovering evidence that leads to information important to the investigation. The patrol force is an important resource to the task force in that its members may be called upon to locate witnesses and contact informants or contacts, tipsters, or possible suspects. This delegation of tasks is necessary because the task force needs help outside of the core group to accomplish their goal.

Four different levels of information are distributed during the course of an investigation. The handling of information and proper dissemination to each level is paramount to a successful investigation. The levels are:

- The task force itself, including command staff, members, and subgroups
- The chiefs and upper-level management within each department and organization
- The line staff and patrol force of all participating agencies
- The media

All levels of distribution are equally important within an investigation, and each receives different amounts, content, and forms of information relative to the case. Information given should be recorded and tracked throughout the timeline of the investigation for obvious reasons. This reinforces the need for one information officer delegated to accomplish this task, assigned to the team to establish accountability and integrity. The task force itself and all of the members hold *all* of the information from all sources.

Regular meetings should be held to relay and discuss findings related to assignments during the course of the investigation. These meetings should be brief and informative, not routine and mundane. This will prevent burnout of staff, maintain interest, and conserve time and energy, thus lifting morale. The meetings should include all members at all times (Keppel & Birnes, 2003).

INVESTIGATIVE ANALYSIS

Cases are sometimes referred to as active, inactive, ongoing, or cold. The complete files in a serial offender murder investigation can be termed case files, murder book, or investigative file. The file incorporates all of the information gleaned in its entirety from all areas and sources. The information collected over the course of the investigation is entered into several databases to match forensic evidence and fingerprints, locate similar crimes or MOs, search for previous incidents, find witnesses, and many other reasons. The main purpose of entering names, biographic data, specific tips and interview notes, witness and suspect statements, and facts is to locate a pattern. This pattern can be found by cross-referencing data from various sources and databases and will hopefully point to a certain individual.

Previous research has found that conducting an analysis of data collected yields the name of the offender and the information, which leads to the offender's capture, arrest, and prosecution. It is therefore necessary for supervisors and administrators (as well as the investigators themselves) within the framework of the task force to conduct a thorough and frequent review of all the information obtained from the investigators assigned to the unit. Reexamining and cross-referencing these files and databases, conducting data analysis, and finding anomalies or similarities could yield a clue or information that would break the case. This process offers an overall picture of the investigation as opposed to a "snapshot" of specific areas.

For instance, one assignment to an investigator or detective may be to answer phones and collect information for follow-up from tips. Another investigator interviews witnesses and canvasses neighborhoods and businesses, another looks for specific vehicles and runs license plates to match registration information with individuals, another researches previous incidents and similar crimes, and another creates a profile based upon the crimes committed and their characteristics; a subgroup collects/tags evidence, categorizes it, and conducts crime scene analysis; and still another subgroup generates a spatial analysis or geographic profile based upon the physical location of the crimes.

Each of these areas is segregated to a certain extent as one task. Any one may yield a valuable clue. This information is passed on to all task force members at regular meetings. New information may stand out to another task force member and turn into the piece of information that breaks the case. When taken together under review and examination, data analysis is one of the most important aspects of long-term, ongoing serial offender investigations. All of the parts equal the sum of the whole. One piece of information may not mean much in and of itself, but when taken in context with the totality of the circumstances, certain information stands out and leads to the suspect.

Process of elimination is a useful means of uncovering a serial offender. The training, education, experience, resources, and past practice of investigators should be employed full force at the outset, utilizing all information as it becomes available. As mentioned earlier, the 48- to 72-hour rule dictates that finding the offender becomes more difficult after this time period is surpassed. After matching all victims with relatives, friends, co-workers, acquaintances, and witnesses and determining motive, means, opportunity, and forensics, one person usually stands out and shows up numerous times. This person is usually the offender.

The Ridgway murders included more than 60 victims involving missing persons, runaways, prostitutes, and combinations of both. These incidents took place between 1982 and 2001. The MO included strangulation, sexual acts with corpses, and piling and concealment of bodies. More than 50 investigators were assigned to a multi-agency task force, and an estimated $2 million was spent annually (Guillen, 2007). As was evidenced by this case, the processing, dissemination, and interpretation of data and information collected over the course of the investigation is the single most important factor in a successful investigation, culminating in an arrest. This is a common theme in previous serial offender investigations.

PREVIOUS STUDIES REGARDING TASK FORCES

Academic Journals

Research has been conducted on single cases and wide-ranging theories in the area of serial rape and serial murder. In one instance, researchers were called in to help assist police investigators in their investigation of a case of serial rape (Strangeland, 2005). The Institute of Criminology at the University of Malaga used their resources through criminological theories and computer software programs to create a profile for the offender. The use of crime mapping and geographic profiling helped to locate and arrest the offender. As a result, the researchers were able to interview and contrast and compare their findings with the offender's actual motivations determined during the interview process. There were 18 cases of sexual assault committed by the same offender (DNA confirmed this) in an area populated by 600,000 people. The methodology used to create a geographic profile shows that in cases of serial rape (and murder) this technique can be useful. More research in this area would be useful to law enforcement, as would the creation of task forces for this purpose.

In 1982, a task force was created to submit recommendations (to the Attorney General) for the alleviation of violent crime in the United States. The resulting report is interesting but represents a different type of task force than is discussed in this chapter. It is useful for research and comparative purposes to the topic addressed here. The task force consisted of numerous informed, experienced, and knowledgeable criminal justice experts (Thompson, 1982). Seven cities, 80 witnesses, and thousands of written reports were received from scholars, the Department of Justice, and members of the general public from across the country. The task force formulated an agenda for dealing with violent crime in the United States from these data. This approach is also a useful tool and method in finding answers to some of the questions investigators have within a task force.

In a study conducted by Rutgers University, the authors present the explanation of applicable theories, stating that "both behavioral and situational elements interact to produce the criminal event, a social exchange between people who find themselves in particular circumstances" (Sherley, 2005). This study presents a unique aspect that is informative as to the motivation of the offender as learned from the offenders themselves as well as the victim and witness statements. This information would be useful to a task force in the profile stage to target and locate an offender who is still at large.

The U.S. Senate created a 28-member task force to make recommendations concerning the interrelationship between drugs and violence (Denno, 2000). Most previous studies only addressed one issue or the other, not both. This study provided a set of recommendations to the U.S. Sentencing Commission for several criminal justice policy implementations.

Another example is provided in the area of spatial analysis and methodology for geographic profiling in a study conducted by the University of Maryland (Harries & LeBeau, 2007). This study specifically discusses the process used to discover the most probable area in which a serial offender may reside or operate. Spatial interrelatedness is put into a criminal context to assist investigators in determining a geographic location for locating and targeting an individual. The examples provided here on this topic are used sporadically, and the knowledge from these studies would be useful to incorporate into every task force for the serial offender.

As previously mentioned, there are many types and compositions of task forces. The next study is included as an example of a worldwide effort to address national problems. The G-7 (Canada, France, Germany, Italy, Japan, the United Kingdom, and the United States) created a task force to address the problem of transnational drug trafficking (Gilmore, 1998). This task force hoped to make local policy changes that would help to eradicate international issues related to the production of drugs with the use of chemicals and their shipment. They sought to institute chemical regulation at the policy level. While this study has no bearing on the composition of the current topic, it does demonstrate the new-age move to address serious issues by using a task force concept.

One of the more notable task force formations was in response to the terrorist attacks of September 11, 2001. It was an international task force on bioterrorism established to improve cooperation between the member states and to facilitate collaboration in regard to public health preparedness (Tegnell et al., 2003). This was a 15-member task force under the Directorate General for Health and Consumer Protection, with nine national experts participating. The most important contribution of this task force (for law enforcement) was the creation and implementation of emergency preparedness through the National Incident Management System (NIMS) and the Incident Command System (ICS). This established a uniform means and organizational structure for response to critical incidents, natural disasters, and terrorist threats. These types of outcomes and guidelines can be used to increase the success rate and overall effectiveness of task forces set up to combat serial offenders.

Findings

There is very little written on the intricate details relating to the formation, structure, organization, and methodology of task forces set up for the pursuit of violent criminal offenders (e.g., serial murder and serial rape). Extensive research has failed to yield literature on the subject of serial offenders and targeting through the use of a criminal justice task force set up exclusively for that purpose.

There is a need associated with this subject for law enforcement to gain knowledge and increase the effectiveness of current-day methods in catching a serial offender. The trend toward task forces is apparent and necessary for future success. How is a task force formed? Who makes the decision to create a task force locally? How are the member agencies and personnel chosen? What is the structure and organizational hierarchy of a task force? These are just some of the questions that should be answered to accomplish these goals.

Once we have answers to these questions, we can provide empirical data and a solid foundation to law enforcement to produce a uniformly effective means of creating this type of task force. It would also provide a national policy that all areas of law enforcement could use for this purpose, and all participating members could be properly trained. This effort would increase the likelihood of success, decrease the timeline to successful completion, decrease extended costs, and prevent future crimes.

CONCLUSION

The task force concept has come a long way in recent years, and we have learned from previous studies and working groups. This progress is evident in considering the 1982 task force set up by the American Bar Association in an attempt to confront the issue of gun control in the United States (Middleton, 1982). If you contrast this task force with more recent examples, the differences are notable. In a task force by law enforcement for serial offenders, there is a collaborative effort for investigative purposes with a single common goal. There are not (or should not be) any politics involved with the process. There are no recommendations or policy decisions. The task force is a cohesive unit specifically designated for one purpose: to catch the serial offender, protect the public, and prevent future crimes.

It is nearly impossible to establish a standardized procedure, manual, or policy in conducting an investigation on serial offenders; similarly, it is not feasible to apply these same standards to the formation of a task force, local or multijurisdictional. However, it is possible to form a framework or basic foundation for an investigation in these areas. This effort is based upon past experience, research, and successes and failures in investigating similar crimes all over the world. Law enforcement has evolved in the past 20 years to meet the needs and challenges presented in current-day society. Technology has advanced to aid authorities in ways that were previously unattainable.

Several agencies, states, and countries have established a process based upon these elements that will eventually be standardized or used as models by future task forces. Regardless, an important consideration is that the same procedures be followed by all member departments and agencies that comprise the task force. Future studies in criminology should focus on the formation of task forces and the results associated with these endeavors. Data, statistics, and analysis in this area would be useful in determining the overall effectiveness of task forces. It would also allow law enforcement to adjust formation, structure, and methodology to maximize effectiveness based upon previous successes. Criminologists and researchers can apply theoretical concepts, and the emergence of new theories is a possibility based upon these studies.

CHAPTER 13

Conclusion

Kristen Kuehnle and Kevin Borgeson

One of the key points of this book has been about the role of the media in the blurring of fact and fiction of crime and criminal investigation. Serial homicide, while one of the rarest crimes, has been extensively covered, capturing the public's interest. In actuality, any type of serial crime generally attracts a group of crime "fans." For example, it was difficult to separate fact from fiction with the intense media coverage with the day-care sexual abuse cases in the 1980s. Starting with the McMartin trial in California, new cases popped up throughout the United States, and some compared the abuse cases to the Salem witchcraft trials of 1692. In Bakersfield, California, John Stoll, along with two other men and a woman were accused of molesting children in group-sex parties. Forty six people were arrested, alleged to be participating in four to eight separate child abuse rings. Television and newspapers extensively covered the stories as if the existence of new cases provided evidence that the abuse was occurring. Out of the 46 arrested, 30 were convicted, though 22 had their convictions reversed. Of the remaining individuals, one died in prison and the rest served their time. In particular, John Stoll remained in prison for 20 years. As of 2004, most of the six witnesses against Stoll have admitted to lying about the charges. In 1985, 1 million people were falsely accused of child abuse (Ramsland, n.d.).

Viewing the media's portrayal, the American public is led to believe they have a sense of crime and guilt, though they may not understand the legal process. "Innocent until proven guilty" is frequently forgotten when the public views a mug shot or watches on television the alleged perpetrator being transported. Many individuals feel that they have an intuitive sense of guilty, especially when the alleged perpetrator is apprehended. An example that comes to mind is a comment made by a graduate student in counseling at a prestigious university. Class discussion was about the 1986 Fells Acre day care in Malden, the sex scandal that shocked the Boston area. This female student informed the class that Gerald Amirault was guilty because she could tell by how he looked as he was led to court for an arraignment. "He looked evil," she said. "You could tell by his eyes, I know that he did it." In the Fells Acre case, Gerald Amirault was convicted of molesting eight children at his family's Fells Acre day care in Malden, Massachusetts, despite the fact that the day care had been in business for 18 years without a complaint. One day in 1984, Gerald, who did maintenance for the school, was asked to change the pants of a boy who had wet himself; that was the source of the initial allegations. All three members of the family were convicted, with Gerald receiving a sentence of 30 to 40 years and his mother and sister receiving sentences of 8 to 20 years (Ramsland, n.d.).

Recognizing that technologic advances have greatly enhanced the criminal justice system's investigative techniques, it must also be noted that the media concurrently have advanced dissemination of this technologic knowledge. The public has become actively engaged in the process of crime solving, either through the news or true crime shows or through movies and television shows. Early television shows, such as *Dragnet* and *Perry Mason* focused upon the characters' ability to detect lying from witnesses and suspects. Timelines were established by a dated receipt. The early sleuths provided some insight into the "art" of detection. Now, as media portrayals become increasingly sophisticated, incorporating technology into shows and movies, many viewers have become even more "pseudo"-sophisticated armchair crime fighters. The American public believes they are knowledgeable about solving a crime and gathering the evidence needed to do so.

In the past 10 years, shows and movies that have focused more upon the techniques involved in the actual investigation have been called "infotainment" (Surette, 2007) and may actually blur facts with fiction. By watching infotainment, the viewer perceives that he or she has gained expertise about the inside working of a crime lab and the various ways to analyze miniscule pieces of evidence, the "*CSI* effect." The phrase "*CSI* effect" has emerged referring to the impact of *CSI* and related shows on potential jurors. But does it exist?

At a new training center in forensic science in South Wales, pathologist Bernard Knight states that "because of television crime dramas, jurors today expect more categorical proof than forensic science is capable of delivering" (Forensic Science, 2010). Other researchers have actually investigated the impact on other branches of the criminal justice system. Durnal (2010) suggests that the media help create the illusion that most crimes can be easily solved with the technology currently available. These shows lead many to expect the availability of the same resources to solve any crime, an unrealistic expectation. If we actually compare the number of homicides solved over the past 30 to 40 years, the number has significantly dropped. And as we watch "scientifically based crime solvers," as Knight suggests, we have an "extremely skewed view of the resources available to law enforcement." In his review of the research on the *CSI* effect, Durnal (2010) discusses the effects on all the players in the criminal justice system—law enforcement, jurors, prosecutors, defense attorneys, and judges. Durnal (2010) indicates that the most serious aspect of *CSI* is the knowledge that criminals obtain. For example, the use of bleach, which destroys DNA, is not unusual in homicide cases, and there is greater use of gloves or taping envelopes (Durnal, 2010).

Some take their detecting even further and pressure agencies to investigate certain individuals, and this pressure has led to erroneous arrests, as with Steven Hatfill, the alleged "anthrax doctor." In 2001, anthrax-contaminated letters were anonymously sent to various news sources and public officials, leading to five deaths and numerous injuries. Only a limited number of American scientists had a working knowledge of anthrax, and one was Steven Hatfill. Hatfill, a medical doctor, had once worked at the Medical Research Institute of Infectious Diseases, which had stocks of anthrax. After surveying publicly available evidence and documents supplied by the FBI, the consultant felt that Hatfill was the offender.

Hatfill had been in Rhodesia during an anthrax outbreak in the 1970s, and he attended medical school near a Rhodesian suburb, Greendale. This was the name of the school in the return address (Freed, 2010). In addition, another individual came to similar conclusions. She was an outspoken opponent of the use of bioweapons and became convinced that Steven Hatfill was responsible for the anthrax attacks. She pushed for a meeting with senate staff members, where she criticized the FBI for not being aggressive enough. (Her interpretation of these events, it should be noted, differed following the ruin of this innocent man.) To compound matters, the media were used to pressure the arrest of Hatfill. Law enforcement leaked his name to the press with the result that inflammatory innuendoes dominated television and the front page of newspapers. Kristof, a columnist for *The New York Times*, wrote a scathing article about a Dr. Z, who clearly resembled Hatfill, with distortion of Hatfill's past and current life. Kristof never identified his sources but urged the FBI to make a move in his op-eds (Freed, 2010).

In addition, the media extensively cover crimes involving foreigners or visitors in other countries without any understanding about the cultural differences in defining crime, its elements and the methods of investigation, and the legal process. These differences are poorly understood or appreciated by individuals outside the country, representing a "legal" ethnocentrism. For example, consider the case of Amanda Knox, a college student who was living abroad for a semester. She, along with two men, supposedly engaged in drugs and risky sex, resulting in the murder of her roommate. The media on both sides of the ocean were literally obsessed with the case. After Amanda Knox's arrest, the trial was widely publicized internationally. The verdict shocked many people, drawing commentaries from the United Kingdom and the United States. From the beginning, there was public discussion, and disapproval, over the handling of the crime scene. When she was sentenced, the sentence was viewed as unusually harsh by others. Many U.S. analysts denounced the verdict, claiming that the jury was not screened for bias and was allowed to read newspapers and watch television reports and that there was a lack of forensic evidence. Some who followed the complex case suggested that the outcome was more about the prosecutor and the media than a lack of forensic evidence. Many Italians, however, viewed Americans' responses as arrogant for questioning the Italian legal process (Vargas & James, 2009).

In addition, Americans feel that they have an understanding of the law and the process and that anyone in the United States should want to be law abiding, even if they recently immigrated. In a criminal justice class, students are presented a case about a Romani offender whose crime was to share the clan social security number to legitimately purchase a car in the United States. Students consistently agree that this is a crime and that if someone is in the United States, it is his or her responsibility to "to learn the laws of the country." When asked if they are aware of the laws in another country before they go on a trip, typically only those individuals in the military or law enforcement are aware of some of the laws. Evidently, Amanda Knox did not know or understand Italian law or the legal system.

This "legal" ethnocentrism can be detrimental when faced with the globalization of crime. Knowledge about investigative techniques used in other countries broadens the perspective of the public and the individuals in the criminal justice system in regard to potential motives for offenders, especially considering the mobility of people. Reviewing the social and cultural context of serial offenses broadens our knowledge base, rather than relying on the fictionalization of an offense via the media.

Cyberpredators, sex offenders, serial arsonists, and serial stalkers cause significant psychological and physical harm to the victim and the surrounding community, even injuries resulting in death. When there is an alleged serial offender in a community, the community essentially feels terrorized by the unknown. These people depend on the media for an ongoing update, and they pressure law enforcement for an arrest. By reviewing the chapters in this book, they may develop a better understanding of serial offenders and the difficulties law enforcement faces regarding apprehension and conviction. In addition, the chapters provide detailed case studies about different types of offenders for more elaboration.

As Levin indicates, homicide is not the only serial offense worthy of examining. Serial offenders are found in a variety of offenses, and repeat offenders can both terrorize a community and raise the anxiety level of an entire society. In Chapter 1, Borgeson and Kuehnle share their perspective—i.e., the rationale for the study of serial offenders. Serial offenders have a major impact on society while they are at large and require massive efforts, bringing together other agencies. Apprehension of serial offenders requires a concerted methodological effort that brings together the most sophisticated tools and databases. The media have provided insight to the general public about serial offenders and their investigations; however, these authors suggest that the media's portrayal distorts facts with fiction, often raising unreasonable expectations.

Levin and Fox, in Chapter 2, take the position that the distinguishing characteristics of sadistic serial killers may be found in the vast majority of humankind; namely, the inability to empathize, the ability to compartmentalize and dehumanize victims, concern with impression management, and the need for power and control can be found in some form throughout most of human society. The authors suggest that a serial killer's ability to torture and kill multiple victims with extreme violence makes the killer qualitatively different from the average person. However, the authors suggest that the sociopathic designation may be incorrectly applied to sadistic serial killers and that researchers may have missed other important differences.

In Chapter 3, Poland, Kilburn, and Alvarez-Rivera indicate that serial rape is difficult to define and measure because many rapes are unreported and the actual definitions of rape and attempted rape may vary. As they indicate, serial rapists differ in their motives, in their social skills, and in developmental factors, sharing no common characteristics. However, research and profiles indicate that serial rapists do have common aspects related to the crime, the selection of victims and process of attack, the signature of sexuality in the act, and the staging of the crime.

In Chapter 4, Bernier, Kuehnle, and Howerton introduce the variation in types of adult sex offenders, including adult offenders with adult victims and adult offenders with child victims. The authors review the difficulty when processing and convicting sex offenders throughout the criminal justice system. They provide past studies about the obstacles present in law enforcement, prosecution, defense, jury, and judicial decision making. The authors discuss the difficulty with rehabilitation, particularly with pedophiles. As they explain, rehabilitation of sex offenders varies in types of treatment, including drug treatment and counseling, and may occur while incarcerated or on an outpatient basis. This chapter also introduces the impact of social networking for this type of offender, with research indicating that most online sex offenders are not registered offenders.

Lanning, in Chapter 5, continues with the sex offender continuum, focusing specifically upon cyber "pedophiles." Based upon his extensive experience studying this deviant behavior, he provides insight into the behavioral patterns of offenders and victims in the sexual exploitation of children, involving computer. He makes a distinction between pedophile and child molester, two terms that are frequently misused by the general public and the media. Pedophiles are significantly older individuals who prefer to have sex with children, whereas child molesters may decide to have sex with a child because of availability or curiosity. Lanning identifies three types of offenders who use the computer to sexually exploit children: situational offenders, preferential offenders, and miscellaneous offenders. The author suggests that in computer cases, it is often easier to determine the type of offender than in other kinds of child sexual exploitation.

As indicated by Spitzberg, Dutton, and Kim in Chapter 6, the dynamics of stalking suggest that it emerges out of a relatively normal relationship and that these dynamics may not be applicable to serial stalkers. Serial stalkers demonstrate a consistency and a deviance in their behaviors across situations. Serial stalkers invest time and resources to victimize multiple parties. The authors review the underlying dynamics of stalkers, identifying the different typologies that can be utilized. This chapter carefully examines the characteristics of serial stalkers and their victims, and the possible effects on victims. The authors also review the research on the criminal justice system's response to serial stalking. Stalkers, in general, are often not prosecuted even when identified; when prosecuted, they are not always convicted; and when convicted, they do not receive long sentences.

Parenteau indicates in Chapter 7 that serial arson is a severe problem and may be even more serious and common for those under 18 years of age. Acknowledging that arson has a low clearance rate, Parenteau identifies the reasons for these low clearance rates for arson. Clearance rates for serial arson are even more difficult to establish because of the lack of record keeping by various agencies for this type of offense. Specifically, serial arsonists (fire setters) take time off between each offense, a cooling time. In addition, the serial arsonist began his or her career as a juvenile, indicating that young males and young females engage in this offense. Parenteau looks at the motivations of the serial arsonists, also considering the characteristics of pyromania. Clearly, serial arson results in massive destruction and economic loss as well as injury or death. The author proposes that by sharing this research with agencies, serial arsonists can be apprehended.

Chapter 8 introduces a topic about which little empirical evidence is available. Specifically, Labuschagne introduces a comparative, cross-cultural perspective on the intentional killing of another individual, muti murder. Muti murder is an element of bewitchment beliefs in South Africa. Many societies, including Western societies, believe in the existence of good and evil spiritual entities. Muti murder has been practiced for centuries as part of a subculture of traditional African beliefs. With the introduction of the Western criminal justice system, these practices became illegal. Labuschagne indicates that it is important for law enforcement agencies to be able to distinguish between muti murders, cult-related murders, sadistic murders, serial murders, and other types of murder that may involve mutilation but may require different approaches when conducting an investigation. Labuschagne indicates that each of these crimes has a different context; for example, some are group related, such as a cult murder; others are part of a broader belief system, such as muti murder and honor killings; and others are unique to the offender's own psyche, such as sadistic killings. Without knowledge of muti murder, an investigator could initial an inappropriate investigative approach and focus upon an incorrect type of offender. The author provides ways to identify muti murders, as well as details regarding the typical offender, victim, and body part used.

In Chapter 9, the cross-cultural perspective continues, specifically with South Africa. Labuschagne and Borgeson look at the following areas of criminal profiling: history of profiling, types of profiling, and the profiling unit for the South African Police Service. As the authors indicate, a history of profiling is needed because it places into context that profiling is not a new tool for criminal justice agencies but one that has been used over a period of time under various circumstances. An emphasis on the different types of profiling is warranted so the public has an understanding that there are several types of profiling. The media have frequently demonstrated the FBI's approach to profiling. Undoubtedly, the FBI can be credited for placing offender profiling on the map and initiating scientific interest in the field. Their earlier training programs for U.S. and foreign law enforcement agencies have helped establish the concept of behavioral advisers throughout the world. Other types of profiling are introduced in this chapter, such as geographic profiling, along with their contributions to investigative methods. Lastly, the authors introduce the Investigative Psychology Unit of the South African Police Service that has been in existence since 1996. They provide examples of cases solved by this unit.

Chapter 10, also by Labuschagne, introduces case linkage analysis, a form of behavioral analysis that is used to determine whether a series of crimes has been committed by one offender. Instead of focusing upon forensic evidence, linkage analysis, or comparative case analysis, focuses upon the behavior of the offender, thus allowing investigators to exclude possible offenders and communities from investigative efforts and suggesting areas upon which to focus in their investigation. In this chapter, an additional valuable aspect is added to the five assessment procedures suggested by Hazelwood and Warren (2003)—the offender's behavior. The author suggests that the offender's behavior, specifically the geographic behavior, can be crucial to an investigation. Identifying the offender's residence along with proximity of crimes is an important part of linkage analysis. Labuschagne indicates that linkage analysis can be valuable in different ways throughout the various stages of the investigation and through the trial phase.

Estimates of the number of victims for serial killers is difficult to ascertain. Historically, figures have been inflated, and in Chapter 11 Quinet discusses the reasons for the inflation. She indicates that all estimates neglect the victim that may be uncounted; namely, the victim has not been reported as missing, the serial killer disposes of a body in such a way that it cannot be identified, or serial killers choose victims from a marginalized population, such as prostitutes, homeless, and illegal aliens. The importance in establishing a more accurate estimate is that it would aid police prevention and intervention. The author suggests that serial murder is not increasing; rather, some victims have always been missed, and better quantification is required.

The serial offender has been a constant source of problems to members of law enforcement. According to Schmink in Chapter 12, the apprehension and prosecution of a serial offender is "paramount." This effort requires collaboration of federal, state, and local agencies, an organized task force. Task forces were originally established by the U.S. military for maximum efficiency during war times. Today, the term is used for law enforcement to establish a "temporary" collaborative assigned the task of investigating, targeting, locating, and apprehending the serial offender. Schmink makes the distinction between the formations of "work groups," "ad-hoc committees," and "initiatives" that address problems such as domestic violence or child abuse. While it may not be possible to establish a standardized procedure, manual, or policy for conducting an investigation of serial offenders, past experience, research, and success/failures in investigating similar crimes can provide a basic foundation.

Extensive research has been reviewed in these chapters. What is clearly indicated is the necessity for ongoing research of the serial offender. Serial offenders cause psychological distress, physical harm, and economic losses to individuals as well as society.

Because estimates of the number of serial offenders and their victims are hard to quantify, research needs to continue developing a larger database that can be used in the apprehension of the serial offender. To establish policies about prevention and detection of the serial offender, legislative bodies require up-to-date, accurate information about serial offenses. Knowing when to establish a task force and managing the cost also requires accurate information. Overall, effective policy needs to be based upon methodological research that is disseminated to law enforcement, legislators, mental health and social service agencies, as well as the general public. This type of information is in marked contrast to the media's portrayal of serial crime and is required to provide a more balanced perspective.

APPENDIX A Estimates Related to Prevalence of Serial Stalking

Estimate	Operationalization & Notes	Sample size	Sample description	Source
54%	Modified NVAWS stalking behavior items, referring to the year prior to Time 1 (T1) (personal communication with lead author, 10/30/09)	406	Intimate partner violence victims seeking help from a shelter, civil court assistance, or criminal court assistance in a mid-Atlantic city	Bell et al. (2008)
39%	Claimed their stalker had targeted at least one other person	124	Stalking cases derived from self-help U.K. support groups to aid stalking victims	Boon & Sheridan (2001)
48.5%	"stalked at least one other former intimate in the past" (p. 27)	187	Former stalking victim women identified through victim service agencies and law enforcement and newspaper advertisements	Brewster (1998)
8%	"prior stalking"	120	Michigan batterers in treatment or subjects of police incident reports for felony arrests for domestic violence and stalking	Burgess et al. (1997)
5%	"Respondents were also asked if they thought their pursuer had ever pursued others" (p. 116).	233	Undergraduates at two small, private Japanese universities	Chapman & Spitzberg (2003)
2%	"Pursued new victim" was the reason attributed to stalking having stopped.	130	Stalking victims reported on by mental health professionals	Coleman (1999)
14%	"reported previously obtaining a protective order" (p. 641)	90	Women seeking a protective order in a Texas district attorney's office regarding family violence	Gist et al. (2001)
4%	"In [these] files more than one victim lodged a complaint against the stalker" (p. 284).	204	Stalking ("beleaguering") cases in Belgium randomly drawn from the available 2000 stalking cases "treated by the public prosecutor between 1999 and 2004" in Leuven	Groenen & Vervacke (2009)
46%	Stalkers "had a history of prior offenses for the same charge, sometimes with the same object, but sometimes with different objects" (p. 194). 33% stalkers had multiple victims.	48	New York cases charged with harassment and menacing	Harmon, Rosner, & Owens (1995)

APPENDIX A Estimates Related to Prevalence of Serial Stalking cont'd

Estimate	Operationalization & Notes	Sample size	Sample description	Source
25%	"re-offending rate" involving attempting to contact the victim	64	District attorney case files of persons charged with stalking and convicted of stalking or related offense in San Diego	Huffhines (2001)
28%	"had engaged in previous stalking behavior" (p. 434)	85	Stalkers referred to London psychiatric evaluation, derived from 600 case files reviewed	James & Farnham (2003)
28%	"The person had harassed others" (p. 263).	50	Women who had been harassed by a male after informing him they were not interested in dating	Jason et al. (1984)
30%	Had a previous restraining order in effect	63	Family justice center closed stalking case files.	Johnson & Spitzberg (2006)
6%	Rearrested for stalking (Note: approximately 50% were rearrested for *some* domestic violence offense, most often for restraining order violations.)	268	Police-identified and researcher-identified stalkers based on case analyses in Rhode Island	Klein et al. (2009)
15.5%	Were subsequently charged with stalking	346	"Males charged with stalking" in Kentucky.	Logan et al. (2002)
18%	Based on those who experienced stalking before and after obtaining a protective order (personal communication with lead author, 10/30/09)	210	A 12-month longitudinal study of 709 women obtaining a protective order, of which 210 claimed stalking by the person named in the order	Logan & Walker (2009)
50%	Had a "record documenting past criminal charges or convictions incurred *prior* to the current investigation for criminal harassment" (p. 70). Only 8.5% had been convicted of a prior "stalking" related offense (Table 2).	241	All cases investigated for criminal harassment in Vancouver police department for 1997	Lyon (2006)
25%	"pursuit of others" (p. 79, Table 7)	152	Stalking case files obtained from the Ontario Provincial Police Threat Assessment Unit in Ontario, using Zona et al. typology	Maksymchuk (2001)

APPENDIX A Estimates Related to Prevalence of Serial Stalking cont'd

Estimate	Operationalization & Notes	Sample size	Sample description	Source
about 50%	"convicted before for, among others, theft, destruction of property, stalking and threatening the victim. The case files did not clarify whether these crimes were committed against the present victim or against others" (pp. 205-206)	77	Stalking cases adjudicated by Dutch courts	Malsch (2007)
23%	65 "previously engaged in stalking behaviors, 19 of these against the same victim" (p. 153).	200	"stalkers referred to a community forensic mental health clinic" (p. 151)	McEwan, Mullen, & MacKenzie (2008)
16%	"had one to four prior arrests for stalking other individuals" (p. 213)	82	Cases from solicitation of research collaborators for case files from United States, Canada, and Australia of female stalkers	Meloy & Boyd (2003)
18%	Reported "prior stalking victims"	65	"Obsessional followers" selected from among 2300 Superior Court of San Diego County case files of persons referred for forensic evaluation.	Meloy et al. (2000)
about 58%	92% of cases at T1 (case closure) had indicated stalking within the prior 6 months; 56.3% at 6 months after case closure, and 58.1% at 1 year after case closure.		Ratings of frequency of experiencing 10 stalking behaviors, and a general definition as "willful, repeated, and malicious following, harassing, or threatening" (p. 89)	Melton (2004)
31%	"Subject has harassed others" (p. 149). Note: 19% "unknown," 50% had "not harassed others." 15% had been "arrested previously for obsessional harassment behaviors" (p. 149, Table 1).	1005	Stalking cases, from review of "2300 files dealing with instances of stalking, criminal harassment, menacing, terrorist threats, or domestic violence behaviors" (p. 148) from North America and Canada	Mohandie et al. (2006)
41%	"of victims in this study indicated knowledge of at least one other victim and the remainder were unsure about whether their stalker had victimized anyone else in this way" (p. 29)	1024	Respondents to a nationally representative sample in Scotland	Morris et al. (2002)

APPENDIX A Estimates Related to Prevalence of Serial Stalking cont'd

Estimate	Operationalization & Notes	Sample size	Sample description	Source
29%	Alleged stalking behavior in past relationships" with 18% "previous stalking/criminal harassment charge" (p. 745)	103	"Perpetrators charged with criminal harassment" in Canada (p. 744)	Morrison (2008)
21%	"had at different times directed their affections at different women" (p. 471)	14	Counseling cases involving at least one extended episode involving stalking and a pathology of love—all cases had also involved the police	Mullen & Pathé (1994)
13%	"Do you have reason to believe that this person has stalked others before or after you?" (n = 62).	1068	College students at a large public southwestern university	Nguyen & Spitzberg (2009)
11% victims; 7% pursuers	Subsequent "episode" of stalking. Note: "it is impossible to conclude that subsequent episodes involved the same victims and/or offenders because identifying information was not provided" (p. 491)	1921	College students randomly sampled from a university population of 48,237 students at a large southeastern university	Nobles et al. (2009)
12%	"had a prior arrest for stalking the victim, 8% had a prior arrest for assaulting the victim, and 5% had a prior arrest for harassing the victim" (p. 9)	267	"cases with a stalking charge reported to Alaska State Troopers from 1994 to 2005"	Rosay et al. (2007)
22%	8% "harassed more than one different woman," and in 14% "both men and women were harassed by the same offender" (p. 257).	189	"Individuals were evaluated for crimes reflecting stalking or harassment" (p. 256) "derived from several sources: case files of stalking offenders referred to the New York City Forensic Psychiatry Clinic, court documents, records from the Department of Probation" (p. 253)	Rosenfeld (2003)

APPENDIX A Estimates Related to Prevalence of Serial Stalking cont'd

Estimate	Operationalization & Notes	Sample size	Sample description	Source
17%	"have been charged more than once with stalking" (p. 32)	242	Cases charged with stalking in Delaware between 1992 and 1994	Scocas et al. (1996)
48%	"claimed . . . stalker had also targeted at least one person other than themselves"	29	Self-identified stalking victims who had sought help from a "Survivors of Stalking" organization in England	Sheridan (2001)
54%	"their stalker had stalked someone else, or was doing so"	95	Self-defined British stalking victims	Sheridan, Davies & Boon (2001)
13%	"had a history of previous charges or convictions for stalking-related offenses targeted at other victims" (p. 239)	61	Adult males, convicted of stalking-related offenses under Canada criminal code	Storey et al. (2008)
75%	Developed subsequent obsessions regarding an attachment object	4	Clinical case studies of erotomanic males	Taylor et al. (1983)
8%	"offenders each stalked two targets" (p. 149)	40	Court case transcripts of stalking prosecutions in Australia	Thompson (2009, study 1)
20%	28% classified as a "recidivist" stalking charge (p. 73, Table 4); 20% of recidivist cases had no prior relationship with victim (combining data from Tables 7 and 11)	240	Stalking cases evaluated at the Center for Forensic Psychiatry in Michigan	Tonin (1998)
16%	"made more than one stalking arrest against the same offender," with 9% of cases "unknown" (p. 676)	90	Law enforcement departments (sheriff's, municipal, university police) in Florida	Tucker (1993)
8%	"Known pursuit of others" (p. 899, Table 4); 14%: Erotomanic; 15%: Love obsessional; 0%: Simple obsessional	74	Los Angeles Threat Management Unit case files of "obsessional" pursuers	Zona et al. (1993)

References

Abel, G. G. (1985). A Clinical Evaluation of Possible Sex Offenders. Retrieved May 20, 2010 from http://mhawestchester.org

Ace, A. (2004). *Stalking victims: Appraisals and coping strategies.* Unpublished Doctoral Dissertation, University of South Carolina. Columbia, SC.

Adams, S. (1999, December 13). Serial batterers (Domestic Violence Special Report). *Probation Research Bulletin.* Office of the Commissioner of Probation, Massachusetts Trial Court, MA.

Agency for Healthcare Research and Quality. (2003). 2001 national statistics, results, outcomes by patient and hospital characteristics for all discharges. Retrieved November 11, 2003, from www.ahcpr.gov/data/hcup/hcupnet.htm

Ainsworth, P. B. (2002). *Offender profiling and crime analysis.* Devon: Willan.

Alison, L., & Canter, D. (1999). Profiling in policy and practice. In D. V. Canter, & L. J. Alison (Eds.), *Offender profiling series: Vol. II. Profiling in policy and practice* (pp. 3–20). Aldershot: Dartmouth.

Almond, L., Alison, L., & Porter, L. (2007). An evaluation and comparison of claims made in behavioural investigative advice reports compiled by the National Policing Improvements Agency in the United Kingdom. *Journal of Investigative Psychology and Offender Profiling, 4*(2), 71–83.

American Hospital Association. (2003). Fast facts on U.S. hospitals from hospital statistics. Retrieved June 30, 2003, from http://www.hospitalconnect.com

Arluke, A., Levin, J., Luke, C., & Ascione, F. (1999).The relationship of animal abuse to violence and other forms of antisocial behavior. *Journal of Interpersonal Violence, 14,* 963–975.

American Psychiatric Association. (2000). *Diagnostic and statistical manual of mental disorders* (4th ed., text revision). Washington DC: Author.

Ashton, E. H. (1943). *Medicine, magic, and sorcery among the Southern Sotho.* Cape Town: University of Cape Town.

Australian Institute of Criminology. (2005). *The arsonist's mind: Part 2—pyromania.* Australian Institute of Criminology: Bushfire Arson Bulletin. Retrieved September 7,   2009, from http://www.aic.gov.au/documents/5/B/C/{5BC81644-BAEA-4297-A518-B71C33C29C90}bfab009.pdf

Balachandra, K., & Swaminath, S. (2002). Fire fetishism in a female arsonist. *Canadian Journal of Psychiatry, 47*(5).

Barbaree, H. E., Seto, M. C., Serin, R., Amos, N., & Preston, D. (1994). Comparisons between sexual and nonsexual rapist subtypes. *Criminal Justice and Behavior, 21,* 95–114.

Bartol, C. R., & Bartol, A. M. (2005). *Current perspectives in forensic psychology and criminal justice.* Thousand Oaks, CA: Sage Publications.

Basile, K. C. (1999). Rape by acquiescence: The ways in which women "give in" to unwanted sex with their husbands. *Violence Against Women 5*(9):1017–1035.

Basile, K. C., Swahn, M. H., Chen, J., & Saltzman, L. E. (2006). Stalking in the United States: Recent national prevalence estimates. *American Journal of Preventative Medicine, 31,* 172–175.

Bateman, A. L., & Salfati, C. G. (2007). An examination of behavioral consistency using individual behaviors of groups of behaviors in serial homicide. *Behavioral Sciences and the Law, 25,* 527–544.

Baum, K., Catalano, S., Rand, M., & Rose, K. (2009, January). *Stalking victimization in the United States* (NCJ 224527). Washington DC: Bureau of Justice Programs, U.S. Department of Justice.

Beatty, D. (2003). Stalking legislation in the United States. In M. P. Brewster (Ed.), *Stalking: Psychology, risk factors, interventions, and law* (pp. 2.1–2.55). Kingston, NJ: Civic Research Institute.

Beauregard, E., Rossmo, D. K., & Proulx, J. (2007). A descriptive model of the hunting process of serial sex offenders: A rational choice perspective. *Journal of Family Violence, 22,* 449–463.

Becker, S. (2007). Race and violent offender "propensity": Does the intraracial nature of violent crime persist on the local level? *Justice Research and Policy, 9*(2), 53–86.

Bell, G. (1993). Testing of the national crime information center missing/unidentified persons computer comparison routine. *Journal of Forensic Sciences, 38,* 13–22.

Bell, M. E., Cattaneo, L. B., Goodman, L. A., & Dutton, M. A. (2008). Assessing the risk of future psychological abuse: Predicting the accuracy of battered women's predictions. *Journal of Family Violence, 23,* 69–80.

Bennel, C., & Canter, D. V. (2002). Linking commercial burglaries by modus operandi: Tests using regression and ROC analysis. *Science and Justice, 42,* 1–12.

Bergen, R. K. (1995). Surviving wife rape. *Violence Against Women, 1,* 117–138.

Bergen, R. K. (1996). *Wife rape.* Thousand Oaks, CA: Sage.

Bernat, F. P. (2002). Rape law reform. In J. F. Hodgson & D. S. Kelley (Eds.), *Sexual violence* (pp. 51–72). Westport, CT: Praeger.

Berrios, G. E., & Kennedy, N. (2002). Erotomania: A conceptual history. *History of Psychiatry, 13,* 381–400.

Beyer, K.R., & Beasley, J.O. (2003). Nonfamily child abductors who Murder Their Victims. *J. Interpersonal Violence.* 18, 1167–1188.

Bjerregaard, B. (2000). An empirical study of stalking victimization. *Violence and Victims, 15,* 389-406.

Blackburn, E. J. (1999). *"Forever yours": Rates of stalking victimization, risk factors and traumatic responses among college women.* Unpublished doctoral dissertation, University of Massachusetts, Boston.

Boles, G. S. (2001). Developing a model approach to confronting the problem of stalking: Establishing a threat management unit. In J. A. Davis (Ed.), *Stalking crimes and victim protection: Prevention, intervention, threat assessment, and case management* (pp. 337–350). Boca Raton, FL: CRC Press.

Boon, J. C. W., & Sheridan, L. (2001). Stalker typologies: A law enforcement perspective. *Journal of Threat Assessment, 1,* 75–97.

Boon, J., & Sheridan, L. (Eds.), (2002). *Stalking and psychosexual obsession: Psychological perspectives for prevention, policing and treatment.* West Sussex, England: John Wiley & Sons.

Borgeson, K. (2008, May 10). Non-sharing of data enables serial killings. *Boston Globe,* p. 15.

Brewster, M. P. (1998). *Exploration of the experiences and needs of former intimate stalking victims.* Final report submitted to the National Institute of Justice (NCJ 175475). Washington DC: U.S. Department of Justice.

Brewster, M. P. (2002). Trauma symptoms of former intimate stalking victims. *Women & Criminal Justice, 13,* 141–161.

Brewster, M. P. (2003). Power and control dynamics in prestalking and stalking situations. *Journal of Family Violence, 18,* 207–217.

Brooks, P. R., Devine, M. J., Green, T. J., Hart, B. L. & Moore, M. D. (1987). Serial murder: A criminal justice response. *Police chief,* 40–44.

Budd, T., & Mattinson, J. (2000). *Stalking: Findings from the 1998 British Crime Survey* (Home Office Research, Research Findings No. 129). London: Research Development and Statistics Directorate.

Buckles, T. (2007). *Crime scene investigation, criminalistics, and the law.* Clifton Park, NY: Thompson Delmar Learning.

Buckley, D. M. (2006). How to identify, interview and interrogate child sex offenders. Guildord, CT: Hahn Printing.

Bureau of Justice Statistics. (n.d.). *Homicide trends in the US.* Retrieved March 16, 2010, from http://bjs.ojp.usdoj.gov/content/homicide/multiple.cfm

Burgess, A. W., Baker, T., Greening, D., Hartman, C. R., Burgess, A. G., Douglas, J. E., & Halloran, R. (1997). Stalking behaviors within domestic violence. *Journal of Family Violence, 12,* 389–403.

California v. Bogard, (1996, February). California Supreme Court hearing in San Diego.

California v. Prince, 9 CAL.App.4th 1176, 10 CAL.Rptr.2D 855 (1992).

Callebs, S. (2005). Police admit computer mix-up in serial rape case: Colorado man suspected in at least six attacks. Retrieved May 23, 2009 from http://www.cnn.com/2005/LAW/02/21/colorado.rapes/index.html.

Campbell, J. C., & Soeken, K. L. (1999). Forced sex and intimate partner violence. *Violence Against Women, 5*(9).

Canter, D. (1994). *Criminal shadows: Inside the mind of the serial killer*. London: HarperCollins.

Canter, D. (2000). Offender profiling and criminal differentiation. *Legal and Criminal Psychology, 5*, 23–46.

Canter, D. (2003). *Mapping murder: The secrets of geographical profiling*. London: Virgin.

Canter, D. (2004a). Offender profiling and investigative psychology. *Journal of Investigative Psychology and Offender Profiling, 1*(1), 1–15.

Canter, D. (2004b). Geographical profiling of criminals. *Medico-Legal Journal, 72*(2), 53–66.

Canter, D. (2009). Developments in geographical offender profiling: Commentary on Bayesian Journey-to-Crime modeling. *Journal of Investigative Psychology and Offender Profiling, 6*(3), 161–166.

Canter, D. V., Alison, L. J., Alison, E., & Wentink, N. (2004). The organized/disorganized typology of serial murder: myth or model? *Psychology, Public Policy and Law, 10*(3), 293–320.

Canter, D., Heritage, R., & King-Johannessen, K. (1989). *Offender profiling: Second Interim Report to the Home Office*. Unpublished Home Office Report.

Canter, D., & Larkin, P. (1993). The environmental range of serial rapists. *Journal of Environmental Psychology, 13*, 63–69.

Carlisle, A. C. (1998). The divided self: Toward understanding of the dark side of the serial killer. In R. M. Holmes & S. T. Holmes (Eds.), *Contemporary perspectives on serial murder* (pp. 85–100). Thousand Oaks, CA: Sage.

Chapman, D. E., & Spitzberg, B. H. (2003). Are you following me? A study of unwanted relationship pursuit and stalking in Japan: What behaviors are prevalent? *Bulletin of Hijiyama University, 10*, 89–138.

Chavunduka, G. L. (2001). The reality of witchcraft. *African Legal Studies, 2*, 163–169.

Child Predatory Characteristics, (n.d.) Retrieved May 20, 2010 from http://childprotection.lifetips.com

Clay-Warner, J., & Burt, C. H. (2005). Rape reporting after reforms: Have times really changed? *Violence Against Women, 11*, 150–176.

Coleman, F. L. (1999). *Clinical characteristics of stalkers*. Dissertation (UMI Dissertation Services No. 9949961), University of Memphis, Memphis, TN.

Coleman, C., & Norris, C. (2000). *Introducing criminology*. Cullompton: Willan.

Cooperman, J. B. (2005, August). Chasing Rabbitt: Why was the South Side Rapist so hard to catch—and why do his motives still elude us? *St. Louis Magazine*. Retrieved May 23, 2009, from http://www.stlmag.com/media/St-Louis-Magazine/August-2005/Chasing-Rabbitt/

Conklin, J. E. (2004). *Criminology* (8th ed.). Boston: Allyn & Bacon.

Costigan, S. M. (2006). *Post-relationship stalking and harassment: The "reasonable person" standard of fear*. PhD thesis, Department of Psychology, University of Saskatchewan, Saskatoon, Saskatchewan, Canada.

Crossley, T., & Guzman, R. (1985). The relationship between arson and pyromania. *American Journal of Forensic Psychology, 3*(1), 39–44.

Cupach, W. R., & Spitzberg, B. H. (2000). Obsessive relational intrusion: Incidence, perceived severity, and coping. *Violence and Victims, 15*, 1–16.

Cupach, W. R., & Spitzberg, B. H. (2004). *The dark side of relationship pursuit: From attraction to obsession to stalking*. Mahwah, NJ: Lawrence Erlbaum Associates.

Dale, A., Davies, A., & Wei, L. (1997). Developing a typology of rapists' speech. *Journal of Pragmatics, 27*, 653–669.

Dan, B., & Kornreich, C. (2000). Talmudic, Koranic, and other classic reports of stalking. *British Journal of Psychiatry, 177*, 282.

Davis, J., & Lauber, K. (1999). Criminal behavioral assessments of arsonists, pyromaniacs, and multiple firesetters. *Journal of Contemporary Criminal Justice,15*(3), 273–290.

Davis, K. E., Ace, A., & Andra, M. (2000). Stalking perpetrators and psychological maltreatment of partners: Anger-jealousy, attachment insecurity, need for control, and break-up context. *Violence and Victims, 15*, 407–425.

Davis, K. E., Coker, A. L., & Sanderson, M. (2002). Physical and mental health effects of being stalked for men and women. *Violence and Victims, 17*, 429–443.

Davis, K. E., & Frieze, I. H. (2000). Research on stalking: What do we know and where do we go? *Violence and Victims, 15*, 473-491.

Davis, L. (1996, June 5). The nameless and the dead: Connecting the unidentified dead with their relatives is no easy task—especially when John Doe has 25 aliases. *The San Francisco Weekly.*

De Fazio, L. (2009). The legal situation on stalking among the European member states. *European Journal of Criminal Policy Research, 15*, 229–242.

Delaware v. Pennel, 584 A.2d 513 (Del.Super, 1989).

Del Ben, K. (2000). *Stalking: Developing an empirical typology to classify stalkers.* Unpublished master's thesis, Department of Psychology, West Virginia University, Morgantown.

Dennison, S., & Thomson, D. M. (2000). Community perceptions of stalking: What are the fundamental concerns? *Psychiatry, Psychology and Law, 7*, 159–169.

Dennison, S. M., & Thomson, D. M. (2002). Identifying stalking: The relevance of intent in commonsense reasoning. *Law and Human Behavior, 26*, 543–561.

Dennison, S. M., & Thomson, D. M. (2005). Criticisms or plaudits for stalking laws? What psycholegal research tells us about proscribing stalking. *Psychology, Public Policy and Law, 11*, 384–406.

Denno, D. (2000). When bad things happen to good intentions: The development and demise of a task force examining the drugs–violence interrelationship. *Albany Law Review, 63*(3), 749.

Derber, C. (1992). *Money, murder and the American dream: Wilding from Wall Street to Main Street.* Boston: Faber & Faber.

Devapriam, J., Raju, L., Singh, N., Collacott, R., & Bhaumik, S. (2007). Arson: Characteristics and predisposing factors in offenders with intellectual disabilities. *The British Journal of Forensic Practice, 9*(4), 23–27.

De Wet, J. (2008). *An exploratory analysis of serial rape in South Africa.* Unpublished Doctoral Thesis, University of Pretoria, Pretoria, South Africa.

Doe Network. (2006). The unidentified victims chronological index. Retrieved September 10, 2004, from http://www.doenetwork.org

Doley, R. (2003). Pyromania fact or fiction? *British Journal of Criminology. 43*(4), 797–807.

Douglas, J. E., Burgess, A. W., Burgess, A. G., & Ressler, R. K. (1992). *Crime classification manual.* New York: Macmillan.

Douglas, J. E., Burgess, A. W., Burgess A. G., & Ressler, R. K. (1997). *Crime classification manual: A standard system for investigating and classifying violent crimes.* San Francisco: Jossey-Bass.

Douglas, J. E., & Munn, C. (1992a). Violent crime scene analysis: Modus operandi, signature, and staging. *FBI Law Enforcement Bulletin.* February, 1–10.

Douglas, J. E., & Munn, C. M. (1992b). Modus operandi and the signature aspects of violent crime. In J. E. Douglas, A. W. Burgess, A. G. Burgess, & R. K. Ressler (Eds.), *Crime Classification Manual* (pp. 259–268). New York: Lexington Books.

Dressing, H., Küehner, C., & Gass, P. (2005). Prävalenz von stalking in Deutschland. *Psychiatric Praxis, 32,* 73–78.

Durnal, E. W. (2010). Crime scene investigation (as seen on TV). *Forensic Science International,* doi: 10.1016/j.forsciint.2010.02.015

Dussuyer, I. (2000, December). *Is stalking legislation effective in protecting victims?* Paper presented to the Criminal Justice Responses Conference, Australian Institute of Criminology, Sydney, Australia.

Dutton, L. B., & Spitzberg, B. H. (2007). Stalking: Its nature and dynamics. In Kendall-Tacket, K., & Giaccamoni, S. (Eds.), *Intimate partner violence,* Kingston, NJ: Civic Research Institute.

Dutton, L. B., & Winstead, B. A. (2006). Predicting unwanted pursuit: Attachment, relationship satisfaction, relationship alternatives, and break-up distress. *Journal of Social and Personal Relationships, 23,* 565–586.

Egger, S. A. (1984). A working definition of serial murder and the reduction of linkage blindness. *Journal of Police Science and Administration, 12,* 348–357.

Egger, S. (2002). *The killers among us. An examination of serial murder and its investigation* (2nd ed.). Upper Saddle River, NJ: Prentice Hall.

Egger, S. A. (2003). *The need to kill: Inside the world of the serial killer.* Upper Saddle River, NJ: Prentice Hall.

Eke, A. W. (1999). *Stalking offences and victim impact in a forensic sample of Ontario stalking survivors.* Unpublished master's thesis, Graduate Programme in Psychology, York University, Toronto, Ontario, Canada.

Esparza, S. (2009, December 16). Lack of money delays Wayne County anti-arson project. *The Detroit News.*

Families of Missing Loved Ones. (2002). Missing persons statistics 2001–2002. Retrieved October 31, 2004, from http://www.fomlo.homestead.com

Farrell, G., Weisburd, D., & Wyckoff, L. (2000). Survey results suggest need for stalking training. *The Police Chief, 67*(10), 162–167.

Federal Bureau of Investigation. (1990). Quantico, VA: Unpublished behavioral science unit file. In D. Kim Rossmo, *Geographic Profiling.* Boca Raton, FL: CRC Press.

Federal Bureau of Investigation. (2001). *Crime in the United States, 2000, Uniform Crime Reports.* Retrieved June 30, 2010, from http://www.fbi.gov/filelink.html?file=/ucr/cius_00/contents.pdf

Federal Bureau of Investigation. (2003). *Crime in the United States, 2002, Uniform Crime Reports.* Retrieved June 30, 2010, from http://www.fbi.gov/ucr/cius_02/pdf/02crime.pdf

Federal Bureau of Investigation. (2005). *Crime in the United States, 2005, uniform crime report.* Retrieved from http://www.fbi.gov/ucr/05cius/data/table_25.html

Federal Bureau of Investigation. (2009). *Crime in the United States, 2008, Uniform Crime Report.* Retrieved June 30, 2010, from http://www.fbi.gov/ucr/cius2008/index.html

Feldman-Summers, S., & Palmer, G. C. (1980). Rape as viewed by judges, prosecutors, and police officers. *Criminal Justice and Behavior, 7,* 19–40.

feminist.com. (2008). Facts about violence. Retrieved June 28, 2010, from http://feminist.com/antiviolence/facts.html

Ferraro, K. F. (1995). *Fear of crime: Interpreting victimization risk.* Albany, NY: State University of New York Press.

Few looking for missing foster children. (2002, October 27). *The Oklahoman.*

Finch, E. (2001). *The criminalization of stalking: Constructing the problem and evaluating the solution.* London: Cavendish Publishing.

Finn, J., & Banach, M. (2000). Victimization online: The down side of seeking human services for women on the Internet. *CyberPsychology & Behavior, 3,* 243–254.

Fisher, B. F., Cullen, F. T., & Turner, M. G. (2000). *The sexual victimization of college women* (NIJ No. 182369). Washington DC: National Institute of Justice.

Forensic science: The *CSI* effect. (2010, April 24). *The Economist*, pp. 77–78.

Fox, J. A. (2004). Homicide trends in the U.S. Retrieved September, 2004, from U.S. Department of Justice Bureau of Justice Statistics Web site: www.ojp.usdoj.gov/bjs/homicide/homtrnd.htm

Fox, J. A., & Levin, J. (1985). *Mass murder: America's growing menace*. New York: Plenum Press.

Fox, J. A., & Levin, J. (1998). Multiple murder: Patterns of serial and mass murder. In M. Tonry (Ed.), *Crime and justice: A review of research*. Chicago: University of Chicago Press.

Fox, J. A., & Levin, J. (2001). *The will to kill: Makings sense of senseless murder*. Boston: Allyn & Bacon.

Fox, J. A., & Levin, J. (2005). *Extreme killing: Understanding serial and mass murder*. Thousand Oaks, CA: Sage.

Fox, J. A., Levin, J., & Quinet, K. (2005). *The will to kill: Making sense of senseless murder* (2nd ed.). Boston: Allyn & Bacon.

Freed, D. (2010) The wrong man. Retrieved July 13, 2010, from http://www.theatlantic.com/magazine/archive/2010/05/the-wrong-man/8019/

Fritzon, K. (2000). The contribution of psychological research to arson investigation. In D. Canter & L. Alison (Eds.), *Offender profiling series: Profiling property crimes* (Vol IV, pp.149–184). Burlington, VT: Ashgate.

Frohmann, L. (1991). Discrediting victims' allegations of sexual assault: Prosecutorial accounts of case rejection. *Social Problems, 38*, 213–226.

Gabbard, G. O. (2003). American Psychiatric Association's Institute on Psychiatric Services, Boston.

Galeai, G. M., Bu ar-Ru man, A., De Fazio, L., Groenen, A. (2009). Experiences of stalking victims and requests for help in three European countries. A survey. *European Journal of Criminal Policy Research, 15*, 243–260.

Galeai, G. M., Elkins, K., & Curci, P. (2005). The stalking of mental health professionals by patients. *Psychiatric Services, 56*, 137–138.

Gartner, R., & Macmillan, R. (1995). The effect of victim-offender relationship reporting crimes of violence against women. *Canadian Journal of Criminology, 37*, 393–429.

Geberth, V. J. (2003). *Sex-related homicide and death investigations: Practical and clinical perspectives*. Boca Raton, FL: CRC Press.

Geller, J., McDermeit, M., & Brown, J. (1997). Pyromania? What does it mean? *Journal of Forensic Sciences, 42*(6), 1052–1057.

Gentile, S. R., Asamen, J. K., Harmell, P. H., & Weathers, R. (2002). The stalking of psychologists by their clients. *Professional Psychology Research & Practice, 33*, 490–494.

Geshiere, P. (2000). *The modernity of witchcraft: Politics and the occult in postcolonial Africa*. Charlottesville, VA: University Press of Virginia.

Gill, R., & Brockman, J. (1996). *A review of section 264 (criminal harassment) of the Criminal Code of Canada*. Working document WD 1996–7e. Research, Statistics and Evaluation Directorate. Ottawa, Ontario, Canada: Department of Justice, Canada.

Gilmore, W. (1998). The G-7 and transnational drug trafficking: The task force experience. *Hume Papers on Public Policy, 6*(1/2), 30.

Gerbner, G., & Gross, L. (1976). Living with television: The violence profile. *Journal of Communication, 26*, 76.

Gerbner, G., & Morgan, M. (2002). *Against the mainstream: Selected works of George Gerbner*. New York: Peter Lang Publishing.

Gerbner, G., & Signorielli, N. (1988). *Violence and terror in the mass media: An annotated bibliography*. Westport, CT: Greenwood Press.

Gist, J. H., McFarlane, J., Malecha, A., Fredland, N., Schultz, P., & Willson, P. (2001). Women in danger: Intimate partner violence experienced by women who qualify and do not qualify for a protective order. *Behavioral Sciences and the Law, 19*, 637–647.

Glassner, B. (2000). *The culture of fear.* New York: Basic Books.

Godwin, G. M. (1999). *Hunting serial predators: A multivariate classification approach to profile violent behavior.* Boca Raton, FL: CRC Press.

Godwin, G. M. (2000). *Hunting serial predators: A multivariate classification approach to profiling violent behavior.* Boca Raton, FL: CRC Press.

Goffman, E. (1959). *The presentation of self in everyday life.* Garden City, NY: Doubleday.

Graham, R. (2006). Male rape and the careful construction of the male victim. *Social and Legal Studies, 15*, 187–208.

Graney, D. J., & Arrigo, B. A. (2002). *Power serial rapist.* Springfield, IL: Charles C Thomas.

Green, E. J., Booth, C. E., & Biderman, M. D. (1976). Cluster analysis of burglary M/O's. *Journal of Police Science and Administration, 4*, 382–388.

Greenfield, L. A. (1997). *Sex offenses and offenders: An analysis of data on rape and sexual assault.* Washington DC: U.S. Department of Justice Office of Justice Programs Bureau of Justice Statistics.

Groenen, A., & Vervacke, G. (2009). Violent stalkers. Detecting risk factors by the police. *European Journal of Criminal Policy Research, 15*, 279–291.

Grossman, D. (1996). *On killing.* Boston: Back Bay Books.

Groth, N. (1985). The incest offender. In S. Sgroi, *Handbook of clinical intervention In child sexual abuse.* Lexington, MA: Lexington Books.

Groth, A. N., & Birnbaum, H. J. (1979). *Men who rape.* New York: Plenum Press.

Groth, A. N., Burgess, A., & Holmstrom, L. (1977). Rape, power, anger and sexuality. *American Journal of Psychiatry, 134*, 1239–1243.

Grové, H. V. A. (1950). Sluipende dood. Ontsettende wreedheid van rituele moored in Basoetoland. *Die Huisgenoot*, Januarie.

Grubin, D., & Gunn, J. (1990). *The imprisoned rapist and rape.* London: Institute of Psychiatry.

Grubin, D., Kelly, P., & Brunsdon, C. (2001). *Linking serious sexual assaults through behaviour.* London: Home Office.

Gudjonsson, G. H., & Haward, L. R. C. (1999). *Forensic psychology: A guide to practice.* East Sussex, England: Routledge.

Guillen, T. (2007). *Serial killers: Issues explored through the Green River murders.* Upper Saddle River, NJ: Prentice Hall.

Haglund, W. D. (1993). The national crime information center (NCIC) missing and unidentified persons system revisited. *Journal of Forensic Sciences, 38*, 365–378.

Häkkänen, H., Hagelstam, C., & Santtila, P. (2003). Stalking actions, prior offender—victim relationships and issuing of restraining orders in a Finnish sample of stalkers. *Legal and Criminological Psychology, 8*, 189–206.

Hall, D. M. (1998). The victims of stalking. In J. R. Meloy (Ed.), *The psychology of stalking* (pp. 113–137). San Diego, CA: Academic Press.

Hare, R. D. (1993) *Without conscience: The disturbing world of the psychopaths among us.* New York: Pocket Books.

Harmon, R. B., Rosner, R., & Owens, H. (1995). Obsessional harassment and erotomania in a criminal court population. *Journal of Forensic Sciences, 40*, 188–196.

Harmon, R. B., Rosner, R., & Owens, H. (1998). Sex and violence in a forensic population of obsessional harassers. *Psychology, Public Policy, and Law, 4*, 236–249.

Harries, K., & LeBeau, J. (2007). Issues in the geographic profiling of crime: Review and commentary. *Police Practice & Research, 8*(4), 321–333.

Harrington, A. (1972). *Psychopaths*. New York: Simon & Schuster.

Haugaard, J. J., & Seri, L. G. (2003). Stalking and other forms of intrusive contact after the dissolution of adolescent dating or romantic relationships. *Violence and Victims, 18*, 279–297.

Hazelwood, R. R., & Burgess, A. W. (1987a). An introduction to the serial rapist: Research by the FBI. *FBI Law Enforcement Bulletin, 56*, 16–24.

Hazelwood, R. R., & Burgess, A. W. (1987b). *Practical aspects of rape investigation: A multidisciplinary approach*. New York: Elsevier.

Hazelwood, R. R., & Burgess, A. W. (1989). The serial rapist: His characteristics and victims. (Part I). *FBI Law Enforcement Bulletin, 58*, 11–17.

Hazelwood, R. R., & K. V. Lanning. (2001). Collateral materials in sexual crimes. In R. R. Hazelwood & A. Burgess (Eds.), *Practical aspects of rape investigation* (3rd ed.). Boca Raton, FL: CRC Press.

Hazelwood, R. R., Reboussin, R., & Warren, J. I. (1989). Serial rape: Correlates of increased aggression and the relationship of offender pleasure to victim resistance. *Journal of Interpersonal Violence, 4*, 65–78.

Hazelwood, R. R., & Warren, J. (1989). The serial rapist: His characteristics and victims (Part 2). *FBI Law Enforcement Bulletin, 58*, 18–25.

Hazelwood, R. R., & Warren, J. (1990). The criminal behavior of the serial rapist. *FBI Law Enforcement Bulletin, 59*, 11–16.

Hazelwood, R. R., & Warren, J. (1995). The serial rapist. In R. R. Hazelwood & A. W. Burgess (Eds.), *Practical aspects of rape investigation: A multidisciplinary approach* (2nd ed.). Boca Raton, FL: CRC Press.

Hazelwood, R. R., & Warren, J. (2000). The sexually violent offender: Impulsive or ritualistic? *Aggression and Violent Behavior, 5*, 267–279.

Hazelwood, R. R., & Warren, J. I. (2003). Linkage analysis: Modus operandi, ritual, and signature in serial sexual crime. *Aggression and Violent Behaviour, 8*, 587–598.

Heilbrun, A. B. (1982). Cognitive models of criminal violence based upon intelligence and psychopathy levels. *Journal of Consulting and Clinical Psychology, 50*, 546–557.

Hickey, E. W. (1997). *Serial murderers and their victims*. Belmont, CA: Wadsworth.

Hickey, E. W. (2002). *Serial murderers and their victims* (3rd ed.). Belmont, CA: Wadworth-Thompson Learning.

Hickey, E. W. (2004). *Serial murderers and their victims*. Belmont, CA: Wadsworth.

Hickman, M. J., Hughes, K. A., Strom, K. J., & Ropero-Miller, J. D. (2007). Medical examiners and coroners' offices, 2004. Bureau of Justice Statistics special report. Washington DC: U.S. Department of Justice, Office of Justice Programs, Bureau of Justice Statistics.

Hills, A. M., & Taplin, J. L. (1998). Anticipated responses to stalking: Effect of threat and target-stalker relationship. *Psychiatry, Psychology and Law, 5*, 139–146.

Hodgskiss, B. (2001). *A multivariate model of the offence behaviours of South African serial murderers*. Unpublished master's thesis, Rhodes University, Grahamstown, South Africa.

Hodgskiss, B. (2004). Lessons from serial murder in South Africa. *Journal of Investigative Psychology and Offender Profiling, 1*(1), 67–94.

Hoffman, L. H., & Zeffert, D. (1988). *The South African Law of Evidence* (4th ed.). Durban, South Africa: Butterworths.

Hollander, Z. (2009, March 13). Man accused of serial rape gets May trial date. *Anchorage Daily News*.

Holmes, R. M. (1998a). Sequential predation: Elements of serial fatal victimization. In R. M. Holmes & S. T. Holmes (Eds.), *Contemporary perspectives on serial murder* (pp. 101–112). Thousand Oaks, CA: Sage.

Holmes, R. M. (1998b). Stalking in America: Types and methods of criminal stalkers. In R. M. Holmes & S. T. Holmes (Eds.), *Contemporary perspectives on serial murder* (pp. 137–148). Thousand Oaks, CA: Sage.

Holmes, R. M. (2001). Criminal stalking: An analysis of the various typologies of stalkers. In J. A. Davis (Ed.), *Stalking crimes and victim protection: Prevention, intervention, threat assessment, and case management* (pp. 19–29). Boca Raton, FL: CRC Press.

Holmes, R. M., & DeBurger, J. (1988). *Serial murder*. Newbury Park, CA: Sage.

Holmes, R. M., & Holmes, S. T. (2002). *Profiling violent crimes: An investigative tool*. Thousand Oaks, CA: Sage Publications.

Holmes, S. T., & Holmes, R. M. (2008). *Sex crimes: Patterns and behaviors* (3rd ed.). Thousand Oaks, CA: Sage Publications.

Holmes, R. M., & Holmes, S. T. (2009). *Profiling violent crimes* (4th ed.). Thousand Oaks, CA: Sage.

Huffhines, D. M. (2001). *Recidivism rates of convicted stalkers in San Diego County*. Unpublished master's thesis, Department of Public Administration, San Diego State University, CA.

Icove, D., & Estepp, M. (1987). Motive-based offender profiles of arson and fire-related crimes. *FBI Law Enforcement Bulletin, 56*(4), 17–23.

Inciardi, J. (1970). The adult firesetter: A typology. *Criminology, 8*, 145–155.

Indianapolis Police Department (IPD). (2005). Interviews of missing persons detectives, June 2005.

Innes, B. (2003). *Profile of criminal mind: How psychological profiling helps solve true crimes*. London: Amber Books.

Insurance Information Institute. (2009a). *Arson*. Retrieved December 30, 2009, from http://www.iii.org/media/hottopics/insurance/arson/

Insurance Information Institute. (2009b). *Insurance fraud*. Retrieved December 18, 2009, from http://www.iii.org/media/hottopics/insurance/fraud/

Ivey, G., & Myers, T. (2008). The psychology of bewitchment (Part 1): A phenomenological study of the experience of bewitchment. *South African Journal of Psychology, 38*(1), 54–74.

James, D. V., & Farnham, F. R. (2003). Stalking and serious violence. *Journal of the American Academy of Psychiatry and the Law, 31*, 432–439.

Jasinski, J. L., & Dietz, T. L. (2003). Domestic violence and stalking among older adults: An assessment of risk markers. *Journal of Elder Abuse & Neglect, 15*, 3–18.

Jason, L. A., Reichler, A., Easton, J., Neal, A., & Wilson, M. (1984). Female harassment after ending a relationship: A preliminary study. *Alternative Lifestyles, 6*, 259–269.

Jenkins, P. (1994). *Using murder: The social construction of serial homicide*. New York: Aldine de Gruyter.

Jenkins, P. (2005). Myth and murder: The serial killer panic. In V. E. Kappeler & G. W. Potter (Eds.), *The mythology of crime and criminal justice* (4th ed.). Prospect Heights, IL: Waveland Press.

Jensen, G. F., & Kapros, M. M. (1993). Managing rape: Exploratory research on the behavior of rape statistics. *Criminology, 31*, 363–385.

Johnson, S. M., & Spitzberg, B. H. (2006, July). *Mapping predatory pursuit: Investigating stalker case files*. Paper presented to the International Association of Relationship Research, Rethymnon, Crete, Greece.

Jordan, C. E., Logan, TK, Walker, R., & Nigoff, A. (2003). Stalking: An examination of the criminal justice response. *Journal of Interpersonal Violence, 18*, 148–165.

Kamb, L. (2003, February 22). In their own words: The twisted art of murder. *Seattle Post-Intelligencer*.

Kamir, O. (2001). *Every breath you take: Stalking narratives and the law*. Ann Arbor, MI: University of Michigan Press.

Kamphuis, J. H., Galeai, G. M., De Fazio, L. Emmelkamp, P. M. G., Farnham, F., Groenen, A., James, D., & Vervaeke, G. (2005). Stalking—Perceptions and attitudes amongst helping professions. An EU cross-national comparison. *Clinical Psychology and Psychotherapy, 12*, 215–225.

Kapley, D. J., & Cooke, J. R. (2007). Trends in antistalking legislation. In D. A. Pinals (Ed.), *Stalking: Psychiatric perspectives and practical approaches* (pp. 141–163). New York: Oxford University Press.

Karchmer, C. (1984). Young arsonists. *Society, 22*(1), 78–83.

Karger, B., Rand, S. P., & Brinkman, B. (2000). Criminal anticipation of DNA investigations resulting in mutilation of a corpse. *International Journal of Legal Medicine, 113*(4), 247–248.

Kelly, L. (1988). How women define their experiences of violence. In K. Yllo & M. Bograd (Eds.), *Feminist perspectives on wife abuse* (pp. 114–132). Newbury Park, CA: Sage.

Keen, S. (1986). *Faces of the enemy.* New York: Harper & Row.

Keppel, R. D. (2000a). Signature murders: A report of the 1984 Cranbrook, British Colombia cases. *Journal of Forensic Sciences, 45*(2), 500–503.

Keppel, R. D. (2000b). Investigation of the serial offender: Linking cases through modus operandi and signature. In L. B. Schlesinger (Ed.), *Serial offenders: Current thoughts, recent findings* (pp. 121–133). Boca Raton, FL: CRC Press.

Keppel, R. (2006). *Offender profiling* (2nd ed.). New York: Thomson Press.

Keppel, R. D., & Birnes, W. J. (2003). *The psychology of serial killer investigations: The grisly business unit.* San Diego, CA: Academic Press.

Keppel, R. D., & Birnes, W. J. (2009). *Serial violence. Analysis of modus operandi and signature characteristics of killers.* Boca Raton, FL: CRC Press.

Keppel, R. D., & Weis, J. G. (2004). The rarity of "unusual" dispositions of victim bodies: Staging and posing. *Journal of Forensic Science, 49*(6), 1–5.

Keppel, R. D., Weis, J. G., Brown, K. M., & Welch, K. (2005). The Jack the Ripper murders: A modus operandi and signature analysis of the 1888–1891 Whitechapel murders. *Journal of Investigative Psychology and Offender Profiling, 2,* 1–21.

Kienlen, K. K., Birmingham, D. L., Solberg, K. B., O'Regan, J. T., & Meloy, J. R. (1997). A comparative study of psychotic and nonpsychotic stalking. *Journal of the American Academy of Psychiatry and Law, 25,* 317–334.

Kiger, K. (1990). The darker figure of crime: The serial murder enigma. In S. Egger (Ed.), *Serial murder: An elusive phenomenon* (pp. 35–52). New York: Praeger.

Kilpatrick, D. G. (2000). *Rape and sexual assault. National Violence Against Women Prevention Research Center. Medical University of South Carolina.*

Kingsnorth, R. (2006). Intimate partner violence: Predictors of recidivism in a sample of arrestees. *Violence Against Women, 12.*

Kinkade, P., Burns, R., & Fuentes, A. I. (2005). Criminalizing attractions: Perceptions of stalking and the stalker. *Crime & Delinquency, 51,* 3–25.

KMBC.com. (2010). Police: Don't become vigilantes in rapist search: Residents on high alert searching for Waldo rapist. Retrieved March 26, 2010, from http://www.kmbc.com/news/22672141/detail.html

Knight, R. A., & Prenky, R. A. (1987). The developmental antecedents and adult adaptations of rapist subtypes. *Criminal Justice and Behavior, 14*(4), 403–426.

Knight, R. A., & Prentky, R. A. (1990). Classifying sexual offenders: The development of corroboration of taxonomic models. In W. L. Marshall, D. R. Laws, & H. E. Barbaree (Eds.), *Handbook of sexual assault* (pp. 23–52). New York: Plenum.

Knox, K., & Roberts, A. R. (2003). Crisis intervention for victims in stalking cases. In M. P. Brewster (Ed.), *Stalking: Psychology, risk factors, interventions, and law* (pp. 10.1–10.18). Kingston, NJ: Civic Research Institute.

Kocsis, R. N. (1997). Criminal profiling the residence location of serial rape and arson offenders. *Australian Police Journal, 51*(4), 250–253.

Kocsis, R. N. (2002). *Arson: Exploring motives and possible solutions.* Retrieved June 30, 2010, from the Australian Institute of Criminology Web site, http://www.aic.gov.au/documents/A/1/8/{A18209AF-C67E-4E5E-9FCD-D5413DCA4686}ti236.pdf

Kocsis, R. N. (2006).*Criminal profiling: Principals and practice*. Totowa, NJ: Humana Press.

Kocsis, R. N., & Irwin, H. J. (1998). The psychological profile of serial offenders and a redefinition of the misnomer of serial crime. *Psychiatry, Psychology, and Law, 5*, 197–213.

Kohn, M., Flood, H., Chase, J., & McMahon, P. M. (2000). Prevalence and health consequences of stalking—Louisiana, 1998–1999. *Morbidity and Mortality Weekly Report, 49*(29), 653–655.

Koss, M. P., Gidycz, C. J., & Wisniewski, N. (1987). The scope of rape: Incidence and prevalence of sexual aggression and victimization in a national sample of higher education students. *Journal of Consulting and Clinical Psychology, 55*, 162–170.

Krauland, W., Schneider, V., Smerling, M., & Ludwig, W. R. (1980). Defensive Leichenzerstückelung. *Arch Kriminol, 166*, 1–17.

Labuschagne, G. N. (2003). Offender profiling in South Africa: Its definition and context. *Acta Criminologica: Southern African Journal of Criminology, 16*(3), 67–74.

Labuschagne, G. N. (2004). Features and investigative implications of muti murder in South Africa. *Journal of Investigative Psychology and Offender Profiling, 1*(3), 191–206.

Labuschagne, G. N. (2006). The use of a linkage analysis in the conviction of the Newcastle Serial Murderer, South Africa. *Journal of Investigative Psychology and Offender Profiling, 3*, 183–191.

Lambrecht, I. (1998). *A psychological study of shamanic trance states in South African shamanism*. Unpublished doctoral dissertation, University of the Witwatersrand, Johannesburg, South Africa.

Langan, P. A., Schmitt, E. L. & Durose, M. R. (2003). Recidivism of sex offenders released from prison in 1994. United States Department of Justice, NCJ 198281.

Langer, W. C. (n.d.). *A psychological analysis of Adolf Hitler: His life and legend*. Retrieved July 9, 2010, from http://www.nizkor.org/hweb/people/h/hitler-adolf/oss-papers/text/profile-index.html

Langhinrichsen-Rohling, J. (2006). An examination of sheltered battered women's perpetration of stalking and other unwanted pursuit behaviors. *Violence and Victims, 21*, 579–595.

Langhinrichsen-Rohling, J., Palarea, R. E., Cohen, J., & Rohling, M. L. (2000). Breaking up is hard to do: Unwanted pursuit behaviors following the dissolution of a romantic relationship. *Violence and Victims, 15*, 73–90.

Lanning, K. (1992a). *Child molesters: A behavioral analysis* (3rd ed.). Arlington, VA.: National Center for Missing & Exploited Children.

Lanning, K. (1992b). *Child sex rings: A behavioral analysis* (2nd ed.). Arlington, VA: National Center for Missing & Exploited Children.

Lanning, K. (2002). *Child molesters: A behavioral analysis* (4th ed.). Arlington, VA.: National Center for Missing & Exploited Children.

Lavendera, E. (2004, February 27). Six states track possible serial killer. Retrieved June 19, 2004 from http://www.cnn.com/2004/us/02/27/possible.serial.killer

Lavrakas, P. J. (1982). Fear of crime and behavioral restrictions in urban and suburban neighborhoods. *Population and Environment, 5*, 242–246.

LeBeau, J. L. (1985). Some problems with measuring and describing rape presented by the serial offender. *Justice Quarterly, 2*(3), 385–398.

LeBeau, J. L. (1987). Patterns of stranger and serial rape offending: Factors distinguishing apprehended and at large offenders. *The Journal of Criminal Law and Criminology, 78*(2), 309–326.

LeBeau, J. L. (2005). Geographic profiling. In L. E. Sullivan & M. S. Rosen (Eds.), *Encyclopedia of law enforcement* (Vol. 1, pp. 380–381). Thousand Oaks, CA: Sage.

Lee, M. R., & Dehart, E. (2007). The influences of a serial killer on changes in fear of crime and the use of protective measures: A survey-based case study of Baton Rouge. *Deviant Behavior, 28*(1), 1–28.

Leong, G. (1992). Psychiatric study of persons charged with arson. *Journal of Forensic Sciences, 37*(5), 1319–1326.

Levin, J., & Fox, J. A. (1985). *Mass murder: America's growing menace*. New York: Plenum Press.

Levine, N. (2002). Crimestat: A spatial statistics program for the analysis of crime incident locations (v2.0). Ned Levine and Associates, Houston, TX and the National Institute of Justice, Washington DC.

Lewis, S. F., Fremouw, W. J., Del Ben, K., & Farr, C. (2001). An investigation of the psychological characteristics of stalkers: Empathy, problem-solving, attachment and borderline personality features. *Journal of Forensic Sciences, 46*, 80–84.

Lifton, R. J. (1986). *The Nazi doctors: Medical killing and the psychology of genocide*. New York: Basic Books.

Lloyd-Goldstein, R. (1998). De Clérambault on-line: A survey of erotomania and stalking from the old world to the world wide web. In J. R. Meloy (Ed.), *The psychology of stalking* (pp. 193–212). San Diego, CA: Academic Press.

Lloyd-Goldstein, R. (2000). Serial stalkers: Recent clinical findings. In L. B. Schlesinger (Ed.), *Serial offenders: Current thought, recent findings* (pp. 167–185). Boca Raton, FL: CRC Press.

Logan, TK, & Cole, J. (2007). The impact of partner stalking on mental health and protective order outcomes over time. *Violence and Victims, 22*, 546–562.

Logan, TK, Cole, J., Shannon, L., & Walker, R. (2006). *Partner stalking: How women respond, cope, and survive*. New York: Springer.

Logan, TK, Nigoff, A., Walker, R., & Jordan, C. (2002). Stalker profiles with and without protective orders: Reoffending or criminal justice processing. *Violence and Victims, 17*, 541–553.

Logan, TK, Shannon, L., Cole, J., & Swanberg, J. (2007). Partner stalking and implications for women's employment. *Journal of Interpersonal Violence, 22*, 268–291.

Logan, TK, Shannon, L., Walker, R., & Faragher, T. M. (2006). Protective orders: Questions and conundrums. *Trauma, Violence & Abuse, 7*, 175–205.

Logan, TK, & Walker, R. (2009). Civil protective order outcomes: Violations and perceptions of effectiveness. *Journal of Interpersonal Violence, 24*, 675–692

Logan, TK, Walker, R., Stewart, C., & Allen, J. (2006). Victim service and justice system representative responses about partner stalking: What do professionals recommend? *Violence and Victims, 21*, 49–66.

Lord, V. B., & Rassel, G. (2002). Law enforcement responses to sexual assault. In J. F. Hodgson & D. S. Kelley, *Sexual violence* (pp. 155–172). Westport, CT: Praeger.

Louisiana v. Code, 627 So.2d 1373 (1994).

Lowney, K. S., & Best, J. (1995). Stalking strangers and lovers: Changing media typifications of a new crime problem. In J. Best (Ed.), *Images of issues: Typifying contemporary social problems* (2nd ed., pp. 33–57). New York: Aldine de Gruyter.

Lundrigan, S., & Canter, D. (2001). A multivariate analysis of serial murderers' disposal site location choice. *Journal of Environmental Psychology, 21*, 423–432.

Lyon, D. R. (2006). *An examination of police investigational files for criminal harassment (stalking): Implications for case management.* Unpublished Ph.D. dissertation, Simon Fraser University, British Columbia, Canada.

Madden, M. A. (n.d.). George Metesky: New York's Mad Bomber. Retrieved July 9, 2010, from http://www.trutv.com/library/crime/terrorists_spies/terrorists/metesky/4.html

Maksymchuk, L. (2001). *A comparative study of a stalker typology: An analysis of the stalking case files of the Ontario Provincial Police*. Unpublished Master of Arts Thesis, Department of Criminology, University of Ottowa, Ontario.

Makwe, E. R. (1985). *Western and indigenous psychiatric help-seeking in an urban African population.* Unpublished master's dissertation, University of the Witwatersrand, Johannesburg, South Africa.

Magid, K., & McKelvey, C. A. (1988). *High risk: Children without a conscience*. New York: Bantam Books.

Mahoney, P. (1999). High Rape Chronicity and Low Rates of Help Seeking among Wife Rape Survivors in a Nonclinical Sample. *Violence Against Women 5*, 993–1016.

Malsch, M. (2007). Stalking: Do criminalization and punishment help? *Punishment & Society, 9*, 201–209.

Martinez, B. (2004). Interstate arson: Catching the traveling serial arsonist. *Fire Engineering, 157*(6), 109–114.

Maryland Coalition Against Sexual Assault. (2007). Sexual assault in-service training for law enforcement. Retrieved June 28, 2010, from http://www.mcasa.org/uploads/docs/MCASA_Victim_Interviews_07.ppt

Matthews, T. (2006). FBI-NCIC unidentified dead statistics. Retrieved April 30, 2006, from http://www.doenetwork.org

Mavromatis, M. (2000) Serial arson: Repetitive firesetting and pyromania. In L. L. Schlesinger (Ed.), *Serial offenders: Current thoughts, recent findings* (pp. 67–101). Boca Raton, FL: CRC Press.

Maxwell, C. D., Garner, J. H., & Fagan, J. A. (2002). The preventative effects of arrest on intimate partner violence: Research, policy and theory. *Criminology and Public Policy, 2*, 51–80.

Maxey, W. (2001). Stalking the stalker: Law enforcement investigation and intervention. In J. A. Davis (Ed.), *Stalking crimes and victim protection: Prevention, intervention, threat assessment, and case management* (pp. 351–374). Boca Raton, FL: CRC Press.

Maxey, W. (2002). The San Diego Stalking Strike Force: A multi-disciplinary approach to assessing and managing stalking and threat cases. *Journal of Threat Assessment, 2*, 43–53.

McCabe, M., & Wauchope, M. (2005). Behavioral characteristics of men accused of rape: Evidence for different types of rapists. *Archives of Sexual Behavior, 34*(2), 241–253.

McCarroll, J. E., Thayer, L. E., Liu, X., Newby, J. H., Norwood, A. E., Fullerton, C. S., et al. (2000). Spouse abuse recidivism in the U. S. Army by gender and military status. *Journal of Consulting and Clinical Psychology, 68*, 521–525.

McClain, P., Sacks, J., Froehlke, R., & Ewigman, B. (1993). Estimates of fatal child abuse and neglect, United States, 1979–1988. *Pediatrics, 91*, 338–343.

McCutcheon, L. E., Scott, V. B., Jr., Aruguete, M. S., & Parker, J. (2006). Exploring the link between attachment and the inclination to obsess about or stalk celebrities. *North American Journal of Psychology, 8*, 289–300.

McEwan, T., Mullen, P. E., & MacKenzie, R. (2009). A study of the predictors of persistence in stalking situations. *Law and Human Behavior, 33*, 149–158.

McLennan, W. (1996). *Women's safety, Australia, 1996.* Canberra, Commonwealth of Australia: Australian Bureau of Statistics.

Mead, G. H. (1934). *Mind, self, and society.* Chicago: University of Chicago Press.

Mele, M. (2009). The time course of repeat intimate partner violence. *Journal of Family Violence, 24*, 619–624.

Meloy, J. R. (Ed.). (1998). *The psychology of stalking.* Boston: Academic Press.

Meloy, J. R. (1999). Erotomania, triangulation, and homicide. *Journal of Forensic Sciences, 44*, 421–424.

Meloy, J.R. (1997). The clinical risk management of stalkers: "Someone is watching over me…" The *American Journal of Psychotherapy, 51*, 174–184.

Meloy, J. R. (2007). Stalking: The state of the science. *Criminal Behaviour and Mental Health, 17*, 1–7.

Meloy, J. R., & Boyd, C. (2003). Female stalkers and their victims. *Journal of the American Academy of Psychiatry and the Law, 31*, 211–219.

Meloy, J. R., Rivers, L., Siegel, L., Gothard, S., Naimark, D., & Nicolini, J. R. (2000). A replication study of obsessional followers and offenders with mental disorders. *Journal of Forensic Sciences, 45*, 147–152.

Meloy, J. R., Sheridan, L., & Hoffman, J. (2008). Public figure stalking, threats, and attacks: The state of the science. In J. R. Meloy, L. Sheridan & J. Hoffman (Eds.), *Stalking, threatening, and attacking public figures: A psychological and behavioral analysis* (pp. 3–34). New York: Oxford University Press.

Melton, H. C. (2004). Stalking in the context of domestic violence: Findings on the criminal justice system. *Women & Criminal Justice, 15*, 33–58.

Ménard, K. S., Anderson, A. L., & Godboldt, S. M. (2009). Gender differences in intimate partner recidivism: A 5-year follow-up. *Criminal Justice and Behavior, 36,* 61–76.

Merry, S. (2000). Crime analysis: Principles for analysing everyday serial crime. In D. Canter & L. Alison (Eds.), *Profiling property crime* (pp. 297–318). Aldershot, England: Ashgate.

Meyers, J. (1998). Cultural factors in erotomania and obsessional following. In J. R. Meloy (Ed.), *The psychology of stalking* (pp. 213–224). San Diego, CA: Academic Press.

Middleton, M. (1982). Crime task force report gets airing. *American Bar Association Journal, 68*(3), 258.

Miller, N. (2001). *Stalking laws and their implementation: What stalking investigators and prosecutors do—A problem solving perspective.* Final Report, available Institute for Law and Justice, Alexandria, VA.

Miller, N., & Nugent, H. (2001). *Stalking laws and implementation practices: A national review for policymakers and practitioners* (NCJ 197066). Washington DC: United States Department of Justice.

Minaar, A. (1998). *Witchpurging and muti murders in South Africa with specific reference to the Northern Province.* Presentation to a SAPS Occult Crime Unit workshop on occult- and witchcraft-related crime, Paarl, South Africa.

Minaar, A. (2001). Witchpurging and muti murder in South Africa: The legislative and legal challenges to combating these practices with specific reference to the Witchcraft Suppression Act (No. 3 of 1957, amended by Act No. 50 of 1970). *African Legal Studies, 2,* 1–21.

Minaar, A., Offringa, D., & Payze, C. (1991). The witches of Venda. Politics in magic potions. *Indicator SA, 9,* 53–56.

Mischel, W. (1999). Personality coherence and dispositions in a cognitive-affective personality system (CAPS) approach. In D. Cervone & Y. Shoda (Eds.), *The coherence of personality: Social-cognitive bases of consistency, variability and organisation* (pp. 37–60). London: Guilford Press.

Modena Group on Stalking. (2005). Recognition and perceptions of stalking by police officers and general practitioners: A multi-centre European study (pp. 82–110). *Female victims of stalking: Recognition and intervention models: A European study.* Milano: Franco Angeli.

Modena Group on Stalking. (2007, April). *Protecting women from the new crime of stalking: A comparison of legislative approaches within the European Union.* Modena Group on Stalking/Daphne Project Final Report 05-1/125/W. Universita Degli Studi Di Modena and Reggio Emilia. Retrieved June 6, 2009, from http://stalking.medlegmo.unimo.it/RAPPORTO_versione_finale_011007.pdf

Mohandie, K. (2004). Stalking behavior and crisis negotiation. *Journal of Police Crisis Negotiations, 4,* 23–44.

Mohandie, K., Meloy, R., McGowan, M. G., & Williams, J. (2006). The RECON typology of stalking: Reliability and validity based upon a large sample of North American stalkers. *Journal of Forensic Sciences, 51,* 147–155.

Montero, M. S. (2003). *Personality characteristics of perpetrators of stalking-like behaviors.* Unpublished master's thesis, University of South Carolina, Columbia.

Morewitz, S. J. (2003). *Stalking and violence: New patterns of trauma and obsession.* New York: Kluwer Academic/Plenum.

Morris, S., Anderson, S., & Murray, L. (2002). *Stalking and harassment in Scotland.* Edinburgh: Scottish Executive Social Research

Morrison, K. A. (2001). Predicting violent behavior in stalkers: A preliminary investigation of Canadian cases in criminal harassment. *Journal of Forensic Sciences, 46,* 1403–1410.

Morrison, K. A. (2008). Differentiating between physically violent and nonviolent stalkers: An examination of Canadian cases. *Journal of Forensic Science, 53,* 742–751.

Mossman, D. (2007). Stalking, competence to stand trial, and criminal responsibility. In D. A. Pinals (Ed.), *Stalking: Psychiatric perspectives and practical approaches* (pp. 164–191). New York: Oxford University Press.

Mott, N. (1999). Serial murder: Patterns in unsolved cases. *Homicide Studies, 3,* 241–255.

Mullen, P. E. (2000). Erotomanias (pathologies of love) and stalking. In F. Flach (Ed.), *The Hatherleigh guide to psychiatric disorders* (Part II, pp. 145–163). New York: Hatherleigh Press.

Mullen, P. E. (2003). Multiple classifications of stalkers and stalking behavior available to clinicians. *Psychiatric Annals, 33,* 651–656.

Mullen, P. E., Pathé, M., & Purcell, R. (2008). *Stalkers and their victims* (2nd ed.). Cambridge: Cambridge University Press.

Muller, D. A. (2000). Criminal profiling: Real science or just wishful thinking? *Homicide Studies, 4,* 234–264.

Mustaine, E. E., & Tewksbury, R. (1999). A routine activity theory explanation for women's stalking victimizations. *Violence Against Women, 5,* 43–62.

Nabors, E. L., Dietz, T. L., & Jasinski, J. L. (2006). Domestic violence beliefs and perceptions among college students. *Violence and Victims, 21,* 779–795.

National Academy of Sciences. (2009). *Strengthening forensic science in the United States: A path forward.* Washington DC: National Academies Press.

National Center for Missing and Exploited Children. (2010). Retrieved May 5, 2010, from http://www.missingkids.com

National Center for Prosecution of Child Abuse. (2007). Practitioner's guide to the Adam Walsh Act. Washington DC: American Prosecutor's Research Institute.

National Crime Information Center. (2004). Active missing person breakdown sex, age and category as of October 1, 2004. Available from the Doe Network Web site: www.doenetwork.org

National Crime Information Center. (2005). Active missing person statistics. Retrieved August 25, 2005, from http://www.doenetwork.org

National Crime Information Center. (2006). Unidentified dead statistics as of April 30, 2006. Retrieved May 17, 2006, from http://www.doenetwork.org

National Vital Statistics System. (2006, April 19). Deaths: Final data for 2003. *National Vital Statistics Reports, 54,* 13.

National Volunteer Fire Council. (2004). *News: 2004 arson awareness week: May 2–8.* Retrieved June 30, 2010, from http://www.nvfc.org/news/hn_2004_arson_awareness.html

Nel, C. J., Verschoor, T., Calitz, F. J. W., & van Rensburg, P. H. J. J. (1992). Die belang van 'n Antropologiese perspektief by toepaslike verhore van oënskynlike motieflose moored. *Suid-Afrikaanse Tydskrif vir Etnologie, 15,* 85–92.

Network of Medicolegal Information Systems. (2006). Network of Medicolegal Information Systems Project. Retrieved June 20, 2006, from http://www.nomisproject.com

New Jersey v. Fortini, 745 A.2d 509 (N.J., 2000).

Ngubane, H. (1986). The predicament of the sinister healer; some observations on "ritual murder" and the professional role of the inyanga. In: M. Last & G. L. Chavunduka (Eds.), *The professionalisation of African medicine.* Manchester: Manchester University Press.

Nguyen, K. N. (2005). Brent J. Brents sentenced to 1,300-plus years in prison: Convicted serial rapist pleads guilty to 68 counts. Retrieved May 23, 2009, from http://www.thedenverchannel.com/news/4688806/detail.html

Nicol, B. (2006). *Stalking.* London: Reaktion.

Nobles, M. R., Fox, K. A., Piquero, N., & Piquero, A. R. (2009). Career dimensions of stalking victimization and perpetration. *Justice Quarterly, 26,* 476–503.

Norris, J. (1988). *Serial killers: The growing menace.* New York: Doubleday.

Olivier, F. (1990, May 4). In Venda is jy skuldig as die mense so sê. *Vrye Weekblad.*

Olsen, L. (2003, February 24). Records often are as hard to find as a body. *Seattle Post-Intelligencer.*

Olsen, L., & Kamb, L. (2003, February 18). Missing person cases are routinely ignored. *Seattle Post-Intelligencer.*

Ormerod, D. (1999). Criminal profiling: Trial by judge and jury, not by criminal psychologist. In D. Canter & L. Alison (Eds.), *Profiling in policy and practice* (pp. 207–261). Aldershot, England: Ashgate Publishing.

Orsos, F. (1940). Leichenzerstückelung. In F. Neureiter, F. Pietrusky, & E., Schütt (Eds.), *Handwörterbuch der gerichtlichen medizin und naturwissenschaftlichen kriminalistik* (pp. 446–451). Berlin: Springer.

Palermo, G. B., & Kocsis, R. (2005). *Offender profiling: An introduction to the sociopolitical analysis of violent crime.* Springfield, IL: Charles C. Thomas.

Park, J., Schlesinger, L. B., Piniotto, A. J., & Davis, E. F. (2008). Serial and single-victim rapists: Differences in crime-scene violence, interpersonal involvement, and criminal sophistication. *Behavioral Sciences & the Law, 26*(2), 227–237.

Pathé, M., & Mullen, P. (2002). The victim of stalking. In J. Boon & L. Sheridan (Eds.), *Stalking and psychosexual obsession: Psychological perspectives for prevention, policing and treatment* (pp. 1–22). West Sussex, England: John Wiley & Sons.

Pathé, M., & Mullen, P. E. (1997). The impact of stalkers on their victims. *British Journal of Psychiatry, 170,* 12–17.

Pathé, M., Mullen, P. E., & Purcell, R. (2000). Same-gender stalking. *Journal of the American Academy of Psychiatry and the Law, 28,* 191–197.

Paulsen, D. (2006). Human versus machine: A comparison of the accuracy of geographic profiling methods. *Journal of Investigative Psychology and Offender Profiling, 3*(2), 77–89.

Pearce, A., & Easteal, P. (1999). The "domestic" in stalking. *Alternative Law Journal, 24,* 165–170.

Peterson, K. (2002). State agencies search for foster kids. Retrieved December 2, 2005, from http://www.pewtrusts.com/news

Petherick, W. (2006). Serial stalking: Looking for love in all the wrong places? In W. Petherick (Ed.), *Serial crime: Theoretical and practical issues in behavioral profiling* (pp. 132–160). Burlington, MA: Elsevier/Academic Press.

Petherick, W., Field, D., Lowe, A., & Fry, E. (2005). Criminal profiling as expert evidence. In W. Patherick (Ed.), *Serial crime: Theoretical and practical issues in behavioral profiling* (pp. 72–73). New York: Elsevier.

Petrus, T. S. (2007). Ritual crime: Anthropological considerations and contributions to a new field of study. *Acta Criminologica, 20*(2), 119–137.

Phoenix Business Group. (1996). *U.S. Fire Administration combats nation's arson problem.* Retrieved April 6, 2010, from http://www.consumer-protection.com/arson.html

Phillips, L., Quirk, R., Rosenfeld, B., & O'Connor, M. (2004). Is it stalking? Perceptions of stalking among college undergraduates. *Criminal Justice and Behavior, 31,* 73–96.

Polinsky, A. M., & Shavell, S. (1997). *On the disutility and discounting of imprisonment and the theory of deterrence.* NBER Working Papers 6259, National Bureau of Economic Research, Inc.

Pollinger, J., Samuels, L., & Stadolnik, R. (2005). A comparative study of the behavioral, personality, and fire history characteristics of residential and outpatient adolescents (ages 12–17) with firesetting behaviors. *Adolescence, 40*(158), 345–353.

Prentky, R. A., Cohen, M., & Seghorn, T. K. (1985). Development of a rational taxonomy for the classification of rapists: The Massachusetts Treatment Center System. *Bulletin of the American Academy of Psychiatry and the Law, 13,* 39–70.

Profile of a Pedophile. (n.d.) Retrieved May 25, 2010 from http://childprotection.lifetips.com

Potterat, J. J., Brewer, D. D., Muth, S. Q., Rothenberg, R. B., Woodhouse, D. E., Muth, J. B., et al. (2004). Mortality in an open cohort of prostitute women. *American Journal of Epidemiology, 159,* 778–785.

Potterat, J., Woodhouse, D., Muth, J., & Muth, S. (1990). Estimating the prevalence and career longevity of prostitute women. *Journal of Sex Research*, *27*, 233–244.

Prinsloo, M. W., & Du Plessis, J. H. (1989). Towermoorde, rituele doding en medisynemoorde in Venda. *Journal for South African Law*, *4*, 617–623.

Profile of a pedophile. Retrieved May 25, 2010, from http://childprotection.lifetips.com/child-predators/index.html

Purcell, R., Pathé, M., & Mullen, P. E. (2001). A study of women who stalk. *American Journal of Psychiatry*, *153*(12), 2056–2060.

Purcell, R., Pathé, M., & Mullen, P. E. (2002). The prevalence and nature of stalking in the Australian community. *Australian and New Zealand Journal of Psychiatry*, *36*, 114–120.

Püschel, K., & Koops, E. (1987). Zerstückelung und verstümmelung (1. und 2. Teil). *Arch Kriminol*, *180*, 29–40, 88–100.

Rabkin, J. G. (1979). The epidemiology of forcible rape. *American Journal of Orthopsychiatry*, *49*(4), 634–647.

Ramirez, D. (2004, February 17). Authorities say slayings in four states could be work of serial killer. *Fort Worth Star Telegram*.

Ramsland, K. (n.d.) The McMartin nightmare and the hysteria puppeteers. Retrieved July 13, 2010, from http://www.trutv.com/library/crime/criminal_mind/psychology/mcmartin_daycare/4.htmlRand, M. R. (2008). *Criminal victimization, 2008*. Bureau of Justice Statistics Bulletin, NCJ 227777.Washington DC: U.S. Department of Justice.

Rajs, J., Lundtröm, M., Broberg, M., Lidberg, L., & Lindquist, O. (1998). Criminal mutilation of the human body in Sweden: A thirty-year medico-legal and forensic psychiatric study. *Journal of Forensic Sciences*, *43*, 653–580.

Regina v. Burlingham, B.C.J.No. 1986, Vancouver Registry: CA006715 (1993).

Renauer, B., & Henning, K. (2005). Investigating intersections between gender and intimate partner violence recidivism. *Journal of Offender Rehabilitation*, *41*, 99–124.

Rennison, C. M. (2002). Rape and sexual assault: Reporting to police and medical attention, 1992–2000. Washington DC: U.S. Department of Justice, NCJ 194530.

Ritter, B. (2002). Research for the cop on the beat: What we can do to help police. In M. D. Smith & P. Blackmun (Eds.), *The relationship between non-lethal and lethal violence: Proceedings of the 2002 meeting of the Homicide Research Working Group*. Chicago: Homicide Research Working Group.

Roberts, A. R. (2006). Changing stalking patterns and prosecutorial decisions: Bridging the present to the future. *Victims and Offenders*, *1*, 47–60.

Roberts, A. R., & Dziegielewski, S. F. (1996). Assessment typology and intervention with the survivors of stalking. *Aggression and Violent Behavior*, *1*, 359–368.

Romans, J. S. C., Hays, J. R., & White, T. K. (1996). Stalking and related behaviors experienced by counseling center staff members from current or former clients. *Professional Psychology: Research and Practice*, *27*, 595–599.

Rosay, A. B., Postle, G., TePas, K., & Wood, D. (2007). Stalking in Alaska. *Alaska Justice Forum*, *24*(1), 1–12.

Rosenfeld, B. (2003). Recidivism in stalking and obsessional harassment. *Law and Human Behavior*, *27*, 251–265.

Rosenfeld, B. (2004). Violence risk factors in stalking and obsessional harassment: A review and preliminary meta-analysis. *Criminal Justice and Behavior*, *31*, 9–36.

Rosenfeld, B., & Lewis, C. (2005). Assessing violence risk in stalking cases: A regression tree approach. *Law and Human Behavior*, *29*, 343–357.

Rossmo, D. K. (1995). Place, space and police investigation: Hunting serial violent criminals. In J. E. Eck & D. Weisburg. (Eds.), *Crime and place. Crime Prevention Studies* (Vol. 4). Monsey, NY: Criminal Justice Press.

Rossmo, D. K. (1997). Geographic profiling. In J. L. Jackson & D. A. Bekerian (Eds.), *Offender profiling: Theory, research and practice* (pp. 159–175). Chichester, England: John Wiley & Sons.

Rossmo, D. K. (2000). *Geographic profiling*. Boca Raton, FL: CRC Press.

Rossmo, K. (2004, November 20). Spatial and temporal patterns of serial murder in the United States. Paper presented to the American Society of Criminology, Nashville, TN.

Rossmo, D. K., Davies, A., & Patrick, M. (2004). *Exploring the geo-demographic relationship between stranger rapists and their offences* (Special Interest Series). London: Policing and Reducing Crime Unit, Home Office.

Rule, A. (2004). *Green River, running red: The real story of the Green River killer—America's deadliest serial murderer*. New York: Free Press.

Saad, L. (2001). Fear of conventional crime at record lows. *Gallup Poll Monthly*, October, 2–10.

Safarik, M. E., Jarvis, J., & Nussbaum, K. (2000). Elderly female serial sexual homicide: A limited empirical test of criminal investigative analysis. *Homicide Studies, 4*, 294–307.

Sakheim, G., & Osborn, E. (1999). Severe vs. nonsevere firesetters revisited. *Child Welfare, 78*(4), 411–434.

Sakheim, G., Vigdor, M., Gordon, M., & Helprin, L. (1985). A pscyhological profile of juvenile firesetters in residential treatment. *Child Welfare, 54*(5), 453–476.

Salfati, C. G., & Bateman, A. L. (2005). Serial homicide: An investigation of behavioural consistency. *Journal of Investigative Psychology and Offender Profiling, 2*(2), 121–144.

Samenow, S. (2004). *Inside the criminal mind*. New York: Random House.

Sandberg, D. A., McNiel, D. E., & Binder, R. L. (1998). Characteristics of psychiatric inpatients who stalk, threaten, or harass hospital staff after discharge. *American Journal of Psychiatry, 155*, 1102–1105.

Santtila, P., Junkkila, J., & Sandnabba, N. K. (2005). Behavioural linking of stranger rapes. *Journal of Investigative Psychology and Offender Profiling, 2*, 87–103.

Sapp, A. D., Huff, T. G., Gary, G. P., & Icove, D. G. (1994). *A motive-based offender analysis of serial arsonists*. Retrieved June 30, 2010, from http://www.interfire.org/features/serialarsonists/Motive_based/cover.asp

Sapp, A. D., Huff, T. G., Gary, G. P., Icove, D. J., & Horbert, P. (1994). *A report of essential findings from a study of serial arsonists*. Quantico, VA: National Center for the Analysis of Violent Crime.

Savino, J. O., & Turvey, B. E. (2005). Serial rape: Investigative issues. In J. O. Savino & B. E. Turvey (Eds.), *Rape investigation handbook* (pp. 301–330). Burlington, MA: Elsevier Academic Press.

Scarce, M. (1997). *Male on male rape: The hidden toll of stigma and shame*. New York: Plenum.

Schapera, I. (1952). Sorcery and witchcraft in Bechuanaland. *African Affairs, 51*, 41–52.

Schneider, A., & O'Connor, P. (2002, October 12). Nation's nursing homes are quietly killing thousands. *St. Louis Post Dispatch*.

Scholtz, H. J., Phillips, V. M., & Knobel, G. J. (1997). Muti or ritual murder. *Forensic Sciences International, 87*, 117–123.

Schwartzman, P., Stambaugh, H., & Kimball, J. (1998). *Special report: Arson and juveniles: Responding to the violence*. Retrieved June 30, 2010, from the United States Fire Administration Web site, http://www.usfa.dhs.gov/downloads/pdf/publications/tr-095.pdf

Schwikkard, P. J. (2002). Similar fact evidence. In P. J. Schwikkard & S. E. van der Merwe (Eds.), *Principles of evidence* (pp. 66–77). Landsdowne, South Africa: JUTA.

Scocas, E., O'Connell, J., Huenke, C., Nold, K., & Zoelker, E. (1996). *Domestic violence in Delaware 1994: An analysis of victim to offender relationships with special focus on stalking*. Dover, DE: Statistical Analysis Center.

Sedlak, A., Finkelhor, D., Hammer, H., & Schultz, D. (2002). National incidence studies of missing, abducted, runaway, and thrownaway children. Washington DC: U.S. Department of Justice, Office of Justice Programs, Office of Juvenile Justice and Delinquency Prevention.

Sex Offender Statistics (n.d.). Retrieved May 25, 2010, from http://childprotection.lifetips.com/child-predators/index.html

Shaw, C., & McKay, H. (1942). *Juvenile delinquency and urban areas.* Chicago: University of Chicago Press.

Sheridan, L. (2001). The course and nature of stalking: An in-depth victim survey. *Journal of Threat Assessment, 1,* 61–79.

Sheridan, L. P., Blaauw, E., & Davies, G. M. (2003). Stalking: Knowns and unknowns. *Trauma, Violence, & Abuse, 4*(2), 148–162.

Sheridan, L., & Boon, J. (2002). Stalker typologies: Implications for law enforcement. In J. Boon & L. Sheridan (Eds.), *Stalking and psychosexual obsession: Psychological perspectives for prevention, policing and treatment* (pp. 63–82). West Sussex, England: John Wiley & Sons.

Sheridan, L., & Davies, G. M. (2001). What is stalking? The match between legislation and public perception. *Legal and Criminological Psychology, 6,* 3–17.

Sheridan, L., Davies, G. M., & Boon, J. C. (2001). The course and nature of stalking: A victim perspective. *Howard Journal of Criminal Justice, 40,* 215–234.

Sherley, A. (2005). Contextualizing the sexual assault event: Images from police files. *Deviant Behavior, 26*(2), 87–108.

Shoenfeld, D. (1936). *The crime and the criminal: A psychiatric study of the Lindbergh case.* New York: Covichi Friede.

Skogan, W. G. (1977). Dimensions of the dark figure of unreported crime. *Crime & Delinquency, 23*(1), 41–50.

Skolnick, A. (1998). Critics denounce staffing jails and prisons with physicians convicted of misconduct. *The Journal of the American Medical Association, 280,* 1391–1392.

Slavkin, M., & Fineman, K. (2000). What every professional who works with adolescents should know about firesetters. *Adolescence, 35*(140), 759–774.

Smartt, U. (2001). The stalking phenomenon: Trends in European and international stalking and harassment legislation. *European Journal of Crime, Criminal Law and Criminal Justice, 9,* 209–232.

Snook, B., Zito, M., Bennell, C., & Taylor, P. (2005). On the complexity and accuracy of geographical profiling strategies. *Journal of Quantitative Criminology, 1*(1), 1–26.

South Dakota v. Anderson, McCook County Court Preliminary Hearing (1998, April 9).

Spence-Diehl, E., & Potocky-Tripodi, M. (2001). Victims of stalking: A study of service needs as perceived by victim services practitioners. *Journal of Interpersonal Violence, 16,* 86–94.

Spencer, A. C. (1998). *Stalking and the MMPI-2 in a forensic population.* Unpublished doctoral dissertation, University of Detroit Mercy, Detroit, MI.

Spitzberg, B. H. (2002). The tactical topography of stalking victimization and management. *Trauma, Violence, & Abuse, 3,* 261–288.

Spitzberg, B. H. (2010). Stalkers, types. In B. Fisher, & S. Lab (Eds.), *Encyclopedia of victimology and crime prevention.* Thousand Oaks, CA: Sage.

Spitzberg, B. H., & Cadiz, M. (2002). The media construction of stalking stereotypes. *Journal of Criminal Justice and Popular Culture, 9,* 128–149.

Spitzberg, B. H., & Cupach, W. R. (2007). The state of the art of stalking: Taking stock of the emerging literature. *Aggression and Violent Behavior, 12,* 64–86.

Spitzberg, B. H., & Cupach, W. R. (2003). What mad pursuit? Conceptualization and assessment of obsessive relational intrusion and stalking-related phenomena. *Aggression and Violent Behavior: A Review Journal, 8,* 345–375.

Spitzberg, B. H., & Rhea, J. (1999). Obsessive relational intrusion and sexual coercion victimization. *Journal of Interpersonal Violence, 14,* 3–20.

Spohn, C., Beichner, D., & Davis-Frenzel, E. (2001). Prosecutorial justifications for sexual assault case rejection. *Social Problems, 48,* 206–235.

Spohn, C., & Spears, J. (1996). The effect of offender and victim characteristics on sexual assault case processing decisions. *Justice Quarterly, 13*, 649–680.

Stangeland, P. (2005). Catching a serial rapist: Hits and misses in criminal profiling. *Police Practice & Research, 6*(5), 453–469.

Stark, C., Paterson, B., Henderson, T., Kidd, B., & Godwin, M. (1997). Counting the dead. *Nursing Times, 93*, 34–37.

Stark, C., Paterson, B., Henderson, T., Kidd, B., & Godwin, M. (2001). Opportunity may be more important than profession in serial homicide. Letter to the editor. *British Medical Journal, 322*, 993.

State v. Nyauza, Case No CC97/2007. Pretoria High Court, South Africa (2007).

State v. Stander, Case No CC37/2008. Eastern Cape High Court, Port Elizabeth, South Africa (2000).

State v. Sukude, Case No 34/2006. Pietermaritzburg High Court, South Africa (2006).

State v. van Rooyen, Case No SS 55/2007. Cape High Court, South Africa (2007).

Steiger, S., Burger, C., & Schild, A. (2008). Lifetime prevalence and impact of stalking: Epidemiological data from Eastern Austria. *European Journal of Psychiatry, 22*, 235–241.

Stephan, J., & Karberg, J. (2003). Census of state and federal correctional facilities, 2000 (NCJ 198272). Washington DC: U.S. Department of Justice, Bureau of Justice Statistics.

Stevens, D. J. (1997). Violence and serial rape. *Journal of Police and Criminal Psychology, 12*(1), 39–47.

Steyn, M. (2005). Muti murders in South Africa: A case report. *Forensic Science International, 151*, 279–287.

Storey, J. E., Hart, S. D., Meloy, J. R., & Reavis, J. A. (2009). Psychopathy and stalking. *Law and Human Behavior, 33*, 237–246.

Surette, R. (2007). *Media, crime, and criminal justice: Images and realities* (3rd ed.). Belmont, CA: Thomson-Wadsworth.

Taylor, P., Mahendra, B., & Gunn, J. (1983). Erotomania in males. *Psychological Medicine, 13*, 645–650.

Taylor, J., Thorne, I., Robertson, A., & Avery, G. (2002). Evaluation of a group intervention for convicted arsonists with mild and borderline intellectual disabilities. *Criminal Behavior and Mental Health, 12*(4), 282–194.

Tegnell, A., Bossi, P., Baka, A., Van Loock, F., Hendriks, J., Wallyn, S., et al. (2003). The European commission's task force on bioterrorism. *Emerging Infectious Diseases, 9*(10), 1330–1332.

Texas Task Force responds to terrorist attack. (2001). *IIE Solutions, 33*(12), 10.

Thompson, C. M. (2009). *Developing and testing an integrated theory of stalking violence.* Ph.D. Thesis, Griffith University, Nathan, Queensland, New Zealand.

Thompson, J. (1982). Foreward: Remarks by Governor James R. Thompson on the Attorney General's task force on violent crime. *Journal of Criminal Law & Criminology, 73*(3), 867–874.

Thornhill, R., & Palmer, C. T. (2000). *A natural history of rape: Biological bases of sexual coercion.* Cambridge, MA: The MIT Press.

Tjaden, P. G. (2009). Stalking policies and research in the United States: A twenty year retrospective. *European Journal of Criminal Policy Research, 15*, 261–278.

Tjaden, P., & Thoennes, N. (1998). *Stalking in America: Findings from the National Violence Against Women Survey.* Washington DC: National Institute of Justice and Centers for Disease Control and Prevention (NCJ 169592).

Tjaden, P., & Thoennes, N. (2000). *Full report of the prevalence, incidence, and consequences of violence against women: Findings from the National Violence Against Women Survey.* Washington DC: National Institute of Justice and Centers for Disease Control and Prevention (NCJ 183781).

Tjaden, P., & Thoennes, N. (2006). Extent, nature and consequences of rape victimization: Findings from The National Violence Against Women Survey. Washington DC: UD Department of Justice, NIJ 210346.

Tonin, E. (2004). The attachment styles of stalkers. *Journal of Forensic Psychiatry & Psychology, 15*, 584–590.

Tonkin, M., Grant, T., & Bond, J. W. (2008). To link or not to link: A test of the case linkage principles using serial car theft data. *Journal of Investigative Psychology and Offender Profiling, 5*, 59–77.

Toulmin, S. (1958). *The uses of argument*. Cambridge, England: Cambridge University Press.

Trowbridge, B. (2009). Does sex offender treatment work? Retrieved May 24, 2010, from http:// trowbridgefoundation.org/articles.htm

Truman, J. L., & Mustaine, E. E. (2009). Strategies for college student stalking victims: Examining the information and recommendations available. *American Journal of Criminal Justice, 34*, 69–83.

Tucker, J. T. (1993). Stalking the problems with stalking laws. *Florida Law Review, 45*, 609–707.

U.S. Department of Justice. (2008). Forcible rape. *Uniform crime report: Crime in the United States, 2007*. Washington DC: U.S. Department of Justice; Federal Bureau of Investigation. Retrieved June 27, 2010, from http://www.fbi.gov/ucr/cius2007/documents/forciblerapemain.pdf

United States Fire Administration. (2009). *Arson for profit*. Retrieved September 7, 2009, from http://www. usfa.dhs.gov/downloads/pdf/arson/aaw09_media_kit.pdf

van der Berg, E., & van der Merwe, S. E. (2002). Opinion evidence. In P. J. Schwikkard, & S. E. van der Merwe (Eds.), *Principles of evidence* (pp. 79–99). Landsdowne, South Africa: JUTA.

van Dijk, J., van Kesteren, J., & Smit, P. (2008). *Criminal victimization in international perspective*. The Hague: United Nations Office of Drugs and Crime.

Vargas, E., & James, M. S. (2009). A tale of two cultures: Amanda Knox case reveals a stark divide. Retrieved May 31, 2010, from http://abcnews.go.com

Vendel, C. (2010, February 25). Black men feeling persecuted by broad suspicions over Waldo serial rapes. *The Kansas City Star*. Retrieved March 26, 2010, from http://www.kansascity. com/2010/02/25/1774739/black-men-feeling-persecuted-by.html#ix0jJR9l3zN

Virginia Commission on Youth. (2003). *Maladaptive behaviors*. Retrieved October 13, 2009, from http:// coy.state.va.us/Modalities/firesetting.htm

Vold, G. B. (1981). *Theoretical criminology* (2nd ed). New York: Oxford University Press.

Wachi, T., Watanabe, K., Yokota, K., Suzuki, M., Hoshino, M., Sato, A., et al. (2007). Offender and crime characteristics of female serial arsonists in Japan. *Journal of Investigative Psychology an Offender Profiling, 4*, 29–52.

Walby, S., & Allen, J. (2004, March). *Domestic violence, sexual assault and stalking: Findings from the British Crime Survey*. London: Home Office Research, Development and Statistics Directorate.

Warr, M. (1985). Fear of rape among urban women. *Social Problems, 32*, 238–250.

Warr, M., & Ellison, C. (2000). Rethinking social reactions to crime: Personal and altruistic fear in family households. *American Journal of Sociology, 3*, 551–578.

Warren, J., Reboussin, R., Hazelwood, R. R., Gibbs, N. A., Trumbetta, S. L., & Cummings, A. (1999). Crime scene analysis and the escalation of violence in serial rape. *Forensic Science International, 100*, 37–56.

Washington v. Russel, 125 Wash.2d 24, 882 P.2D 747 (1994).

Weinrott, M. R., & Saylor, M. (1991). Self report of crimes committed by sex offenders. *Journal of Interpersonal Violence, 6*, 286–300.

Wells, K. (2001). Prosecuting those who stalk: A prosecutor's legal perspective and viewpoint. In J. A. Davis (Ed.), *Stalking crimes and victim protection: Prevention, intervention, threat assessment, and case management* (pp. 427–456). Boca Raton, FL: CRC Press.

Wentink, N. (2001). *Serial sexual murder: Classification and development over a series of offences*. Unpublished master's thesis, University of Liverpool, Liverpool, England.

White, R. (2009, February 26). Valley cook accused of serial rape. *Anchorage Daily News*.

Williams, K. R. (1981). Few convictions in rape cases. *Journal of Criminal Justice, 9*, 29–40.

Willing, R. (2007, June 24). Report: Authorities have about 14,000 sets of human remains. *USA Today*, p. 1.

Wilson, J. Q., & Kelling, G. L. (1982, March). Broken windows: The police and neighborhood safety. *Atlantic Monthly, 249*, 29–38.

Wolak, J., Finkelhor, D., & Mitchell, K. (2009). Trends in arrests of "online predators." Retrieved on May 10, 2010, from http://www.unh.edu/ccrc/pdf/CV194.pdf

Woodhams, J., & Grant, T. (2006). Developing a categorization system for rapists' speech. *Psychology, Crime & Law, 12*(3), 245–260.

Woodhams, J., Grant, T. D., & Price, A. R. (2007). From marine ecology to crime analysis: Improving the detection of serial sexual offences using a taxonomic similarity measure. *Journal of Investigative Psychology and Offender Profiling, 4*, 17–27.

Woodhams, J., Hollin, C. R., & Bull, R. (2007). The psychology of linking crimes: A review of the evidence. *Legal and Criminological Psychology, 12*, 233–249.

Woodhams, J., Hollin, C. R., & Bull, R. (2008). Incorporating context in linking crimes: An exploratory study of situational similarity and if-then contingencies. *Journal of Investigative Psychology and Offender Profiling, 5*, 1–23.

Woodhams, J., & Toye, K. (2007). An empirical test of the assumptions of case linkage and offender profiling with serial commercial robberies. *Psychology, Public Policy, and Law, 13*(1), 59–85.

Wooldredge, J., & Thistlethwaite, A. (2005). Court dispositions and rearrest for intimate assault. *Crime & Delinquency, 51*, 71–102.

World Health Organization. (2002). *Sexual violence facts.* Geneva, Switzerland: Author.

Wright, C., & Gary, G. (1995, winter). Paul Kenneth Keller: A profile comparison with typical serial arsonists. *International Association of Arson Investigators Newsletter*, 10–19.

Wright, J., & Hensley, C. (2003). From animal cruelty to serial murder: Applying the graduation hypothesis. *International Journal of Offender Therapy and Comparative Criminology, 47*, 71–88.

Zipper, P., & Wilcox, D. (2005). Juvenile arson: The importance of early intervention. *The FBI Law Enforcement Bulletin, 74*(4), 1–9.

Zona, M. A., Sharma, K. K., & Lane, J. (1993). A comparative study of erotomanic and obsessional subjects in a forensic sample. *Journal of Forensic Sciences, 38*, 894–903.

Author Index

Subject Index

Note: Tables are noted with a *t*.